God's word is not chained.

2 TIMOTHY 2:9

THE COMPLETE

Bible
Discussion
Guide

GROUP DISCUSSION
QUESTIONS FOR EVERY CHAPTER
IN THE BIBLE

IN TWO VOLUMES:
NEW TESTAMENT • OLD TESTAMENT & TOPICAL INDEX

MACK THOMAS

The Complete
Bible Discussion Guide
© 1992 by Questar Publishers, Inc.

Multnomah Press Books
from Questar Publishers, Inc.
Sisters, Oregon

Printed in the United States of America

International Standard Book Numbers:
Volume One (Old Testament): 0-945564-54-6
Volume Two (New Testament & Topical Index): 0-945564-55-4

to
Howard G. Hendricks

STUDENT OF GOD'S WORD
TEACHER OF TEACHERS

FIND THESE HELPFUL FEATURES IN THE BACK OF THIS BOOK:

➤ *HELPFUL GROUP GUIDELINES for greater effectiveness in your Bible study discussion group*

➤ *A STUDY SCHEDULE for each book of the Bible*

➤ *PRAYERS AND PROMISES from the Scriptures to pray and believe as you study the Bible, as a group or on your own*

AND IN THE BACK OF VOLUME ONE:

➤ *A THOROUGH TOPICAL INDEX, for personal and group Bible study by topics, using the questions in both volumes (Old Testament & New Testament) of THE COMPLETE BIBLE DISCUSSION GUIDE*

CONTENTS

QUESTIONS TO ASK AS YOU STUDY <u>EACH CHAPTER</u>:

➤ Since the ultimate aim of Bible study is *to know God better,* what does this chapter tell me about God's character and personality?

➤ Since God has given me the Bible to change my life, what needed corrections or adjustments in my habits or character come to mind as I explore this chapter?

➤ In this chapter, what are...
the key verses, the key phrases, the key words?
the key points or principles—*and how do they*
work in my life?

➤ In this chapter, do I see any...
commands to obey?
promises to claim?
standards to live by?

➤ What three-to-six word title would I give to this chapter, to help me remember its teaching?

Everyone's Best Preparation for Discussing Each Chapter:
Read the chapter...reread it...and reread it again.

Questions to Ask as You Begin Your Study of <u>Each Book</u>:

➤ If you're already familiar with this book, which passages are your favorite parts of it?

➤ If this were the only book in the Bible you knew about or had access to, what things could you still find out about God?

➤ As you scan this book, what *types* of Bible literature does it appear to contain? (You may want to review together the different types, such as those listed here:)
- poetry
- historical or biographical narrative (a record of people and events)
- teaching or sermons
- laws or covenant agreements
- parables (short stories and word pictures with a moral point)
- proverbs (short, wise sayings)
- prophecy (statements from God about the present and future)

➤ What appear to be the main divisions in this book?

➤ From what you understand about this book, *who* wrote it, about *when* did he write it, and for what *original audience* was it written?

➤ From what you see in looking over this book, what would you say the author was trying most to accomplish?

➤ Which chapter in this book would you say is the key chapter, the one that best summarizes or reflects or unlocks the meaning of the entire book?

➤ From what you see in looking over this book, what kinds of answers and guidelines and solutions in life do you think we can reasonably expect to find in this book?

➤ What four- to six-word title would you give to this book, to best summarize its content and significance?

➤ When you get to heaven, if you asked God, "Why did You include this book in the Bible?" how do you think He would answer?

A sampling of the subjects you'll find in the Topical Index

(in the back of Volume One)

confidence

counseling

decision making

faith

family

fellowship

forgiveness

friendship

holiness

humility

integrity

joy

leadership

love

maturity

obedience

patience

peace

prayer

purpose

repentance

reward

service

spiritual gifts

strength

success

temptation

unity

wisdom

witnessing

work

worship

Matthew

OVERVIEW

(Discuss these OVERVIEW questions both at the beginning of your study of Matthew, and again after you've studied together all 28 chapters. Your answers may change significantly once you've looked more closely at the entire book.)

Startup: Together, list aloud the most positive images and concepts that come to your mind when you think of these words: *king* and *kingdom.*

SEEING WHAT'S THERE

1. It's been said that while the *death* of Christ relates primarily to the *penalty* of sin, the *life* of Christ tells us more about overcoming sin's *power* in everyday life. If that's true, what kind of answers and guidelines would you like to discover as you study the life of Jesus in the book of Matthew?

2. God's *kingdom* is a key concept in Matthew. Scan through the book together (especially chapters 5, 13, and 18—21) to find where the word *kingdom* occurs. From what you see there, what definition could you give for the word as it's used by Matthew?

3. To learn more about the author of this gospel, the apostle Matthew (also known as Levi), look together at 9:9-13. From this evidence, what kind of person would you guess Matthew to be? What differences in Matthew's life do you think his friends were probably talking about after Matthew decided to follow Jesus?

4. Take a few minutes to scan through this book together, and notice how many times you can find an instance where Jesus *healed* someone. (You may want to divide into two groups —one group to start scanning at the beginning of Matthew, and the other to start at the end and work backwards.)

5. Look also at the list of "Questions to Ask as You Begin Your Study of Each Book" on page 393.

CAPTURE THE ESSENCE

6. Matthew's gospel is noted for its emphasis on presenting Jesus as *King*—the King of the Jews, and Ruler of God's Kingdom. What passages can you point to that bring out this theme?

FOR LIFE TODAY

7. Since Matthew's gospel portrays Jesus as the King, can this book still be meaningful and relevant to a society today that has no royal officials? Why or why not?

8. How can you ensure that your study of Matthew is not merely theoretical and intellectual, but is instead truly practical and useful? Talk together about this. What can you do to help keep the process alive and interesting?

FOR GOING DEEPER

The book of Matthew is sometimes referred to as the most Jewish of the four gospels. From what you know of all four gospels, how does the "Jewishness" of Matthew come through, especially in comparison with the other three gospels?

MATTHEW 1

Startup: Talk together about any time you can recall in the past when you were faced with a particularly tough dilemma, and saw no positive way out of it.

SEEING WHAT'S THERE

1. From the long list of names in verses 2-16, identify all the people you're familiar with, and tell the most interesting facts you know about them.

2. For helpful background on the dilemma Joseph faced in verses 18-19, look together at Deuteronomy 22:22-24.

3. For background on the name "Immanuel" for Jesus in verse 23, look together at Isaiah 7:14.

4. Bible teachers often note that the apostle Matthew wrote this gospel essentially for a Jewish audience. How do you see that reflected in this chapter?

5. EYE FOR DETAIL—*If everyone in the group has read the entire chapter, try answering the following question without looking at your Bible:* The first part of this chapter is a genealogy of Jesus. Besides Jesus, the names of two outstanding biblical heroes are repeated in both the sentence that introduces the genealogy, and in the summary sentence at the end of the genealogy. Who are these two important men? (For the answer, see verses 1 and 17.)

6. Look also at the list of "Questions to Ask as You Study Each Chapter" on page 392, which you may want to do for each chapter in Matthew.

CAPTURE THE ESSENCE

7. If you were Joseph and had the dream he had and heard the words he heard in verses 20-21, what thoughts and questions might come to your mind?

8. Why did Joseph marry Mary, though under the circumstances it did not appear socially or morally proper for him to do so?

9. From what you see in this chapter, how would you describe Joseph's relationship with God?

FOR LIFE TODAY

10. In verses 18-25 we are presented with the fact of Jesus' virgin birth. Why is this an important truth for us to know and believe?

11. How could you use this chapter to help explain to someone why Jesus came to earth?

FOR GOING DEEPER

Compare the way in which this gospel begins (verses 1-17), with the way the other three gospels begin (in Mark 1:1, Luke 1:1-4, and John 1:1-18). What do these different "start-up styles" tell you about the *purpose* of each gospel?

MATTHEW 2

Startup: From all the Christmases you've known and all the times you've heard the Christmas story, what images do you have of the "wise men" or "magi" or "kings," as they're variously called?

SEEING WHAT'S THERE

1. What things did the magi or wise men apparently know and understand about the identity of Jesus?

2. Compare verse 3 with verse 10 and notice the difference in *attitude* reflected in these verses. How would you explain the *reasons* for each attitude?

3. From what you see in verses 9-10, do you think the magi (or wise men) had lost sight of the star mentioned in verse 2? Or could the star in verse 9 have been a different star from the one in verse 2?

4. How could you use this chapter to illustrate to a new Christian the concept of God's *protection* for His people?

5. How do these first two chapters show the *uniqueness* of Jesus the King?

6. EYE FOR DETAIL—*If everyone in the group has read the entire chapter, try answering the following question without looking at your Bible:* How many dreams are mentioned in this chapter? (See verses 12, 13, 19, and 22.)

CAPTURE THE ESSENCE

7. What patterns do you see in the way Joseph responds to the different situations he faces in life?

8. How would you describe Joseph's basic *mindset* or *attitude* in life?

9. How would you describe Herod's basic *mindset* or *attitude* in life?

10. How is Joseph a model of a good father?

11. Look again at the tragic incident recorded in verses 16-18. Why do you think God allowed this to happen, and why did He include it in the Bible?

FOR LIFE TODAY

12. What guidelines for *obedience* can you draw from Joseph's example in Matthew 1 and 2?

13. What guidelines for *depending on God* can you draw from these chapters?

14. What helpful insights do you find in chapter 2 regarding the right way to approach God in worship?

FOR GOING DEEPER

Compare the Christmas story in Matthew 1 and 2, which focuses more on *Joseph* and the *magi,* with the Christmas story as told in Luke 1 and 2, which focuses more on *Mary* and the *shepherds.* What are the most important ways in which they complement each other?

MATTHEW 3

Startup: According to your personality, are you a person who usually welcomes new ideas, or one who tends to resist changes?

SEEING WHAT'S THERE

1. In what ways do you see John the Baptist fulfilling the prophecy mentioned in verse 3?

2. John's popular appeal is mentioned in verse 5. How would you explain the reasons for his appeal?

3. Express in your own words the picture you get of Jesus in verses 11 and 12.

4. In verse 12, what does John the Baptist mean by the words *wheat* and *chaff?*

5. In what ways do you think Jesus' baptism could "fulfill all righteousness," according to His words in verse 15?

6. What do we learn in verses 16-17 about the relationships between God the Father, God the Son, and God the Holy Spirit?

7. Think carefully about verse 17. What was it about Jesus that was "pleasing" to God, and why did God want to tell Him?

8. Who do you think God most wanted to hear His words in verse 17?

9. As you think about this chapter, how would you state in your own words the response required from people upon the arrival of the kingdom of heaven?

10. EYE FOR DETAIL—*If everyone in the group has read the entire chapter, try answering the following question without looking at your Bible:* Where did Jesus come *from* when He came to John at the Jordan River to be baptized? (See verse 13.)

CAPTURE THE ESSENCE

11. In your own words, what was the essential message that John the Baptist proclaimed?

12. How would you describe the *tone* of John's message—and how do *you* tend to respond to others who speak in that tone?

13. From the evidence you see in this chapter, what would you say John the Baptist considered to be the most important things in life?

14. Look together at verse 11. In what way does Jesus baptize with the Holy Spirit and with fire?

15. What does this chapter teach us about baptism?

16. In verse 16, what significance do you see in the Holy Spirit's appearance in the form of a *dove?*

FOR LIFE TODAY

17. In verse 8, John told the Sadducees and Pharisees to produce "fruit" in their lives that was consistent with repentance. For people in our churches today, what kind of "fruit" do you think this should be?

18. Look again at verse 11. What *fire* have you seen in your life?

19. Jesus' preparation for His ministry will continue in the next chapter. Taking Jesus' example as a model for us, what kind of preparation would you say *we* need for having an effective ministry for God?

FOR GOING DEEPER

Look ahead to Matthew 21:32, where Jesus describes the purpose for John the Baptist's ministry. How do John's words and actions in this chapter compare with the description Jesus gives later?

MATTHEW 4

Startup: In your adult life, what have been the most valuable "preparation" times for work or ministry or family responsibilities that you later took on?

SEEING WHAT'S THERE

1. Take a "walk" together through the incidents that happen in this chapter: Using your imagination, talk about the kinds of sights, smells, sounds, and feelings you might experience.

2. For useful background to the answers Jesus gave to the devil's temptations (verses 1-11), look together at Deuteronomy 8:3, 6:16, and 6:13.

3. What truths from Scripture did Jesus use to defy the devil?

4. In verse 11, what do you think the angels actually did to minister to Jesus?

5. On a map, look together at the places mentioned in verses 24-25. Why do you think Jesus was having such widespread appeal?

6. From what you've seen so far in Matthew, how does the message Jesus preached compare with the one John the Baptist preached?

7. EYE FOR DETAIL—*From what you recall seeing in this chapter, try answering the following question without looking at your Bible:* How many days and nights did Jesus fast in the desert before the devil came to tempt Him? (See verse 2.)

8. AND MORE DETAIL—*Another question to try answering without looking at your Bible:* What were the three ways in which the devil tempted Jesus? (See verses 3, 5-6, and 8-9.)

CAPTURE THE ESSENCE

9. After reviewing the three ways in which the devil tempted Jesus (verses 3-9), how would you comment on the devil's *strategy* against Jesus at this time, as it appears in this passage?

What were the devil's desires, and how did he plan to achieve them?

10. For each of the three temptations, discuss what you think would have happened next if Jesus had yielded to Satan's wishes.

11. If Satan had succeeded in getting Jesus under his control, what do you think is the worst thing he could have done to Jesus?

12. From the evidence you see in this temptation passage (verses 1-11), how would you describe Jesus' relationship to God, His Father?

13. From what you see in verses 3-11, how would you describe the devil's character and personality?

14. From the way Jesus answered the devil each time, what conclusions can you draw about the *value* and the *reliability* of the Scriptures?

15. Think about the imagery in the words of verse 16. In what different ways can you see Jesus fulfilling this prophecy?

16. In verse 23 we read that Jesus was preaching the gospel—the good news of the kingdom. From what you see elsewhere about His teachings and ministry, what was this good news?

17. In this chapter, which of these character qualities in Jesus comes through most strongly to you: His compassion, His power, or His wisdom? (Explain your answer.)

18. What in this chapter do you think might be the most interesting to someone who was learning about Jesus Christ for the first time?

FOR LIFE TODAY

19. Notice again the three ways in which Jesus was tempted by Satan (verses 3-9). In what ways have you experienced similar temptations?

20. If the three answers Jesus gave to the devil (verses 4, 7, and 10) were the only Scripture verses you knew, how much would each one help you as you faced various temptations? Are there any temptations you face for which you find no help at all in these three verses quoted by Jesus?

21. What kind of *living* was Jesus talking about in verse 4? How would you describe someone today who truly lives on every word of God?

22. Think about the temptation Jesus overcame in verses 5-7. In what ways today do we sometimes try to bind God to human plans?

23. Look again at verse 7, and decide how much you agree or disagree with this statement: We can't "box God in" by putting Him to the test, but He is probably pleased if we ask in true faith for signs and indications of His guidance.

24. Let the words of Jesus in verse 10 resound in your mind. Then discuss this question: Who or what do people sometimes worship today instead of God?

25. How could you paraphrase verse 16 and make it into a prayer for your family or friends or community?

26. Review verse 19. What things do we need to learn from Jesus in order to become "fishers of men"?

27. In light of how you're doing spiritually in your life today, which verse in this chapter do you think is the most important to you—and why?

FOR GOING DEEPER

Jesus quotes the Old Testament three times in this chapter. Look together at the following additional verses in Matthew in which Jesus referred to the Old Testament, then discuss what they show us about how Jesus regarded the Scriptures: Matthew 8:4, 12:39-42, 19:3-6, and 24:37-39.

MATTHEW 5

Startup: How do you think most people today would define true happiness in life?

SEEING WHAT'S THERE

1. What in this chapter do you think might be most surprising to a new Christian reading it for the first time?

2. Use any of the following verses to help you put together a definition for the word *blessed,* as it's used in verses 3-11 in this chapter: Psalms 94:12-13, 112:1-3, 128:1-4, and 144:12-15; Jeremiah 17:7-8; James 1:12; and Revelation 19:9, 20:6, and 22:14.

3. How would you describe the basic *mindset* or *attitude* in life which Jesus is teaching in this chapter?

4. What teachings in this chapter do you find hardest to understand?

5. In verses 6, 10, and 20, the word *righteousness* is given great importance. How would you define this word?

6. Suppose you were a Bible translator for a remote tribe on a faraway continent, and this tribe did not have any experience or knowledge of salt. How would you explain what salt is, so they could understand the meaning of verse 13?

7. Beginning with verse 21, six sections take up the rest of this chapter, and they all begin in much the same way. Notice this pattern as you take turns reading aloud the first two verses in each section: 21-22, 27-28, 31-32, 33-34, 38-39, and 43-44. From what you see in these verses, what is Jesus criticizing: the Old Testament law, or the people's *understanding* of the Old Testament law? (Explain your answer.)

8. In your own words, how would you explain the meaning of verse 48?

9. EYE FOR DETAIL—*From what you recall seeing in this chapter, try answering the following question without looking at your Bible:* What three words will complete this quotation from Jesus: "Blessed are the pure in heart, for they…" (See verse 8.)

CAPTURE THE ESSENCE

10. What do you think is the Lord's *intent* as He gives us the standards for Christian living included in this chapter?

11. Would you say verses 3-10 are more about *values* and *attitudes,* or more about *actions?* Explain your answer.

12. From what you see in verses 3-11, express in your own words what Jesus is looking for in His followers.

13. Jesus tells us in verses 11-12 to be glad when we are persecuted. What good things does persecution accomplish in our lives?

14. What can we conclude about *our purpose in life* from verses 13-16?

15. In verse 17, Jesus said He came to fulfill the Old Testament Scriptures, and not to destroy or abolish them. What ways can you think of in which Jesus fulfilled the Old Testament, and why are these important?

16. If Jesus did not come to abolish or destroy the Old Testament Scriptures, does that mean they still apply to us today? Explain your answer.

17. How could you use verses 23-24 to help someone who told you about an offense that was committed against him by another Christian brother or sister?

18. From what Jesus says in verses 27-30, how do you think He would define the term *purity of mind?*

19. From the evidence you see in this chapter, how do you think Jesus would define the terms *success* and *ultimate significance?*

20. What are the most important things this chapter communicates about God's character?

FOR LIFE TODAY

21. If you were asked to summarize the most important "marks of Christian maturity" as taught in this chapter, which ones would you mention first?

22. Which of the qualities and conditions in verses 3-10 are the hardest for you to experience in your own life?

23. What implications do you find in verses 17-19 for the way we view the Scriptures?

24. Look again at verses 29-30. Do you think there's a danger of responding too drastically to sin? If so, how commonly does this seem to happen in the lives of Christians you know?

25. How would you use verses 31-32 to help a Christian who was considering divorce?

FOR GOING DEEPER

Look again at what Jesus said in verse 17, and compare it with the following list of passages. What do they reveal about how Jesus fulfilled the Old Testament Scriptures?—Matthew 12:39-40, 13:13-15, 13:34-35, and 22:34-40.

Matthew 6

Startup: What kind of responsibilities or relationships in life are the easiest for you *not* to be anxious and troubled about?

SEEING WHAT'S THERE

1. How would you describe the basic *mindset* or *attitude* in life which Jesus is teaching in this chapter?

2. What teachings in this chapter do you find hardest to understand?

3. Does the word *righteous* mean the same thing in verse 1 as it does in verse 33? (Explain your answer.)

4. Jesus speaks three times in this chapter about God's reward for those who please Him (verses 4, 6, and 18). What do you think this reward is?

5. Review verses 5-15. From what you see here, what perspective does Jesus want us to have about prayer?

6. Review the "Lord's Prayer" in verses 9-13, then try restating it in completely different language, without using any words from the original (except those that are three letters or less). You may want to go around the group and have each person paraphrase one line from the prayer.

7. What do you think Jesus means in the last verse in this chapter when He says that tomorrow will "worry about itself" or "care for itself"?

8. EYE FOR DETAIL—*From what you recall seeing in this chapter, try answering the following question without looking at your Bible:* What five words will complete this quotation from Jesus: "For where your treasure is, there…" (See verse 21.)

CAPTURE THE ESSENCE

9. With verses 4, 6, and 18 in mind, discuss how much you agree or disagree with this statement: It is only what we do *privately* for God that will bring us a reward from Him.

10. Think about verses 14 and 15. Why is *forgiveness* so important for us to practice in life?

11. In verses 22-23, what would you say the lamp represents, and what does the eye represent?

12. In verses 22-23 would you say Jesus' main point is more about salvation, more about spiritual understanding, or more about warfare against Satan? Explain your answer.

13. If you were asked to summarize the most important "marks of Christian maturity" as taught in this chapter, which ones would you mention first?

14. What are the most important things this chapter communicates about God's character?

FOR LIFE TODAY

15. On a scale of one to ten (one = "very poor," ten = "very fulfilling and meaningful"), how would you rate the quality of your "secret life" with God—the things you do in service to Him that only He really knows about?

16. How could you use verses 5-15 to help teach a new Christian how to pray?

17. Think again about verses 14-15. How hard is it for you to forgive others? How hard is it for you to ask for forgiveness?

18. What treasures would you like to be storing in heaven?

19. Is the "seeking" which Jesus mentions in verse 33 meant to be a life-long seeking? If so, how much "finding" should we expect to experience in this life on earth? Will we ever be able to get by with less and less seeking?

20. What insight does this chapter offer regarding a godly perspective toward material possessions?

21. How could you use this chapter to help a new Christian who doubted his or her worth in God's eyes?

Compare verse 34 with Proverbs 27:1. What underlying principles would you say are the same for both verses?

MATTHEW 7

Startup: Talk about any memories you may have of not receiving something valuable simply because you failed to ask for it, or to ask for it enough.

1. How would you restate the "Golden Rule" (verse 12) in your own words?

2. In the familiar illustration which Jesus gives in verses 24-27, what does He mean by the "rock"?

3. How would you describe the basic *mindset* or *attitude* in life which Jesus is teaching in this chapter?

4. Which teachings in this chapter do you find hardest to understand?

5. EYE FOR DETAIL—*From what you recall seeing in this chapter, try answering the following question without looking at your Bible:* What is it that made the crowds of people so amazed or astonished by the teachings of Jesus? (See verses 28-29.)

6. Once again, if you were asked to summarize the most important "marks of Christian maturity" as taught in this chapter, which ones would you mention first?

7. Verses 7-8 teach us to pray with confidence. What is the true basis of that confidence?

8. Do you think verses 21-23 were meant to scare us, to comfort us, or something else entirely? (Explain your answer.)

9. What are the most important things this chapter communicates about God's character?

10. If we fully obey verses 1-2, do you think it's a guarantee that we won't be unfairly criticized by others? If not, then what does this verse really mean?

11. Jesus tells us to ask and to seek and to knock (verses 7-8). Look together at each of the following verses in this chapter, and think carefully about what Jesus is teaching us there. Then express each one in the form of a model prayer that any Christian could use—or a prayer that specifically fits your life right now: verses 2, 5, 12, 14, 21, and 24.

12. Think about verses 13-14. What is "narrow" about the path in life which you have chosen?

13. Review verses 15-20. Has there been a time when you have followed these guidelines and have recognized false Christian teaching?

14. Look at the amazement or astonishment mentioned in verses 28-29. What surprises *you* about the teaching of Jesus?

FOR GOING DEEPER

Compare what verses 13-14 imply about our *security* in life with what verses 24-27 teach about the same subject. How do these passages complement each other?

MATTHEW 8

Startup: The stigma often associated today with the AIDS virus is sometimes compared with the way in which people with leprosy were treated in the past. What have been your own thoughts about associating with persons with AIDS?

SEEING WHAT'S THERE

1. Once again, take a "walk" together through the incidents in this chapter. Using your imagination, talk about the kinds of sights, smells, sounds, and feelings you might experience.

2. How do you see the *power* of Jesus demonstrated in this chapter?

3. How is the *character* of Jesus demonstrated in this chapter?

4. How is the *purpose* of Jesus demonstrated in this chapter?

5. EYE FOR DETAIL—*From what you recall seeing in this chapter, try answering the following question without looking at your Bible:* In the incident where Jesus calmed the furious storm while He and the disciples were out on the Sea of Galilee, does the passage (verses 22-27) tell us who got into the boat first? If so, who was it?

CAPTURE THE ESSENCE

6. From what you see in this chapter, what does it really mean to "follow Jesus"?

7. In the incident in verses 23-27, how do you think the disciples would have responded to the storm if they had had more faith? How exactly did Jesus *want* them to respond?

8. If the disciples in the boat had truly responded in faith when the storm hit, do you think there were some even greater lessons they could have learned? If so, what might these have been?

9. How would you compare the power of the storm in verse 24 with the

power of the demons in verses 28-32?

10. In this chapter, which of these character qualities in Jesus comes through most strongly to you: His compassion, His power, or His wisdom? (Explain your answer.)

11. Imagine you were helping to produce a film based on this chapter. Describe the kinds of scenery, supporting characters, background music, lighting effects, etc., you would use to portray this chapter's central message.

FOR LIFE TODAY

12. In Colossians 3:1 we read this command: "Since you have been raised with Christ, set your hearts on things above, where Christ is seated at the right hand of God." What have you personally observed about Jesus Christ in this chapter that would be worthy of setting your heart on?

13. Look at the command Jesus gave in verse 22. How might this verse apply to us? How should we "let the dead bury their own dead"?

14. Think again about verses 23-27, especially the words Jesus spoke in verse 26. Is it wrong to ever be afraid? Is it possible to have faith and yet still experience fear?

15. What are some "storms" in your life —the " winds" and "waves" that have given you fear or anxiety? How have you seen that the Lord has power over them?

FOR GOING DEEPER

In verse 20, Jesus calls Himself "the Son of Man." This is the title Jesus uses most often for Himself in the gospels. Look at any or all of the following additional passages in Matthew in which Jesus calls Himself this. Discuss together the significance of this title—9:6, 11:19, 12:8, 12:40, 13:41, 16:13, 16:27-28, 17:9, 17:22, 20:28, 24:30, 24:44, and 26:64.

MATTHEW 9

Startup: Talk about any experiences you've had with people who had some kind of physical paralysis. How did it affect them mentally and emotionally?

SEEING WHAT'S THERE

1. Imagine that you are a roving reporter for the "Jerusalem Journal." In a few sentences, how would you describe what happened in this chapter?

2. Review verses 1-8, especially the reaction of the crowds in verse 8. What exactly was it that impressed these people about Jesus?

3. What does Jesus mean by the word *righteous* in the way He uses it in verse 13?

4. Look again at the story of the two blind men in verses 27-30 whose sight was restored by Jesus. What kind of words do you think came from their mouths as they suddenly were able to *see* each other (and everything and everyone else as well)?

5. What does this chapter teach us about the *power* of Jesus?

6. EYE FOR DETAIL—*From what you recall seeing in this chapter, try answering the following question without looking at your Bible:* In the last verse of this chapter, Jesus gave His disciples a brief, specific request to ask of God. What was that request?

7. In light of what you've seen so far in Matthew, how would you describe one of the "workers" or "laborers" which Jesus talks about in verse 38?

CAPTURE THE ESSENCE

8. From the evidence you see in this chapter, what would you say the disciple Matthew considered to be the most important things in life?

9. From what you've seen in this chapter, what does it really mean to "follow Jesus"?

10. Notice the encounters Jesus had in this chapter with both sexes. In what ways do you see that following Jesus Christ enhances your manhood or your womanhood?

11. Look again at verse 8. How does Jesus demonstrate His authority today, so that people can see and give praise to God?

12. Look at Jesus' answer to John's disciples in verse 15. Is the Bridegroom still with us? Is it now time to feast, or to fast?

13. The command in verse 38 is tied to verse 37. To what degree is what Jesus said in verse 37 still true today?

FOR GOING DEEPER

In verse 13, Jesus quotes a statement God makes in Hosea 6:6, and tells the Pharisees to go and learn what it means. Look ahead to Matthew 12:7, where Jesus quotes the verse again. Why do you think this was such an important verse to Jesus at this time?

MATTHEW 10

Startup: Recall a time in your life when you started on some new and challenging job or project or mission. What was it exactly that made it exciting for you?

SEEING WHAT'S THERE

1. Imagine that you are the disciple Peter, and that you're writing a quick letter to your family back home. Give a few sample lines of how you would describe what it was like to experience what the disciples experienced in this chapter.

2. Look again at verse 5. Why do you think Jesus at this time sent His disciples only to the Jews?

3. Look in verse 7 at the preaching message which Jesus gave to the disciples. How does it compare with the message He Himself preached, and the message John the Baptist preached? (Refer back to 3:2 and 4:17.)

4. Look at the last part of verse 8. What exactly had the disciples received for "free"?

5. Look together at verse 41. How would you define what a "righteous man" really is?

6. EYE FOR DETAIL—*From what you recall seeing in this chapter, try answering the following question without looking at your Bible:* In the first verse of the chapter, Jesus gave His disciples authority to do two things. What were they?

CAPTURE THE ESSENCE

7. What do you think Jesus meant by his command in the last part of verse 16?

8. From what you've seen in this chapter, what does it mean —or what *can* it mean, for some people—to "follow Jesus"?

9. Again, if you were asked to summarize the most important "marks of Christian maturity" as taught in this

chapter, which ones would you mention first?

FOR LIFE TODAY

10. In verse 1, look at the authority which Jesus gave to His twelve disciples. Do we have this same authority today?

11. Look again at the last sentence in verse 8. How does that principle apply to us today?

12. Look at the last part of verse 10. How would you say that this principle applies today in our churches and ministries?

13. Look again at the command in the last part of verse 16. What are some valid ways in which we could apply this principle today?

14. Look at what Jesus promised His disciples in verse 22. How hard is it for you to endure hatred from others?

15. Jesus encouraged us in Matthew 7:7 to ask and to seek and to knock. With this confidence in mind, look together at verses 32, 37, 38, and 39 in this chapter, and think carefully about what Jesus is teaching us there. Then express each verse in the form of a model prayer any Christian could use—or a prayer that specifically fits your life right now.

FOR GOING DEEPER

Review the prophetic words which Jesus spoke to the disciples in verses 17-18. Then look together at how these words came true in Acts 5:27-41, and Acts 12:1-5. Look also in Acts 26:9-11 at the confession of someone who persecuted Christians.

MATTHEW 11

Startup: Talk about any time you can remember when you needed or wanted more proof of how *reliable* someone or something was.

SEEING WHAT'S THERE

1. What do you think might have caused the doubts about Jesus which John the Baptist expressed in verse 2?

2. In your own words, how would you state what Jesus said in verse 11?

3. In verse 14, Jesus compared John the Baptist to the prophet Elijah. For helpful background on Elijah, look at Malachi 4:5, 1 Kings 19:3-19, and 2 Kings 2:11. Also look ahead to Matthew 17:11-13.

4. Would you describe the words of Jesus in verses 28 and 29 as a command, an invitation, a plea—or all three? Explain your answer.

5. Try stating the passage in verses 28-30 in completely different language, without using any words from the original (except those that are three letters or less).

6. EYE FOR DETAIL—*From what you recall seeing in this chapter, try answering the following question without looking at your Bible:* In this chapter, Jesus offers all of His listeners a specific *gift.* What is that gift? (See verse 28.)

CAPTURE THE ESSENCE

7. What do we learn in this chapter about the relationship between John the Baptist's ministry and the ministry of Jesus?

8. Look at the last sentence in verse 19, then look together at James 3:13. What do these verses teach us about wisdom?

9. Look closely at verses 25-27. What does this passage teach us about (a) Jesus' relationship to God, (b) God's

relationship to us, and (c) our relationship to Jesus?

10. Would you say that the rest Jesus promises in verse 28 is available at all times for Christians, or are there times when God does not want us to experience this kind of "rest"?

11. What do you think might be the most interesting thing in this chapter to someone who was learning about Jesus Christ for the first time, and why?

FOR LIFE TODAY

12. How could you use verses 2-6 to help a young believer who was beginning to have doubts about Jesus?

13. Look at the words Jesus spoke about His generation in verses 16-18. In what ways could these verses apply to our generation today?

14. In verses 20-24, look at the reasons for which Jesus pronounced judgment upon certain cities. In what ways could some of our cities today fall under the same judgment?

15. Look at the two kinds of people Jesus mentions in His prayer in verse 25. In what ways do you fit into either or both of these categories?

FOR GOING DEEPER

Compare the words of Jesus in verses 28-30 with His words in John 6:37. What attitudes or attributes of Jesus do you see in both passages?

MATTHEW 12

Startup: Talk about any experience you've had with "bending" or breaking a rule or law in order to do something you felt was right and important.

SEEING WHAT'S THERE

1. In the incident described in verses 1-8, what one or two words would you say best describe the disciples here? What one or two words best describe the Pharisees in this incident? What one or two words best describe Jesus here?

2. For helpful background on verse 2, look together at Exodus 34:21.

3. For helpful background on verses 3-4, look together at 1 Samuel 21:1-6 and Deuteronomy 23:25. Take a look also at God's instructions for baking the Sabbath bread in Leviticus 24:5-9.

4. For helpful background on verse 5, look together at Numbers 28:9-10, where God talks about some "work" to do (offering sacrifices) on the Sabbath.

5. From all that you see in verses 9-14, what one or two words would you say best describe the people Jesus spoke to in verse 11? What one or two words best describe Jesus here? What one or two words best describe the man with the injured hand?

6. In verses 17-21, what images stand out most to you in the words quoted from Isaiah 42?

7. If verses 17-21 were the very first and only words you had ever heard about the Messiah—the Son of God—how would you describe His character, in your own words?

8. From what you've seen so far in Matthew, how would you describe the attitude which the Pharisees and religious teachers have toward Jesus at this point in His ministry?

9. EYE FOR DETAIL—*From what you recall seeing in this chapter, try answering the following question without looking at your Bible:* In this chapter, Jesus compared Himself to two well-known Old Testament characters, saying that He was greater than either of them. Who were these two men? (See verses 41-42.)

CAPTURE THE ESSENCE

10. In verse 7, Jesus quotes a statement that God makes in Hosea 6:6, and says that the Pharisees did not know the meaning of these words. Look carefully at this statement Jesus quoted; what *does* it mean?

11. Why do you think the Pharisees did not understand the verse Jesus quoted in verse 7?

12. Jesus says in verse 8 that He is "Lord of the Sabbath." By saying this, what was He trying to communicate to the Pharisees?

13. What does verse 8 imply about Jesus' relationship to the Old Testament law?

14. How do you think the man with the injured hand would have answered the question in verse 10?

15. Explain how much you agree or disagree with this statement: In verses 1-14, the most important lesson for both the Pharisees and the disciples had to do with their understanding of Jesus, not their understanding of the Sabbath.

16. Why do you think Jesus did what He did in verse 16?

17. In this chapter, which of these character qualities in Jesus comes through most strongly to you: His compassion, His power, or His wisdom? (Explain your answer.)

18. Matthew 12 is often considered a key chapter, a key turning point in the book of Matthew. Why do you think this is so?

FOR LIFE TODAY

19. How might verse 6 be applied to the way we worship God today?

20. As you think about verse 7, ask yourself this question: In the way I live my Christian life, which (if either) is more important to me: sacrifice, or showing mercy and compassion?

21. What does the Sabbath mean to you in your life?

FOR GOING DEEPER

Notice in verses 24-28 that the devil is called both "Satan" and "Beelzebub" or "Beelzebul." Matthew's gospel teaches us much about the devil. Discuss together what we can learn about him in these verses: 4:1-11, 13:37-39, 16:22-23, and 25:41.

Matthew 13

Startup: Talk about any experiences you've had with farming or gardening—and focus on what you may have learned about the best planting methods.

1. Review the parable of the sower and the soils in verses 3-9. In what ways is this parable a *warning* to us? In what ways is it an *encouragement?*

2. In verse 9, what kind of "ears" is Jesus talking about?

3. What does verse 11 imply about the choices God makes?

4. What does the last verse in this chapter imply about the power and the will of God?

5. EYE FOR DETAIL—*From what you recall seeing in this chapter, try answering the following question without looking at your Bible:* In His explanation of the parable of the sower and the soils, what did Jesus say the thorns stood for? (See verse 22.)

6. Look closely at verses 34-35. What kinds of things were "hidden" for all of history until Jesus began His teaching ministry?

CAPTURE THE ESSENCE

7. If this chapter was the only Scripture portion you had, what biblical definition would you give for the term *kingdom of heaven?*

8. From what you see in verses 10-13, is it accurate to say that Jesus was hiding the truth from some people?

9. Look at the last half of verse 15. What lessons could be drawn from this verse about what it means to truly know God?

10. From what you see in this chapter, what is a *parable,* and what is its purpose?

FOR LIFE TODAY

11. Jesus encouraged us in Matthew 7:7 to ask and to seek and to knock. With this confidence in mind, look together at verses 44-46 in this chapter, and think carefully about what Jesus is teaching us there. Then express this passage in the form of a model prayer that any Christian could use—or a prayer that specifically fits your life right now.

12. Look at what Jesus said to His disciples in verse 11. Has the Lord also given to you what was given to the disciples?

13. How could you paraphrase the last half of verse 15 and make it into a prayer for yourself?

14. In line with what Jesus says in verse 23, describe as fully as possible what it takes for us to be "good soil"?

15. Notice how the parable of the weeds in verses 24-30 is explained later by Jesus in verses 36-43. From what you see here, is it right for us to try to seek out and destroy the "weeds" in the church today?

16. Look at verses 44-46. Have you ever felt like either of these two men?

FOR GOING DEEPER

Notice the use of the word *fulfilled* in verses 14 and 35. This is an important and frequently used word in Matthew's gospel. Review together the principle of fulfillment which Jesus expressed in 5:17, then discuss together the following passages where the words *fulfill* or *fulfilled* are used: 1:21-23, 2:14-15, 3:13-15, 4:13-16, 8:16-17, 12:15-21, 21:1-5, and 26:54-56.

MATTHEW 14

Startup: Talk about hardships you may have experienced that were due to your standing up for what you believed was right.

SEEING WHAT'S THERE

1. This chapter focuses on three very different events in very different circumstances. Take a "walk" together through all three incidents, being observant of everything around you. Using your imagination, talk about the kinds of sights, smells, sounds, and feelings you might experience.

2. Focus in particular on the incident in verses 22-33. Imagine that you're Peter, and you're explaining later on to others what happened here. How would you describe it?

3. From what you see in this chapter, how would you describe the character and personality of King Herod?

4. What do verses 13-14 reveal about the character of Jesus?

5. From what you've seen so far in Matthew, how much of His schedule was Jesus able to spend alone? Why did He make time for this?

6. EYE FOR DETAIL—*From what you recall seeing in this chapter, try answering the following question without looking at your Bible:* When Jesus fed the five thousand, how many bread loaves and how many fish did He begin with, and how many basketfuls of leftovers were there? (See verses 19-20.)

CAPTURE THE ESSENCE

7. From the evidence in verses 16-21, draw as many conclusions as you can about the *power* of Jesus.

8. From the evidence in verses 22-33, draw as many conclusions as you can about *faith.*

9. From what you see in this chapter, why did Jesus perform miracles?

10. In this chapter, which of these character qualities in Jesus comes through most strongly to you: His compassion, His power, or His wisdom? (Explain your answer.)

FOR LIFE TODAY

11. What guidelines for people in ministry today can you find in Jesus' example in this chapter?

12. From the way Jesus seemed to handle the news of John's death (in verses 13-14, and 22-23), what possible guidelines can you discover for dealing with grief in our lives today?

FOR GOING DEEPER

What else do you learn about this King Herod from Mark 6:20, from the prayer in Acts 4:27, and from Acts 12:19-23?

MATTHEW 15

Startup: What kind of difficulties can you recall having in trying to go against the traditions and routines of others?

SEEING WHAT'S THERE

1. Together, list aloud all the different kinds of people represented in this chapter. What would you say are the most prominent characteristics of each one?

2. Imagine yourself being present in the situation described in verses 1-20. In light of your own personality, what words spoken by Jesus in this passage stand out most to you?

3. What different tones of voice do you think Jesus may have used in the various places where He is quoted in this chapter?

4. What do the words of Jesus in verses 3-6 tell us about how God views our responsibility toward our parents?

5. Read again verses 29-32, and notice how long Jesus was ministering at this particular place. How would you describe a typical day for Him at this time?

6. EYE FOR DETAIL—*From what you recall seeing in this chapter, try answering the following question without looking at your Bible:* When Jesus fed the four thousand, how many loaves of bread did He begin with, and how many basketfuls of leftovers were there? (See verses 34-37.)

CAPTURE THE ESSENCE

7. Think about verses 16-20, then discuss how much you agree or disagree with this statement: God is just as concerned with the "internals" of our lives as He is with the "externals"— He cares as much about what we are thinking as He does about what we are doing.

8. Review what Jesus says in verses 17-20 about what makes a person "unclean." If this is what makes us unclean, what is it that makes us *clean?*

9. How complete would you say is the list of unclean actions in verse 19?

10. Think carefully about the incident in verses 21-28. What does this passage show us about Jesus' obedience to His Father, and also about God's compassion? Are these two qualities in conflict here?

11. In verse 23, why do you think Jesus was silent?

FOR LIFE TODAY

12. Read over again verses 8-9. Does this mean that when we feel inwardly distant from God, we should not try to worship Him?

13. Look again at verse 12. In what ways are Jesus' words offensive to some today?

14. Could Jesus' words in verse 14 be spoken about anyone today?

15. Hear again the words of commendation which Jesus spoke to the Canaanite woman in verse 28. What was so great about this woman's faith?

FOR GOING DEEPER

Compare the list of sinful deeds and qualities in verse 19 with the lists you see in these passages: Romans 1:29-31; 1 Corinthians 6:9-10; Galatians 5:19-21; and Revelation 22:15.

Matthew 16

Startup: What have been the most important "turning points" in your life?

SEEING WHAT'S THERE

1. Consider carefully verses 1-4. Why didn't Jesus just go ahead and show these people a miracle or two?

2. What is the "yeast" Jesus speaks of in verses 5 and 11-12, and why is it so dangerous?

3. From what you've seen in the most recent chapters in Matthew, how would you summarize the attitude the Pharisees and religious teachers have toward Jesus at this point in His ministry?

4. Verse 18 is the first time in the New Testament that the word *church* is used. What does this verse teach us about the church?

5. EYE FOR DETAIL—*From what you recall seeing in this chapter, try answering the following question without looking at your Bible:* Jesus asked the disciples, "Who do people say the Son of Man is?"—and the answer from the disciples included three names. What were those three names? (See verse 14.)

CAPTURE THE ESSENCE

6. In the second half of this chapter, Jesus has begun to focus His ministry upon His disciples. What guidelines for today's discipleship training do you see in the way Jesus taught His disciples in verses 13-19?

7. Imagine yourself as Peter in the scene recorded in the last half of this chapter. As you hear the words of Jesus spoken directly to you in verses 17-19, what thoughts and questions would come to your mind?

8. Compare what Jesus says in verse 19 with Matthew 18:17-20. What do these passages together tell us about the privileges and responsibilities of the church?

9. What would you say verses 24 and 25 have to teach us about self-esteem?

10. If you were asked to summarize the most important "marks of Christian maturity" as taught in this chapter, which ones would you mention first?

FOR LIFE TODAY

11. Look at the first question Jesus asks in verse 9. In what ways might the Lord be justified in asking this question of you today?

12. Is the "yeast" still around today which Jesus describes in verses 5 and 11-12? If so, where?

13. Jesus gives the true source of faith in verse 17. In your life, what has been the process in which God the Father "revealed" to you the truth about His Son?

14. Restate in your own words—and in the context of our lives today—the three things Jesus asks us to do in verse 24.

15. Remember again how Jesus encouraged us in Matthew 7:7 to ask and to seek and to knock. With this confidence in mind, look together at verses 24-25 in this chapter, and think carefully about what Jesus is teaching us there. Then express this passage in the form of a model prayer any Christian could use—or a prayer that specifically fits your life right now.

FOR GOING DEEPER

Compare Jesus' words about the church in verses 18-19 with the teaching in Ephesians 2:19-22 and 1 Timothy 3:15.

Matthew 17

Startup: What memorable experiences have you had mountain-climbing?

1. Using your imagination, how would you describe the probable "atmosphere" of the incident recorded in verses 1-8?

2. In verse 3, what do you know about Moses and Elijah that explains the significance of their presence here?

3. Examine closely the words God spoke about Jesus in verse 5. Notice the different phrases that make up this quotation. What would you say is the significance of each phrase?

4. Notice Jesus' instructions to Peter, James, and John in verse 9. Imagine that you are one of these three disciples, and that the time is now at the end of this gospel, after Jesus had risen from the dead. You are now free to tell them about the mountaintop experience which we see in Matthew 9. How would you go about explaining what happened that day to the other disciples?

5. Were the words Jesus spoke in verse 17 meant to sound harsh? Why or why not?

6. In what ways did Jesus have to "put up with" the disciples (verse 17)?

7. Take turns in your group saying aloud the answer Jesus gave in verse 20, and try to capture the tone of voice you think Jesus probably used.

8. EYE FOR DETAIL—*From what you recall seeing in this chapter, try answering the following question without looking at your Bible:* Can you name all six men who were on the high mountain in the incident described at the beginning of this chapter? (See verses 1-3.)

9. From God's point of view, what was the purpose of Jesus' transfiguration (in verses 1-8)?

10. Look at what Peter, James, and John did in verse 6. How much would you say their actions qualify as a picture and example for us of true worship?

11. To see what Peter wrote later about his experiences in verses 1-8, look together at 2 Peter 1:16-18. What seem to be the most important things Peter learned from being a witness to this transfiguration of Jesus?

12. Why do you think Jesus told the disciples (in verse 9) not to tell anyone what they had seen?

13. Look again at verse 20. Why does God place so much value on faith?

14. In verse 22 we come to the second instance in Matthew's gospel where Jesus tells the disciples about His coming death and resurrection. The first time was in Matthew 16:21. For both of those references, look at the verses which follow to see how the disciples responded. What thoughts do you think were on their minds?

15. What guidelines for today's discipleship training do you see in the way Jesus taught His disciples in verses 19-23?

16. With the last sentence in verse 20 in mind, discuss some "impossibilities" which you have seen God accomplish in your life, or in the life of someone close to you.

Compare the account in verses 1-8 of Jesus' transfiguration with the passage about His baptism in 3:13-17. What similarities do you see in both events? And how do they relate to one another?

MATTHEW 18

Startup: Talk about the most recent time you can recall hearing a young child say something that struck you as humorous.

SEEING WHAT'S THERE

1. Again in this chapter, the focus of Jesus' ministry is on the training of the disciples. What would you say are the main discipleship concepts in verses 1-9?

2. In as few words as possible, how would you summarize the principle Jesus is teaching in verses 8 and 9?

3. Practically speaking, what exactly is Jesus warning us not to do in verse 10?

4. In the parable of the lost sheep (verses 10-14), how would you summarize the main discipleship concepts?

5. How would you summarize the main discipleship concepts in verses 15-20?

6. How would you summarize the main discipleship concepts in the parable of the unmerciful servant (verses 21-35)?

7. Imagine yourself being present in the situation described in this chapter. In light of your own personality, what words spoken by Jesus in these verses stand out most to you?

8. EYE FOR DETAIL—*From what you recall seeing in this chapter, try answering the following question without looking at your Bible:* In the last verse of the chapter, Jesus mentioned a specific manner in which we are to forgive our brothers. What was it?

CAPTURE THE ESSENCE

9. As you consider the words of Jesus in verses 3-4, give as full a definition as you can of what it means to "become like children."

10. Recall once more how Jesus encouraged us in Matthew 7:7 to ask and to seek and to knock. With this confidence in mind, look together at verses 3-4 in Matthew 18, and think carefully about what Jesus is teaching us there. Then express this passage in the form of a model prayer any Christian could use—or a prayer that specifically fits your life right now.

11. What kind of actions do you think Jesus is talking about in verses 6-7—things people do that cause others to sin?

12. Reflect on verses 19-20, and decide together all it means for Christians to "agree" about what they ask God for.

13. Again, if you were asked to summarize the most important "marks of Christian maturity" as taught in this chapter, which ones would you mention first?

FOR LIFE TODAY

14. Look at the question which the disciples asked Jesus in verse 1. In what ways, if any, do we sometimes ask this question today?

FOR GOING DEEPER

Jesus gives important information about angels in verse 10. To study more about what angels do, look together at these verses: Genesis 16:7, Exodus 14:19, Judges 2:1-5, 2 Samuel 24:16, Daniel 6:22, and Revelation 20:1-2.

MATTHEW 19

Startup: What do you feel is the most important choice you've made in the last 24 hours? In the last week? In the last year?

SEEING WHAT'S THERE

1. For helpful background on the divorce passage in verses 3-9, look together at Deuteronomy 24:1-4. Look also at Matthew 5:31-32.

2. What "statement" or "word" is Jesus talking about in verse 11, which He says that not everyone can accept?

3. How would you explain verse 14 in your own words?

4. EYE FOR DETAIL—*From what you recall seeing in this chapter, try answering the following question without looking at your Bible:* When Jesus stated that a man who divorced his wife and married another woman was guilty of adultery, He also mentioned an exception. What was the exception? (See verse 9.)

CAPTURE THE ESSENCE

5. In verses 6 and 9 Jesus speaks of the binding permanence of marriage, while in verse 12, He speaks about those who stay single for the sake of God's kingdom. How do these passages fit together? What foundational principles seem to underlie this entire section on divorce, marriage, and singleness?

6. As you look over the last half of the chapter (from verse 16 on), discuss this question: Is this passage mostly about *possessions,* mostly about *relationships,* or equally about both?

7. Would you say verse 21 is mostly about *actions,* mostly about *attitudes,* or equally about both?

8. What would you say is the "ultimate truth" Jesus is trying to teach in this last half of the chapter?

9. What in this chapter do you think might be the most interesting to someone who was learning about Jesus Christ for the first time, and why?

10. What would you say is the key word or phrase in the statement Jesus makes in verse 29?

FOR LIFE TODAY

11. Review what Jesus commanded in verse 21. For whom, if anyone, is this command still valid today?

12. Think about verse 22, then discuss how much you agree or disagree with this statement: Material possessions always have more potential for causing sadness than for causing happiness.

13. In light of what Jesus says in verse 30, what kind of surprises do you think we're in for (even though Jesus has told us this beforehand)?

FOR GOING DEEPER

Look together at the opening phrase in verse 1. The same statement, or one similar to it, occurs also in 7:28, 11:1, 13:53, and later in 26:1. Bible teachers often use these statements as the dividing marks between the six main parts of the book of Matthew. Look up these other verses, and notice together the context in which each one occurs. What clues do they give of the way Matthew put together this book?

MATTHEW 20

Startup: Can you recall a time in your work history when you felt you were being paid unfairly?

SEEING WHAT'S THERE

1. In this chapter's opening parable of the vineyard owner and his workers, who do you think the landowner represents, and who do the workers represent?

2. In verses 17-19 we find the third instance in Matthew where Jesus predicts His death and resurrection. How does the wording here compare with the previous two predictions in 16:21 and 17:22-23? What additional information is Jesus now giving to His disciples?

3. In verses 22 and 23, what "cup" do you think Jesus is talking about?

4. How would you explain the meaning of the word *ransom* in verse 28?

5. EYE FOR DETAIL—*From what you recall seeing in this chapter, try answering the following question without looking at your Bible:* In the incident at the end of the chapter, what were the two blind men in Jericho shouting to Jesus? (See verses 30-31.)

CAPTURE THE ESSENCE

6. What does the opening parable (verses 1-16) teach us about God's character, and about the way He does things?

7. Would you say this opening parable is more about *judgment* and *rewards*... or more about *grace* and *salvation?*

8. In verse 15, the landowner speaks about his legal "rights." How would you describe and define the "rights" God has? Are these the same as what is always *right* for Him to do?

9. In verse 28, Jesus said He came to give His life as a *ransom* for us. If we need a ransom—what does that say about *us?*

10. Was it wrong for the mother of James and John to ask what she did in verse 21? Why or why not?

FOR LIFE TODAY

11. Think again about this chapter's opening parable. What possible surprises in heaven does this passage help you anticipate?

12. From what Jesus says in verse 16, should we actually *try* to be "last"? And if so, what does that mean?

13. Discuss whether you think there's any danger for us today in applying verses 26-27 too literally.

FOR GOING DEEPER

Jesus spoke in verses 22-23 about the "cup" He was to drink. To see how this phrase is used vividly in other Scriptures, look at Jeremiah 25:15-16, Ezekiel 23:32-34, Habakkuk 2:16, and Revelation 14:9-10.

Matthew 21

Startup: What experience have you had with growing fruit trees or vines?

SEEING WHAT'S THERE

1. Keep the events of verses 1-11 in mind, as you discuss how much you agree or disagree with this statement: The cheering welcome and praise which Jesus received as He entered Jerusalem was rooted only in the people's misunderstanding of what kind of king He truly was, and this was proven by the way the crowds turned against Him later in the week.

2. Imagine that you are a reporter for the "Jerusalem Journal." How would you describe the events of this chapter?

3. Review what was said and done in verses 12-17. How did this incident compare with an earlier one recorded in John 2:13-17?

4. For background on Jesus' words about the Temple being a "house of prayer" (verse 13), look together at Isaiah 56:7.

5. Notice in verses 45-46 how the Jewish religious leaders responded to the parables of Jesus (perhaps especially the last one in this chapter). Beginning with verse 33, identify each person or group of people in this last parable, and who each one represents.

6. EYE FOR DETAIL—*From what you recall seeing in this chapter, try answering the following question without looking at your Bible:* In this chapter Jesus told His disciples that they would receive whatever they asked for in prayer, but He attached a condition to that promise. What was the condition? (See verse 22.)

CAPTURE THE ESSENCE

7. In this chapter, how could the Temple be compared with the fig tree Jesus cursed?

8. What do you think was the *motive* Jesus had for doing what He did in verses 12-17?

9. Why do you think Jesus cursed the fig tree in verse 19?

10. Explain *why* you agree or disagree with this statement: Verses 21-22 in this chapter prove that Jesus approved of the practice of magic.

11. Is Jesus giving us a "blank check" in verse 22? If not, then why does He make this statement?

FOR LIFE TODAY

12. Remember again the command in Colossians 3:1—"Since you have been raised with Christ, set your hearts on things above, where Christ is seated at the right hand of God." What have you personally observed about Jesus Christ in this chapter that would be worthy of setting your heart on?

13. Think again about verses 12-17. Do you feel there is anything in our churches today that corresponds to the activities of the people whom Jesus drove out of the Temple?

14. In verses 23-27, the focus is on the *authority* of Jesus and the *authority* of John the Baptist, both of which came from God. What authority do *you* have from God?

15. Which of the two sons in verses 28-32 are you most like?

16. With the closing parable of this chapter in mind, compare it with another interesting parable about a vineyard in Isaiah 5:1-7. What are the similarities, and what are the differences?

Compare what you see in this chapter's opening scene with Psalm 45:4. How much does this psalm seem to describe Jesus?

MATTHEW 22

Startup: Can you recall a time when you felt someone was trying to trap you with a question ?

SEEING WHAT'S THERE

1. In your own words, how would you summarize the main point of the parable in verses 1-14? Why did Jesus tell this parable?

2. Verse 15 says that the Pharisees had laid a trap for Jesus. How do you think they expected the trap to work?

3. Does the question from the Sadducees in verse 23 appear to be a trap as well? Why or why not?

4. For background on verse 24, look together at Deuteronomy 25:5-10.

5. EYE FOR DETAIL—*From what you recall seeing in this chapter, try answering the following question without looking at your Bible:* In the parable Jesus told about the wedding banquet, the king commanded his servants to tie up a certain man who was there, and to throw him out of the wedding hall. What was it about this man that caused the king to do this? (See verses 11-13.)

6. Imagine you're a devout Jew from Rome and have come across the sea for the first time to visit Jerusalem for the Passover festival. The events in Matthew 21 and 22 are your first exposure to Jesus of Nazareth; in fact, as far as you know, no one back home in Rome has even heard of this Man. What kind of impressions would you now have of Jesus, based on all you've seen these past few days? (Look back over these two chapters to help you keep in mind all these events.)

CAPTURE THE ESSENCE

7. In verses 11-12, what do you think the wedding clothes are meant to represent?

8. In your opinion, how important was the question which Jesus asked the Pharisees in verses 41-42?

9. Did the Pharisees give the right or wrong answer to Jesus' question in verse 42? Why did Jesus respond the way He did in the next three verses?

10. The Jesus we see in this gospel is not only fully God, but also fully human. From what you've seen so far in Matthew, in what ways does Jesus show Himself to be the perfect model of manhood?

11. Think about verse 21. In your life, what things belong to God, and yet still must be given up to Him?

12. Recalling verse 37, what portions of your heart or your soul or your mind are the hardest to love God with?

13. Remember again how Jesus encouraged us to ask and to seek and to knock (in Matthew 7:7). With this confidence in mind, look together at verses 37-39 in Matthew 22, and think carefully about what Jesus is teaching us there. Then express this passage in the form of a model prayer any Christian could use—or a prayer that specifically fits your life right now.

FOR GOING DEEPER

Compare the "wedding clothes" in verses 11-12 with the imagery you discover when you look up these verses: Isaiah 61:10, Romans 13:14, Galatians 3:27, and Revelation 3:4-5 and 19:7-8

MATTHEW 23

Startup: What's more important to you: Doing things the right way, or doing the right things even if they're done the wrong way?

SEEING WHAT'S THERE

1. Six times in this chapter Jesus uses the word *hypocrites* to describe the Pharisees and the religious teachers. How would you define this word?

2. Imagine yourself being present in the situation described in this chapter. In light of your own personality, what words spoken by Jesus in these verses stand out most to you?

3. Discuss how much you agree or disagree with this statement: In verses 8-12, Jesus teaches us that leadership is much less important than people often think it is.

4. EYE FOR DETAIL—*From what you recall seeing in this chapter, try answering the following question without looking at your Bible:* Jesus accused the Pharisees and religious teachers of neglecting the three most important matters of the law—the provisions of the law that carry the most weight in God's eyes. What are those three things? (See verse 23.)

CAPTURE THE ESSENCE

5. In verse 12, Jesus promises specific consequences both for those who exalt themselves and for those who humble themselves. When do you think these consequences will occur —mostly in eternity, or mostly in this life?

6. Look at Jesus' words in verse 34. When He speaks of "prophets and wise men and teachers," who is He referring to?

FOR LIFE TODAY

7. From what Jesus says about the Pharisees in this chapter, rank the following three things according to how

you see their importance to God: (a) what we say, (b) what we know, and (c) what we do.

8. What do you feel is the best *cure* for hypocrisy? What do you feel is the best *prevention* against hypocrisy?

9. What similarities would you point out between being a Jewish religious leader in the days when Jesus lived on earth, and being a pastor or other Christian leader today? What major differences would there be?

10. Look over the long list of criticisms in this chapter which Jesus had for the religious leaders of His day. Then discuss which of these faults and failures are, in your opinion, the biggest dangers for Christian leaders today.

11. Look at the first statement Jesus makes in verse 5. Has there ever been a time when that charge could have been accurately made against you?

FOR GOING DEEPER

Look at the two men mentioned in verse 35, then turn together to Genesis 4:1-8 and 2 Chronicles 24:17-22 to learn more about them.

MATTHEW 24

Startup: What experience have you had in reading the predictions of people who claim to see into the future? How much credibility do you tend to attach to them?

SEEING WHAT'S THERE

1. Who is Jesus speaking to in this chapter?

2. Review carefully verses 1-3. What things do the disciples specifically want to know?

3. What questions are raised in your mind by the words of Jesus in this chapter?

4. Bible teachers have presented various outlines of this chapter to indicate how Jesus is speaking at times about the end of this present age (as in verses 4-14), then about the coming destruction of Jerusalem later in the First Century (as in verses 15-21), and finally about His second coming (as in verses 22-31). What to you are the verses with the *clearest* meaning and time reference in this chapter?

5. From what Jesus tells His disciples in verses 4-14, does He want them to think it will be a *long* time or a *short* time before the end of the present age?

6. Many Bible teachers regard verse 22 as one of the most important statements in this chapter. Why do you think this is so?

7. What exactly do you think Jesus means in verse 44 about being "ready"?

8. EYE FOR DETAIL—*From what you recall seeing in this chapter, try answering the following question without looking at your Bible:* Most of the words in this chapter were spoken when Jesus and His disciples were sitting in a particular location. Where

was it, and what do you know about this place? (See verse 3.)

CAPTURE THE ESSENCE

9. What would you say is the most important concept this chapter teaches us about our *responsibility*, as we wait for the end?

10. Verse 14 focuses our attention on the entire world. Look again at verses 9-14, with Christians around the world in mind. Which of the predictions mentioned in this passage are taking place now?

11. Who are "the elect" in verse 22, and what does this passage show us about them?

FOR LIFE TODAY

12. Discuss how you respond inwardly to what you see in this chapter. Is it with anticipation? Fear? Confusion?

13. How susceptible do you think you might be to the deceptions which Jesus warns about in verses 4 and 23-26?

14. As you think about verses 9-14, what effect would you say persecution can have on our evangelism efforts? (See also Acts 8 and 1 Timothy 2:1-4.)

15. Look at the statement Jesus makes in verse 36. What difference in your life do you think it would make if you *did* know the exact day or hour when Jesus will return?

16. Review verses 42-44. Practically speaking, how do we stay alert and watchful today, in obedience to these words from Jesus?

FOR GOING DEEPER

To discover more about the Mount of Olives, where Jesus gave most of the teaching in this chapter, look at 2 Samuel 15:30, Zechariah 14:3-4, Luke 19:29, Luke 22:39-43, John 8:1, Acts 1:12, and Revelation 14:1-5.

MATTHEW 25

Startup: What would you say are the most important gifts and abilities you've been given?

SEEING WHAT'S THERE

1. Notice how this chapter divides almost equally into three parts: the parable of the ten virgins (1-13), the parable of the talents (14-30), and a final passage about the Lord's judgment (31-46). What would you say is the main point of each of these three parts?

2. What do these three parts together show us about the *kingship* of Jesus?

3. Who is Jesus speaking to in this chapter? (Go back to the beginning of chapter 24 to find out.)

4. What kind of wrong thinking or actions do you think Jesus may be trying to prevent by telling the disciples these things?

5. EYE FOR DETAIL—*From what you recall seeing in this chapter, try answering the following question without looking at your Bible:* In His teaching about the sheep and the goats, Jesus mentions six different physical needs which His righteous servants were meeting in the lives of others. Can you name all six? (See verses 35-36.)

CAPTURE THE ESSENCE

6. Once again, if you were asked to summarize the most important "marks of Christian maturity" as taught in this chapter, which ones would you mention first?

7. From what you see in this chapter, how would you define the word *faithful*?

FOR LIFE TODAY

8. Discuss how much you agree or disagree with this statement: If we aren't multiplying our gifts from God, then we don't really have them at all.

9. If the parable of the ten virgins is at least partially a picture of our lives today, what does the oil represent?

10. Think again of Philippians 4:8, where we're given this command: "Whatever is true, whatever is noble, whatever is right, whatever is pure, whatever is lovely, whatever is admirable—if anything is excellent or praiseworthy—*think about such things.*" What food for thought can you find in this chapter that especially strikes you as being *true,* or *noble,* or *right,* or *pure,* or *lovely,* or *admirable,* or *excellent,* or *praiseworthy?*

11. From what you've learned so far in the book of Matthew, summarize what you think it means for Christians today to "follow in the footsteps of Jesus."

12. In verse 13, just as He did in the last chapter (24:42-44), Jesus tells His followers to stay alert for His coming. He surely knew how difficult this alertness could be for us. What kind of obstacles to this alertness do you see in your own life?

13. With the parable of the talents in mind (in verses 14-30), in what ways can you honestly say your gifts from the Lord are increasing and multiplying?

FOR GOING DEEPER

Compare the judgment mentioned in the passage about the sheep and the goats (verses 31-46) with the judgment described in Revelation 20:10-15. What similarities do you see?

MATTHEW 26

Startup: What is most important to you about the celebration of the Lord's Supper?

SEEING WHAT'S THERE

1. In what ways, if any, do you see the worthiness and nobleness and purity of Jesus in this chapter?

2. How would you explain what Jesus means by the word *covenant* in verse 28?

3. Notice in verse 38 how deep was the sorrow which Jesus experienced. How would you explain this verse to a child?

4. EYE FOR DETAIL—*From what you recall seeing in this chapter, try answering the following question without looking at your Bible:* When Peter heard the rooster crow after he had denied Jesus three times, what did Peter do next? (See verse 75.)

CAPTURE THE ESSENCE

5. The woman mentioned in verses 6-13 is identified in John 12:1-3 as being Mary, the sister of Martha and Lazarus. From what you see in this chapter, what would you say Mary considered to be the most important things in life?

6. When Jesus told His disciples that one of them would betray Him, notice their response in verse 22. Contrast their response with that of Judas Iscariot in verse 25. In what detail was Judas's reply different, and what did it reveal about his heart?

7. From the evidence you see in this chapter, how would you describe Simon Peter's relationship with Jesus?

8. Why do you think Jesus gave no answer to the high priest's questioning in verse 62, and yet immediately gave a clear and extended answer to the high priest's question in verse 63?

9. How would you explain the meaning of what Jesus did and said in verses 26-28 to someone who had never seen or heard this passage?

10. What actions can we do that, in God's eyes, would be equivalent to what the woman did with the perfume in verse 7? Or is it truly too late?

11. Is there any sense today in which we are called upon to "keep watch" with Jesus, as the disciples were called to do in verses 38-41?

12. Look again at the action (or lack of action) by the disciples in verse 56. What warning, if any, do you see for us today in their example?

13. Review the high priest's verdict about the guilt of Jesus in verse 65. What do people "accuse" Jesus of today?

FOR GOING DEEPER

Study the regulations for the high priest in Leviticus 21:10, and compare it to the high priest's action in verse 65. What does this imply about the opinion the high priest had of Jesus and His words?

MATTHEW 27

Startup: Have you ever seen someone die? What was it like?

SEEING WHAT'S THERE

1. Read aloud verses 1 and 2. Then begin with verse 11, and walk your way through the events of this chapter as if you were Jesus Himself, feeling what He felt, seeing what He saw, hearing what He heard. Describe to one another the sensations that come to your imagination.

2. This chapter records only two brief sentences spoken by Jesus. Investigate them, and talk about their significance for Jesus Himself, and for all Christians.

3. For background on Jesus' silence in verses 12 and 14, look together at the prophecy in Isaiah 53:7.

4. What miracles do you see taking place in the last half of this chapter?

5. EYE FOR DETAIL—*From what you recall seeing in this chapter, try answering the following question without looking at your Bible:* After they crucified Jesus, the Roman soldiers placed a sign above Him that contained the so-called "charge" against Him. What did this sign say? (See verse 37.)

CAPTURE THE ESSENCE

6. Look in verse 4 at how the religious leaders responded to Judas's confession. How correct was their answer?

7. From God's perspective, would you say the actions of the chief priests in verses 6-8 were good and commendable?

8. From what you see in verses 11-26, what kind of a man was Pilate?

9. Look together at verses 11, 37, and 42. From what you've noticed so far in the book of Matthew, how would you describe the *kingship* of Jesus?

10. From what you see in verse 19, what kind of woman was Pilate's wife?

11. How do you think verse 46 relates to what Jesus prayed in Matthew 26:39?

FOR LIFE TODAY

12. No one is trying to physically crucify us today—but what does Jesus' *example* in this chapter mean personally for your life?

13. Of the most important events and truths in this chapter, which do you think are the easiest for Christians to forget about?

FOR GOING DEEPER

For prophetic background on this chapter, read together Psalm 22. What are the strongest themes in this psalm that find their fulfillment in Matthew 27?

MATTHEW 28

Startup: Practically speaking, what would you say is the most important thing you have to do in the time you have remaining on earth?

SEEING WHAT'S THERE

1. In verse 2, why do you think the angel rolled back the stone from the entrance to the tomb?

2. Examine each part of the angel's message to the women in verses 5-7. What was the importance of each part?

3. Review verses 11-15. From what you see there, what kind of thoughts may have been running through the minds of the Jewish leaders after they heard the report from the guards?

4. What do you think Jesus means by the term "make disciples" in verse 19?

5. EYE FOR DETAIL—*From what you recall seeing in this chapter, try answering the following question without looking at your Bible:* The final words of Jesus in this gospel are known as "the Great Commission." How much of it can you recall?

CAPTURE THE ESSENCE

6. Look closely at verses 18-20, a passage traditionally known as "The Great Commission." What is your strongest response to this passage—hope, excitement, a sense of responsibility, or something else?

7. Compare verses 19-20 with what Jesus told His disciples earlier in Matthew 10:5-7. Give as many reasons as you can for the change in His instructions to them.

8. Why do you think Jesus included all three Persons of the Trinity in verse 19? What thoughts do you think came to the minds of the apostles when they heard these words?

9. What to you personally is the most important *command* in the "Great Commission" passage (verses 18-20)?

10. Look once more at the final words of Jesus in this book. Then identify together the kinds of people in your community whom you would say probably know the least about the living Lord Jesus Christ. What else are these people like? What do they do in daily life? Where do they live? Now imagine that God has brought you together with a small group of these people, and in this meeting they indicate a genuine desire to understand who Jesus is and what He has done. From what you have seen in the gospel of Matthew, what are the most important things you would want to communicate to them, and how would you word it?

FOR GOING DEEPER

Analyze the importance of Jesus' resurrection as you think together about this chapter, and about these supporting passages: Romans 4:25, 1 Corinthians 15:17, and Revelation 1:18.

MATTHEW:

THE BIG PICTURE

(Discuss again the questions in the "Overview," plus the questions below.)

1. Look together at each of these passages, and discuss which one you believe is the best candidate for "KEY VERSE" in the book of Matthew— the one which brings into sharpest focus what this book is most about: 1:1, 3:11-12, 5:17, 16:15-16, 16:19 and 28:18-20.

2. In what ways do you see this book serving as a bridge between the Old Testament and the New Testament?

3. Even more than the other gospel writers, Matthew is said to be a skilled *teacher*. How would you evaluate his teaching skills, as you've observed them in this book?

4. What would you say are the most important ways in which this book is *unique* in all the Bible?

5. In James 1:23-24 we're told that "anyone who listens to the word but does not do what it says is like a man who looks at his face in a mirror and, after looking at himself, goes away and immediately forgets what he looks like." In what important ways has the book of Matthew been a "mirror" for you—showing you what you can and should do?

6. What to you are the most important ways in which this book proves that Jesus is the King of the Jews?

7. What does the kingship of Jesus mean to you personally? How is He *your* king?

Mark

OVERVIEW

(Discuss these OVERVIEW questions both at the beginning of your study of Mark, and again after you've studied together all 16 chapters. Your answers may change significantly once you've looked more closely at the entire book.)

Startup: What pictures or words come to your mind when you think of the term *servant?*

SEEING WHAT'S THERE

1. Look together at 1 Peter 2:21. Suppose you had never read any of the gospels before, but someone told you this verse was an excellent summary of what's written in the Bible about Jesus. What would you therefore expect to find while reading through the gospel of Mark for the first time?

2. If anyone in your group has a Bible with the words of Jesus in red, look on together as you scan through the pages of Matthew and Mark. Which of these gospels puts more emphasis on Jesus' teachings, and which one seems to emphasize His actions?

3. To learn more about the author of this gospel, Mark (also known as John Mark, or simply John), look together at Acts 12:25—13:5, 13:13, and 15:36-40; Colossians 4:10; 2 Timothy 4:11; Philemon 24; and 1 Peter 5:13. From this evidence, what kind of person would you guess Mark to be? What were, perhaps, the major events of his life?

4. Bible teachers often point out the fast pace with which the narrative moves along in Mark. For example,

scan the first chapter, and notice how many times the words *immediately* or *at once* or *straightway* are used to describe the action.

5. Look also at the list of "Questions to Ask as You Begin Your Study of Each Book" on page 393.

CAPTURE THE ESSENCE

6. Compare the way in which this gospel begins (Mark 1:1), with the way the other three gospels begin (in Matthew 1:1-17, Luke 1:1-4, and John 1:1-18). What do these different "start-up styles" tell you about the *purpose* of each gospel?

7. Scan this book together to see how many *miracles* of Jesus you can find. As you identify them this way, what kind of impression do they give you of Jesus?

FOR LIFE TODAY

8. How can you ensure that your study of Mark is not merely theoretical and intellectual, but is instead truly practical and relevant? Talk together about this. What can you do to help keep the process alive and interesting?

FOR GOING DEEPER

Bible teachers often present Mark as the gospel that especially presents Jesus as "the Servant of God"; in Mark, the *servanthood* of Jesus—serving both God and man—is clearly apparent, along with His power and authority. From what you know of all four gospels, how does this emphasis in Mark come through in comparison?

MARK 1

Startup: The first verse in this chapter is like a title to the entire gospel of Mark. If you were able to write down a full account of what the Lord has done in *your* life, what title would you like to give it?

SEEING WHAT'S THERE

1. In what ways do you see John the Baptist fulfilling the prophecy mentioned in verses 2-3?

2. Review together verses 12-13. You'll find longer accounts of Satan's temptation of Jesus in Matthew 4:1-11 and Luke 4:1-13. In Mark's shorter version, what might have been Mark's reasons for emphasizing the particular points he chose to tell about?

3. In verse 14 we read that Jesus was proclaiming the gospel—the good news of God. From what you see in verse 15 and what you read elsewhere about His teachings and ministry, what really was this good news Jesus preached?

4. Mark's gospel does not include information about Jesus' birth or childhood. But what are the most important things it *does* say about Jesus before His ministry begins in verse 14?

5. What does verse 35 tell us about the character and personality of Jesus?

6. EYE FOR DETAIL—*If everyone in the group has read the entire chapter, try answering the following question without looking at your Bible:* How does this chapter describe John the Baptist's clothing and his food? (For the answer, see verse 6.)

7. What do we learn in verses 10-11 about the relationships between God the Father, God the Son, and God the Holy Spirit?

8. Look also at the list of "Questions to Ask as You Study Each Chapter" on page 392, which you may want to do for each chapter in Mark.

CAPTURE THE ESSENCE

9. In your own words, what was the essential message John the Baptist proclaimed?

10. John's popular appeal is mentioned in verse 5. How would you explain the reasons for his appeal?

11. Look together at verse 11. In your opinion, what was it about Jesus that was "pleasing" to God, and why did God want to tell Him?

12. In this chapter, which of these character qualities in Jesus comes through most strongly to you: His compassion, His power, or His wisdom? (Explain your answer.)

13. What in this chapter do you think might be the most interesting to someone who was learning about Jesus Christ for the first time?

FOR LIFE TODAY

14. Review verses 16-17. In your opinion, what are the most important things we need to learn from Jesus in order to become "fishers of men"?

15. Look at the amazement or astonishment mentioned in verse 22. What surprises *you* about the teaching of Jesus?

16. In light of how you're doing spiritually in your life today, which verse in this chapter do you think is the most important—and why?

17. This chapter shows the growing fame of Jesus in His early ministry. For people today, how would you define the difference between *admiring* Jesus and *loving* Him?

18. Jesus' life has been called the most *exciting* life ever lived. Are you convinced this is true? Why or why not? How important to you personally is this dimension of Jesus?

Authority (also translated as *power* in some versions) is a key word in this gospel. Notice how it's used in connection with Jesus in verses 22 and 27. Look also at the following passages later in Mark where this word is used, and describe how they together teach us about the authority Jesus *possesses,* and the authority He *gives*—2:8-12, 3:14-15, 6:7-13, and 11:27-33.

MARK 2

Startup: Talk together about any times when you may have been bedridden because of an illness or injury. What was going on in your mind while your body was so confined?

SEEING WHAT'S THERE

1. Take a "walk" together through the incidents that happen in this chapter: Using your imagination, talk about the kinds of sights, smells, sounds, and feelings you might experience.

2. Review verses 1-12, especially the reaction of the crowds in verse 12. What exactly was it that impressed these people about Jesus?

3. In the way Jesus uses the word *righteous* in verse 17, what does He mean by it?

4. In the incident described in verses 23-28, what one or two words would you say best describe the disciples here? What one or two words best describe the Pharisees in this incident? What one or two words best describe Jesus here?

5. For helpful background on verse 24, look together at Exodus 34:21.

6. For helpful background on verses 25-26, look together at 1 Samuel 21:1-6 and Deuteronomy 23:25. Take a look also at God's instructions for baking the Sabbath bread in Leviticus 24:5-9.

7. Jesus says in verse 27 that God made the Sabbath for man, not man for the Sabbath. As you understand it, what use for man does the Sabbath serve? (You may want to look together at Exodus 20:8-11 and 31:12-17.)

8. TEACHABLE MOMENT: Often in the gospel of Mark, Jesus' teaching appears to be prompted by a specific circumstance or question that will help His listeners to better understand His message. In verses 18-22,

what's the main point Jesus is making, and what circumstance or question prepares His listeners to understand it?

9. EYE FOR DETAIL—*From what you recall seeing in this chapter, try answering the following question without looking at your Bible:* What city is the location of this chapter's opening scene, in which the paralyzed man is lowered through the roof? (See verse 1.)

CAPTURE THE ESSENCE

10. What lessons about *faith* can you draw from the incident in verses 3-12?

11. Explain how much you agree or disagree with this statement: In verses 23-28, the most important lesson for both the Pharisees and the disciples had to do with their understanding of Jesus, not their understanding of the Sabbath.

12. What does verse 28 imply about Jesus' relationship to the Old Testament law?

13. Jesus says in verse 28 that He is "Lord even of the Sabbath." By saying this, what was He trying to communicate to the Pharisees?

14. Imagine you were helping to produce a film based on this chapter. Describe the kinds of scenery, supporting characters, background music, lighting effects, etc., which you would use to portray this chapter's central message.

FOR LIFE TODAY

15. Look again at verse 12. How does Jesus demonstrate His authority today so people can see and give praise to God?

16. Look at Jesus' answer to John's disciples in verses 19-20. Is the Bridegroom still with us? Is it time now to feast, or to fast?

17. What does the Sabbath mean to you in your life?

18. In Colossians 3:1 we read this command: "Since, then, you have been raised with Christ, set your hearts on things above, where Christ is seated at the right hand of God." What have you personally observed about Jesus Christ in this chapter that would be worthy of setting your heart on?

FOR GOING DEEPER

Jesus asks many questions in the gospel of Mark; in this chapter, for example, look at verses 8-9 and 19. Look also at the questions in the following list of verses in Mark, and discuss together what they tell us about Jesus' teaching style—3:4, 3:23, 3:33, 4:13, 4:21, 4:30, 4:40, 8:17-21, 8:27-29, 9:33, 10:18, 10:38, 11:29-30, 12:15-16, and 14:48.

MARK 3

Startup: What's the most unusual thing you used your *hand* for today?

SEEING WHAT'S THERE

1. TEACHABLE MOMENT: In verses 1-6, What would you say is the main point Jesus makes in what He says, and what circumstance or question prepares His listeners to understand it?

2. From all you see in verses 1-6, what one or two words would you say best describe the people Jesus spoke to in verse 4? What one or two words best describe Jesus here? What one or two words best describe the man with the injured hand?

3. From what you see in verse 2, how did these people view the power of Jesus?

4. On a map, look together at the places mentioned in verse 8. Why do you think Jesus was having such widespread appeal?

5. Imagine you are one of the men mentioned in verses 16-18, and that you're writing a letter to a friend. Give a few sample lines of how you would describe to your friend all that happened in this chapter.

6. Another Teachable Moment: In verses 20-30, what would you say is the main point Jesus makes in what He says, and what circumstance or question prepares His listeners to understand it?

7. In your own words, how would you explain what Jesus is saying in verses 34-35?

8. From what you've seen so far in Mark, how would you describe the attitude which the Pharisees and religious teachers have toward Jesus, at this point in His ministry?

9. EYE FOR DETAIL—*From what you recall seeing in this chapter, try answering the following question without looking at your Bible:* In this chapter we read that when the evil spirits saw Jesus, they fell down and cried out to Him. What is it that they cried out to Jesus? (See verse 11.)

CAPTURE THE ESSENCE

10. How do you think the man with the injured hand would have answered the question in verse 4?

11. What would you say verse 5 tells us about the emotions, the values, and the character of Jesus?

12. Why do you think Jesus did what He did in verse 12?

FOR LIFE TODAY

13. Review the question Jesus asked in verse 4. Then tell how much you agree or disagree with this statement: If we are not doing good, we are doing evil; and if we are not saving life, we are destroying life.

14. Look in verses 14-15 at what the twelve disciples were supposed to do and learn. Are we supposed to be doing and learning the same things?

15. Keep in mind what Jesus says in verses 33-34 as you answer together this question: How can we experience more of a "family" feeling with other Christians?

16. In light of how you're doing spiritually in your life today, which verse in this chapter do you think is the most important at this time—and why?

FOR GOING DEEPER

In verse 5, notice the emotions or human feelings which are evident in Jesus. Look together also at the following verses in Mark, and discuss together the picture they give of the *human* and *emotional* side of Jesus Christ: 4:38, 6:6, 6:34, 7:34, 8:12, 10:14, 10:21, 11:12, 14:34, and 15:34.

MARK 4

Startup: When someone is doing something for you, what in general is more important to you: the *speed* with which it is done, or the *quality?*

SEEING WHAT'S THERE

1. Review the parable of the sower and the soils in verses 1-25. In what ways is this parable a *warning* to us? In what ways is it an *encouragement?*

2. In verse 9, what kind of "ears" is Jesus talking about?

3. The parable of the growing seed in verses 26-29 is found only in the gospel of Mark. What's the major point of this parable?

4. What in this chapter do you think might be most surprising to a new Christian reading it for the first time?

5. EYE FOR DETAIL—*From what you recall seeing in this chapter, try answering the following question without looking at your Bible:* Before the disciples and Jesus got into the boat (which was later nearly swamped in the storm), what did Jesus say to them? (See verse 35.)

CAPTURE THE ESSENCE

6. In what ways can you see Jesus demonstrating His *authority* in this chapter?

7. From what you see in verses 10-12, is it accurate to say Jesus was hiding the truth from some people?

8. Imagine you have a friend who has been blind for life. Tell how you would explain to this friend the meaning of verses 21-22.

9. In the incident in verses 35-41, how do you think the disciples would have responded differently to the storm if they had had more faith? How exactly did Jesus *want* them to respond?

10. If the disciples in the boat had truly responded in faith when the storm hit, do you think there were some even greater lessons they could have learned? If so, what might these have been?

11. From what you see in this chapter, what really is a *parable,* and what is its purpose?

12. If this chapter was the only Scripture portion you had, what biblical definition would you give for the term *kingdom of God?*

FOR LIFE TODAY

13. Look at what Jesus said to His disciples in verse 11. Has the Lord also given to you what was given to the disciples?

14. In line with what Jesus says in verse 20, describe as fully as possible what it takes for us to be "good soil"?

15. Look closely at verses 24-25. What practical suggestions can you give for how to obey these words of Jesus?

16. Think again about verses 35-41, especially the words Jesus spoke in verse 40. Is it wrong to ever be afraid? Is it possible to have faith and yet still experience fear?

17. What are some "storms" in your life —the " winds" and "waves" that have given you fear or anxiety? How have you seen the Lord's power over them?

FOR GOING DEEPER

The *kingdom of God* is a central concept in the gospel of Mark. Notice how the phrase is used by Jesus in verses 11, 26, and 30. Then look together at the following additional passages in Mark, and discuss these questions: What really *is* the kingdom of God, and how exactly does a person enter it?—1:15, 9:1, 9:47, 10:14-15, 10:23-25, 12:24, and 14:25.

MARK 5

Startup: Recall any time when you met someone who was either very scary or very repulsive, or both.

SEEING WHAT'S THERE

1. In three very different ways in this chapter, Jesus heals three very different people in three very different conditions. Despite these differences, what *similarities* can you see in all three situations?

2. In verse 34, Jesus told the woman that her faith had healed her. Was faith involved in the other two healings in this chapter?

3. Imagine you are a reporter for the "Galilee Gazette." In a few sentences, how would you describe what happened in verses 1-20?

4. EYE FOR DETAIL—*From what you recall seeing in this chapter, try answering the following question without looking at your Bible:* The opening scene in the chapter tells about the demon-possessed man who lived in the tombs. What did he use to cut himself with? (See verse 5.)

CAPTURE THE ESSENCE

5. In this chapter, which of these character qualities in Jesus comes through most strongly to you: His compassion, His power, or His wisdom? (Explain your answer.)

FOR LIFE TODAY

6. Notice the encounters Jesus had in this chapter with both sexes. In what ways do you see that following Jesus Christ enhances your manhood or your womanhood?

7. Which verse in this chapter do you think God wants you to understand best?

FOR GOING DEEPER

Look again at the strict orders Jesus gave in the last verse in this chapter. Then evaluate together these other verses in Mark, and discuss what Jesus' "publicity" strategy seemed to be, and how it developed: 1:34, 1:43-45, 3:11-12, 7:36-37, 8:29-30, 9:9, 11:7-11, 12:35-37, 14:60-62, and 15:2.

MARK 6

Startup: Talk about any times when you may have felt overwhelmed by the spiritual needs you saw in a crowd of people.

SEEING WHAT'S THERE

1. This chapter focuses around some very different events in very different circumstances. Take a "walk" together through them, being observant of everything around you. Using your imagination, talk about the kinds of sights, smells, sounds, and feelings you might experience.

2. TEACHABLE MOMENT: In verses 1-6, what would you say is the main point Jesus makes in what He says, and what circumstance or question prepares His listeners to understand it?

3. Look in verse 12 at the message which the disciples preached. How does it compare with the message Jesus Himself preached, and the message John the Baptist preached? (Refer back to 1:4 and 1:15.)

4. From what you see in verses 14-29, how would you describe the character and personality of King Herod?

5. What picture do you get in verses 30-34 of the character of Jesus?

6. Imagine you are a roving reporter for the "Jerusalem Journal." In a few sentences, how would you describe what happened in verses 30-44?

7. From what you've seen so far in Mark, how much time was Jesus able to spend alone? And why did He make time for this?

8. EYE FOR DETAIL—*From what you recall seeing in this chapter, try answering the following question without looking at your Bible:* In the opening scene of this chapter, in which Jesus visits his hometown of Nazareth, we are told He was surprised by something here. What was it that caused

Him to "marvel" or "wonder" or to be "amazed," as various translations put it? (See verse 6.)

CAPTURE THE ESSENCE

9. In what ways can you see Jesus demonstrating His *authority* in this chapter?

10. What do verses 5-6 imply about the power and the will of God?

11. From the evidence in verses 39-44, draw as many conclusions as you can about the *power* of Jesus.

12. What do you think may have caused the hardening of the disciples' hearts mentioned in verse 52?

13. From what you see in this chapter, why did Jesus perform miracles?

14. What in this chapter do you think might be the most interesting to someone who was learning about Jesus Christ for the first time, and why?

FOR LIFE TODAY

15. In light of how you're doing spiritually in your life today, which verse in this chapter do you think is the most important at this time—and why?

16. In verse 7, look at the authority which Jesus gave to His twelve disciples. Do we have this same authority today?

17. If you are, or ever plan to be, a teacher, what instruction and inspiration could you draw from verse 34?

18. From what Jesus did for the people with the loaves and fish in verses 35-44, what principles can you derive to give you confidence in your own ministry?

19. What guidelines for people in ministry today can you find in Jesus' example in this chapter?

20. If God had written this chapter only for you, which words or phrases do

you think He would have underlined?

Look together at the prophecy of
Ezekiel 34:23-31, and also at Psalm
23:1. To what degree would you say
these Old Testament passages find fulfillment in Mark 6:30-44?

MARK 7

Startup: What traditions in your family
or from your background are the most
meaningful to you?

1. Together, list aloud all the different
   kinds of people represented in this
   chapter. What would you say are the
   most prominent characteristics of
   each one?

2. What different tones of voice do you
   think Jesus may have used in the various places where He is quoted in
   this chapter?

3. Imagine yourself being present in the
   situation described in verses 1-23. In
   light of your own personality, what
   words spoken by Jesus in this passage
   stand out most to you?

4. TEACHABLE MOMENT: In verses 1-8, what would you say is the
   main point Jesus makes in what He
   says, and what circumstance or question prepares His listeners to understand it?

5. What do the words of Jesus in verses
   9-13 tell us about how God views
   our responsibility toward our parents?

6. With your mind on what Jesus says
   in verses 20-23, look together at Jeremiah 17:9. To what degree would
   you say Jesus here is teaching the
   same message found in this Old Testament passage?

7. Look at the last verse in the incident
   described in verses 24-30. What
   questions or thoughts do you think
   may have been in the mind of this
   woman as she made her way home?

8. The account in verses 32-36 of how
   Jesus healed a deaf and mute man is
   found only in Mark's gospel. Why
   do you think Jesus took this man
   away from the crowd to heal him, as
   verse 33 tells us?

9. Why do you think Mark recorded the "sigh" of Jesus in verse 34? (Look together also at His sigh in 8:11-12, and compare the two situations.)

10. EYE FOR DETAIL—*From what you recall seeing in this chapter, try answering the following question without looking at your Bible:* Near the middle of this chapter, Jesus gave a long list of the evil things that come out of a person's heart. How many of these can you name? (See verses 21-22.)

CAPTURE THE ESSENCE

11. Think about verses 17-23, then discuss how much you agree or disagree with this statement: God is just as concerned with the "internals" of our lives as He is with the "externals"— He cares as much about what we are thinking as He does about what we are doing.

12. Review what Jesus says in verses 18-23 about what makes a person "unclean." If this is what makes us unclean, what makes us *clean?*

13. How complete would you say is the list of unclean actions in verses 21-22?

14. Think carefully about the incident in verses 24-30. What does this passage show us about Jesus' obedience to His Father, and also about God's compassion? Are these two qualities in conflict here?

15. From what you see in this chapter, how would you define the kind of religion that pleases God?

FOR LIFE TODAY

16. Read over again verses 6-7. Does this mean that when we feel inwardly distant from God, we should not try to worship Him?

17. How might our churches today be guilty of what Jesus condemns in verse 13?

18. In light of how you're doing spiritually in your life today, which verse in this chapter do you think is the most important at this time—and why?

19. What evidence do you find in verse 16 that could be used to help a Christian friend who had doubts about whether the Bible is truly God's Word?

FOR GOING DEEPER

Compare the list of sinful deeds and qualities in verses 21-22 with the lists you see in these passages: Romans 1:29-31; 1 Corinthians 6:9-10; Galatians 5:19-21; and Revelation 22:15.

MARK 8

Startup: Talk about any memorable lessons in life that you recall having had to learn more than once.

SEEING WHAT'S THERE

1. Compare the miraculous meal in verses 1-10 with the similar incident in Mark 6:30-44. How many differences can you find between these two incidents?

2. Once again, take a "walk" together through the incidents that happen in this chapter. Using your imagination, talk about the kinds of sights, smells, sounds, and feelings you might experience in each scene that's presented here.

3. How is the *character* of Jesus demonstrated in this chapter?

4. How is the *purpose* of Jesus demonstrated in this chapter?

5. Consider carefully verses 11-13. Why didn't Jesus just go ahead and show these people a miracle or two?

6. What really is the "yeast" Jesus speaks of in verse 15, and why is it so dangerous?

7. The story of the healing of the blind man in Bethsaida in verses 22-26 is recorded only in the gospel of Mark. Together as a group, summarize the sequence of events in this incident, then discuss why you think Jesus chose to accomplish this miracle in stages, instead of all at once.

8. From what you've read about Jesus in Mark 7 and 8, how would you describe a typical day for Him at this time in His ministry?

9. From what you've seen in the most recent chapters in Mark, how would you summarize the attitude which the Pharisees and religious teachers have toward Jesus, at this point in His ministry?

10. EYE FOR DETAIL—*From what you recall seeing in this chapter, try answering the following question without looking at your Bible:* In the city of Bethsaida, a blind man was brought to Jesus to be healed. Jesus led the man by the hand to the spot where this healing took place. Where was it? (See verse 23.)

CAPTURE THE ESSENCE

11. What do you think might be most surprising in this chapter to a new Christian reading it for the first time?

12. Mark 8 is often considered a key chapter and a key turning point in the book of Mark. Why do you think this is so?

13. Is the "yeast" still around today which Jesus describes in verse 15? If so, where?

14. In much of this chapter, Jesus has begun to focus His ministry upon His disciples. What guidelines for today's discipleship training do you see in the way Jesus taught His disciples in verses 27-38?

15. Why do you think Jesus gave the disciples the warning recorded in verse 30?

16. Listen again to the sharp words Jesus spoke to Peter in verse 33. In your own understanding, what specifically were the "things of man" which Peter had in mind, and what were the "things of God" which he *should* have had in mind?

17. Restate in your own words—and in the context of our lives today—the three things Jesus asks us to do in verse 34.

18. What would you say verses 34-37 have to teach us about self-esteem?

19. If you were asked to summarize the most important "marks of Christian maturity" as taught in this chapter, which ones would you mention first?

20. Thinking again of the "yeast" in verses 15-21, is it as hard for us to recognize this yeast today as it was for the disciples? Why or why not?

21. Look at the question Jesus asks in verse 21. In what ways might the Lord be justified in asking this question of you today?

22. As a group, answer as fully as possible the question Jesus asks in verse 29, as it relates to your lives today.

23. How could you use verses 35-38 to help an unsaved friend who was afraid of being persecuted if he became a Christian?

24. In light of how you're doing spiritually in your life today, which verse in this chapter do you think is the most important at this time—and why?

FOR GOING DEEPER

In verse 31, Jesus calls Himself "the Son of Man." This is the title Jesus uses most often for Himself in the gospels. Look at any or all of the following additional passages in Mark in which Jesus calls Himself this, and discuss together the significance of this title: 2:10, 2:28, 8:31, 9:12, 10:45, 13:26, 14:41, and 14:62.

MARK 9

Startup: What experiences in nature or among people can you recall in which you sensed especially that you were witnessing a display of *power?*

SEEING WHAT'S THERE

1. Using your imagination, how would you describe the probable "atmosphere" of the incident recorded in verses 2-13?

2. In verse 4, what do you know about Moses and Elijah that explains the significance of their presence here?

3. What do you think might have been actually *said* by Moses and Elijah in their conversation with Jesus mentioned in verse 4? (You may want to look also at Luke 9:30-31.)

4. Examine closely the words God spoke about Jesus in verse 7. Notice the different phrases that make up this quotation. What would you say is the significance of each phrase?

5. Think carefully about verse 1, then explain how much you agree or disagree with this statement: The experience of the disciples in seeing Jesus transfigured on the mountain was a direct fulfillment of what Jesus said they would see in verse 1.

6. Imagine you are a Bible-times version of a private detective, hired by the religious leaders in Jerusalem to spy on Jesus. What would you say in your latest report to them, based on what you observe in verses 14 to the end of the chapter?

7. Were the words Jesus spoke in verse 19 meant to sound harsh? Why or why not?

8. Look again at verse 19. In what ways did Jesus have to "put up with" the disciples?

9. Imagine yourself being present in the situation described in verses 33-37. In light of your own personality,

what words spoken by Jesus in these verses stand out most to you?

10. What does it really mean to "welcome" a child in Jesus' name, as He tells us to do in verse 37?

11. In as few words as possible, how would you summarize the principle Jesus is teaching in verse 37?

12. TEACHABLE MOMENT: In verses 38-50, what are the main points Jesus makes in what He says, and what circumstance or question prepares His listeners to understand them?

13. In as few words as possible, how would you summarize the principle Jesus is teaching in verses 43-48?

14. Suppose you were a Bible translator for a remote tribe on a faraway continent, and this tribe did not have any experience or knowledge of salt. How would you explain what salt is, so they could understand the meaning of verse 50?

15. EYE FOR DETAIL—*From what you recall seeing in this chapter, try answering the following question without looking at your Bible:* In this chapter, what words does Jesus use to describe hell? (See verses 43-48.)

CAPTURE THE ESSENCE

16. From God's point of view, what was the purpose for Jesus' transfiguration (in verses 2-8)?

17. Notice Jesus' instructions to Peter, James, and John in verse 9. Imagine you are one of these three disciples, and Jesus has risen from the dead. You are now free to tell others about the mountaintop experience which we see in Matthew 9. How would you go about explaining what happened that day to the other disciples?

18. To see what Peter wrote later about his experiences in verses 1-8, look together at 2 Peter 1:16-18. What

seem to be the most important things Peter learned from being a witness to this transfiguration of Jesus?

19. In the incident recorded in verses 14-29, what are the main lessons to be learned about *faith?*

20. Again, if you were asked to summarize the most important "marks of Christian maturity" as taught in this chapter, which ones would you mention first?

FOR LIFE TODAY

21. Look at the topic of the argument mentioned in verse 34. In what ways, if any, do we sometimes continue this argument today?

22. Look closely at verse 40, and tell how much you agree or disagree with this statement: Unless you are actively working *against* the Lord and His will, then it's the same as working *for* His will. (You may want to also look together at Matthew 12:30.)

23. What are some ways in which it might be easy or tempting for us to violate what Jesus warns us against in verse 42?

24. If a non-Christian friend told you he didn't believe there was any life after death, how could you use verses 43-48 to help you give a meaningful reply?

25. What guidelines for today's discipleship training can you glean from the way Jesus taught His disciples in this chapter?

26. If God had written this chapter only for you, which words or phrases do you think He would have underlined?

FOR GOING DEEPER

In verses 30-32 we see the second time in Mark when Jesus gives His disciples a prediction of His death and resurrection. Look also at the first of these predictions in 8:31-32, and another yet to come in 10:32-34. Look together at all three of them. What is the context for these predictions, how similar is each one, and what would you say is Jesus' apparent purpose or strategy in telling them?

MARK 10

Startup: In the way we read and study the Bible, what kind of mental habits can most easily block this gospel of Mark from coming alive in our minds and hearts?

SEEING WHAT'S THERE

1. Again, imagine you are a private detective hired by the religious leaders in Jerusalem to spy on Jesus. What would you say in your latest report to them, based on what you observe in this chapter?

2. For helpful background on the divorce passage in verses 1-12, look together at Deuteronomy 24:1-4. Look also at Matthew 5:31-32.

3. How would you explain verse 14 in your own words?

4. As you look over verses 17-31 (about conversations Jesus had with the rich young man, and then with the disciples), discuss this question: Is this passage more about *possessions,* more about *relationships,* or equally about both?

5. Would you say verse 21 is more about *actions,* more about *attitudes,* or equally about both?

6. TEACHABLE MOMENT: In verses 35-45, what would you say is the main point Jesus makes in what He says, and what circumstance or question prepares His listeners to understand it?

7. In verses 38 and 39, what "cup" do you think Jesus is talking about?

8. How would you explain the meaning of the word *ransom* in verse 45?

9. EYE FOR DETAIL—*From what you recall seeing in this chapter, try answering the following question without looking at your Bible:* In this chapter, a man called Jesus "Good Teacher," and then asked Jesus what he needed to do to inherit eternal life. Before he

asked this question, the man did something else. What was it? (See verse 17.)

CAPTURE THE ESSENCE

10. What foundational principles about marriage do you see in verses 6-12?

11. What would you say is the most important truth which Jesus is trying to teach in verses 21-30?

12. Think about Peter's statement in verse 28. What does it imply about the disciples, and what does it imply about Jesus?

13. What would you say is the key word or words in the statement Jesus makes in verses 29-30?

14. Was it wrong for James and John to ask what they did in verse 37?

15. Focus together on verses 41-45. In light of what you've seen in the book of Mark, how do you think Jesus would define the words *serve* and *servant?*

16. In verse 45, Jesus said He came to give His life as a *ransom* for us. If we need a ransom—what does that say about *us?*

17. Once more, if you were asked to summarize the most important "marks of Christian maturity" as taught in this chapter, which ones would you mention first?

FOR LIFE TODAY

18. In Philippians 4:8 we're given the following command: "Whatever is true, whatever is noble, whatever is right, whatever is pure, whatever is lovely, whatever is admirable—if anything is excellent or praiseworthy—*think about such things.*" What food for thought can you find in this chapter that especially strikes you as being *true,* or *noble,* or *right,* or *pure,* or *lovely,* or *admirable,* or *excellent,* or *praiseworthy?*

19. Look again at verses 11-12. How would you use this passage to help a Christian who was considering divorce?

20. Review what Jesus commanded in verse 21. For whom, if anyone, is this command still valid today?

21. With verse 27 in mind, discuss some "impossibilities" which you have seen God accomplish in your life, or in the life of someone close to you.

22. In light of what Jesus says in verse 31, what kind of surprises do you think we're in for (even though Jesus has told us this beforehand)?

23. From what Jesus says in verse 31, should we actually *try* to be "last"? If so, what does that mean?

24. Would it be wrong for us today to ask the question which James and John asked in verse 37? Why or why not?

25. Looking at verse 43, do you think it's right in God's eyes to want to be great in His kingdom? Why or why not?

26. Discuss whether you think there's any danger for us today in applying verses 43-44 too literally.

27. What guidelines for today's discipleship training can you glean from the way Jesus taught His disciples in this chapter?

28. In light of how you're doing spiritually in your life today, which verse in this chapter do you think is the most important at this time?

FOR GOING DEEPER

In the list in verse 30, the word *persecutions* often catches the eye. Look together at the following verses in Mark, and discuss what they teach about the place of *suffering* in our discipleship: 8:34, 10:33-35, 10:38-39, and 13:11-13.

MARK 11

Startup: If you discovered you had only one week to live, what questions would you ask yourself to help you live that last week wisely?

SEEING WHAT'S THERE

1. Keep the events of verses 7-10 in mind, as you discuss how much you agree or disagree with this statement: The cheering welcome and praise which Jesus received as He entered Jerusalem was rooted only in the people's misunderstanding of what kind of king He truly was, and this was proven by the way the crowds turned against Him later in the week.

2. Imagine you are a roving reporter for the "Jerusalem Journal." In a few sentences, how would you describe what happened in the first half of this chapter?

3. Review what was said and done in verses 12-17. How did this incident compare with an earlier one recorded in John 2:13-17?

4. For background on Jesus' words about the Temple being a "house of prayer" (verse 17), look together at Isaiah 56:7.

5. TEACHABLE MOMENT: In verses 20-25, what would you say is the main point Jesus makes in what He says, and what circumstance or question prepares His listeners to understand it?

6. How would you describe in your own words what Jesus teaches about *faith* in verses 22-24?

7. What in this chapter do you think might be most surprising to a new Christian reading it for the first time?

8. How is the *character* of Jesus demonstrated in this chapter?

9. How is the *purpose* of Jesus demonstrated in this chapter?

10. EYE FOR DETAIL—*From what you recall seeing in this chapter, try answering the following question without looking at your Bible:* In this chapter's account of Jesus in the temple, we read that He began driving out the buyers and sellers, and overturned the tables of the money-changers and the benches of those selling doves. This account also mentions one more thing Jesus did, besides reminding them about the true meaning of the temple. What was this other action that Jesus took? (See verse 16.)

CAPTURE THE ESSENCE

11. In this chapter, which of these character qualities in Jesus comes through most strongly to you: His *compassion,* His *power,* or His *wisdom?* (Explain your answer.)

12. Look together at verses 12-14 and 20-25. This cursing of the fig tree is the last miracle recorded in Mark before Jesus' death. As you recall the other miracles you've seen in this book, what would you say are the *reasons* Jesus performed miracles?

13. What do you think was the *motive* Jesus had for doing what He did in verses 12-17?

14. Why do you think Jesus cursed the fig tree in verse 14?

15. Look again at verses 22-24. Why does God place so much value on faith?

16. Explain *why* you agree or disagree with this statement: Verse 23 in this chapter proves that Jesus approved of the practice of magic.

17. Is Jesus giving us a "blank check" in verse 24? If not, then why does He make this statement?

18. Think together about verse 25. Why is *forgiveness* so important for us to practice in life?

19. What in this chapter do you think might be the most interesting to someone who was learning about Jesus Christ for the first time, and why?

20. The Jesus we see in this gospel is not only fully God, but also fully human. From what you've seen so far in Mark, in what ways does Jesus show Himself to be the perfect model of manhood?

21. In what ways can you see Jesus demonstrating His *authority* in this chapter?

22. In this chapter, how could the Temple be compared with the fig tree Jesus cursed?

23. Imagine that you saw earlier today a message written in fire in the sky. It was addressed to you by name, then continued with these words: Thus saith the Lord: "Read xxx, for I have something for you there." Which verse or verses in this chapter do you think He most likely would be referring to?

FOR LIFE TODAY

24. Think again about verses 12-17. Do you feel there is anything in our churches today that corresponds to the activities of the people whom Jesus drove out of the Temple?

25. Look again at verse 24. How will a person know whether or not he has enough faith when he's praying?

26. Think again about verse 25. How hard is it for you to forgive others? How hard is it for you to ask for forgiveness?

27. In verses 27-33 the focus is on the *authority* of Jesus and the *authority* of John the Baptist, both of which came from God. What authority do *you* have from God?

FOR GOING DEEPER

Compare what you see in verse 24 with the prayer principles in James 4:3. How do the principles from both passages work together?

MARK 12

Startup: If you could have been with Jesus during this last week before He was crucified, what question would you have most wanted to ask Him?

SEEING WHAT'S THERE

1. With the opening parable of this chapter in mind, compare it with another interesting parable about a vineyard in Isaiah 5:1-7. What are the similarities, and what are the differences?

2. Notice in verse 12 how the Jewish religious leaders responded to the parable Jesus tells at the beginning of this chapter. Then go back through the parable and identify each person or group of people, and who each one represents.

3. Verse 13 says the religious leaders had laid a trap for Jesus. How do you think they expected the trap to work?

4. Imagine you are one of the Pharisees or Herodians mentioned in verse 13. What kind of report would you make to the religious leaders who sent you, based on what you observe in this chapter?

5. Does the question from the Sadducees in verse 18 appear to be a trap as well? Why or why not?

6. For background on verse 19, look together at Deuteronomy 25:5-10.

7. Imagine yourself being present in the situation described in verses 38-39. In light of your own personality, what words spoken by Jesus in these verses stand out most to you?

8. Imagine you're a devout Jew from Rome, and you've come across the sea for the first time to visit Jerusalem for the Passover festival. The events in Mark 11 and 12 are your first exposure to Jesus of Nazareth; in fact, as far as you know, no one back home in Rome has even heard of this Man. What kind of impressions would you now have of Jesus, based on all you've seen in these last few days? (Look back over these two chapters to help you keep in mind all these events.)

9. EYE FOR DETAIL—*From what you recall seeing in this chapter, try answering the following question without looking at your Bible:* What did the poor widow put into the temple treasury as her offering? (See verse 42.)

CAPTURE THE ESSENCE

10. How important would you say was the question which Jesus asked in verses 35-37?

11. Why did Jesus have to suffer and die? Look again at verse 12. Then look ahead to 14:1-2, 14:61-64, and 15:9-13, and discuss together what they show about the *human* reason for the suffering and death of Jesus.

12. Now think about *God's* reason for the suffering and death of His Son, Jesus. Look back at these verses in Mark and discuss how clear these reasons were for Jesus: 8:31, 9:30-31, 10:32-34, and 10:45.

13. From the evidence you see in this chapter, how do you think Jesus would define the terms *success* and *ultimate significance*?

14. In what ways can you see Jesus demonstrating His *authority* in this chapter?

15. From what you see in verses 41-44, how does God calculate the size of our gifts to Him?

FOR LIFE TODAY

16. Think about verse 17. In your life, what things belong to God, and yet still must be given up to Him?

17. Recalling verse 30, what portions of your heart or your soul or your mind are the hardest to love God with?

18. What similarities would you point out between being a Jewish religious leader in the days when Jesus lived on earth, and being a pastor or other Christian leader today? What major differences would there be?

19. Think carefully again about what Jesus says in verses 43-44. Then imagine Him evaluating the significance of your own giving on a scale of one to ten, in which ten equals the example of the poor widow in this passage, and one equals the example of the other rich people here. What score do you think He would probably assign to you?

20. In light of how you're doing spiritually in your life today, which verse in this chapter do you think is the most important at this time?

FOR GOING DEEPER

When Jesus stated (in verses 29-31) the two most important commands, He used the word *love* in both of them. This word is used less in Mark than in any of the other three gospels. But look together at these other passages in Mark, and discuss how much you see the *concept* of love in them, even though the word isn't there—1:40-42, 3:31-35, 6:30-31, 9:38-41, and 14:4-9.

MARK 13

Startup: What are the biggest questions you have about the second coming of Christ?

SEEING WHAT'S THERE

1. In his long discourse in this chapter, who is Jesus speaking to?

2. Review carefully verses 1-4. What things do the disciples specifically want to know?

3. What questions are raised in your mind by the words of Jesus in this chapter?

4. EYE FOR DETAIL—*From what you recall seeing in this chapter, try answering the following question without looking at your Bible:* The very last thing Jesus says in this chapter is a brief command, and it could easily be considered the most important thing in the chapter. In many Bible translations this command is only one word. What is it?

CAPTURE THE ESSENCE

5. From what Jesus tells His disciples in this chapter, does He want them to think it will be a *long* time or a *short* time before the end of the present age?

6. Who are "the elect" in verse 20, and what does this passage show us about them?

7. Many Bible teachers regard verse 20 as one of the most important statements in this chapter. Why do you think this is so?

FOR LIFE TODAY

8. Discuss how you respond inwardly to what you see in this chapter. Is it with anticipation? Fear? Confusion?

9. How susceptible do you think you might be to the deceptions which Jesus warns about in verses 6 and 21-23?

10. As you think about verses 9-13, what effect would you say persecution can have on our evangelism efforts?

11. Look at what Jesus promised His disciples in verse 13. How hard is it for you to endure hatred from others?

12. What exactly is the lesson to learn from the fig tree in verses 28-29, as it relates to us today?

13. Review verses 32-37. Practically speaking, how do we stay alert and watchful today, in obedience to these words from Jesus?

14. Look at the statement Jesus makes in verse 32. What difference in your life do you think it would make if you *did* know the exact day or hour when Jesus will return?

15. Which of the predictions mentioned in this chapter would you say are taking place now?

16. What would you say is the most important concept this chapter teaches us about our *responsibility*, as we wait for the end?

17. How could you use verses 34-37 to help a friend whom you felt was living a "lazy" Christian life?

18. Summarize the most important principles you've seen so far in Mark that tell Christians today how to "follow in the footsteps of Jesus."

FOR GOING DEEPER

In verse 32, Jesus speaks of "that day." Look together in these Old Testament passages and discuss the dramatic ways in which two of God's prophets also describe "that day"—Amos 8:3, 8:9-10, 8:13, and 9:11; and Micah 4:6-7, 5:10-15, and 7:12-13.

MARK 14

Startup: Talk about a particularly costly gift you can recall either giving or receiving.

SEEING WHAT'S THERE

1. TEACHABLE MOMENT: In verses 1-9, what would you say is the main point Jesus makes, and what circumstance or question prepares His listeners to understand it?

2. The woman mentioned in verses 3-9 is identified in John 12 as being Mary, the sister of Martha and Lazarus. From what you see in this chapter, what did Mary consider to be the most important things in life?

3. For helpful background on Judas Iscariot, look together at Matthew 26:14-16, Luke 22:47-48, and John 6:70-71, 12:4-6, and 17:12. In these passages, what *choices* do you see Judas making?

4. How would you explain what Jesus means by the word *covenant* in verse 24?

5. In verse 34, notice how deep the sorrow was which Jesus experienced. How would you explain this verse to a child?

6. If you were able to ask Mark, "Why did you include verses 51-52 in your gospel?" how do you think he would answer?

7. How is the *character* of Jesus demonstrated in this chapter?

8. How is the *purpose* of Jesus demonstrated in this chapter?

9. What in this chapter do you think might be most surprising to a new Christian reading it for the first time?

10. EYE FOR DETAIL—*From what you recall seeing in this chapter, try answering the following question without looking at your Bible:* As Jesus gave bread and wine to His disciples, He called the bread His "body," and

then gave a longer description of the cup. What was this longer description? (See verses 23-24.)

CAPTURE THE ESSENCE

11. From the evidence you see in this chapter, how would you describe Simon Peter's relationship with Jesus?

12. How would you explain the meaning of what Jesus did and said in verses 22-24 to someone who had never seen or heard this passage?

13. With verse 36 in mind, look back at Mark 11:24. In His prayer in Gethsemane, is Jesus now violating the guideline which He earlier gave His disciples? Explain your answer.

14. Why do you think Jesus gave no answer to the high priest's questioning in verse 60, and yet immediately gave a clear and extended answer to the high priest's question in verse 61?

15. In what ways can you see Jesus demonstrating His *authority* in this chapter?

FOR LIFE TODAY

16. What actions can we do that, in God's eyes, would be equivalent to what the woman did with the perfume in verse 3? Or is it truly too late?

17. Is there any sense today in which we are called upon to "keep watch" with Jesus, as the disciples were called to do in verses 34-38?

18. Look again at the action (or lack of action) by the disciples in verse 50. What warning, if any, do you see for us today in their example?

19. Review in verses 63-65 the guilty verdict against Jesus from the high priest and the other religious leaders. What do people "accuse" Jesus of today?

20. In light of how you're doing spiritually in your life today, which verse in this chapter do you think is the most important at this time—and why?

21. Remember again the command in Colossians 3:1—"Since you have been raised with Christ, set your hearts on things above, where Christ is seated at the right hand of God." What have you personally observed about Jesus Christ in this chapter that would be worthy of setting your heart on?

FOR GOING DEEPER

Look at the following other gospel passages, and discuss these other events in the trial of Jesus which Mark does not record: John 18:12-14 and 18:19-24; and Luke 23:6-12.

MARK 15

Startup: Discuss together the times in life when you felt most *alone.*

SEEING WHAT'S THERE

1. As best as you can, walk your way through the events of this chapter as if you were Jesus Himself, feeling what He felt, seeing what He saw, hearing what He heard. Describe to one another the sensations that come to your imagination.

2. This chapter records only two brief sentences spoken by Jesus. Investigate them, and talk about their significance for Jesus Himself, and for all Christians.

3. For background on Jesus' silence in verse 5 (see also verse 61 in the last chapter), look together at the prophecy in Isaiah 53:7.

4. From what you see in verses 2-15, what kind of a man was Pilate?

5. EYE FOR DETAIL—*From what you recall seeing in this chapter, try answering the following question without looking at your Bible:* Joseph of Arimathea was the man who took down Jesus' body from the cross and placed it in a tomb. Mark describes Joseph as a prominent member of the Jewish ruling council, and also gives a detail about Joseph's spiritual life. What detail was this? (See verse 43.)

CAPTURE THE ESSENCE

6. How do you think verse 34 relates to what Jesus prayed in Mark 14:36?

FOR LIFE TODAY

7. No one is trying to physically crucify us today—but what does Jesus' *example* in this chapter mean personally for your life?

8. Of the most important events and truths in this chapter, which do you think are the easiest for Christians to forget about?

FOR GOING DEEPER

For the disciples of Jesus, His trial, crucifixion, and burial—and soon afterward, His resurrection—were traumatic events that pounded their senses and emotions, and affected each of them in a different and powerful way. This is reflected well in the four different accounts of these events which the gospel writers give. For example, look up the following references to see together how each gospel records what happened from the time Jesus arrived at Golgotha (Calvary), to the moment He died. What unique details does each gospel bring out?—Matthew 27:33-50, Mark 15:22-37; Luke 23:33-46; and John 19:17-30.

MARK 16

Startup: Practically speaking, what would you say is the most important thing you have to do in the time you have remaining on earth?

1. Examine each part of the angel's message to the women in verses 6-7. What was the importance of each part?

2. For examples of what Jesus spoke about in verses 17-18, look together at these passages in the book of Acts —3:2-8, 5:15-16, 8:6-7, and 28:3-5.

3. EYE FOR DETAIL—*From what you recall seeing in this chapter, try answering the following question without looking at your Bible:* What are the names of the three women who are mentioned here as taking spices to the tomb of Jesus? (See verse 1.)

CAPTURE THE ESSENCE

4. What would you say this chapter teaches us about *faith* and about *baptism?*

FOR LIFE TODAY

5. How could you use verse 16 to help an unsaved friend who seemed to understand his need for salvation, but kept postponing a definite decision to entrust his life to Christ?

6. Look again at verses 15-16. Then identify together the kinds of people in your community whom you would say probably know the least about the living Lord Jesus Christ. What else are these people like? What do they do in daily life? Where do they live? Now imagine God has brought you together with a small group of these people, and in this meeting they indicate a genuine desire to understand who Jesus is and what He has done. From what you have seen in the gospel of Mark, what are the most important things you would want to communicate to them, and how would you word it?

FOR GOING DEEPER

Tell in your own words the importance of Jesus' resurrection as you think together about this chapter, and about these supporting passages: Romans 4:25, 1 Corinthians 15:17, and Revelation 1:18.

MARK:

THE BIG PICTURE

(Discuss again the questions in the "Overview," plus the questions below.)

1. Look together at each of these verses, and discuss which one you believe is the best candidate for "KEY VERSE" in the book of Mark—the one which brings into sharpest focus what this book is most about: 1:1, 3:35, 8:34, and 10:45.

2. What would you say are the strongest themes in the way this book portrays Jesus Christ?

3. In what passages in Mark did you especially notice Jesus backing up His words with action?

4. Which passages in this gospel gave you the strongest impression about the *power* of Jesus?

5. Even more than the other gospel writers, Mark is said to be a skilled *storyteller.* How would you evaluate his storytelling skills, as you've observed them in this book?

6. What would you say are the most important ways in which this book is *unique* in all the Bible?

7. In James 1:23-24 we're told that "anyone who listens to the word but does not do what it says is like a man who looks at his face in a mirror and, after looking at himself, goes away and immediately forgets what he looks like." In what important ways has the book of Mark been a "mirror" for you—showing you what you can and should do?

Luke

(Discuss these OVERVIEW questions both at the beginning of your study of Luke, and again after you've studied together all 24 chapters. Your answers may change significantly once you've looked more closely at the entire book.)

Startup: What qualities come to your mind when you think of the phrase *ideal manhood?*

SEEING WHAT'S THERE

1. It's been said that there's no better pathway to maturity in Christ than to carefully study the life of Christ. If that's true, what kinds of answers and guidelines and solutions would you like to discover as you study the book of Luke?

2. Look together at the following passages to learn more about Luke, the author of this gospel: Colossians 4:14, 2 Timothy 4:9-11, Philemon 23-24, and Luke 1:1-4.

3. Luke may well have been a Gentile, and if so, he was the only non-Jewish author of any of the books in Scripture. Look together at the following accounts (which are found in Luke's gospel, but not in the other three), and discuss how they might reflect Luke's sensitivity to the broader world beyond the Jewish people: 2:1; 2:10; 2:27-32; 10:30-37; 13:1-3; 13:28-30; 17:11-19; and 18:8.

4. Look also at the list of "Questions to Ask as You Begin Your Study of Each Book" on page 393.

CAPTURE THE ESSENCE

5. Compare the way in which this gospel begins (Luke 1:1-4), with the way the other three gospels begin (in Matthew 1:1-17, Mark 1:1, and John 1:1-18). What do these different "start-up styles" tell you about the *purpose* of each gospel?

FOR LIFE TODAY

6. Look together at the description of Jesus given in Hebrews 12:2-3. What goals and motivation can this verse give you as you begin studying the life of Christ as recorded by Luke?

7. How can you ensure that your study of Luke is not merely theoretical and intellectual, but is instead truly practical and relevant? Talk together about this. What can you do to help keep the process alive and interesting?

FOR GOING DEEPER

Bible teachers often present Luke as the gospel that especially presents Jesus as "the Son of Man"; in Luke, the *humanity* of Jesus is clearly apparent along with His divinity. From what you know of all four gospels, how does this side of Luke come through, especially in comparison with the other three gospels?

LUKE 1

Startup: Tell about a recent time when you spontaneously began singing aloud because of the happiness you felt.

SEEING WHAT'S THERE

1. From his introduction to this gospel in verses 1-4, what is Luke trying to accomplish in this book?

2. From what Luke says in verses 1-4, what kind of person would you say he seems to be?

3. Again with verses 1-4 in mind, what kind of hopes and expectations does Luke raise about what we'll see in the rest of the book?

4. From what you see in this chapter, how would you describe the kind of person Zechariah is, and in what ways can you identify with him?

5. From what you see in this chapter, how would you describe the kind of person Elizabeth is, and in what ways can you identify with her?

6. From what you see in this chapter, how would you describe the kind of person Mary is, and in what ways can you identify with her?

7. EYE FOR DETAIL—*If everyone in the group has read the entire chapter, try answering the following question without looking at your Bible:* In introducing this gospel, Luke addresses it to someone named "Theophilus." What title does Luke give to this man? (For the answer, see verse 3.)

8. Look also at the list of "Questions to Ask as You Study Each Chapter" on page 392, which you may want to do for each chapter in Luke.

CAPTURE THE ESSENCE

9. Keep in mind the way Gabriel described the son to be born to Zechariah and Elizabeth (verses 13-17), as you answer this question in your own words: What was God's purpose for the ministry of John the Baptist, and why was this ministry needed?

10. The name *John* means "The Lord is gracious." In light of what John the Baptist would accomplish in his life, in what ways would you say his God-given name was a good fit?

11. In verses 34-35, and in the events that follow in chapter 2 (and also in Matthew 1:18-25), we see how Jesus was conceived and born of a virgin. Why is the virgin birth of Jesus an important truth for us to know and believe?

12. What do you see as the strongest themes in Mary's song in verses 46-55?

13. What do you see as the strongest themes in Zechariah's song in verses 67-79?

14. What *choices* can you see Mary making in this chapter?

15. How would you describe Mary's faith?

16. Imagine you were helping to produce a film based on this chapter. Describe the kinds of scenery, supporting characters, background music, lighting effects, etc., which you would use to portray this chapter's central message.

17. How could you use this chapter to help explain to someone why Jesus came to earth?

FOR LIFE TODAY

18. Luke addressed this gospel to "Theophilus," whose name means "friend of God." Perhaps Luke was even thinking that others who were interested in reading this book would also be "friends of God." Do you feel comfortable applying that term to yourself? Why or why not?

FOR GOING DEEPER

When the angel Gabriel appeared to Zechariah and later to Mary, he quickly told them both not to be afraid (in verses 13 and 30). Notice how these same words are spoken by the angel to the shepherds in 2:10. Then look together at the following additional passages in Scripture where the angel of the Lord says much the same thing. What other similarities do you see in these passages that could link them with Luke 2?—Genesis 15:1, Daniel 10:18-19; and Acts 27:23-24 (see also the words of Jesus in Revelation 1:17-18).

LUKE 2

Startup: From all the Christmases you've known and all the times you've heard the Christmas story, what images have formed in your mind of the shepherds? the angels? Mary and Joseph? the baby Jesus? the city of Bethlehem?

SEEING WHAT'S THERE

1. Make a list together of all the *people* who are actually mentioned in this chapter. Notice also those who are *not* mentioned here—the innkeeper, and the wise men (magi), and Herod, for example.

2. What in this chapter do you think might be most surprising to a new Christian reading it for the first time?

3. Compare verse 25 with verse 26. What does each one say that Simeon was waiting for? Is this two different ways of saying the same thing?

4. Looking again at verses 25 and 26, how would you explain in your own words Simeon's spiritual condition?

5. If this chapter were the only Scripture portion you had ever read or heard, and you did not know any facts about the adult life of Jesus, what would you expect this child to be like when He grew up?

6. EYE FOR DETAIL—*From what you recall seeing in this chapter, try answering the following question without looking at your Bible:* The Holy Spirit revealed to Simeon that he would not die until he had seen "the Lord's Christ." After Simeon saw Jesus, he prayed and said, "My eyes have seen ———" What two words complete that sentence? (See verse 30.)

CAPTURE THE ESSENCE

7. From what you see in this chapter, how would you describe Mary and Joseph's relationship with God?

8. Why do you think God chose *shepherds* to receive the announcement

from His angels of the birth of Christ?

9. Look at verse 49. What would you say the boy Jesus at this time understood about Himself, and about His purpose in life?

10. How does this chapter demonstrate God's control over history?

FOR LIFE TODAY

11. What aspects of the story of Christ's birth as presented here do you think are most easily overlooked in the way the Christmas holiday is celebrated?

12. Think again about the description of Simeon in verses 25 and 26. In what ways could this be an example for us?

FOR GOING DEEPER

Compare the Christmas story in Luke 1 and 2—which focuses more on *Mary* and the *shepherds*—with the Christmas story as told in Matthew 1 and 2, which focuses more on *Joseph* and the *magi*. What are the most important ways in which these accounts complement each other?

LUKE 3

Startup: What are your favorite fruits?

SEEING WHAT'S THERE

1. In what ways do you see John the Baptist fulfilling the prophecy mentioned in verse 4?

2. What kind of "fruit" do you think John was speaking of in verse 8?

3. Express in your own words the picture of Jesus you get in verses 16 and 17.

4. In verse 17, what does John the Baptist mean by the words *wheat* and *chaff?*

5. Imagine yourself being present in the crowd to hear John's words spoken in verses 16 and 17, and that you were one of the many Jews looking forward to the coming of Christ (the Messiah). In light of your own personality, what expectations and questions would be in your mind?

6. Luke says that John's message to the people was "the gospel," or "good news" (verse 18). What is the good news in his message?

7. What do we learn in verses 21-22 about the relationships between God the Father, God the Son, and God the Holy Spirit?

8. Think carefully about verse 22. What was it about Jesus that was "pleasing" to God, and why did God want to tell Him?

9. From the long list of names in verses 23-38, identify all the people you're familiar with, and tell the most interesting facts you know about them.

10. EYE FOR DETAIL—*From what you recall seeing in this chapter, try answering the following question without looking at your Bible:* What did John the Baptist tell the soldiers to do? (See verse 14.)

11. From what John told the crowds of people to *do* in verses 10-14, what principles can you draw that summarize the kind of lifestyle God wants His people to have?

12. In your own words, what was the essential message John the Baptist proclaimed?

13. How would you describe the *tone* of John's message—and how do *you* tend to respond to others who speak in that tone?

14. From the evidence you see in this chapter, what would you say John the Baptist considered to be the most important things in life?

15. Look together at verse 17. In what way does Jesus baptize with the Holy Spirit and with fire?

16. What does this chapter teach us about baptism?

17. In verse 22, what significance do you see in the Holy Spirit's appearance in the form of a *dove?*

18. If this chapter was the only Scripture portion you had, what biblical definition would you give for the word *repentance?*

19. In verse 8, John told the Sadducees and Pharisees to produce "fruit" in their lives that was consistent with repentance. For people in our churches today, what kind of "fruit" do you think this should be?

20. Look again at verse 10. If masses of people today asked sincerely, "What should we do?" how do you think a messenger from God would answer?

21. Look again at verse 16. What *fire* have you seen in your life?

22. Jesus' preparation for His ministry will continue in the next chapter. But from all you've seen in Luke so far, and taking Jesus' example as a model for us, what kind of preparation would you say we need for having an effective ministry for God?

Only the gospel of Luke mentions that Jesus was *praying* when the Holy Spirit came upon him like a dove after His baptism. Look together at the following additional passages in Luke, and discuss what they tell us about Jesus' prayer life —6:12, 9:18, 9:28-29, 11:1, 22:39-44, 23:34, and 23:46.

LUKE 4

Startup: What's the *hungriest* you ever remember being?

SEEING WHAT'S THERE

1. For useful background to the answers Jesus gave to the devil's temptations (verses 1-13), look together at Deuteronomy 8:3, 6:16, and 6:13.

2. How would you express in your own words the truths from Scripture that Jesus used to defy the devil?

3. Imagine you are a reporter for the "Nazareth News." In a few sentences, how would you describe what happened in verses 14-30?

4. Look at the reaction of the people mentioned in verses 28-29. How would you explain the cause for this reaction?

5. EYE FOR DETAIL—*From what you recall seeing in this chapter, try answering the following question without looking at your Bible:* In the synagogue at Nazareth, Jesus stood, and was handed the scroll of the prophet Isaiah. After reading a short passage from this book, what did Jesus immediately do? (See verses 20-21.)

CAPTURE THE ESSENCE

6. As you think about the way Jesus handled the devil's temptations (in verses 1-13), imagine yourself being present with the disciples when Jesus first told them about this encounter. What would impress you most about what Jesus said, and what thoughts and questions would come to your mind?

7. After reviewing the three ways in which the devil tempted Jesus (verses 3-8), how would you comment on the devil's *strategy* against Jesus, as it appears in this passage? What were the devil's desires, and how did he plan to achieve them?

8. For each of the three temptations, discuss what you think would have happened next if Jesus had yielded to Satan's wishes.

9. If Satan had succeeded in getting Jesus under his control, what do you think is the worst thing he could have done to Jesus?

10. From the evidence you see in this temptation passage (verses 1-13), how would you describe Jesus' relationship to God His Father?

11. From what you see in verses 1-13, how would you describe the devil's character and personality?

12. From the way Jesus answered the devil each time, what conclusions can you draw about the *value* and the *reliability* of the Scriptures?

13. What does this chapter communicate to us about the *purpose* Jesus had for His ministry?

FOR LIFE TODAY

14. Think once more about the three ways in which Jesus was tempted by Satan (verses 3-11). In what ways have you experienced similar temptations?

15. If the three answers Jesus gave to the devil (verses 4, 8, and 12) were the only Scripture verses you knew, how much would each one help you as you faced various temptations? Are there any temptations you face for which you find no help at all in these three verses quoted by Jesus?

16. What kind of *living* was Jesus talking about in verse 4?

17. How do you see that Jesus lived on *every* word of God? How would you describe someone today who truly lives on every word of God?

18. Let the words of Jesus in verse 8 resound in your mind. Then discuss this question: Who or what do peo-

ple sometimes worship today instead of God?

19. Think together about the temptation Jesus overcame in verses 9-12. In what ways today do we sometimes try to bind God to human plans?

20. Look again at verse 12, and decide how much you agree or disagree with this statement: We can't "box God in" by putting Him to the test, but He is pleased if we ask in true faith for signs and indications of His guidance.

21. In light of how you're doing spiritually in your life today, which verse in this chapter do you think is the most important at this time—and why?

22. Look at the amazement or astonishment mentioned in verses 32 and 36. What surprises *you* about the teaching of Jesus?

FOR GOING DEEPER

Compare the three approaches Satan used in tempting Jesus (verses 5-12) with the three forms of worldliness mentioned in 1 John 2:16. How closely do they match?

LUKE 5

Startup: What do you think Jesus actually looked like? In your own mind, how do you like to think of His appearance when He lived on earth?

SEEING WHAT'S THERE

1. Take a "walk" together through the incidents that happen in this chapter: Using your imagination, talk about the kinds of sights, smells, sounds, and feelings you might experience.

2. Look at the similarity in verses 11 and 28. When the disciples "left everything" to follow Jesus, what specific things do you think were included in the "everything"?

3. Review verses 17-26, especially the reaction of the crowds in verse 26. What exactly was it that impressed these people about Jesus?

4. Thinking again of verses 11 and 28, imagine yourself in the sandals of Simon or John or Levi. What is it about Jesus that would attract you enough to leave your worldly belongings and follow Him?

5. What does Jesus mean by the word *righteous* in verse 32?

6. How do you see the *power* of Jesus demonstrated in this chapter?

7. How is the *character* of Jesus demonstrated in this chapter?

8. How is the *purpose* of Jesus demonstrated in this chapter?

9. What do you think might be most surprising in this chapter to a new Christian reading it for the first time?

10. EYE FOR DETAIL—*From what you recall seeing in this chapter, try answering the following question without looking at your Bible:* Four disciples are named in this chapter; who are they? (See verses 8-11 and 27-28.)

11. What does verse 16 tell us about the character and personality of Jesus?

12. Look at Jesus' answer to John's disciples in verses 34-35. Is the Bridegroom still with us? Is it time now to feast, or to fast?

13. In this chapter, which of these character qualities in Jesus comes through most strongly to you: His compassion, His power, or His wisdom? (Explain your answer.)

FOR LIFE TODAY

14. Look again at verses 12-13. Perhaps Jesus spent all night in prayer before choosing His twelve apostles, because choosing those twelve men was such an important task. What future decisions of yours could be as important in your own life as the selection of the twelve disciples was to Jesus?

15. Look again at verse 26. How does Jesus demonstrate His authority today, so that people can see it and give praise to God?

16. In light of how you're doing spiritually in your life today, which verse in this chapter do you think is the most important at this time—and why?

FOR GOING DEEPER

Look again at Peter's words to Jesus in verse 8, and compare these with Job 42:6 and Isaiah 6:5. What do these verses together teach us?

LUKE 6

Startup: Talk about something you may have made or built which lasted a much shorter time than you wanted it to.

SEEING WHAT'S THERE

1. In the incident described in verses 1-5, what one or two words would you say best describe the disciples here? What one or two words best describe the Pharisees in this incident? What one or two words best describe Jesus here?

2. For helpful background on verse 2, look together at Exodus 34:21.

3. For helpful background on verses 3-4, look together at 1 Samuel 21:1-6 and Deuteronomy 23:25. Take a look also at God's instructions for baking the Sabbath bread in Leviticus 24:5-9.

4. From all that you see in verses 6-11, what one or two words would you say best describe the Pharisees and the teachers of the law? What one or two words best describe Jesus here? What one or two words best describe the man with the injured hand?

5. From what you see in verse 7, how did the Pharisees view the power of Jesus?

6. What do you think Jesus was looking for at the beginning of verse 10?

7. What does verse 12 tell us about the character and personality of Jesus?

8. Imagine that you are one of the men mentioned in verses 14-15, and that you're writing a quick letter to a friend. Give a few sample lines of how you would describe to your friend all that happened in the first half of this chapter.

9. Compare the various lists of the twelve apostles in Matthew 10:2-4, Mark 3:16-19, here in Luke 6:14-16, and Acts 1:13. What differences do you see in these lists? Which persons

are always listed in the same place on each list?

10. Use any of the following verses to help you put together a definition for the word *blessed*, as it's used in verses 20-22 in this chapter: Psalms 94:12-13, 112:1-3, 128:1-4, and 144:12-15; Jeremiah 17:7-8; James 1:12; and Revelation 19:9, 20:6, and 22:14.

11. How would you restate the "Golden Rule" (verse 31) in your own words?

12. In the familiar illustration which Jesus gives in verses 46-49, what really is the "rock" that is mentioned there?

13. How would you describe the basic *mindset* or *attitude* in life which Jesus is teaching in this chapter?

14. EYE FOR DETAIL—*From what you recall seeing in this chapter, try answering the following question without looking at your Bible:* Jesus said to His disciples, "Woe to you when all men speak well of you—" How did He finish that sentence? (See verse 26.)

CAPTURE THE ESSENCE

15. Jesus says in verse 5 that He is "Lord of the Sabbath." By saying this, what was He trying to communicate to the Pharisees?

16. What does verse 5 imply about Jesus' relationship to the Old Testament law?

17. Why do you think Jesus said what He did to the man in verse 8?

18. How do you think the man with the injured hand would have answered the question in verse 9?

19. Explain how much you agree or disagree with this statement: In verses 1-11, the most important lesson for both the Pharisees and the disciples had to do with their understanding of Jesus, not their understanding of the Sabbath.

20. What do you think is the Lord's *intent* as He gives us these standards for Christian living in verse 20 and continuing to the end of this chapter?

21. Would you say verses 20-26 are more about *values* and *attitudes,* or more about *actions?* Explain your answer.

22. From what you see in verses 20-23, express in your own words what Jesus is looking for in His followers.

23. Jesus tells us in verse 23 to be glad when we are persecuted. What good things does persecution accomplish in our lives?

24. Compare verse 37 with verses 43-45. How do we recognize "bad fruit" without violating what Jesus says about judging and condemning in verse 37?

FOR LIFE TODAY

25. If you were asked to summarize the most important "marks of Christian maturity" as taught in this chapter, which ones would you mention first?

26. Which of the qualities and conditions in verses 20-23 are the hardest for you to experience in your own life?

27. Discuss how much you agree or disagree with this statement: Although verses 27-36 present important basic principles, we are not to take them 100 percent literally in the way we apply them to our lives.

28. Review the question Jesus asked in verse 9. Then tell how much you agree or disagree with this statement: If we are not doing good, we are doing evil; and if we are not saving life, we are destroying life.

29. What principles from verses 39-40 could be applied as you evaluate the choices you've made about what church to attend, and what Bible teachers to listen to?

30. In light of how you're doing spiritually in your life today, which verse in this chapter do you think is the most important at this time?

FOR GOING DEEPER

What were these men getting themselves into? Think again about the selection Jesus made (in verses 13-16) of the twelve apostles, then look at these other verses in Luke in which this group of twelve is mentioned. Discuss how much of these experiences the twelve apostles might have anticipated at the time they were chosen—Luke 9:1-6, 9:10-13, 17:5-6, 18:31-34, 22:14-16, and 24:9-11.

LUKE 7

Startup: If you've had military experience, talk about anything interesting you learned about the giving and carrying out of orders.

SEEING WHAT'S THERE

1. Review the incident recorded in verses 11-17. Take turns briefly retelling this story from these three different points of view: first, as if you were the widow retelling the story; second, as if you were the young man who had been dead; and finally, as if you were Jesus. Use your imagination to throw in details of sight, sound, smells, etc.

2. What do you think might have caused the doubts about Jesus which John the Baptist expressed in verses 18-19?

3. In your own words, how would you state what Jesus said in verse 28?

4. Look over also the incident recorded in verses 36-50. Then take turns briefly retelling this story from these three different points of view: first, as if you were the woman telling the story; second, as if you were Simon the Pharisee; and finally, as if you were Jesus. Again, use your imagination to throw in details of sight, sound, smells, etc.

5. EYE FOR DETAIL—*From what you recall seeing in this chapter, try answering the following question without looking at your Bible:* What was the name of the town where Jesus raised the widow's dead son to life as his body was being carried away? (See verses 11-15.)

CAPTURE THE ESSENCE

6. What do we learn in this chapter about the relationship between John the Baptist's ministry and the ministry of Jesus?

7. Look at verse 35, then look together at James 3:13. What do these verses together teach us about wisdom?

8. How could you use the account in verses 36-50 to help a non-Christian who said he was too great a sinner to be accepted by God?

9. In this chapter, which of these character qualities in Jesus comes through most strongly to you: His compassion, His power, or His wisdom? (Explain your answer.)

FOR LIFE TODAY

10. Notice the encounters Jesus had in this chapter with both sexes. In what ways do you see that following Jesus Christ enhances your manhood or your womanhood?

11. How could you use verses 18-23 to help a young believer who was beginning to have doubts about Jesus?

12. Look at the words Jesus spoke about His generation in verses 31-35. In what ways could these verses apply to our generation today?

FOR GOING DEEPER

Notice Jesus' attitude toward two women in verses 13 and 44-48. Luke 7 is a good example of the prominence this gospel—more than the other three—gives to women. Look together at the following verses. From what you discover there together, discuss how you would summarize your impression of *Luke's* view of women, and *Jesus'* view of women—1:41-42, 2:19, 2:36-37, 8:1-3, 8:47-48, 10:38-42, 11:27-28, 13:10-16, 15:8-9, 23:27-31, 23:48-49, 23:55-56, and 24:1-11.

LUKE 8

Startup: What's the stormiest weather you can recall having been in?

SEEING WHAT'S THERE

1. Review the parable of the sower and the soils in verses 4-15. In what ways is this parable a *warning* to us? In what ways is it an *encouragement?*

2. In verse 8, what kind of "ears" is Jesus talking about?

3. Imagine that you are a reporter for the "Galilee Gazette." In a few sentences, how would you describe what happened in verses 26-39?

4. Notice again in this chapter the encounters Jesus had with both sexes. From what you've seen in this gospel, how would you define what *manhood* and *womanhood* mean to Jesus?

5. What in this chapter do you think might be most surprising to a new Christian reading it for the first time?

6. EYE FOR DETAIL—*From what you recall seeing in this chapter, try answering the following question without looking at your Bible:* After casting out the demons from the man who lived in the tombs, what did Jesus tell this man to do? (See verses 38-39.)

CAPTURE THE ESSENCE

7. From what you see in the first part of this chapter, what is a *parable,* and what is its purpose?

8. From what you see in verse 10, is it accurate to say that Jesus was hiding the truth from some people?

9. Imagine that you have a friend who has been blind for life, and tell how you would explain to this friend the meaning of verses 16-17.

10. In the incident in verses 22-25, how do you think the disciples would have responded differently to the storm if they had had more faith?

How exactly did Jesus *want* them to respond?

11. If the disciples in the boat had truly responded in faith when the storm hit, do you think there were some even greater lessons they could have learned? If so, what might these have been?

12. How would you compare the power of the storm in verses 23-24 with the power of the demons in verses 27-29?

13. In this chapter, which of these character qualities in Jesus comes through most strongly to you: His compassion, His power, or His wisdom? (Explain your answer.)

FOR LIFE TODAY

14. Look at what Jesus said to His disciples in verse 10. Has the Lord also given to you what was given to the disciples?

15. If a loyal friend mentioned to you a concern that you were living life too carelessly, how could you use verse 14 to help you evaluate whether or not that was so?

16. In line with what Jesus says in verse 15, describe as fully as possible what it takes for us to be "good soil"?

17. Think again about verses 22-25, especially the question Jesus asked in verse 25. Is it wrong to ever be afraid? Is it possible to have faith and yet still experience fear?

18. What are some "storms" in your life —the " winds" and "waves" that have given you fear or anxiety? How have you seen that the Lord has power over them?

19. In light of how you're doing spiritually in your life today, which verse in this chapter do you think is the most important at this time—and why?

FOR GOING DEEPER

Verse 12 mentions one of the strategies used by the devil. Look together also at the following verses in Luke, and discuss what they tell us about Satan's work and power—10:17-18, 11:18, 13:16, 22:3-4, and 22:31-32.

LUKE 9

Startup: Who or what has authority over you, in one degree or another? Make a list together of the different authorities you recognize in your life.

SEEING WHAT'S THERE

1. Imagine that you are a Bible-times version of a private detective, hired by the religious leaders in Jerusalem to spy on Jesus. What would you say in your latest report to them, based on what you observe in the first seventeen verses of this chapter?

2. How is the *character* of Jesus demonstrated in this chapter?

3. How is the *purpose* of Jesus demonstrated in this chapter?

4. What clues do you see in verses 7-9 about the character and personality of King Herod?

5. What picture do you get in verses 10-11 of the character of Jesus?

6. Using your imagination, how would you describe the probable "atmosphere" in the incident recorded in verses 28-36?

7. In verses 30-31, what do you know about Moses and Elijah that explains the significance of their presence here?

8. What do you think might have been actually *said* by Moses and Elijah in the conversation with Jesus mentioned in verse 31?

9. Examine closely the words God spoke about Jesus in verse 35. Notice the different phrases that make up this quotation. What would you say is the significance of each phrase?

10. Were the words Jesus spoke in verse 41 meant to sound harsh? Why or why not?

11. Look again at verse 41. In what ways did Jesus have to "put up with" people?

12. What does it really mean to "welcome" a child in Jesus' name, as He tells us to do in verse 48?

13. What image of Jesus does verse 51 bring to your mind?

14. In verses 51-55, compare the behavior of the Samaritan villagers, the disciples James and John, and Jesus. How well would you say they all understood each other?

15. EYE FOR DETAIL—*From what you recall seeing in this chapter, try answering the following question without looking at your Bible:* A man told Jesus that he would follow wherever Jesus went. In His answer, Jesus mentioned two kinds of animals. What were they? (See verse 58.)

CAPTURE THE ESSENCE

16. If you were asked to summarize the most important "marks of Christian maturity" as taught in this chapter, which ones would you mention first?

17. Why do you think Jesus gave the disciples the warning recorded in verse 21?

18. What would you say verses 23-25 have to teach us about self-esteem?

19. Look again at verses 28-36. From God's point of view, what was the purpose for Jesus' transfiguration?

20. Notice Luke's words about Peter, James, and John in verse 36. Imagine that you are one of these three disciples after Jesus had risen from the dead. How would you go about explaining to the other disciples what you had witnessed that day on the mountain?

21. To see what Peter wrote later about his experiences in verses 28-36, look together at 2 Peter 1:16-18. What seem to be the most important things Peter learned from being a witness to this transfiguration of Jesus?

22. In as few words as possible, how would you summarize the principle Jesus is teaching in verse 48?

23. From what you've seen in this chapter, what does it really mean to "follow Jesus"?

24. From what you've seen so far in Luke, why did Jesus perform miracles?

FOR LIFE TODAY

25. In verse 1, look at the authority which Jesus gave to His twelve disciples. Do we have this same authority today?

26. In much of this chapter, Jesus has begun to focus His ministry upon His disciples. What guidelines for today's discipleship training do you especially see in the way Jesus taught His disciples in verses 18-27?

27. Restate in your own words—and in the context of our lives today—the three things Jesus asks us to do in verse 23.

28. Look at the topic of the argument mentioned in verse 46. In what ways, if any, do we sometimes continue this argument today?

29. Look closely at verse 50, and tell how much you agree or disagree with this statement: Unless you are actively working *against* the Lord and His will, then it's the same as working *for* His will. (You may want to also look together at Matthew 12:30.)

30. Look again at verses 51-56, and compare what you see there with Mark 10:35-45. How would you describe the personalities of James and John, and in what ways can you identify with them?

31. Look at the command Jesus gave in verse 60. In what ways, if any, might this verse apply to us? How should *we* "let the dead bury their own dead"?

32. Look at the statement Jesus makes in verse 62. In what ways can we sometimes be guilty of "looking back" while our hands are on the plow?

33. What guidelines for people in ministry today can you find in Jesus' example in this chapter?

34. In light of how you're doing spiritually in your life today, which verse in this chapter do you think is the most important at this time—and why?

FOR GOING DEEPER

Compare the account in verses 28-36 of Jesus' transfiguration with the passage about His baptism in 3:21-22. What similarities do you see in both events? How do they relate to one another?

LUKE 10

Startup: What's the most dangerous assignment you've ever received?

SEEING WHAT'S THERE

1. In verses 1-16, compare the instructions Jesus gave for this ministry campaign with the instructions He gave to a smaller group—the twelve apostles—in Luke 9:1-5. How are these instructions alike, and how are they different?

2. How would you describe the ministry strategy of Jesus at this time?

3. In light of what you've seen so far in Luke, how would you describe one of the "workers" or "laborers" which Jesus talks about in verse 2?

4. In the parable in verses 30-35, how would you summarize the attitude toward the wounded man of each person mentioned there?

5. Jesus said in verse 42 that Mary had made a choice—and a good choice. From what you see in verses 38-42, what choices had her sister Martha made already?

6. EYE FOR DETAIL—*From what you recall seeing in this chapter, try answering the following question without looking at your Bible:* In this chapter, Jesus sent out a large contingent of disciples two-by-two on a ministry trip. When they returned, what did they say to Jesus? (See verse 17.)

7. What in this chapter do you think might be the most interesting to someone who was learning about Jesus Christ for the first time, and why?

CAPTURE THE ESSENCE

8. Look closely at verses 21-22. What does this passage teach us about (a) Jesus' relationship to God, (b) God's relationship to us, and (c) our relationship to Jesus?

9. What principles about *love* can you draw from the parable in verses 30-35?

10. From what you see in verses 38-42, discuss how much you agree or disagree with this statement: Martha was doing her best to serve Jesus, but His compliment for Mary shows us that there are more important things than serving the Lord.

FOR LIFE TODAY

11. To what degree is what Jesus said in the first part of verse 2 still true today?

12. Jesus tells His disciples in verse 3 that He's sending them out like "lambs among wolves." To what degree would you say those words also apply to us?

13. Jesus gives a principle in verse 7 about the wages deserved by His laborers. How would you apply that principle to His workers today?

14. In verses 13-15, look at the reasons for which Jesus pronounced judgment upon certain cities. In what ways could some of our cities today fall under the same judgment?

15. Look at the two kinds of people Jesus mentions in His prayer in verse 21. In what ways do you fit into either or both of these categories?

16. Look together at verses 38-41, and compare what you see there with John 11:17-40. How would you describe the personalities of Mary and Martha, and in what ways can you identify with either of them?

17. Think together about Philippians 4:8, where we're given this command: "Whatever is true, whatever is noble, whatever is right, whatever is pure, whatever is lovely, whatever is admirable—if anything is excellent or praiseworthy—*think about such things.*" What food for thought can you find in this chapter that especial-

ly strikes you as being *true,* or *noble,* or *right,* or *pure,* or *lovely,* or *admirable,* or *excellent,* or *praiseworthy?*

FOR GOING DEEPER

More than any other gospel, the book of Luke emphasizes *joy* and *rejoicing.* Notice in this chapter the joy experienced by the disciples in verse 17, and especially by Jesus in verse 21. Then consider together these other verses in Luke that speak of joy or rejoicing, and discuss how we, too, can have a share in it: 1:46-48, 2:10, 6:22-23, 15:3-10, 19:37-38, and 24:50-52.

LUKE 11

Startup: What's the earliest prayer you remember praying as a child?

SEEING WHAT'S THERE

1. Review verses 1-12. From what you see here, what perspective does Jesus want us to have about prayer?

2. Review the "Lord's Prayer" in verses 2-4, then try restating it in completely different language, without using any words from the original (except those that are three letters or less). You may want to go around the group and have each person paraphrase one line from the prayer.

3. Is Jesus saying in verse 13 that we need to *ask* God for the Holy Spirit before we can receive Him? Explain your answer.

4. Imagine yourself being present at the meal described in verses 37-53. In light of your own personality, what words spoken by Jesus in these verses stand out most to you?

5. In what Jesus says about the Pharisees in verses 39-52, is He more displeased with their *actions* or with their *attitudes*—or is He equally displeased about both?

6. What in this chapter do you think might be most surprising to a new Christian reading it for the first time?

7. EYE FOR DETAIL—*From what you recall seeing in this chapter, try answering the following question without looking at your Bible:* In this chapter, what does Jesus say God will give us, if we'll ask Him? (See verse 13.)

CAPTURE THE ESSENCE

8. Verses 9-10 teach us to pray with confidence. What is the true basis of that confidence?

9. What would you say is the main point in the parable Jesus tells in verses 16-22?

10. In verses 33-36, what would you say the lamp represents, and what does the eye represent?

11. In verses 33-36, would you say Jesus' main point is more about salvation, more about spiritual understanding, or more about warfare against Satan? Explain your answer.

12. Based on all that Jesus says about them in verses 39-52, what one-word adjectives would you use to describe the Pharisees?

13. Look at Jesus' words in verse 49. When He speaks of "prophets and apostles," who is He referring to?

14. What similarities would you point out between being a Jewish religious leader in the days when Jesus lived on earth, and being a pastor or other Christian leader today? What major differences would there be?

15. How could you use verses 1-13 to help teach a new Christian how to pray?

16. Jesus encourages us in verses 9-10 to ask and to seek and to knock. With this confidence in mind, look together at each of the following verses in this chapter, thinking carefully about what Jesus teaches us there. Then express each verse in the form of a model prayer that any Christian could use—or a prayer that specifically fits your life right now: verses 13, 28, and 34.

17. Look over the long list of criticisms which Jesus had for the religious leaders of His day (verses 39-52), and answer this question: Which of these faults and failures are the biggest dangers for Christian leaders today?

18. From what Jesus says about the Pharisees in verses 39-52, rank the following three things according to how you see their importance to God: (a) what we say, (b) what we know, and (c) what we do.

Compare what you see in verses 5-8 with the parable about the unjust judge in Luke 18:1-8. How are these passages alike, and how are they different? What do these passages together teach about *prayer?*

LUKE 12

Startup: What lessons do you recall learning (perhaps the hard way) which have helped you to look beyond today when making choices?

SEEING WHAT'S THERE

1. Look closely at verses 13-15, then discuss how much you agree or disagree with this statement: Jesus' answer in verse 14 shows us that the Lord will not judge us for how we set up our wills or estates, or for what we do with anything we receive through an inheritance.

2. Jesus tells us in verse 22 to not worry about life. In the verses that follow, what valid reasons can you find for not worrying?

3. What do you think Jesus is talking about in verses 58 and 59?

4. EYE FOR DETAIL—*From what you recall seeing in this chapter, try answering the following question without looking at your Bible:* What did God call the man who told himself to "eat, drink and be merry"? (See verses 12:19-20.)

CAPTURE THE ESSENCE

5. In your own words, how would you define the "yeast" which Jesus speaks of in verse 1?

6. Would you say the man in verses 16-19 was someone who enjoyed inner peace? Why or why not?

7. What does verse 32 tell you about God's character? How easy is it for you to understand and remember this about Him?

8. From what you've seen in this chapter, what does it really mean to "follow Jesus"?

FOR LIFE TODAY

9. Is the "yeast" still around today which Jesus describes in verse 1? If so, where?

10. Think carefully about the parable Jesus told in verses 16-21. At this time in life, how much would you say you're involved in building "bigger barns"?

11. How could you use verses 16-21 to help an unsaved friend who was afraid he would have to give up too much if he became a Christian?

12. How would you describe a person today who is "rich toward God," as Jesus says in verse 21.

13. In the passage that begins in verse 22, which statement of Jesus gives you the most powerful reason not to worry about life's common concerns?

14. Is the "seeking" which Jesus mentions in verse 31 meant to be a lifelong seeking? If so, how much "finding" should we experience in this life on earth, and will we be able to get by with less and less seeking?

15. In your life, how do you think verse 35 should be applied?

16. Look at the statement Jesus makes in verse 40. What difference in your life do you think it would make if you *did* know the exact day or hour when Jesus will return?

17. Look again, carefully, at verses 54-56. In what way might it be valid for Jesus to call *us* "hypocrites," because we haven't interpreted correctly the time in which we live?

18. What insight does this chapter offer regarding a godly perspective toward material possessions?

19. In light of how you're doing spiritually in your life today, which verse in this chapter do you think is the most important at this time—and why?

20. Jesus encouraged us in Luke 11:9-10 to ask and to seek and to knock. With this confidence in mind, look together at each of the following verses in chapter 12, thinking care-

fully about what Jesus teaches us there. Then express each verse in the form of a model prayer that any Christian could use — or a prayer that specifically fits your life right now: verses 8, 22, 40, 42, and 49.

Verse 33 is a good example of how Luke (even more than the other gospel writers) reveals the special concern God has for the poor. Look also at how this concern is portrayed in the following verses in Luke. Then decide together how they should influence your own attitude toward the poor — 4:17-18, 6:20, 6:24, 7:22, 11:41, 14:12-14, 16:19-31, 18:22-25, and 21:1-4.

LUKE 13

Startup: Talk about any memorable experiences you've had of getting locked out of a place where you needed to be inside.

SEEING WHAT'S THERE

1. What do you think is the main point of the parable in verses 6-9?

2. For background on verses 6-9, look together at Psalm 1:1-3 and Jeremiah 17:7-8. How do these Old Testament passages compare to the parable Jesus told?

3. In each of the two brief parables in verses 18-21, what is the big point Jesus is making?

4. Look again at the question Jesus was asked in verse 23, and the answer He made in the verses that follow. Explain whether you would summarize His answer to the question as a "Yes" or a "No"?

5. In your own words, how would you explain what Jesus said in verse 33?

6. EYE FOR DETAIL — *From what you recall seeing in this chapter, try answering the following question without looking at your Bible:* In this chapter, Jesus healed a crippled woman on the Sabbath. How long had the woman been crippled? (See verse 11.)

CAPTURE THE ESSENCE

7. In this chapter, which of these character qualities in Jesus comes through most strongly to you: His compassion, His power, or His wisdom? (Explain your answer.)

8. If this chapter was the only Scripture portion you had, what biblical definition would you give for the term *kingdom of God?*

FOR LIFE TODAY

9. With the parable in verses 6-9 in mind, discuss which of these state-

ments best describes each of you: (a) I am now bearing fruit in my Christian life. (b) I'm not now bearing fruit in my Christian life, but I will in the future. (c) It may be too late for me to bear fruit in my Christian life.

10. Look again at what Jesus calls the people in verse 15. What do you feel is the best *cure* for hypocrisy? What do you feel is the best *prevention* against hypocrisy?

11. Think about verses 23-24. What is "narrow" about the doorway in life which you have chosen to enter?

12. How could you use verses 24-25 to help an unsaved friend who seemed to understand his need for salvation, but kept postponing a definite decision to entrust his life to Christ?

13. In light of what Jesus says in verse 30, what kind of surprises do you think we're in for (even though Jesus has told us this beforehand)?

14. Again with verse 30 in mind, should we actually *try* to be "last"? If so, what does that mean?

15. In light of how you're doing spiritually in your life today, which verse in this chapter do you think is the most important at this time—and why?

FOR GOING DEEPER

Picture again the last scene in this chapter, in which Jesus weeps over the city that persecuted the messengers sent to her from God. Look together at 2 Chronicles 24:20-21 and Jeremiah 26:20-23 and discuss these two instances of Jerusalem's sin against God's prophets.

LUKE 14

Startup: Recall your most unusual experiences while you were someone's dinner guest.

SEEING WHAT'S THERE

1. In your own words, how would you summarize the main point of the parable in verses 16-24, and how does it relate to the question Jesus was asked in verse 15?

2. Suppose you were a Bible translator for a remote tribe on a faraway continent, and this tribe did not have any experience or knowledge of salt. How would you explain what salt is, so they could understand the meaning of verse 34?

3. EYE FOR DETAIL—*From what you recall seeing in this chapter, try answering the following question without looking at your Bible:* When Jesus asked the Pharisees and teachers of the law whether it was lawful to heal on the Sabbath or not, how did they answer? (See verses 3-4.)

CAPTURE THE ESSENCE

4. If you were asked to summarize the most important "marks of Christian maturity" as taught in this chapter, which ones would you mention first?

5. From what you've seen in this chapter, what does it really mean to "follow Jesus"?

FOR LIFE TODAY

6. Jesus encouraged us in Luke 11:9-10 to ask and to seek and to knock. With this confidence in mind, look together at each of the following verses in chapter 14, thinking carefully about what Jesus teaches us there. Then express each verse in the form of a model prayer that any Christian could use—or a prayer that specifically fits your life right now: verses 11, 26, 27, and 33.

As this chapter opens, Jesus once again heals someone on the Sabbath. In the verses listed here, look together at the other instances in Luke where Jesus works a miracle on the Sabbath. Besides being on the Sabbath, how else are these miracles alike? How are they different? —4:31-37 and 4:38-41, 6:6-11, and 13:10-17.

LUKE 15

Startup: When is the last time you can remember searching for something valuable that you had misplaced or lost?

SEEING WHAT'S THERE

1. In what ways are the three parables in this chapter all alike?

2. How would you summarize the main discipleship concepts in these three parables—principles that tell us how to *follow* Jesus day by day?

3. What in this chapter do you think might be most surprising to a new Christian reading it for the first time?

4. EYE FOR DETAIL—*From what you recall seeing in this chapter, try answering the following question without looking at your Bible:* When the prodigal son returned home, what three things did the father ask the servants to bring for the son to wear? (See verse 22.)

CAPTURE THE ESSENCE

5. What principles about God's love are evident in all three of the parables in this chapter? (Find as many as you can.)

6. Luke 15 is considered by some to be the key chapter in this gospel. Why do you think this is so?

FOR LIFE TODAY

7. Choose one of these sentences, and complete it as fully and candidly as you can:

> *What I see and understand in this chapter is important to my life because...*
> *What I see and understand in this chapter does NOT seem important to my life at this time, because...*

8. This chapter has been called "The Lost and Found Chapter." How do you feel most in your life now: *lost,* or *found?*

9. How could you use any of the parables in this chapter to help an unsaved friend who said to you, "I've been seeking God, but I can't find Him"?

10. How could you use any of the parables in this chapter to help a Christian friend who felt overcome by a sin he or she had committed?

11. How could you use the last story in this chapter to help an unsaved friend who felt he needed to become a better person before he could become a Christian?

12. In light of how you're doing spiritually in your life today, which verse in this chapter do you think is the most important—and why?

FOR GOING DEEPER

How well does the father's statement in the last verse of this chapter match the pictures given in Ephesians 2:1-5 and Romans 6:13?

LUKE 16

Startup: If you received tomorrow a tax-free gift of one million dollars, what would you do with the money?

SEEING WHAT'S THERE

1. What do you think are the "true riches" Jesus speaks of in verse 11?

2. In verse 14, Luke mentions a specific attitude of the Pharisees. Why do you think he added this statement, and how do you think this attitude might have been demonstrated in their daily life?

3. As you think about the story of the rich man and Lazarus that begins in verse 19, look back earlier in the chapter to see if you find what it is that prompted Jesus to tell this story.

4. What in this chapter do you think might be the most interesting to someone who was learning about Jesus Christ for the first time, and why?

5. EYE FOR DETAIL—*From what you recall seeing in this chapter, try answering the following question without looking at your Bible:* In the story of the rich man and Lazarus, how many brothers did the rich man have? (See verse 28.)

CAPTURE THE ESSENCE

6. Jesus mentions two specific masters in verse 13. In your own words, how would you define what it means to serve each one?

7. Review again verses 14-15. Besides money, what else would fall clearly into the category Jesus mentions of things that are highly esteemed or valued among men, but detestable or abominable to God?

8. What does this chapter have to tell us about the *power* of money?

9. Discuss how much you agree or disagree with this statement: In light of the teaching in this chapter, it is best

in life to have as little to do with money as possible.

10. Think carefully about verses 27-31. What conclusions can you draw from this passage about the *purpose* and *power* of Scripture, and the human response to it?

FOR LIFE TODAY

11. Jesus speaks in verse 10 of the little things in which we need to be honest, before being entrusted with more. What would you say are some good examples today of these "little" ways in which we might be most tempted to be dishonest?

12. Look again at verse 18. How would you use this verse to help a Christian who was considering divorce?

13. If a non-Christian friend told you he didn't believe there was any life after death, how could you use the story of the rich man and Lazarus to help you give a meaningful reply?

14. With the principles of this chapter in mind, what would you say are the three best uses a Christian can make of his or her money?

FOR GOING DEEPER

Compare the following three parables in Luke, and discuss what they together teach about *wealth*. How are they alike, and how are they different?—the rich fool (12:16-21), the great feast (14:16-24), and the shrewd manager (16:1-9).

LUKE 17

Startup: The stigma often associated today with the AIDS virus is sometimes compared to the way people with leprosy were treated in the past. What have been your own thoughts about how to associate with persons with AIDS?

SEEING WHAT'S THERE

1. State in your own words what verse 2 implies about God's *values.*

2. Discuss how much you agree or disagree with this statement: In verse 4, Jesus teaches us that there should be no limits at all on our forgiveness.

3. What do you think prompted the disciples to say what they did in verse 5?

4. Describe as fully as you can the image and understanding of Jesus which you get from verse 24.

5. From what you've seen in this chapter, what does it really mean to "serve God"?

6. EYE FOR DETAIL—*From what you recall seeing in this chapter, try answering the following question without looking at your Bible:* Jesus said the days just before He returns to earth in judgment will be much like the days of Noah before the flood, and the days of Lot before Sodom was destroyed. Jesus also listed several human activities that were taking place during the times of Noah and of Lot. How many of these can you name? (See verses 26-29.)

CAPTURE THE ESSENCE

7. What kind of actions do you think Jesus is talking about in verses 1-2—the things people do that cause others to sin?

8. Look again at verses 5-6. Why does God place so much value on faith?

9. If you were asked to summarize the most important "marks of Christian

maturity" as taught in this chapter, which ones would you mention first?

10. In what specific ways would you say verses 1-3 apply today to Christian pastors and teachers?

11. Look again at verses 15-19. Can you think of any big blessing from God that you haven't sufficiently thanked Him for?

12. In light of how you're doing spiritually in your life today, which verse in this chapter do you think is the most important at this time—and why?

FOR GOING DEEPER

Compare what you see in verses 7-10 with the parable about the king's ten servants in Luke 19:11-27. How are these passages alike, and how are they different? What do these passages together teach about *service* and *obedience?*

LUKE 18

Startup: Recall a time when you gave in to someone's persistent requests only to stop them from asking you.

SEEING WHAT'S THERE

1. How is the *character* of Jesus demonstrated in this chapter?

2. How is the *purpose* of Jesus demonstrated in this chapter?

3. What in this chapter do you think might be most surprising to a new Christian reading it for the first time?

4. As you look over verses 18-30 (about the conversation Jesus had with the rich ruler, and the discussion that followed), talk about this question: Is this passage more about *possessions,* more about *relationships,* or equally about both?

5. Would you say verse 22 is more about *actions,* more about *attitudes,* or equally about both?

6. In verses 31-33 we find another instance in Luke where Jesus predicts His death and resurrection. How does the wording here compare with His previous predictions in 9:21-22 and 9:43-45? What additional information is Jesus now giving to His disciples?

7. EYE FOR DETAIL—*From what you recall seeing in this chapter, try answering the following question without looking at your Bible:* In his conversations with two very different individuals in this chapter, Jesus had a different question for each one. What did Jesus ask the rich ruler? And what did He ask the blind beggar? (See verses 19 and 41.)

CAPTURE THE ESSENCE

8. Discuss how much you agree or disagree with this statement: In verses 2-8 we learn that God will answer our repeated prayers only when He gets tired of hearing them.

9. Which of the two men in verses 10-13 do you think was experiencing the most inner peace? Explain your answer.

10. Summarize all the differences you see—both outward and inward—between the two men in verses 10-13.

11. In verse 14 Jesus promises specific consequences both for those who exalt themselves, as well as for those who humble themselves. Discuss when you think these consequences will occur—mostly in eternity, or mostly in this life.

12. What would you say is the most important truth which Jesus is trying to teach in verses 22-30?

13. What would you say is the key word or words in the statement Jesus makes in verses 29-30?

14. Consider carefully again the words of verse 1. In the last week, what are the biggest things you've prayed for?

15. How could you use verses 10-14 to help an unsaved friend who felt he needed to become a better person before he could become a Christian?

16. How could you use those same verses (10-14) to help an unsaved friend who felt he lived a good enough life already, and didn't need to believe in Christ?

17. If you were to ask God for *mercy*, as the tax collector did in verse 13, what exactly would you mean by that word?

18. Review what Jesus commanded in verse 22. For whom, if anyone, is this command still valid today?

19. With verse 27 in mind, discuss some "impossibilities" which you have seen God accomplish in your life, or in the life of someone close to you.

20. Jesus encouraged us in Luke 11:9-10 to ask and to seek and to knock.

Now again, in 18:1-8, He tells us to not give up in our praying. With this confidence in mind, look together at each of the following verses in chapter 18, thinking carefully about what Jesus teaches us there. Then express each verse in the form of a model prayer that any Christian could use—or a prayer that specifically fits your life right now: verses 14, 17, and 27.

FOR GOING DEEPER

Compare the following two parables in Luke, and discuss what they together teach about *humility*. How are they alike, and how are they different?—the wedding feast (14:7-11), and the Pharisee and the tax collector (18:9-14).

LUKE 19

Startup: In the way we read and study the Bible, what kind of mental habits can most easily block this gospel of Luke from coming alive in our minds and hearts?

SEEING WHAT'S THERE

1. Imagine that you are a reporter for the "Jericho Journal." In a few sentences, how would you describe what happened in the first half of this chapter?

2. Think carefully about verse 11. Then, in light of it, review the parable that follows in verses 12-27. What are the main points being made in this parable?

3. Keep the events of verses 37-38 in mind, as you discuss how much you agree or disagree with this statement: The cheering welcome and praise which Jesus received as He entered Jerusalem was rooted only in the people's misunderstanding of what kind of king He truly was, and this was proven by the way the crowds turned against Him later in the week.

4. Review what was said and done in verses 45-46. How did this incident compare with an earlier one recorded in John 2:13-17?

5. For background on Jesus' words about the Temple being a "house of prayer" (verse 46), look together at Isaiah 56:7.

6. EYE FOR DETAIL—*From what you recall seeing in this chapter, try answering the following question without looking at your Bible:* How much of his money did Zacchaeus promise to give to the poor, and how much did he promise to pay back to anyone he might have cheated? (See verse 8.)

CAPTURE THE ESSENCE

7. In this chapter, which of these character qualities in Jesus comes through most strongly to you: His compassion, His power, or His wisdom? (Explain your answer.)

8. How could you use verse 10 to help a non-Christian who said he was too sinful to come to Christ?

9. Look over the parable of the king's servants in verses 11-27. What does it show us about the *kingship* of Jesus?

10. What kind of wrong thinking or actions do you think Jesus may be trying to prevent by telling the disciples the parable in verses 11-27?

11. If the people in verse 14 are a picture of people today who reject Jesus as their Lord and King, what do you think is the source of the hatred they have for him?

12. From what you see in this parable of the king's ten servants, how would you define the word *faithful?*

13. What do you think was the *motive* Jesus had for doing what He did in verses 45-46?

14. The Jesus we see in this gospel is not only fully God, but also fully human. From what you've seen so far in Luke, in what ways does Jesus show Himself to be the perfect model of manhood?

FOR LIFE TODAY

15. With the parable in verses 12-27 in mind, in what ways can you honestly say that your gifts from the Lord are increasing and multiplying?

16. Again with the parable of the king's ten servants in mind, discuss how much you agree or disagree with this statement: If we aren't multiplying our gifts from God, then we don't really have them at all.

17. Think again about verses 45-46. Do you feel there is anything in our churches today that corresponds to

the activities of the people whom Jesus drove out of the Temple?

In verse 10, Jesus calls Himself "the Son of Man." This is the title Jesus uses most often for Himself in the gospels. Look at any or all of the following additional passages in Luke in which Jesus calls Himself this, and discuss together the significance of this title: 5:24, 6:5, 7:34, 9:22, 9:44, 9:58, 12:8, 17:22-30, 21:27, 22:22, 22:48, and 22:69.

LUKE 20

Startup: Recall any situation in which you felt someone was improperly assuming authority.

SEEING WHAT'S THERE

1. Imagine that you're a devout Jew from Rome, and that you've come across the sea for the first time to visit Jerusalem for the Passover festival. The events in Luke 19 and 20 are your first exposure to Jesus of Nazareth; in fact, as far as you know, no one back home in Rome has even heard of this Man. What kind of impressions would you now have of Jesus, based on all that you've seen in these last few days? (Look back over these two chapters to help you keep in mind all these events.)

2. Which verse in the parable in verses 9-16 reveals the most about the motives and character of the Pharisees?

3. Notice in verse 19 how the Jewish religious leaders responded to the parable Jesus tells in verses 9-18. Then go back through the parable and identify each person or group of people, and who each one represents.

4. For helpful background on verse 17, look together at Psalm 118:22-24. How does this passage from the Psalms enhance the meaning of this situation in which Jesus quoted it?

5. Verse 20 says that the religious leaders had laid a trap for Jesus. How do you think they expected the trap to work?

6. Imagine that you are one of the spies mentioned in verse 20. What kind of report would you make to the religious leaders who hired you, based on what you observe in this chapter?

7. Does the question from the Sadducees in verse 27 appear to be a trap as well? Why or why not?

8. For helpful background on verse 28, look together at Deuteronomy 25:5-10.

9. Imagine yourself being present in the situation described in verses 45-46. In light of your own personality, what words spoken by Jesus in these verses stand out most to you?

10. EYE FOR DETAIL—*From what you recall seeing in this chapter, try answering the following question without looking at your Bible:* When Jesus asked the religious leaders whether John's authority was from heaven or from men, what reasons did they discuss among themselves for not going with either of those answers? (See verses 5-7.)

CAPTURE THE ESSENCE

11. With the parable in verses 9-19 in mind, compare it with another interesting parable about a vineyard in Isaiah 5:1-7. What are the similarities, and what are the differences?

12. How important would you say was the question which Jesus asked in verses 41-44?

FOR LIFE TODAY

13. In verses 1-8 the focus is on the *authority* of Jesus and the *authority* of John the Baptist, both of which came from God. What authority do *you* have from God?

14. Think about verse 25. In your life, what things belong to God, and yet still must be given up to Him?

FOR GOING DEEPER

Think carefully about what Jesus says in verse 18. How is the meaning of this verse supported and deepened by what you see in Isaiah 8:13-15 and Luke 2:34?

LUKE 21

Startup: What are the biggest questions you have about the second coming of Christ?

SEEING WHAT'S THERE

1. Review carefully verses 5-7. What things do the disciples specifically want to know?

2. In his long discourse beginning in verse 8, who is Jesus speaking to?

3. What questions are raised in your mind by the words of Jesus in this chapter?

4. EYE FOR DETAIL—*From what you recall seeing in this chapter, try answering the following question without looking at your Bible:* Where does this chapter say that Jesus was spending each night during this time? (See verse 37.)

CAPTURE THE ESSENCE

5. From what you see in verses 1-4, how does God calculate the size of our gifts to Him?

6. From what you see in verses 12-19, what's the *purpose* of this persecution which these believers will undergo?

7. From what Jesus tells His disciples in this chapter, does He want them to think it will be a *long* time or a *short* time before the end of the present age?

FOR LIFE TODAY

8. Discuss how you respond inwardly to what you see in this chapter. Is it with anticipation? Fear? Confusion?

9. Which of the predictions mentioned in this chapter would you say are taking place now?

10. What would you say is the most important concept this chapter teaches us about our *responsibility,* as we wait for the end?

11. How susceptible do you think you might be to the deceptions which Jesus warns about in verse 8?

12. As you think about verses 12-19, what effect would you say that persecution can have on our evangelism efforts?

13. Look at what Jesus promised His disciples in verse 17. How hard is it for you to endure hatred from others?

14. Review verses 34-36. Practically speaking, how do we stay alert and watchful today, in obedience to these words from Jesus?

15. Think carefully again about what Jesus says in verses 3-4. Then imagine Him evaluating the significance of your own giving on a scale of one to ten, in which ten equals the example of the poor widow in this passage, and one equals the example of the other rich people here. What score do you think He would probably assign to you?

16. From what you've seen so far in the book of Luke, summarize what you think it means for Christians today to "follow in the footsteps of Jesus."

FOR GOING DEEPER

Consider the promise Jesus makes in verse 19. The same Greek word which is translated here as "standing firm" or "endurance" or "patience" in various translations, is also used in the following verses. Looking at them together, what do they tell you about how to practically live out this concept? Luke 8:15, 2 Corinthians 1:6, 1 Thessalonians 1:3, Hebrews 12:1, and James 1:3-4.

LUKE 22

Startup: If you could have been with Jesus during the night before He died, what's the question you would most have wanted to ask Him?

SEEING WHAT'S THERE

1. What in this chapter do you think might be most surprising to a new Christian reading it for the first time?

2. How would you explain what Jesus means by the word *covenant* in verse 20?

3. For background on verse 37, look together at Isaiah 53:11-12, and summarize the major points of that prophecy in your own words.

4. Notice in verse 44 how deep the sorrow was which Jesus experienced. How would you explain this verse to a child?

5. In what ways, if any, do you see the worthiness and nobleness and purity of Jesus in this chapter?

6. EYE FOR DETAIL—*From what you recall seeing in this chapter, try answering the following question without looking at your Bible:* When Judas led a crowd into Gethsemane to arrest Jesus, what question did Jesus ask him? (See verse 48.)

CAPTURE THE ESSENCE

7. How would you analyze the *choices* Peter makes in this chapter?

8. From the evidence you see in this chapter, how would you describe Simon Peter's relationship with Jesus?

9. How would you explain the meaning of what Jesus did and said in verses 19-20 to someone who had never seen or heard this passage?

10. Look at the topic of the argument in verse 24, and compare it with Luke 9:46. As you try to put yourself into the disciples' situation here, why do you think this argument arose again?

11. Look at Jesus' words to the disciples in verse 40. What temptation do you think the disciples were in the most danger of falling into at this time?

12. Look closely at verses 41-44. In what ways do you think the angel mentioned here might have brought strength to Jesus?

13. Imagine that you were helping to produce a film based on this chapter. Describe the kinds of scenery, supporting characters, background music, lighting effects, etc., which you would use to portray this chapter's central message.

FOR LIFE TODAY

14. Discuss whether you think there's any danger for us today in applying verse 26 too literally.

15. In light of how you're doing spiritually in your life today, which verse in this chapter do you think is the most important at this time—and why?

16. How might you use this chapter to explain to a young friend the love God has for us?

FOR GOING DEEPER

Jesus spoke in verse 42 of the "cup" He had been given to drink. To see how this word is used in other Scriptures, discuss together Jeremiah 25:15-16, Ezekiel 23:32-34, Habakkuk 2:16, and Revelation 14:9-10.

LUKE 23

Startup: What is the worst physical pain you have ever experienced in life?

SEEING WHAT'S THERE

1. As best you can, walk your way through the events of this chapter as if you were Jesus Himself, feeling what He felt, seeing what He saw, hearing what He heard. Describe to one another the sensations that come to your imagination.

2. See how many single-word descriptions you can come up with to appropriately describe each of the following men who appear in this chapter: Pilate (verses 3-7 and 12-25); Herod (7-12); Barabbas (18-19); Simon of Cyrene (26); the first criminal (39); the second criminal (40-42); the centurion (47); and finally, Jesus Himself.

3. What are the most important *choices* that are made in this chapter, and how would you analyze each one?

4. What do you think Jesus meant by His words in verse 31?

5. What exactly do you think prompted the centurion to say what he did in verse 47?

6. For more helpful background on the Joseph mentioned in verses 50-54, look together at John 19:38.

7. EYE FOR DETAIL—*From what you recall seeing in this chapter, try answering the following question without looking at your Bible:* This chapter records two prayers which Jesus spoke from the cross to God the Father. What were these two prayers? (See verses 34 and 46.)

CAPTURE THE ESSENCE

8. What good illustrations would you say this chapter gives us of the most common aspects of human nature?

9. What universal lessons about salvation can you draw from the example of the two criminals in verses 39-43?

FOR LIFE TODAY

10. No one is trying to physically crucify us today—but what does Jesus' *example* in this chapter mean personally for your life?

11. Of the most important events and truths in this chapter, which do you think are the easiest for Christians to forget about?

FOR GOING DEEPER

Jesus spoke of "paradise" in His words on the cross to the repentant thief beside Him (verse 43). Look also at the only other two places in the New Testament where this word is used, and discuss together what it means—2 Corinthians 12:3-4 and Revelation 2:7.

LUKE 24

Startup: Practically speaking, what would you say is the most important thing you have to do in the time you have remaining on earth?

SEEING WHAT'S THERE

1. Examine each part of the angel's message to the women in verses 5-7. What was the importance of each part?

2. From the evidence you see in this chapter, how would you describe the nature of the resurrected body of Jesus Christ?

3. EYE FOR DETAIL—*From what you recall seeing in this chapter, try answering the following question without looking at your Bible:* As the two disciples were walking on the road to Emmaus (without realizing that Jesus Himself was with them), what words did they use to describe Jesus to the "stranger" who was walking with them? (See verses 19-21.)

CAPTURE THE ESSENCE

4. Imagine that you were one of the disciples listening to the words of Jesus in verses 44-49. In light of your own personality, what kinds of thoughts and questions would enter your mind as you heard these words?

5. What can this chapter teach us about *faith?*

6. In this chapter, which of these character qualities in Jesus comes through most strongly to you: His compassion, His power, or His wisdom? (Explain your answer.)

7. What in this chapter do you think might be the most interesting to someone who was learning about Jesus Christ for the first time, and why?

FOR LIFE TODAY

8. In light of how you're doing spiritually in your life today, which verse in

this chapter do you think is the most important at this time—and why?

9. What evidence do you find in this chapter that could be used to help a Christian friend who had doubts whether the Bible was truly God's Word?

10. In verse 47, Jesus says two things are to be preached around the world in His name. What is the true importance of these two things? How prominent are they in the communication that goes out from your church to your community?

11. Look again at the statement Jesus made in verse 47. Then identify together the kinds of people in your community whom you would say probably know the least about the living Lord Jesus Christ. What else are these people like? What do they do in daily life? Where do they live? Now imagine that God has brought you together with a small group of these people, and in this meeting they indicate a genuine desire to understand who Jesus is and what He has done. From what you have seen in the gospel of Luke, what are the most important things you would want to communicate to them, and how would you word it?

12. Think about this command in Colossians 3:1—"Since you have been raised with Christ, set your hearts on things above, where Christ is seated at the right hand of God." What have you personally observed about Jesus Christ in this chapter that would be worthy of setting your heart on?

FOR GOING DEEPER

Analyze the importance of Jesus' resurrection as you think together about this chapter, and about these supporting passages: Romans 4:25, 1 Corinthians 15:17, and Revelation 1:18.

LUKE:

THE BIG PICTURE

(Discuss again the questions in the "Overview," plus the questions below.)

1. Look together at each of these passages, and discuss which one you believe is the best candidate for "KEY VERSE" in the book of Luke—the one which brings into sharpest focus what this book is most about: 1:3-4, 2:14, 9:23, 19:10, 22:69, and 24:44.

2. What would you say are the strongest themes in the way Luke portrays Jesus Christ in this gospel?

3. In what passages of this book have you been most impressed with the *compassion* of Christ?

4. Even more than the other gospel writers, Luke is said to be a skilled *historian*. How would you evaluate his skills in this area, as you've observed them in this book?

5. What would you say are the most important ways in which this book is *unique* in all the Bible?

6. In James 1:23-24 we're told that "anyone who listens to the word but does not do what it says is like a man who looks at his face in a mirror and, after looking at himself, goes away and immediately forgets what he looks like." In what important ways has the book of Luke been a "mirror" for you—showing you what you can and should do?

John

OVERVIEW

(Discuss these OVERVIEW questions both at the beginning of your study of John, and again after you've studied together all 21 chapters. Your answers may change significantly once you've looked more closely at the entire book.)

Startup: Talk together about memorable experiences in your lives which taught you the importance of telling the truth.

SEEING WHAT'S THERE

1. To learn more about the author of this gospel, the apostle John, look together at Mark 1:19-20, 3:17, and 10:35-40; Luke 9:52-56. From this evidence, what kind of person would you guess John to be? And what differences in John's life do you think his friends were probably talking about after John decided to follow Jesus?

2. In this gospel, John describes himself as "the disciple whom Jesus loved." Look together at the following passages where this term is used, and discuss what they reveal about John's personality and about his relationship with Jesus: 13:22-25, 19:25-27, 20:1-9, 21:4-8, and 21:19-24.

3. How would you explain the meaning of the word *light* in verse 4 to someone who had been blind since birth?

4. Compare the way in which this gospel begins (John 1:1-18), with the way the other three gospels begin (in Matthew 1:1-17, Mark 1:1, and Luke 1:1-4). What do these different "start-up styles" tell you about the *purpose* of each gospel?

5. Look also at the list of "Questions to Ask as You Begin Your Study of Each Book" on page 393.

CAPTURE THE ESSENCE

6. The Greek word usually translated as *believe* in English is found 79 times in the gospel of John—always as a verb, never as a noun *(belief)*. Scan this gospel together (or you may want to divide your efforts by having each person in the group look over a certain chapter or chapters) , and find <u>four to six</u> instances where the <u>word is used</u>. What would you say John wants us to understand about this term?

7. Another word John uses often in this gospel (25 times) is the word *truth*. Scan the book together (or you may want to divide your efforts by having each person in the group look over a certain chapter or chapters) , and find three or four instances where the word is used in the book. What does John want us to understand about *truth?*

FOR LIFE TODAY

8. Look together at a verse in another book by John: 1 John 2:6. What goals and motivation can this verse give you as you begin studying the life of Christ as recorded in John's gospel?

9. How can you ensure that your study of John is not merely theoretical and intellectual, but is instead truly practical and relevant? Talk together about this. What can you do to help

keep the process alive and interesting?

FOR GOING DEEPER

Bible teachers often present John as the gospel that especially presents Jesus as "the Son of God"; in John, the *divinity* of Jesus is clearly apparent along with His humanity. From what you know of all four gospels, how does this emphasis in John come through, especially in comparison with the other three gospels?

JOHN 1

Startup: Describe some of the most memorable gifts you've received.

SEEING WHAT'S THERE

1. Look together at verses 1-5 in both John 1 and Genesis 1. How would you say these passages expand each other's meaning?

2. Let the words of verse 14 form a picture in your mind, and then describe that picture.

3. Look again at verse 14. Together as a group, make a mental list of every item of information this verse tell us about Jesus Christ.

4. Suppose you and a non-Christian friend were looking together at verses 1-18. In your own words, how would you explain this passage in order to help your friend understand who Jesus is?

5. In what ways do you see John the Baptist fulfilling the prophecy mentioned in verse 23?

6. Imagine yourself one of the Jews who have come out from Jerusalem to listen to John the Baptist. You watch as he directs everyone's attention to a man walking up at the back of the crowd, and you hear John call this man "the Lamb of God who takes away the sin of the world!" (verse 29). What images and thoughts and questions would this trigger in your mind?

7. What would you say were the most important things John the Baptist wanted his hearers to understand about Jesus?

8. In what ways was the ministry of John the Baptist's *unique* among the work of all the Bible's prophets?

9. What did John the Baptist want the Jews to understand about his identity and his ministry?

10. Together, list aloud everything we learn about Jesus from His words and actions in verses 35-51.

11. What incident from the Old Testament is brought to mind by Jesus' words in verse 51? (See Genesis 28:12.)

12. If a non-Christian asked you, "How can I know there's a God?" how could you use this chapter to help you give an answer?

13. EYE FOR DETAIL—*If everyone in the group has read the entire chapter, try answering the following question without looking at your Bible:* What was the name of the future disciple who asked in verse 46 if anything good could come from Nazareth?

14. Look also at the list of "Questions to Ask as You Study Each Chapter" on page 392, which you may want to do for each chapter in John.

CAPTURE THE ESSENCE

15. If you were hospitalized with cancer and your doctors told you to expect only a few more weeks of life, which verses in this chapter do you think would be the most significant to you?

16. What good reasons can you find in this chapter for why we should study the life of Christ?

17. From what this chapter says, what would you say God wants people on earth to *know?*

18. From what this chapter says, what would you say God wants people on earth to *do?*

19. From what this chapter says, what would you say God wants people on earth to *be?*

20. Why do you think John chose in this chapter to call Jesus "the Word"?

21. If this chapter was the only Scripture portion you had, what biblical definition would you give for each of these words: *grace, truth, glory* , and *light.*

22. If this chapter was the only Scripture portion you had, how would you describe God's personality?

23. From what you see in this chapter, how would you describe the kind of relationship which John the Baptist had with God?

24. In verses 32-33, what significance do you see in the Holy Spirit's appearance in the form of a *dove?*

25. In verses 35-51, what do you notice about the way Jesus approaches and responds to people?

26. If you had only this chapter in Scripture to refer to, how would you use it to help show someone that Jesus is truly *God?*

FOR LIFE TODAY

27. What can you find in verses 1-18 that you can truly call God's *personal* gifts to *you?*

28. How could you use verse 12 to help an unsaved friend who expressed a desire to become a Christian?

29. As you think about the ministry of John the Baptist, discuss any time you can recall when you needed someone to "prepare the way for the Lord" in your life.

30. Discuss any time you can recall when God used you to "prepare the way for the Lord" in someone else's life.

31. How could you use this chapter to help explain to someone why Jesus came to earth?

FOR GOING DEEPER

Look ahead to 20:30-31, where John writes about his purpose for writing this gospel. How does he begin accomplishing that purpose in chapter 1?

JOHN 2

Startup: What do you enjoy most about weddings? And what, if anything, do you enjoy least?

SEEING WHAT'S THERE

1. Suppose you were a guest at the wedding in Cana mentioned in verses 1-12. Using your imagination, talk about the kinds of sights, smells, sounds, and feelings you might experience.

2. Why things do you think might have gone through the mind of Jesus and His disciples when they decided to attend this wedding?

3. What do you think Jesus meant by his words in verse 4? What "time" or "hour" is He speaking of?

4. From her words and actions in the first part of this chapter, what do you learn about Mary?

5. When Jesus turned the water into wine, why do you think He made it of such good quality?

6. We see only one response in this chapter from anyone who knew about the miracle Jesus did at Cana. What was that response? (You'll find it in verse 11.)

7. In verses 13-16, what was actually *wrong* about what the money-changers and livestock dealers were doing in the temple?

8. In verses 13 to the end of the chapter, what one-word adjectives would you use to best describe Jesus as you see Him here? What one-word descriptions would best fit the Jews in this passage?

9. John says in verses 24-25 that Jesus knew all about people. Try to summarize what you think John was talking about: *What exactly did Jesus know about people?*

10. Verses 13-16 tell of an incident which Jesus repeated toward the end of His earthly ministry. Compare this passage in John with the later incident recorded in Mark 11:15-18. What similarities do you see in the two events? What differences?

11. EYE FOR DETAIL— *From what you recall seeing in this chapter, try answering the following question without looking at your Bible:* In verse 20, the Jews in Jerusalem mentioned to Jesus how long it had taken to build their temple. How many years was it?

CAPTURE THE ESSENCE

12. In 1:18, John said it is Jesus who makes God known to us—Jesus shows us what God is like. From what you see in chapter 2, *what is God like?*

13. In verse 11, John says that Jesus revealed or demonstrated His glory by this miraculous sign. What do you think John means by this?

14. Jesus *changed* something in this miracle: He changed water into wine. Think about other miracles which Jesus performed. What did He *change* in those miracles?

15. Look closely at verse 17. What help does it give in understanding *why* Jesus did what He did in verses 15-16?

16. Look closely at verses 19-21. Why do you think Jesus responded in this way to the question the Jews asked in verse 18?

17. In this chapter, which of these character qualities in Jesus comes through most strongly to you: His compassion, His power, or His wisdom? (Explain your answer.)

18. What in this chapter do you think might be the most interesting to someone who was learning about Jesus Christ for the first time, and why?

19. If you had only this chapter in Scripture to refer to, how would you use it to help show someone that Jesus is truly *God?*

FOR LIFE TODAY

20. What do you think are the most important things this chapter has to teach us about *faith?*

21. Think again about verses 13-16. Do you feel there is anything in our churches today that corresponds to the activities of the people whom Jesus drove out of the Temple?

22. Discuss why you agree or disagree with this statement: The actions of Jesus in John 2:15-16 shows us that it's legitimate to use use force to accomplish a righteous goal.

23. What can we learn from this chapter about the right way to approach God in worship?

FOR GOING DEEPER

Look together at the prophecy in Malachi 3:1-3. How would you match this prophecy to all that you've seen so far in the gospel of John?

JOHN 3

Startup: If some in the group are parents, talk about your most meaningful memories of seeing your child born.

SEEING WHAT'S THERE

1. What do we learn about the man Nicodemus in this chapter?

2. In verse 12 Jesus uses the terms "earthly things" and "heavenly things." As He continues speaking to Nicodemus, is He speaking of earthly things, heavenly things, or both?

3. How would you summarize the main points of what Jesus told Nicodemus?

4. What would you say are the most important things this chapter teaches about the Holy Spirit?

5. Imagine how Nicodemus might have felt after hearing the words Jesus spoke in verses 10-12. How would you describe those feelings?

6. For background on the reference to Moses and the snake in verse 14, look together at Numbers 21:4-9. What similarities do you see between the situation of the Israelites in this Numbers passage, and the situation of unbelievers today?

7. Let the words of verse 18 form a picture in your mind, and then describe that picture.

8. In verses 22-36, what one-word adjectives would you use to best describe John the Baptist as you see him here?

9. Look at the words of John the Baptist in verse 27. What exactly had John received from heaven?

10. Are John's words in verse 27 true also of the Man Jesus? If so, what did God the Father give to Jesus?

11. Review again verse 18 in chapter 1 —where John said Jesus makes God known to us, and shows us what

God is like. From what you see in Jesus in chapter 3, *what is God like?*

12. EYE FOR DETAIL— *From what you recall seeing in this chapter, try answering the following question without looking at your Bible:* As He was speaking with Nicodemus, what did Jesus note about the wind? (See verse 8.)

CAPTURE THE ESSENCE

13. From what you see in verses 5-8, how would you describe what it means to be a *spiritual* man or woman?

14. What do you think Jesus meant when He said we must be born "of water and the Spirit" in verse 5? (For interesting background, look at an Old Testament Scripture that both Jesus and Nicodemus would have been familiar with: Ezekiel 36:25-27.)

15. Many people consider verse 16 to be the key verse in the entire Bible. Try compressing the content of this verse into a statement that uses as few words as possible.

16. Compare the message in verse 16 with Romans 5:8 and 1 John 4:9-10. Why do you think so many people in the world do not believe this message?

17. Together, list aloud all the character traits of God for which you find evidence in this chapter.

18. From what you see in chapter 1 and in verses 22-36 in chapter 3, how much did John the Baptist understand about who Jesus really was?

19. John the Baptist speaks in verse 29 of the joy that was his. How would you describe this joy he felt?

20. What do the last three verses in this chapter indicate about the relationship between the three Persons of the Trinity—Father, Son, and Holy Spirit?

21. If you had only this chapter in Scripture to refer to, how would you use it to help show someone that Jesus is truly *God?*

FOR LIFE TODAY

22. What kind of mental habits do you think could most easily block the words of Jesus in this chapter from coming alive in our minds and hearts?

23. How could you use verses 16-17 to help an unsaved friend who expressed a desire to become a Christian?

24. If a non-Christian said to you, "But God is too good and loving to condemn anyone to hell," how could you use verses 18 and 36 in reply?

25. Look closely at the statement John the Baptist makes in verse 27. Is this statement true also of you? If so, what exactly have you been given from heaven?

26. In light of how you're doing spiritually in your life today, which verse in this chapter do you think is the most important at this time—and why?

FOR GOING DEEPER

Look ahead to John 7:50-51 and 19:39-40. What else do you learn about Nicodemus in these passages? (You may want to look also at Romans 8:5-9, 1 Corinthians 12:13, and 2 Corinthians 5:5.)

JOHN 4

Startup: What is the most pleasantly surprising encounter you can recall having with a stranger?

SEEING WHAT'S THERE

1. Take a "walk" together through the incidents that happen in this chapter: Using your imagination, talk about the kinds of sights, smells, sounds, and feelings you might experience.

2. What *choices* can you see the Samaritan woman making in this chapter?

3. What is "the gift of God" which Jesus spoke of in verse 10?

4. Is Jesus saying in verse 10 that we need to *ask* for the gift of God before we can receive it? Explain your answer.

5. How would you explain verse 24 to a young child?

6. Review verse 30, in light of what has happened earlier in this chapter. What thoughts and questions do you think may have been in the minds of these Samaritan villagers as they made their way out to the well?

7. What are the most important *choices* that are made in this chapter, and how would you analyze each one?

8. What one-word adjectives would you use to best describe Jesus as you see Him in this chapter?

9. Think again about 1:18—where John said that Jesus makes God known to us, and shows us what God is like. From what you see in chapter 4, *what is God like?*

10. EYE FOR DETAIL— *From what you recall seeing in this chapter, try answering the following question without looking at your Bible:* In the account of the meeting between Jesus and the Samaritan woman at Jacob's well, what time of day was it? (See verse 6.)

CAPTURE THE ESSENCE

11. What do verses 46-53 teach us about *faith?*

12. In this chapter, which of these character qualities in Jesus comes through most strongly to you: His compassion, His power, or His wisdom? (Explain your answer.)

13. What in this chapter do you think might be the most interesting to someone who was learning about Jesus Christ for the first time, and why?

14. If you had only this chapter in Scripture to refer to, how would you use it to help show someone that Jesus is truly *God?*

15. From the evidence you see in this chapter, how do you think Jesus would define the terms *success* and *ultimate significance?*

FOR LIFE TODAY

16. Jesus said in verse 34 that His "food" was doing God's will and finishing His work. What do you think Jesus meant by phrasing it that way?

17. Realistically speaking, do you think doing God's will and finishing His work is supposed to be *your* food too? Why or why not?

18. Again with verse 34 in mind, what are some good examples of God's will and His work for *you?*

19. Notice the encounters Jesus had in this chapter with both sexes. In what ways do you see that following Jesus Christ enhances your manhood or your womanhood?

20. In Colossians 3:1 we read this command: "Since, then, you have been raised with Christ, set your hearts on things above, where Christ is seated at the right hand of God." What have you personally observed about Jesus Christ in this chapter that

would be worthy of setting your heart on?

21. In light of how you're doing spiritually in your life today, which verse in this chapter do you think is the most important at this time—and why?

FOR GOING DEEPER

In the following verses, look together at other places in this gospel where Jesus talked about doing God's work and will. What kind of patterns and unifying concepts do you see? 6:38, 9:4, 12:49, 14:31, 15:10, and 17:4.

JOHN 5

Startup: Talk together about your greatest frustrations and your greatest "breakthroughs" in the past week.

SEEING WHAT'S THERE

1. Imagine you are a reporter for the "Jerusalem Journal." In a few sentences, how would you describe what happens in this chapter?

2. What clues does this chapter offer about the relationship between Jesus' human nature and His divine nature?

3. From what you see in verse 39, how would you describe the perspective Jesus had on the Scriptures?

4. What exactly is the "praise" or "glory" or "honor" that comes only from God, which Jesus speaks of in verse 44?

5. What in this chapter do you think might be most surprising to a new Christian reading it for the first time?

6. Review again John's statement in 1:18. From what you see in chapter 5, *what is God like?*

7. EYE FOR DETAIL—*From what you recall seeing in this chapter, try answering the following question without looking at your Bible:* Before Jesus healed the man who was lying at the pool, for how many years had he been sick? (See verse 5.)

CAPTURE THE ESSENCE

8. If you were hospitalized with cancer and your doctors told you to expect only a few more weeks of life, which verses in this chapter do you think would be the most significant to you?

9. How might you use verse 14 to help a non-Christian who wanted to believe in Jesus, but who did not want to give up sinful behavior in his life?

10. What do you think were the *motives* and the *strategy* behind what Jesus said in verses 31-47?

11. Review the words of Jesus in verses 39-40. What do you think it was that made these religious Jews refuse to come to Jesus?

FOR LIFE TODAY

12. How could you use verse 24 to explain to a non-Christian the meaning of the gospel?

13. How could you use that same verse to help someone who believed in Christ, but who was afraid he might lose his salvation and life in heaven if he sinned?

14. How would you use verses 28-29 to help a new Christian who wanted to know if the Bible teaches reincarnation?

15. How could you use verse 39 to help a new Christian understand the value of the Scriptures?

16. If you had only this chapter in Scripture to refer to, how would you use it to help show someone that Jesus is truly *God?*

FOR GOING DEEPER

In verse 27, Jesus calls Himself "the Son of Man." This is the title Jesus uses most often for Himself in the gospels. Look at any or all of the following additional passages in John in which Jesus calls Himself this, and discuss together the significance of this title: 1:51, 3:13, 6:27, 6:53, 6:62, 8:28, 9:35, 12:23, and 12:34.

JOHN 6

Startup: What do you enjoy most about picnics? And what, if anything, do you enjoy least?

SEEING WHAT'S THERE

1. Once again, take a "walk" together through the incidents that happen in this chapter. Using your imagination, talk about the kinds of sights, smells, sounds, and feelings you might experience.

2. The topics of *manna* and *bread* are prominent in the conversation between Jesus and the Jews in verses 25-58. From what you know about the manna in the Old Testament (and for helpful background, you may want to review together Exodus 16:13-15 and 16:31, and Numbers 11:7-9), how would you compare it with the "true bread from heaven" which Jesus speaks of in verse 32? What are the similarities, and what are the differences?

3. Look at verse 44. What exactly does God do to "draw" people to Himself?

4. Review verse 66, in light of what has happened earlier in this chapter. What thoughts and questions do you think may have been in the minds of these disciples as they turned back toward their homes and their past?

5. From what you've seen so far in the gospel John, how much of His schedule was Jesus able to spend alone? Why did He make time for this?

6. What are the most important *choices* made in this chapter, and how would you analyze each one?

7. EYE FOR DETAIL— *From what you recall seeing in this chapter, try answering the following question without looking at your Bible:* Which one of the disciples told Jesus about the boy

who had five barley loaves and two fish? (See verse 8.)

CAPTURE THE ESSENCE

8. If you expected to live only a few more weeks, which verses in this chapter do you think would be the most significant to you?

9. How could you use verse 51 in response to a false teacher who said Jesus was not actually a sacrifice or substitute for us when He died?

10. In what ways can you see verses 53-56 expanding the meaning of John 1:18?

11. From what you see in this chapter, why did Jesus perform miracles?

12. In this chapter, which of these character qualities in Jesus comes through most strongly to you: His compassion, His power, or His wisdom? (Explain your answer.)

13. What in this chapter do you think might be the most interesting to someone who was learning about Jesus Christ for the first time, and why?

14. If you had only this chapter in Scripture to refer to, how would you use it to help show someone that Jesus is truly *God?*

15. From what you've seen in this chapter, what does it really mean to "follow Jesus"?

FOR LIFE TODAY

16. What kind of mental habits do you think could most easily block the words of Jesus in this chapter from coming alive in our minds and hearts?

17. What guidelines for today's discipleship training do you especially see in the way Jesus worked with His disciples in verses 5-13?

18. How could you use verses 28-29 to help an unsaved friend who felt he lived a good enough life already, and didn't need to believe in Christ?

19. How could you use verse 37 to help an unsaved friend who felt he was too sinful for God to accept him?

20. Look again at verses 60-61. In what ways today do some people find Jesus' words to be offensive?

21. In what ways, if any, do you agree with what the people said in verse 60?

22. In light of how you're doing spiritually in your life today, which verse in this chapter do you think is the most important at this time—and why?

FOR GOING DEEPER

How does the message in verses 44 and 65 relate to the words of Jesus in Matthew 11:28-30?

JOHN 7

Startup: Talk about any time in life when it seemed hardest for other family members to understand a decision or plans you had made.

SEEING WHAT'S THERE

1. What in this chapter do you think might be most surprising to a new Christian reading it for the first time?

2. When Jesus speaks of "the world" in verse 7, who is included in that?

3. From what you see in verses 8, 10, and 14, what was the strategy Jesus was following at this time?

4. Describe in your own words the misconceptions about Jesus which are reflected in verses 12, 15, 20, and 27. Discuss also which of these misconceptions were the most serious, and why.

5. From what you see in verses 12-13, describe both the power of the Jewish leaders, and the courage of the common people.

6. Notice the controversy regarding the Sabbath which Jesus speaks of in verses 21-24. From what you see here, what was the difference between how Jesus viewed the Sabbath, and how these Jews viewed it?

7. The Jews did not understand what Jesus was saying in verses 33-34, as we see in the following two verses. What *was* Jesus talking about here?

8. In verse 39, notice how John defines the "living water" which Jesus spoke of in the previous verse. Is this the same living water which Jesus mentioned to the woman at the well in John 4:10?

9. From the evidence you see in this chapter, discuss how much you agree or disagree with this statement: As seen in this chapter, the Jewish people and leaders in general were open-minded, but they could not quickly accept who Jesus really was because He talked about Himself in such mysterious terms.

10. Think again of the statement about Jesus in John 1:18. From what you see in chapter 7, *what is God like?*

11. EYE FOR DETAIL— *From what you recall seeing in this chapter, try answering the following question without looking at your Bible:* What did Jesus say in this chapter about "living water"? (See verse 38.)

CAPTURE THE ESSENCE

12. How would you describe the *motives* and *values* of Jesus' brothers, from the evidence you see in verses 3-5?

13. Notice what Jesus says about timing in verses 6 and 8, and see also verse 30 in this chapter and verse 20 in chapter 8. What picture do these verses give you of the way Jesus was living His life?

14. What are the most important things we learn about the Holy Spirit in verses 37-39?

15. How could you use verse 17 to help a non-Christian who expressed uncertainty about whether Jesus was God's Son?

16. Look together at verse 32, and then at the report given by the temple guards in verses 45-46. If the Pharisees had given the guards the chance to say more, what else do you think they might have said about the words Jesus spoke?

17. If you had only this chapter in Scripture to refer to, how would you use it to help show someone that Jesus is truly *God?*

FOR LIFE TODAY

18. Look at what Jesus says in verse 7, and relate it to yourself. To what degree does the world have reason to hate you?

19. How could you use what Jesus says in verses 16-18 to evaluate the message of religious teachers and preachers today?

20. Notice again all the conflicting things said about Jesus in this chapter —you'll find a good variety of them in verses 12, 20, 26, and 31. To what degree are there conflicting views in your own mind about Jesus? What are the strongest convictions and conclusions you have about Him?

FOR GOING DEEPER

In much of this chapter, the focus of the Jews is on Jesus as a *man*—see, for example, verses 12, 15, 25, 27, 35, and 40. Look also at these other passages in John, and discuss what they tell us about both the *humanity* and the *manhood* of Jesus, and His example for men today—2:25, 4:6-7, 4:34, 5:6, 5:30, 6:15, 7:37, 8:29, 9:6, 11:35, 11:38, 11:53-54, 12:44, 13:4-5, 18:4-5, 19:26-27, 19:28-30, then back to 1:14.

JOHN 8

Startup: Talk about any time you can recall when some discipline or correction you received was much less severe than what you expected.

SEEING WHAT'S THERE

1. In the opening scene in this chapter, what one-word adjectives would you use to best describe the Jews? What one-word descriptions would best fit Jesus in this scene? What one-word description would you give to the woman?

2. For helpful background on verses 1-6, look together at Leviticus 20:10 and Deuteronomy 22:22-24, and discuss how faithfully you feel the Jews in John 8 were carrying out these provisions in the law.

3. How would you compare the words of Jesus in verses 14-18 with what He said in 5:31-40? Is the main point the same in both passages? If not, how do they differ?

4. How would you describe the *freedom* Jesus speaks of in verses 32 and 36?

5. For helpful background on verses 58-59, look together first at Exodus 3:14, then at Leviticus 24:16. Then try to put yourself in the position of one of the Jews in this passage. Why were so upset by what Jesus says here?

6. As you read this chapter, what's the strongest impression or image it leaves in your mind?

7. Which important details in this chapter do you think might be the easiest to overlook?

8. Think again of the statement about Jesus in John 1:18. From what you see in chapter 8, *what is God like?*

9. EYE FOR DETAIL— *From what you recall seeing in this chapter, try answering the following question without looking at your Bible:* As the scene be-

gins in which the Jews bring before Jesus a woman caught in adultery, what time of day is it? (See verse 2.)

10. When the incident in verses 2-11 was over, what thoughts and questions do you think might well have been in the woman's mind? And what thoughts and questions might well have been in the minds of the Jews who had taken her to Jesus?

11. What kind of mental habits do you think could most easily block the words of Jesus in verses 31-32 from coming alive in our minds and hearts?

12. How would you define and describe the *freedom* which Jesus speaks of in verses 31 and 36?

13. What in this chapter do you think might be the most interesting to someone who was learning about Jesus Christ for the first time, and why?

14. If you had only this chapter in Scripture to refer to, how would you use it to help show someone that Jesus is truly *God?*

FOR LIFE TODAY

15. In Philippians 4:8 we're given the following command: "Whatever is true, whatever is noble, whatever is right, whatever is pure, whatever is lovely, whatever is admirable—if anything is excellent or praiseworthy—*think about such things.*" What food for thought can you find in this chapter that especially strikes you as being *true,* or *noble,* or *right,* or *pure,* or *lovely,* or *admirable,* or *excellent,* or *praiseworthy?*

16. How could you use verses 24 and 34 to help an unsaved friend who felt no constraints against living an immoral lifestyle?

17. How could you use verse 36 to help an unsaved friend who felt he could not become a Christian because he didn't have the power to give up his sinful ways?

18. Look again at verse 47. In what ways, if any, does God actually "speak" to us today, so we can hear Him?

19. How could you use verse 47 to help an unsaved friend who said he didn't believe the Bible was truly God's Word?

FOR GOING DEEPER

The concept of *testimony* or *witness* is a key one not only in this chapter (as you see in verses 13-18), but also throughout the gospel of John. Look together at these other verses in John where the concept appears. Then discuss whether this concept is as important in your life as it was to Jesus and John—1:6-8, 1:32-34, 3:11, 3:32, 4:39, 5:31-39, 15:26-27, 18:37, 19:35, and 21:24.

JOHN 9

Startup: What's the *darkest* situation you can recall having ever been in?

SEEING WHAT'S THERE

1. *Who* would you say this chapter is most about?

2. From what you see in this chapter, how would you describe the personality of the blind man?

3. From the evidence you see in this chapter, what would you say the Pharisees considered to be the most important things in life?

4. Suppose you were one of the Pharisees in this chapter who were questioning the man who claimed to be healed by Jesus. Looking only at the evidence presented in verses 13-34, how would you summarize the *facts* in this case?

5. In verse 39, who are the blind people Jesus speaks of, and who are those who see?

6. What are the most important *choices* made in this chapter, and how would you analyze each one?

7. Think again of the statement about Jesus in John 1:18. From what you see in chapter 9, *what is God like?*

8. What in this chapter do you think might be most surprising to a new Christian reading it for the first time?

9. EYE FOR DETAIL— *From what you recall seeing in this chapter, try answering the following question without looking at your Bible:* What method did Jesus use to give sight to the blind man? (See verses 6-7.)

CAPTURE THE ESSENCE

10. Discuss how much you agree or disagree with what the formerly blind man said about God in verse 31.

11. Discuss how much you agree or disagree with what the man said about Jesus in verse 33.

12. When the man in verse 38 said to Jesus, "Lord, I believe"…*what* exactly would you say he believed?

13. Immediately after the events of this chapter, if you talked with the man who was once blind and asked him to define the word *faith*, how do you think he would have answered?

14. Imagine you were helping to produce a film based on this chapter. Describe the kinds of scenery, supporting characters, background music, lighting effects, etc., which you would use to portray this chapter's central message.

15. In this chapter, which of these character qualities in Jesus comes through most strongly to you: His compassion, His power, or His wisdom?

16. If you had only this chapter in Scripture to refer to, how would you use it to help show someone that Jesus is truly *God?*

FOR LIFE TODAY

17. Look at Jesus' words about day and night in verse 4. In the sense Jesus used, would you say the times in which we live represent the *day,* or the *night?*

18. Look at the statement of purpose which Jesus gives about Himself in verse 39. How would you say it relates to *your* purpose in life?

19. How free are you from spiritual blindness? Think carefully again about what Jesus says in the last three verses of this chapter. Then imagine Him evaluating your spiritual sight on a scale of one to ten, in which ten equals perfect spiritual vision, and one equals complete spiritual blindness. What score do you think He would probably assign to you?

FOR GOING DEEPER

Look at the words of Jesus in verse 5, which is one of several "I am" statements which He makes in this gospel. Look also together at these other verses and make a list together of all that Jesus claimed to be. Then discuss what picture they give of Jesus when taken all together—6:35, 8:12, 10:7, 11:25, 14:6, and 15:1.

JOHN 10

Startup: What kind of pictures come to your mind when you think of the word *security?*

1. In this chapter Jesus speaks much about sheep and shepherds. From what you know about the Old Testament, what kinds of thoughts and pictures probably came into the minds of the Jews as Jesus spoke of Himself as a "Shepherd"? (For helpful background, you may want to look together at Psalm 23:1-4, Isaiah 40:10-11, and Ezekiel 34:11-16.)

2. Jesus says in this chapter that He is both the gate for the sheep (verse 7) and the good shepherd (verse 11). How do these two concepts fit together?

3. Who would you identify with the "thieves and robbers" in verse 8, and with the "thief" in verse 10?

4. Who are the "other sheep" in verse 16?

5. What in this chapter do you think might be the most interesting to someone who was learning about Jesus Christ for the first time, and why?

6. Think again of the statement about Jesus in John 1:18. From what you see in chapter 10, *what is God like?*

7. EYE FOR DETAIL—*From what you recall seeing in this chapter, try answering the following question without looking at your Bible:* The last conversation Jesus has with the Jews in this chapter takes place in the temple area of Jerusalem. What time of year was it? (See verses 22-23.)

CAPTURE THE ESSENCE

8. If you expected to live only a few more weeks, which verses in this chapter do you think would be the most significant to you?

9. Look again at verse 14. In the sense Jesus is using here, what are some good examples of the ways in which He "knows" His sheep?

10. Read again verse 17, then discuss how much you agree or disagree with this sentence: God's reason for loving Jesus had more to do with *what Jesus did* than with *who Jesus was*.

11. In the mental perspective which the Jews displayed in verses 22-39, how much wrong thinking can you find?

12. If the words of Jesus in verses 27-30 were the only Scriptures you had, what conclusions could you make from them about (a) what Jesus is like, (b) what God is like, and (c) what people are like?

13. Based on what Jesus says in verse 30 (and in other relevant Scriptures you know of), discuss how much you agree or disagree with this statement: God the Father and Jesus His Son are one in nature and essence, but they are *not* one person.

14. If you had only this chapter in Scripture to refer to, how would you use it to help show someone that Jesus is truly *God?*

15. From what you've seen in this chapter, what does it really mean to "follow Jesus"?

16. Look again at what Jesus says in verse 10 about the thief and what he does. In what ways do you see these things going on today?

17. How could you use verses 15-18 in response to a false teacher who said Jesus did not know He was going to be murdered by the Jews, but instead intended to lead an uprising against Roman rule?

18. The closing words of Jesus in verse 10 have been translated as "living life to the full," "having life more abundantly," "life in all its fullness," and, "far more life than before." Here are three questions to think about and answer: (a) To what degree can you say this quality of life is a reality in your experience today? (b) To what degree is it your expectation and hope in the future? (c) What examples can you give to illustrate your answer?

19. Remember again the command in Colossians 3:1 — "Since you have been raised with Christ, set your hearts on things above, where Christ is seated at the right hand of God." What have you personally observed about Jesus Christ in this chapter that is worthy of setting your heart on?

20. In light of how you're doing spiritually in your life today, which verse in this chapter do you think is the most important at this time—and why?

FOR GOING DEEPER

Among the four gospels, the book of John is said to be the one which focuses most on the *principles* in Jesus' teachings. From your studies so far in this book, how do you see John putting emphasis on foundational *principles?*

JOHN 11

Startup: What's the earliest experience in your childhood in which you can recall learning about death?

SEEING WHAT'S THERE

1. See how many single-word descriptions you can come up with to appropriately describe each of the following people in this chapter: Thomas (verse 16); Mary (verses 3, 20, and 29-33); Martha (3, 20-28, and 39); Lazarus; Caiaphas (49-52); and finally, Jesus Himself.

2. What does verse 5 imply about the way Jesus scheduled His work?

3. How would you explain verses 25-26 to a young child?

4. Imagine you're the disciple Thomas, and you're writing a quick letter to your family or a friend back home. Give a few sample lines of how you would describe to your friend what happened in this chapter.

5. Notice again in this chapter the encounters Jesus had with both sexes. From what you've seen in this gospel, how would you define what *manhood* and *womanhood* mean to Jesus?

6. What in this chapter do you think might be most surprising to a new Christian reading it for the first time?

7. Think again of the statement about Jesus in John 1:18. From what you see in chapter 11, *what is God like?*

8. EYE FOR DETAIL— *From what you recall seeing in this chapter, try answering the following question without looking at your Bible:* After Jesus received word from Mary and Martha that Lazarus was sick, how many days did He wait before going to see them? (See verse 6.)

CAPTURE THE ESSENCE

9. Immediately after the events of this chapter, if you talked with Mary and Martha and asked them to define the word *faith,* how do you think they would have answered?

10. As you've studied this gospel so far, in what ways, if any, have you seen Jesus put pressure on people to believe in Him? (Explain your answer.)

11. In this chapter, which of these character qualities in Jesus comes through most strongly to you: His compassion, His power, or His wisdom?

12. What in this chapter do you think might be the most interesting to someone learning about Jesus Christ for the first time, and why?

13. If you had only this chapter in Scripture to refer to, how would you use it to help show someone that Jesus is truly *God?*

FOR LIFE TODAY

14. What mental habits do you think could most easily block the words of Jesus in verses 25-26 from coming alive in our minds and hearts?

15. Look together at Luke 10:38-42, and compare what you see there with John 11:17-40. How would you describe the personalities of Mary and Martha, and in what ways can you identify with either of them?

16. In light of how you're doing spiritually in your life today, which verse in this chapter do you think is the most important at this time—and why?

FOR GOING DEEPER

Notice how Jesus begins His prayer in verse 41. In the gospel of John, the word *Father* is used for God more often than in all the other gospels combined. Scan together other chapters in this book (especially 5, 6, 8, 10, and 14—17), and find several passages in which Jesus addresses God in this way. Discuss what insight they give us about the Father-Son relationship between them.

JOHN 12

Startup: Talk together about how you've learned (or are learning) to be patient in waiting for the right time for making a major decision or launching out on new endeavor.

SEEING WHAT'S THERE

1. From the account in verses 1-11, what would you say Mary considered to be the most important things in life?

2. Keep the events of verses 12-15 in mind, as you discuss how much you agree or disagree with this statement: The cheering welcome and praise which Jesus received as He entered Jerusalem was rooted only in the people's misunderstanding of what kind of king He truly was, and this was proven by the way the crowds turned against Him later in the week.

3. Notice what Jesus says in verses 23 and 27, and compare these statements with what He says in John 2:4 and 7:6. What do these passages together tell you about His sense of timing and purpose?

4. Examine closely the words Jesus spoke in verse 24. Does this statement mean that undergoing death was the only way Jesus could multiply His life into the lives of others?

5. Jesus speaks in verse 25 about the man who loves his life. According to what Jesus means by that expression, which one of these words would be the best synonym for the word "loves" in this verse: *protects; enjoys;* or *values?*

6. What would you say is the relationship between what Jesus said in verse 25, and what He said in verse 26?

7. Look at what Jesus says at the end of verse 26 about honor from God. What do you think this honor is?

8. What exactly is the "light" and the "darkness" which Jesus speaks of in verses 35-36?

9. Think again of the statement about Jesus in John 1:18. From what you see in chapter 12, *what is God like?*

10. EYE FOR DETAIL— *From what you recall seeing in this chapter, try answering the following question without looking at your Bible:* In the middle of this chapter, God's voice speaks from heaven. What did Jesus pray immediately before the voice spoke, and how did the voice answer? (See verse 28.)

CAPTURE THE ESSENCE

11. If you expected to live only a few more weeks, which verses in this chapter do you think would be the most significant to you?

12. If the mind and heart of Judas Iscariot had been genuinely open and submissive to what Jesus said and did in verses 1-8, what lesson do you think he could have learned about the value of money?

13. Notice what John says in verse 16 about the disciples' understanding of the events in this chapter. What do you think are the main reasons why they did not understand until later?

14. Is the principle Jesus gives in verse 24 true only about Himself, or about everyone?

15. From the time of the events in this chapter, it was only a matter of days until Jesus would suffer and die. From what you know about the events soon to come, what evidence do you see that the disciples remembered the words of Jesus in verse 26?

16. With verses 44-45 in mind, discuss how much you agree or disagree with this statement: It is impossible to believe in Jesus without also believing in God.

17. If you had only this chapter in Scripture to refer to, how would you use it to help show someone that Jesus is truly *God?*

18. The Jesus we see in this gospel is not only fully God, but also fully human. From what you've seen so far in John, in what ways does Jesus show Himself to be the perfect model of manhood?

FOR LIFE TODAY

19. What actions can we do that, in God's eyes, would be equivalent to what Mary did with the perfume in verse 3? Or is it truly too late?

20. Look again at verses 23 and 27. How do *you* decide when the time is right for some major task or decision in your life?

21. Consider the statement of Jesus in verse 26, and give the best answer you can think of to these questions: (a) *Where is Jesus now?* (b) *What does that mean about where YOU should be?*

22. Verses 37-41 are about *sight*—a group of people who could not see, and an Old Testament prophet who could. Look again at this passage. How could it apply to your witness for Christ?

23. Look at the statement of purpose which Jesus gives about Himself in verse 46. How would you say it relates to *your* purpose in life?

24. From what you've learned especially in the book of John, summarize what you think it means for Christians today to "follow in the footsteps of Jesus."

25. In light of how you're doing spiritually in your life today, which verse in this chapter do you think is the most important at this time—and why?

FOR GOING DEEPER

Notice again how *light* and *darkness* are contrasted in verses 35-36 and 46. This is a common theme in John's gospel. Look at the other examples listed here, and compare them with the light-and-darkness verses in chapter 12. Then discuss together whether *you* look at life in the same "black-and-white" terms as John and Jesus do— 1:4-5, 3:19-21, and 8:12.

JOHN 13

Startup: Talk about some of the most meaningful and surprising ways in which you have been served by someone, when you felt undeserving of that service.

SEEING WHAT'S THERE

1. In verse 1, John speaks of a certain fact Jesus "knew." How do you think Jesus came to learn this fact?

2. Look also in verse 3 at three additional facts that Jesus "knew" at this time. How would you analyze the importance of each of these three facts, as they relate to Jesus at this time?

3. From what you see in this chapter, what one-word adjectives would you use to best describe the disciples? And what appropriate one-word descriptions would you give to each of these individuals: Peter; Judas; and Jesus?

4. Look at the mention made of the devil in verses 2 and 27, and look back also at verses 70-71 in chapter 6. From the evidence you see, what was the devil's strategy at this point in his warfare against God?

5. Think again of the statement about Jesus in John 1:18. From what you see in chapter 13, *what is God like?*

6. What in this chapter do you think might be most surprising to a new Christian reading it for the first time?

7. EYE FOR DETAIL— *From what you recall seeing in this chapter, try answering the following question without looking at your Bible:* After Jesus got up from the mean He was sharing with the disciples, and before He began washing their feet, what three things did He do? (See verses 4-5.)

CAPTURE THE ESSENCE

8. Notice what John says about the love of Jesus in verse 1. Then discuss together how much you agree or disagree with this statement: There is no limit whatsoever to the love of Christ.

9. Look at what Jesus said to the disciples in verse 7. What do you think prevented them from fully understanding what was going on at that time?

10. With verse 16 in mind, discuss how much you agree or disagree with this statement: When we fail to offer loving service to others, we are in essence proclaiming that we are greater and more important than Jesus Himself.

11. Why do you think Jesus calls His command in verse 34 a new command? In what way is it new?

12. Review what Jesus said about Judas in verse 21, and about Peter in Peter in verse 38. Since Jesus knew Judas would betray Him, and Peter would deny Him, why didn't He do something to prevent them from doing so?

13. Some commentators have felt that Judas Iscariot has been unfairly blamed in history for what he did to Jesus—that he was simply reacting in an understandable, human way to a situation in which he had greater expectations of Jesus than Jesus could meet. From what you see in this chapter, especially in verses 2 and 27-30, how would you respond to that observation?

14. If you were asked to summarize the most important "marks of Christian maturity" as taught in this chapter, which ones would you mention first?

15. If you had only this chapter in Scripture to refer to, how would you use it to help show someone that Jesus is truly *God?*

16. Look at what Jesus says in verse 7. What circumstances in your life now could Jesus speak those same words about?

17. Look again at what Jesus said in verses 14-15. Explain in your own words what this example of Jesus means practically in your own life.

18. In people's love for one another, how well do you think your church is living up to the standard taught by Jesus in verses 34-35?

19. How well do you think the people in your Bible study group are living up to the standard taught by Jesus in verses 34-35?

20. In light of how you're doing spiritually in your life today, which verse in this chapter do you think is the most important at this time—and why?

FOR GOING DEEPER

Love is a major emphasis in John's gospel from chapter 13 until the end. Try to start with a blank slate in your mind as you look together at the following key verses, and use them to come up with a fresh definition for *love*—14:21, 15:13, 16:27, and 17:24.

JOHN 14

Startup: What pictures come to your mind as you imagine heaven?

SEEING WHAT'S THERE

1. Look at the very first sentence in the chapter. For what reasons might the disciples feel troubled at this time?

2. How would you explain verse 6 to a young child? (You may want to include verse 5 as well.)

3. What examples would you give of the "greater things" or "greater works" which Jesus talks about in verse 12?

4. What does Jesus mean by the phrase "in my name" in verse 13?

5. In verse 20, what is "that day" which Jesus speaks of?

6. What are the biggest *promises* which you see Jesus making in this chapter?

7. Think again of the statement about Jesus in John 1:18. From what you see in chapter 14, *what is God like?*

8. EYE FOR DETAIL— *From what you recall seeing in this chapter, try answering the following question without looking at your Bible:* How did Jesus complete this sentence in this chapter: "Because I live, —"? (See verse 19.)

CAPTURE THE ESSENCE

9. Imagine you are the disciple Philip, and you are present with the other disciples and Jesus on the night when the events described in John 13—18 take place. What thoughts and questions do you think might come to your mind after you hear Jesus answer your question the way He does in John 14:9?

10. Keep verse 6 in mind, and answer these questions: *Why* is Jesus "the way"?

11. In verse 13, look at the *process* of glory which Jesus speaks of. On a

practical level, how would you explain how this works?

12. Look at verse 26. Why do you think this third Person of the Godhead is so often called the *Holy* Spirit in Scripture, instead of the *Powerful* Spirit, or the *Loving* Spirit, or the *All-Knowing* Spirit?

13. Look at what Jesus says in verse 31. Why does Jesus consider this love so important for the world to learn about?

14. What would you say are the most important things this chapter teaches about the Holy Spirit?

15. How does this chapter's teachings on the Holy Spirit compare with what you learned in John 3, in the words Jesus spoke to Nicodemus?

16. Again, if you were asked to summarize the most important "marks of Christian maturity" as taught in this chapter, which ones would you mention first?

17. If you had only this chapter in Scripture to refer to, how would you use it to help show someone that Jesus is truly *God?*

FOR LIFE TODAY

18. What kind of mental habits do you think could most easily block the words of Jesus in verses 1-3 from coming alive in our minds and hearts?

19. How could you use verse 6 in response to a false teacher who said Jesus is only one of many ways in which human beings can reach God?

20. From your own experience, why would you say you *need* the kind of Holy Spirit described by Jesus in verses 16-17?

21. From what you see in this chapter, what are the most important things to believe about Jesus?

22. In light of how you're doing spiritually in your life today, which verse in this chapter do you think is the most important at this time—and why?

FOR GOING DEEPER

Verse 6 is one of the best-known examples of how the apostle John uses the word *life* in his gospel. John uses this word more than twice as often as any other New Testament writer. In the listed references here, look at a few other passages in John used this word earlier, and decide together how he would have defined this word—1:4, 3:36, 5:21, 5:24, 6:33, 6:63, 10:10, and 12:25.

JOHN 15

Startup: At this point in your life, how strong is your personal desire to know Jesus better, compared with other times in the past? Use a scale of one to ten (one = "much weaker than ever," ten = "much stronger than ever") to help you decide.

SEEING WHAT'S THERE

1. What *fruit* do you think Jesus is speaking of in verses 5, 8, and 16? Is it the same in each of these verses?

2. In verses 4-6, Jesus speaks of the utter necessity for us to "abide" or "remain" in Him. Explain whether you think this "remaining" or "abiding" has more to do with *faith,* more to do with *love,* or more to do with *hope.*

3. In what practical ways does our bearing "fruit" bring glory to God, as Jesus says in verse 8?

4. From what you see in the verses around it, what is the true source of the joy Jesus speaks of in verse 11?

5. What are the biggest *promises* which you see Jesus making in this chapter?

6. Think again of the statement about Jesus in John 1:18. From what you see in chapter 15, *what is God like?*

7. EYE FOR DETAIL— *From what you recall seeing in this chapter, try answering the following question without looking at your Bible:* How did Jesus complete this sentence in this chapter: "If the world hates you,—"? (See verse 18.)

CAPTURE THE ESSENCE

8. From what you see in verse 15, how would you define the kind of human *friendship* Jesus would approve of and endorse?

9. What do you think was involved in the *choice* Jesus made in verse 16?

10. Keep verse 19 in mind as you discuss how much you agree or disagree with this statement: A person either belongs entirely to God, or entirely to the world; there is no middle ground.

11. In verse 26, look at the words which Jesus uses to describe the Holy Spirit (and notice the same words in verses 16-17 in the previous chapter). By using these words, what does Jesus want us to understand about the Holy Spirit?

12. Once again, if you were asked to summarize the most important "marks of Christian maturity" as taught in this chapter, which ones would you mention first?

13. If you had only this chapter in Scripture to refer to, how would you use it to help show someone that Jesus is truly *God?*

FOR LIFE TODAY

14. Think once more of the command in Colossians 3:1—"Since you have been raised with Christ, set your hearts on things above, where Christ is seated at the right hand of God." What have you personally observed about Jesus Christ in this chapter that would be worthy of setting your heart on?

15. With the picture in verses 1 and 2 in mind, what significant pruning would you say God has already accomplished in your life?

16. Jesus speaks in verse 11 of how our joy can be made "full" or "complete." On a scale of one to ten (one = totally empty, ten = totally full or complete), how full or complete would you say is the joy which you are now experiencing in life?

17. In what way would you say the words of Jesus to His disciples in verse 16 are also true of us today?

18. In light of how you're doing spiritually in your life today, which verse in this chapter do you think is the most important at this time—and why?

FOR GOING DEEPER

Jesus teaches us that we *must* depend on Him (verse 5). Look together at the following verses and discuss how Jesus Himself sets the example for us in the way He depends on His Father—5:30, 6:38, 10:37, 12:49-50, and 14:31.

JOHN 16

Startup: During the time you've been a Christian, what important changes, if any, have there been in your understanding about the Holy Spirit?

SEEING WHAT'S THERE

1. In what important ways would you say Jesus is looking after the best interests of His disciples in this chapter?

2. In your own words, how would you express the main points Jesus makes about the Holy Spirit in verses 7-15?

3. Who is Jesus talking about when He speaks of "the world" in verse 8?

4. From what you see in verses 8-11, explain in your own words what the Holy Spirit does for the world.

5. From what you see in verses 12-15, explain in your own words what the Holy Spirit does for the disciples of Jesus.

6. From what you see in verses 14-15, explain in your own words what the Holy Spirit does for Jesus Himself.

7. Describe as fully as possible the *joy* which Jesus talks about in verses 20-24.

8. In verse 23, what is "that day" which Jesus speaks of?

9. What are the biggest *promises* which you see Jesus making in this chapter?

10. What in this chapter do you think might be most surprising to a new Christian reading it for the first time?

11. Think again of the statement about Jesus in John 1:18. From what you see in chapter 16, *what is God like?*

12. EYE FOR DETAIL—*From what you recall seeing in this chapter, try answering the following question without looking at your Bible:* What names does Jesus give to the Holy Spirit in this chapter? (See verses 7, 13, and 15.)

13. What would you say are the most important things this chapter teaches about the Holy Spirit?

14. What wrong thinking or actions on the part of the disciples do you think Jesus may be trying to prevent by what He says in verses 8-11?

15. In verse 14, look at the *process* of glory which Jesus describes as He talks about the Holy Spirit's work. On a practical level, how would you explain how this works?

16. From what you see in verses 22-24, discuss how much you agree or disagree with this statement: It is impossible to experience the fullest dimension of joy in this life without having a vital prayer life.

17. What wrong thinking or actions on the part of the disciples do you think Jesus may be trying to prevent by what He says in verse 33?

18. Chapters 14, 15, and 16 all contain key verses about prayer. Look at them together, and decide what is the most important prayer principle that s taught in all of them: 14:13-14, 15:7, and 16:23-24.

19. If you had only this chapter in Scripture to refer to, how would you use it to help show someone that Jesus is truly *God?*

FOR LIFE TODAY

20. Look at the promises Jesus makes to the disciples in verse 13. To what degree would you say these promises are true for Christians today?

21. What kind of mental habits do you think could most easily block the invitation of Jesus in verse 24 from coming alive in our minds and hearts?

22. Once more, if you were asked to summarize the most important "marks of Christian maturity" as taught in this chapter, which ones would you mention first?

23. In light of how you're doing spiritually in your life today, which verse in this chapter do you think is the most important at this time—and why?

FOR GOING DEEPER

Look together at the generosity of God which Jesus teaches in verse 23. The gospel of John has much to say about *giving*—especially God's giving. Look at each of these verses, and make a list together of the gifts God has given to His Son, Jesus—5:27, 5:36, 6:39, 10:29, 17:2, 17:9, 17:24, and 18:11.

JOHN 17

Startup: At this time in your life, what do you consider to be the most important concern to bring before the Lord in prayer?

SEEING WHAT'S THERE

1. Jesus speaks in verse 1 of the "time" or "hour" that now has come. In His own mind, what does that mean?

2. What exactly is the "work" Jesus speaks of in verse 4, and how did He bring glory to God through it?

3. How many times is the word *world* used in this chapter? Does it appear to have the same meaning in each instance? If not, what different meanings does it have?

4. Together, list aloud all the actual *requests* which Jesus makes in this prayer. Taking them as a group, what do they reveal about the deepest concerns Jesus has?

5. Jesus begins praying in verse 20 for those who will believe in Him through the "word" or "message" of His disciples. What is this word?

6. What one-word adjectives would you use to best describe Jesus as you see Him in this chapter?

7. Think again of the statement about Jesus in John 1:18. From what you see in chapter 17, *what is God like?*

8. EYE FOR DETAIL— *From what you recall seeing in this chapter, try answering the following question without looking at your Bible:* In His prayer in this chapter, what names does Jesus use to address God? (See verses 1, 11, and 25.)

CAPTURE THE ESSENCE

9. From what you see in this prayer of Jesus, which one of the following words do you think best describes what the *world* is like: *a prison; a mountain; a battleground;* or *a trail?*

10. From what you know of Jesus, with what emotion do you think He spoke the words in verse 5?

11. If you expected to live only a few more weeks, which verses in this chapter do you think would be the most significant to you?

12. If you had only this chapter in Scripture to refer to, how would you use it to help show someone that Jesus is truly *God?*

FOR LIFE TODAY

13. What would make it possible for *you* to say to God at the end of your life what Jesus says in verse 4?

14. In verses 14 and 22, look at what Jesus said He had given to His disciples. In what ways has He also given these things to us today?

15. What principles of prayer can you draw from this chapter that might help us pray more powerfully and more often?

16. Think again of Philippians 4:8, where we're given this command: "Whatever is true, whatever is noble, whatever is right, whatever is pure, whatever is lovely, whatever is admirable—if anything is excellent or praiseworthy— *think about such things."* What food for thought can you find in this chapter that especially strikes you as being *true,* or *noble,* or *right,* or *pure,* or *lovely,* or *admirable,* or *excellent,* or *praiseworthy?*

FOR GOING DEEPER

Notice again the prominence of the word *world* in this chapter. John uses this word far more often than any other New Testament writer. Look carefully at how it is used in each of the following verses in John, then discuss in what ways and to what degree the Lord wants us to "think big" about the whole world — 1:10, 3:17, 8:23, 12:31, 15:19, 16:28, and 16:33.

JOHN 18

Startup: How much can you trust what people say these days? How truthful are they? On a scale of one to ten (one = "totally dishonest," ten = "completely honest"), rank each of the following categories of people according to your general perception of their overall truthfulness: government leaders; public school teachers; scientists; people in the news media; automobile salespeople; people who write TV commercials; business leaders; and pastors.

SEEING WHAT'S THERE

1. Imagine you were one of the disciples in this chapter's opening scene in the olive grove. As you watched these events unfold, what would be your thoughts toward Judas? Toward Jesus? Toward yourself and the other disciples?

2. Why do you think the soldiers and officials responded as they did in verse 6?

3. How fully can you define the "cup" Jesus spoke of in verse 11, and why do you think He used this particular word to express what He meant?

4. In verse 36, Jesus tells Pilate what His kingdom is *not.* What would you add to Jesus' words to tell what His kingdom *is?*

5. What are the most important *choices* made in this chapter, and how would you analyze each one?

6. Think again of the statement about Jesus in John 1:18. From what you see in chapter 18, *what is God like?*

7. EYE FOR DETAIL— *From what you recall seeing in this chapter, try answering the following question without looking at your Bible:* After Jesus was arrested and bound, who did the soldiers take Him to first? (See verse 12.)

CAPTURE THE ESSENCE

8. Discuss how much you agree or disagree with this statement: Peter's actions in verse 10 showed that his basic instincts were brave and righteous.

9. If you knew everything that was going on, and you were standing next to Peter in the high priest's courtyard in verses 25-27, what would you have wanted to say to him?

10. Why do you think Jesus answered Pilate the way He did in verse 34?

11. If you had only this chapter in Scripture to refer to, how would you use it to help show someone that Jesus is truly *God?*

FOR LIFE TODAY

12. As fully and as you can, how would you answer Pilate's question in verse 38? What difference does this definition really make in your life?

13. Think well about the statement of purpose which Jesus gives for His life in verse 37—the reason for which He was born into the world. How much can you identify with this purpose in your own life? To what degree is this *your* purpose also?

14. Look closely also in verse 37 at what Jesus says about those who are "of the truth" or "on the side of truth." Get in mind a picture of yourself one year in the future, as a man or woman who is listens fully to the voice of Jesus. As this kind of person, what kinds of things do you see yourself doing?

FOR GOING DEEPER

Look again at Pilate's question in verse 38. Then look at these other verses in John and discuss how John would answer the question himself—1:17, 4:23-24, 7:18, 8:32, 8:44-46, 14:6, 16:13, and 17:17.

JOHN 19

Startup: What is the most fulfilling accomplishment you can recall having completed?

SEEING WHAT'S THERE

1. As best as you can, walk your way through the events of this chapter as if you were Jesus Himself, feeling what He felt, seeing what He saw, hearing what He heard. Describe to one another the sensations that come to your imagination.

2. Look at the following brief passages in chapters 18 and 19, and for each one, explain what you think Pilate was *trying* to do—18:31, 18:38-39, 19:1-4, and 19:14-15.

3. For background on Jesus' silence in verse 9, look together at the prophecy in Isaiah 53:7.

4. In the three words Jesus spoke in verse 30, what do you think the word "it" refers to, and why?

5. Think again of the statement about Jesus in John 1:18. From what you see in chapter 19, *what is God like?*

6. EYE FOR DETAIL—*From what you recall seeing in this chapter, try answering the following question without looking at your Bible:* As recorded in this chapter, what are the final words of Jesus spoken from the cross? (See verse 30.)

CAPTURE THE ESSENCE

7. Imagine you are Pontius Pilate, the Roman governor in Jerusalem, and you are living when the events described in this chapter take place. What thoughts and questions in your mind would cause the fear which is spoken of in verse 8?

8. In what ways, if any, would you say this chapter is a good illustration of basic human nature?

9. If you had only this chapter in Scripture to refer to, how would you use it to help show someone that Jesus is truly *God?*

FOR LIFE TODAY

10. No one is trying to physically crucify us today—but what does Jesus' *example* in this chapter mean personally for your life?

11. Of the most important events and truths in this chapter, which do you think are the easiest for Christians to forget about?

FOR GOING DEEPER

With the events of this chapter fresh in your mind, look back at the words of Jesus in 10:17-18, indicating His willingness to give His life for the world. Then look together at these other verses in John, and make a list together of what Jesus *can* give or *has* given to us—4:10, 5:21, 6:27, 6:51, 13:34, 14:27, 17:14, and 17:22.

JOHN 20

Startup: Practically speaking, what would you say is the most important thing you have to do in the time you have remaining on earth?

SEEING WHAT'S THERE

1. As you read this chapter, what's the strongest impression or image which it leaves in your mind?

2. What one-word adjectives would best describe Mary Magdalene as you see her in this chapter? What one-word descriptions would you give for Thomas as you see him here?

3. How would you explain verses 30-31 to a young child?

4. Think again of the statement about Jesus in John 1:18. From what you see in chapter 20, *what is God like?*

5. EYE FOR DETAIL— *Try answering the following question without looking at your Bible:* After Jesus showed Himself to Thomas, what did Thomas call Him? (See verse 28.)

CAPTURE THE ESSENCE

6. What are the major lessons this chapter teaches about *faith?*

7. In verses 19 and 21, why do you think Jesus spoke the words "Peace be with you" to His disciples?

8. How could you use verses 24-29 to help an unsaved friend who said he needed more proof about Christ before he could believe in Him?

9. How could you use verses 30-31 to help a new Christian understand the value of the Scriptures?

10. How fully can you define and describe the "life" John speaks of in the final phrase in this chapter?

11. Immediately after the events of this chapter, if you talked with the disciple Thomas and asked him to define the word *faith,* how do you think he would have answered?

12. If you had only this chapter in Scripture to refer to, how would you use it to help show someone that Jesus is truly *God?*

FOR LIFE TODAY

13. Look at each statement Jesus makes in verses 21-23. Then imagine you're one of the disciples in the locked room when Jesus appeared. What thoughts and questions would go through your mind as you heard each of the things which Jesus said?

14. Look again at the two things which Thomas called Jesus in verse 28. How would you define what it means to you personally to call Jesus those two things?

15. With the words of verse 31 in mind, how has this study of John deepened your faith, even though you may have been a believer in Christ Jesus for a long time?

16. Think again about verse 31. Then identify together the kinds of people in your community whom you would say probably know the least about the living Lord Jesus Christ. What else are these people like? What do they do in daily life? Where do they live? Now imagine God has brought you together with a small group of these people, and in this meeting they indicate a genuine desire to understand who Jesus is and what He has done. From what you have seen in the gospel of John, what are the most important things you would want to communicate to them, and how would you word it?

FOR GOING DEEPER

Analyze the importance of Jesus' resurrection as you think together about this chapter, and about these supporting passages: Romans 4:25, 1 Corinthians 15:17, and Revelation 1:18.

JOHN 21

Startup: What are the hardest things to communicate to someone you love?

SEEING WHAT'S THERE

1. Once again, take a "walk" together through the incidents that happen in this chapter. Using your imagination, talk about the kinds of sights, smells, sounds, and feelings you might experience.

2. What one-word adjectives would you use to best describe Peter as you see him in this chapter?

3. If you were able to ask the apostle John, "Why did you include verses 20-23 in your gospel?" how do you think he would answer?

4. From the evidence you see in these last two chapters of John's gospel, how would you describe the nature of the resurrected body of Jesus Christ?

5. If you had only this chapter in Scripture to refer to, how would you use it to help show someone that Jesus is truly *God?*

6. EYE FOR DETAIL— *From what you recall seeing in this chapter, try answering the following question without looking at your Bible:* Which disciples are mentioned specifically by name in this chapter? (See verse 2.)

CAPTURE THE ESSENCE

7. Imagine you were helping to produce a film based on this chapter. Describe the kinds of scenery, supporting characters, background music, lighting effects, etc., which you would use to portray this chapter's central message.

8. What changes do you think might have taken place in Peter's heart as a result of his conversation with Jesus in verses 15-23?

9. In your own opinion, did Peter love Jesus? (Explain your answer.)

10. In this chapter, which of these character qualities in Jesus comes through most strongly to you: His compassion, His power, or His wisdom?

11. Look again at John 1:18. From what you see in chapter 21, *what is God like?* And from all you've learned throughout the gospel of John, how would you summarize what God is like?

12. Immediately after the events of this chapter, if you talked with the disciple Peter and asked him to define what it means to *love Jesus,* how do you think he would have answered?

FOR LIFE TODAY

13. Suppose Jesus asked you today the same question He asked Peter in verse 15—"Do you love me more than these?" With what Jesus knows about your own heart, what would the "these" refer to?

14. In the last verse of the book, John tells us that much, much more could be written about the life Jesus lived on earth. What further details of His earthly life would you like most to know more about?

15. In light of how you're doing spiritually in your life today, which verse in this chapter do you think is the most important at this time—and why?

FOR GOING DEEPER

Notice again (in verse 1 of chapter 1) the way this gospel begins as it speaks of Jesus: "In the beginning was the Word, and the Word was with God, and the Word was God." Think about this concept of Jesus as "the Word" and what it means practically for us as human beings; then discuss together how the following verses in John reinforce that concept—3:12, 5:24-25, 5:28-29, 8:14, 8:18, 8:47, 10:24-27, 12:47-50, and 14:10.

JOHN:

THE BIG PICTURE

(Discuss again the questions in the "Overview," plus the questions below.)

1. Look together at each of these passages, and discuss which one you believe is the best candidate for "KEY VERSE" in the book of John—the one which brings into sharpest focus what this book is most about: 1:11-13, 3:16, 5:24, 10:10, 10:11, 11:25; and 20:30-31.

2. What verses or passages in John's gospel present the strongest evidence to you that Jesus will be coming back to earth?

3. Even more than the other gospel writers, John is said to be a skilled *theologian*. How would you evaluate his theological skills, as you've observed them in this book?

4. What would you say are the strongest themes in the way John portrays Jesus Christ?

5. What would you say are the most important ways in which this book is *unique* in all the Bible?

6. In James 1:23-24 we're told that "anyone who listens to the word but does not do what it says is like a man who looks at his face in a mirror and, after looking at himself, goes away and immediately forgets what he looks like." In what important ways has the book of John been a "mirror" for you—showing you what you can and should do?

Acts

OVERVIEW

(Discuss these OVERVIEW questions both at the beginning of your study of Acts, and again after you've studied together all 28 chapters. Your answers may change significantly once you've looked more closely at the entire book.)

Startup: Get a mental picture in your mind of this book of Acts as a bridge between the gospels on one side, and the teaching books (the epistles) on the other. In your mind's eye, what is the river which the bridge crosses? What is the land like on the gospel side? And what is the land like on the epistle side?

SEEING WHAT'S THERE

1. Look together at the following passages to learn more about Luke, the author of Acts: Colossians 4:14, 2 Timothy 4:9-11, Philemon 23-24, and Luke 1:1-4.

2. In the following list of passages, notice the places where the pronoun "we" is used, indicating that Luke was present with Paul during the events described. What kind of interesting experiences did Luke get to share with Paul?—chapters 16, 20, 21, 27 and 28.

3. What do you know about what the world was like at the time this book was written?

4. Start scanning the book of Acts until you come to a verse that brings a question to your mind. What's the question?

5. Begin scanning the book again until you come to a verse that gives you a smile or a sense of gratitude or joy.

What is pleasing to you about this verse?

6. Make a list together of which chapters in this book involve Peter more than anyone else, and which chapters involve Paul more than anyone else. Since the other apostles were also at work at the same time as Peter and Paul, why do you think the Spirit of God has chosen to give us a book that centers only around those two men?

7. If this book of Acts were not included in the Bible, how would you describe what would be missing in the total picture of the Bible's message?

8. Look also at the list of "Questions to Ask as You Begin Your Study of Each Book" on page 393.

CAPTURE THE ESSENCE

9. What previous impressions, if any, have you had about the book of Acts in regard to (a) its content, (b) its level of difficulty, and (c) its importance?

10. The book of Acts has been called "Power Unleashed," "The Book of Christian Action," and "The Gospel's Momentum." With that reputation for this book, what kinds of answers and guidelines and solutions would you like to gain as you examine it more closely?

11. In Luke 1:3-4, notice how Luke indicates the *purpose* for which he wrote his gospel. Compare that passage with the opening verses in Acts, where no such direct statement is

given. If Luke *had* written a clear summary statement of the purpose for this book, what do you think it might have said?

12. Discuss how much you would agree or disagree with this statement: The book of Acts serves as a faithful and thorough guide for the church today and at all times.

13. If the book of Acts is a record of the birth of Christ's church, and a dependable guide for that church today, then studying this book brings to the fore our own commitment to and involvement with the church. In a brief sentence or two, how would you summarize in practical terms your own commitment to the church, the body of Christ?

14. How can you ensure that your study of Acts is not merely theoretical and intellectual, but is instead truly practical and relevant? Talk together about this. What can you do to help keep the process alive and interesting?

FOR GOING DEEPER

As you watch the dynamic, Spirit-led growth of the church in Acts, remember the commands of the Lord Jesus that motivated the disciples onward. Look together at His strategic teachings in these passages—Matthew 28:18-20, Mark 16:15, and Luke 24:45-49.

ACTS 1

Startup: Picture yourself being present in the situation described in verses 6-11. In light of your own personality, what thoughts or questions would be in your mind after you heard the words in verse 11?

SEEING WHAT'S THERE

1. Acts is a book of many *actions.* What are the most important actions you see in this chapter?

2. Who are the people who play an important part in this chapter?

3. What are the most important things you know about the group of apostles in this chapter?

4. Bible teachers have considered the words of Jesus in verse 8 as a useful summary of the entire book of Acts. If Luke intended it to be so, what does this verse then tell us about his purpose for writing this book?

5. Look also at the list of "Questions to Ask as You Study Each Chapter" on page 392, which you may want to do for each chapter in Acts.

6. From the evidence you see in this chapter, how would you describe the nature of the resurrected body of Jesus Christ?

7. EYE FOR DETAIL—*If everyone in the group has read the entire chapter, try answering the following question without looking at your Bible:* As the disciples watched Jesus ascend into heaven, two men dressed in white appeared and spoke to them. What did these men call the disciples? (See verse 11.)

CAPTURE THE ESSENCE

8. In the following verses in John's gospel, look together at what Jesus said before He was crucified; then discuss how they find fulfillment in the events of this chapter—John 6:61-62, 14:2, 14:12, and 16:28.

9. At the end of verse 1, notice Luke's use of the word *began.* Since the content of Luke's first book continues to the end of Jesus' earthly ministry, what might this phrase indicate about Luke's purpose of this book of Acts?

10. Here in chapter 1, what appropriate *patterns* and *principles* do you see for worship or fellowship in the church today?

11. Picture the book of Acts as a fast-moving train. Chapter 1 is the locomotive in front, and the other chapters represent railway cars that follow behind. From what you see here in chapter 1, what is the *energy* in the locomotive—the point or principle or theme that's the driving force for the locomotive and the entire train?

FOR LIFE TODAY

12. Here in chapter 1, what appropriate *patterns* and *principles* do you see for leadership in the church today?

FOR GOING DEEPER

Verse 6 seems to reveal a fever of expectation among the disciples. Compare this verse with Daniel 7:27. What sorts of world events might they have been anticipating?

ACTS 2

Startup: In the way we read and study the Bible, what kind of mental habits can most easily block this book of Acts from coming alive in our minds and hearts?

SEEING WHAT'S THERE

1. Imagine you were helping to produce a film based on the book of Acts. To film the events recorded in chapter 2, summarize all the scenes to be included, and mention also any special kinds of scenery, background music, lighting effects, etc., that you would use to meaningfully portray the action.

2. Who are the people who play an important part in this chapter?

3. Which important details in this chapter do you think might be the easiest to overlook?

4. In what different ways does this chapter fulfill the words Jesus spoke about the church in Matthew 16:18?

5. EYE FOR DETAIL—*From what you recall seeing in this chapter, try answering the following question without looking at your Bible:* What time of day was it when Peter stood up with the Eleven and addressed the crowd gathered in this chapter? (See verse 15.)

CAPTURE THE ESSENCE

6. What to you is the strongest evidence that Jesus truly is alive?

7. In your own words, how would you summarize the *victory* the church achieved in this chapter, through the power of the Holy Spirit? How was it strategically important for the continued growth of the church?

FOR LIFE TODAY

8. In chapter 2, what appropriate *patterns* and *principles* do you see for evangelism in the church today?

9. Also in this chapter, what appropriate *patterns* and *principles* do you see for worship, for fellowship, and for meeting physical needs in the church today?

10. From what you see in this chapter, what is the appropriate basis for *unity* in the church today?

11. ACTION HERITAGE: What act or attitude of obedience in this chapter is the most meaningful example to you of what it means to follow Christ, through the power of the Holy Spirit?

FOR GOING DEEPER

Verses 46-47 speak of the way the infant church was viewed by a watching nation. How do you see the example of the believers here as a demonstration of the principle taught later by the apostle Paul in Romans 14:17-18?

ACTS 3

Startup: When you get to heaven, and you meet the crippled beggar who was healed by Peter and John, what's the first question you'd like to ask him?

SEEING WHAT'S THERE

1. Who are the people who play an important part in this chapter, and what do they do?

2. From what see in Acts, how would you evaluate Peter's spiritual gifts? (You may want to look at the lists of spiritual gifts in Romans 12:6-8, 1 Corinthians 12:7-11, Ephesians 4:11, and 1 Peter 4:10-11.

3. EYE FOR DETAIL—*From what you recall seeing in this chapter, try answering the following question without looking at your Bible:* What was the name of the temple gate where the crippled man was brought to sit and beg every day? (See verse 2.)

CAPTURE THE ESSENCE

4. How would you analyze the message which Peter gave in verses 12-26? How did it fit both his audience and his commission from the Lord to preach the gospel?

FOR LIFE TODAY

5. Here in chapter 3, what appropriate patterns and principles do you see for (a) evangelism in the church today, and (b) leadership in the church today?

6. ACTION HERITAGE: What act or attitude of obedience in this chapter is the most meaningful example to you of what it means to follow Christ, through the power of the Holy Spirit?

FOR GOING DEEPER

Consider verses 17-18, then look ahead to Acts 13:27. What extra "punch" does Paul add regarding the spiritual blindness of the Jewish leaders?

ACTS 4

Startup: If you were one of the believers present in the prayer meeting mentioned in verses 23-31, what words of prayer might you have added to those written here?

SEEING WHAT'S THERE

1. Who are the people who play an important part in this chapter?

2. Imagine again you were helping to produce a film based on the book of Acts. To film the events recorded in chapter 4, summarize all the scenes to be included, and mention also any special kinds of scenery, background music, lighting effects, etc., that you would use to meaningfully portray the action.

3. Acts is a book not only of many *actions,* but also many *reactions.* What happenings in this chapter could definitely be called reactions, and what is each one a reaction to?

4. EYE FOR DETAIL— *From what you recall seeing in this chapter, try answering the following question without looking at your Bible:* How many nights did Peter and John spend in jail in this chapter? (See verse 3.)

CAPTURE THE ESSENCE

5. In your own words, how would you summarize the *victory* the church achieved in this chapter, through the power of the Holy Spirit? How was it strategically important for the continued growth of the church?

FOR LIFE TODAY

6. In chapter 4, what appropriate *patterns* and *principles* do you see for evangelism in the church today?

7. Also in this chapter, what appropriate *patterns* and *principles* do you see for worship, for fellowship, and for meeting physical needs in the church today?

8. From the evidence you see in this chapter, what is the appropriate basis for *unity* in the church today?

9. ACTION HERITAGE: What act or attitude of obedience in this chapter is the most meaningful example to you of what it means to follow Christ, through the power of the Holy Spirit?

FOR GOING DEEPER

Compare Peter's bold charge in verses 11-12 with his teaching in 1 Peter 2:4-8. How is Christ's identity as "the cornerstone" both an encouragement for believers and a judgment for those who refuse to believe?

ACTS 5

Startup: Picture yourself being present in the situation described in verses 12-16. Using your imagination, talk about the kinds of sights, smells, sounds, and feelings you might experience.

SEEING WHAT'S THERE

1. Who are the people playing an important part in this chapter?

2. Here in Acts, a book of *action,* what are the most important actions you see in this chapter?

3. Acts is a book not only of many *actions,* but also many *reactions.* What happenings in this chapter could definitely be called reactions, and what is each one a reaction to?

4. EYE FOR DETAIL— *From what you recall seeing in this chapter, try answering the following question without looking at your Bible:* In this chapter, what place is mentioned as the meeting place of the believers? (See verse 12.)

CAPTURE THE ESSENCE

5. In your own words, how would you summarize the *victory* the church achieved in this chapter, through the power of the Holy Spirit? How was it strategically important for the continued growth of the church?

FOR LIFE TODAY

6. In chapter 5, what appropriate *patterns* and *principles* do you see for evangelism in the church today?

7. Also in this chapter, what appropriate *patterns* and *principles* do you see for leadership in the church today?

8. ACTION HERITAGE: What act or attitude of obedience in this chapter is the most meaningful example to you of what it means to follow Christ, through the power of the Holy Spirit?

FOR GOING DEEPER

Consider the Pharisee Gamaliel's remarkable words in verses 38-39 in light of Paul's declaration in Acts 22:3. When you realize who was most likely Gamaliel's most prized pupil at that time, what do you find ironic about his warning?

ACTS 6

Startup: Notice the concerns and complaints mentioned in the opening verse of this chapter. What's the last time you can recall complaining to this degree in *your* church?

SEEING WHAT'S THERE

1. Who are the people playing an important part in this chapter?

2. How is Stephen described in this chapter?

3. Here in Acts, a book of *action,* what are the most important actions you see in this chapter?

4. EYE FOR DETAIL— *From what you recall seeing in this chapter, try answering the following question without looking at your Bible:* Luke gives the names of all seven men who were chosen to supervise the church's ministry of food to widows, and for one of them, Nicolas, he also tells where he was from. Where was Nicolas from? (See verse 5.)

CAPTURE THE ESSENCE

5. In your own words, how would you summarize the *victory* the church achieved in this chapter, through the power of the Holy Spirit? How was it strategically important for the continued growth of the church?

FOR LIFE TODAY

6. Here in chapter 6, what appropriate *patterns* and *principles* do you see for leadership in the church today?

7. Also in this chapter, what appropriate *patterns* and *principles* do you see for meeting physical needs in the church today?

8. Look again at the descriptions of Stephen in verses 5 and 8. If a Christian today had these same qualities, how would you be able to tell? What practical differences would it make in this person's life?

9. ACTION HERITAGE: What act or attitude of obedience in this chapter is the most meaningful example to you of what it means to follow Christ, through the power of the Holy Spirit?

FOR GOING DEEPER

Reflect on the descriptions of Stephen in verses 10 and 15 in the context of Christ's promise in Luke 21:12-15. What was the dynamic behind Stephen's powerful witness?

ACTS 7

Startup: When you get to heaven, and you meet Stephen, what's the first question you'd like to ask him?

SEEING WHAT'S THERE

1. Who are the people playing an important part in this chapter?

2. Imagine again you were helping to produce a film based on the book of Acts. To film the events recorded in chapter 7, summarize all the scenes to be included, and mention also any special kinds of scenery, background music, lighting effects, etc., that you would use to meaningfully portray the action.

3. EYE FOR DETAIL— *From what you recall seeing in this chapter, try answering the following question without looking at your Bible:* For each of these Old Testament characters, tell whether or not his name is mentioned in Stephen's speech to the Sanhedrin: Noah, Abraham, Isaac, Jacob, Joseph, Moses, Aaron, Joshua, Samuel, David, Solomon, and Elijah. (See verses 8, 9, 20, 40, and 45-47.)

CAPTURE THE ESSENCE

4. From what you see in Acts, how would you describe Stephen's *spiritual gifts* and his *relationship with God?*

FOR LIFE TODAY

5. ACTION HERITAGE: Think again about Stephen's example in this chapter. What is it about his character and commitment that challenge you most?

FOR GOING DEEPER

Stephen's blistering indictment in verse 51 might well have reminded his listeners of the Lord's words to Israel in Jeremiah 4:4 and 9:26. As you look at those Old Testament verses, consider what that association might have done to make the Jewish leaders even angrier than they already were.

ACTS 8

Startup: When you get to heaven, and you meet the Ethiopian whom Philip spoke with, what's the first question you'd like to ask him?

SEEING WHAT'S THERE

1. Who are the people playing an important part in this chapter?

2. Once again, take a "walk" together through the incidents that happen in this chapter. Using your imagination, talk about the kinds of sights, smells, sounds, and feelings you might experience.

3. EYE FOR DETAIL— *From what you recall seeing in this chapter, try answering the following question without looking at your Bible:* Who buried Stephen? (See verse 2.)

CAPTURE THE ESSENCE

4. In your own words, how would you summarize the *victory* the church achieved in this chapter, through the power of the Holy Spirit? How was it strategically important for the continued growth of the church?

FOR LIFE TODAY

5. Here in chapter 8, what appropriate *patterns* and *principles* do you see for evangelism in the church today?

6. ACTION HERITAGE: What act or attitude of obedience in this chapter is the most meaningful example to you of what it means to follow Christ, through the power of the Holy Spirit?

FOR GOING DEEPER

In verse 3, look at the activities of Saul the persecutor; then refer to Paul the apostle's memories of those days in 1 Corinthians 15:9-10. How did Paul's earlier career impact his later one?

ACTS 9

Startup: When you get to heaven, and you meet Ananias, what's the first question you'd like to ask him?

SEEING WHAT'S THERE

1. Who are the people playing an important part in this chapter?

2. Imagine again you were helping to produce a film based on the book of Acts. To film the events recorded in chapter 9, summarize all the scenes to be included, and mention also any special kinds of scenery, background music, lighting effects, etc., that you would use to meaningfully portray the action.

3. Which important details in this chapter do you think might be the easiest to overlook?

4. EYE FOR DETAIL— *From what you recall seeing in this chapter, try answering the following question without looking at your Bible:* What did Ananias call Saul when he met him for the first time? (See verse 17.)

CAPTURE THE ESSENCE

5. In verse 16, notice what the Lord added in his words to Ananias about Saul. Why do you think the Lord mentioned this to Ananias?

6. In your own words, how would you summarize the *victory* the church achieved in this chapter, through the power of the Holy Spirit? How was it strategically important for the continued growth of the church?

FOR LIFE TODAY

7. ACTION HERITAGE: What act or attitude of obedience in this chapter is the most meaningful example to you of what it means to follow Christ, through the power of the Holy Spirit?

FOR GOING DEEPER

Read again verses 17-18. How might Saul's graphic experience in that instant have shaped his later teaching about the "natural man" and the "spiritual man" in 1 Corinthians 2:14-15?

ACTS 10

Startup: When you get to heaven, and you meet Cornelius, what's the first question you'd like to ask him?

SEEING WHAT'S THERE

1. Who are the people playing an important part in this chapter?

2. Once again, take a "walk" together through the incidents that happen in this chapter. Using your imagination, talk about the kinds of sights, smells, sounds, and feelings you might experience.

3. EYE FOR DETAIL— *From what you recall seeing in this chapter, try answering the following question without looking at your Bible:* What was the name of the military unit in which Cornelius served? (See verse 1.)

CAPTURE THE ESSENCE

4. From what you see in this chapter, how would you describe Peter's relationship with God?

5. From what you see in this chapter, how would you describe Cornelius's relationship with God?

FOR LIFE TODAY

6. In chapter 10, what appropriate *patterns* and *principles* do you see for evangelism in the church today?

7. ACTION HERITAGE: What act or attitude of obedience in this chapter is the most meaningful example to you of what it means to follow Christ, through the power of the Holy Spirit?

FOR GOING DEEPER

In what way did the occurrence in verses 44-46 provide Peter with the irrefutable "ammunition" he needed when we went before a somewhat skeptical Jerusalem church council in Acts 11:15-18?

ACTS 11

Startup: Notice the criticism directed at Peter in verses 2-3. When's the last time you've heard criticism to this degree in *your* church?

SEEING WHAT'S THERE

1. Who are the people playing an important part in this chapter, and what do they do?

3. EYE FOR DETAIL— *From what you recall seeing in this chapter, try answering the following question without looking at your Bible:* Who was the Roman emperor at the time of the worldwide famine which the prophet Agabus predicted? (See verse 28.)

CAPTURE THE ESSENCE

4. In your own words, how would you summarize the *victory* the church achieved in this chapter, through the power of the Holy Spirit? How was it strategically important for the continued growth of the church?

5. What impresses you most in the description of Barnabas in verses 23-24?

FOR LIFE TODAY

6. In chapter 11, what appropriate *patterns* and *principles* do you see for leadership in the church today?

7. ACTION HERITAGE: What act or attitude of obedience in this chapter is the most meaningful example to you of following Christ through the power of the Holy Spirit?

FOR GOING DEEPER

Take a moment to note the progression from verse 21 through verse 29. How, in God's providence, did the spiritual ministry of the church in Jerusalem end up as ministry to *themselves?* How do Paul's words in 2 Corinthians 9:6 help explain this phenomenon?

ACTS 12

Startup: When you get to heaven, and you meet the servant girl Rhoda mentioned in verse 13, what's the first question you'd like to ask her?

SEEING WHAT'S THERE

1. Who are the people playing an important part in this chapter?

2. Imagine again you were helping to produce a film based on the book of Acts. To film the events recorded in chapter 12, summarize all the scenes to be included, and mention also any special kinds of scenery, background music, lighting effects, etc., that you would use to meaningfully portray the action.

3. EYE FOR DETAIL— *From what you recall seeing in this chapter, try answering the following question without looking at your Bible:* What was the name of King Herod's servant who helped the people of Tyre and Sidon to win Herod's favor? (See verse 20.)

CAPTURE THE ESSENCE

4. In your own words, how would you summarize the *victory* the church achieved in this chapter, through the power of the Holy Spirit? How was it strategically important for the continued growth of the church?

5. Suppose you were reading this chapter with a new Christian, and he asked you, "Why did God allow James to be killed, and yet He rescued Peter?" How would you answer?

FOR LIFE TODAY

6. ACTION HERITAGE: What act or attitude of obedience in this chapter is the most meaningful example to you of following Christ through the power of the Holy Spirit?

FOR GOING DEEPER

Several Herods had extraordinary "close encounters" with the person and message of Jesus Christ. Compare the experiences of Herod the Great (Matthew 2:1-8 and 2:16), Herod Antipas (Mark 6:16-28), Herod Agrippa I (Acts 12:1-4 and 12:20-23), and Herod Agrippa II (Acts 25:23 and 26:1-30).

ACTS 13

Startup: If you were present in the prayer meeting described in verse 3, what requests might you offer up for Barnabas and Saul?

SEEING WHAT'S THERE

1. Who are the people playing an important part in this chapter?

2. Here in this book of *action,* how would you summarize the action in this chapter?

3. EYE FOR DETAIL— *From what you recall seeing in this chapter, try answering the following question without looking at your Bible:* What are the two names of the man on Cyprus who was struck blind at a word from Paul?

CAPTURE THE ESSENCE

4. In your own words, how would you summarize the *victory* the church achieved in this chapter, through the power of the Holy Spirit? How was it strategically important for the continued growth of the church?

5. Remember to look also at the list of "Questions to Ask as You Study Each Chapter" on page 392, which can help you explore each chapter in Acts.

FOR LIFE TODAY

6. In chapter 13, what appropriate *patterns* and *principles* do you see for evangelism in the church today?

7. Also in this chapter, what appropriate *patterns* and *principles* do you see for leadership in the church today?

8. ACTION HERITAGE: What act or attitude of obedience in this chapter is the most meaningful example to you of following Christ through the power of the Holy Spirit?

FOR GOING DEEPER

The jealousy and fierce opposition of the Jewish leaders surfaces in both Pisidian Antioch (verses 44-45), later in Iconium (14:1-2), and again and again in the book of Acts. Look over at 1 Thessalonians 2:14-16 for Paul's sobering view of those who sought to block the gospel from reaching heart-hungry Gentiles.

ACTS 14

Startup: Picture yourself being present in Lystra in the situation described in verses 8-18. In light of your own personality, what thoughts or questions would be in your mind after you heard the words of Paul and Barnabas in verse 15-17?

1. Who are the people playing an important part in this chapter?

2. Imagine again you were helping to produce a film based on the book of Acts. To film the events recorded in chapter 14, summarize all the scenes to be included, and mention also any special kinds of scenery, background music, lighting effects, etc., that you would use to meaningfully portray the action.

3. Which important details in this chapter do you think might be the easiest to overlook?

4. In a Bible atlas or on a Bible map of the Mediterranean world or Roman Empire in the first century A.D., trace the journey of Paul and his companions as recorded in Acts 13 and 14. Using the mileage scale, approximately how many miles did Paul travel on this journey?

5. EYE FOR DETAIL— *From what you recall seeing in this chapter, try answering the following question without looking at your Bible:* Luke mentions some Jews who stirred up the people of Lystra, resulting soon in Paul's being attacked and nearly killed. Where did these Jews come from? (See verse 19.)

CAPTURE THE ESSENCE

6. In verses 15-17, as Paul speaks to the people of Lystra, notice everything he says about God. What do you think is the significance of each point which he makes?

7. In your own words, how would you summarize the *victory* the church achieved in this chapter, through the power of the Holy Spirit? How was it strategically important for the continued growth of the church?

FOR LIFE TODAY

8. Here in chapter 14, what appropriate *patterns* and *principles* do you see for evangelism in the church today?

9. ACTION HERITAGE: What act or attitude of obedience in this chapter is the most meaningful example to you of following Christ through the power of the Holy Spirit?

FOR GOING DEEPER

Review the mind-boggling change of heart on the part of the crowds in Lystra (verses 18-19) in the light of the Lord's words in John 2:23-25. What do these passages reveal about human nature?

ACTS 15

Startup: When you get to heaven, and you meet Barnabas, what's the first question you'd like to ask him?

1. Who are the people playing an important part in this chapter?

2. Here in this book of *action,* how would you summarize the action in this chapter?

3. In the last two verses of this chapter, Paul sets out from Antioch on another missionary journey, this time with Silas. Use a map to trace this journey as recorded in Acts 15—18. From the time he left Antioch in Acts 15:40 until the time he returned to that city in Acts 18:22, approximately how many miles did Paul travel on this journey?

4. EYE FOR DETAIL—*From what you recall seeing in this chapter, try answering the following question without looking at your Bible:* Which one of these men is *not* mentioned in this chapter—Paul, Barnabas, Peter, James, Silas, Timothy, or John Mark? (See verse 1, 7, 13, 22, and 37.)

CAPTURE THE ESSENCE

5. From what you've seen in Acts 13—15, how would you describe Paul's *spiritual gifts* and his *relationship with God?*

6. In your own words, how would you summarize the *victory* the church achieved in this chapter, through the power of the Holy Spirit? How was it strategically important for the continued growth of the church?

FOR LIFE TODAY

7. Here in chapter 15, what appropriate *patterns* and *principles* do you see for leadership in the church today?

8. ACTION HERITAGE: What act or attitude of obedience in this chapter is the most meaningful example to you of following Christ through the power of the Holy Spirit?

FOR GOING DEEPER

The church cleared a crucial hurdle with the Jerusalem council's decision to exempt Gentile believers from circumcision and the Law of Moses. But this was an issue that refused to go away! Compare Peter's speech to the apostles and elders (verses 7-21) with Paul's strong words to the church in Galatia years later (Galatians 5:2-11). What similarities and differences do you see in these two strong arguments for salvation by grace alone?

ACTS 16

Startup: Imagine yourself as Paul's new helper Timothy on the morning after Paul's dream of the man from Macedonia calling for help. As Paul related this dream to you, what thoughts or questions would be in your mind?

SEEING WHAT'S THERE

1. Who are the people playing an important part in this chapter?

2. How would you summarize the *action* in this chapter?

3. How would you explain verse 31 to a child who heard you tell this Bible story, then told you he or she wanted to be saved?

4. EYE FOR DETAIL— *From what you recall seeing in this chapter, try answering the following question without looking at your Bible:* In a Sabbath gathering on the riverbank outside the city gate of Philippi, Paul and Silas met the woman Lydia, who opened her heart to the Lord's message. Lydia, however, was from somewhere other than Philippi. Where was she from? (See verse 14.)

CAPTURE THE ESSENCE

5. In your own words, how would you summarize the *victory* the church achieved in this chapter, through the power of the Holy Spirit? How was it strategically important for the continued growth of the church?

FOR LIFE TODAY

6. Here in chapter 16, what appropriate *patterns* and *principles* do you see for evangelism in the church today?

7. ACTION HERITAGE: What act or attitude of obedience in this chapter is the most meaningful example to you of following Christ through the power of the Holy Spirit?

FOR GOING DEEPER

Read verses 35-39, then compare them to Acts 22:22-30 and 25:9-12. What do you learn in these three passages about Paul's willingness to work within and through existing civil law structures to protect himself and advance the gospel?

ACTS 17

Startup: How would you explain the root cause of the Jewish opposition to Paul's message, as seen here in verses 5 and 13?

SEEING WHAT'S THERE

1. Who are the people playing an important part in this chapter?

2. Once again, take a "walk" together through the incidents of this chapter. Using your imagination, talk about the kinds of sights, smells, sounds, and feelings you might experience.

3. EYE FOR DETAIL— *From what you recall seeing in this chapter, try answering the following question without looking at your Bible:* For how many Sabbath days did Paul teach in the synagogue at Thessalonica, before the people in the city began to riot? (See verse 2.)

CAPTURE THE ESSENCE

4. In verse 11, Luke commends the Berean Christians for being "noble" or "noble-minded." If you had never heard that word before, what conclusions would you make about its meaning, based on what you see in this verse?

5. How would you summarize the *victory* the church achieved in this chapter, through the power of the Holy Spirit? How was it strategically important for the continued growth of the church?

FOR LIFE TODAY

6. Here in chapter 17, what appropriate *patterns* and *principles* do you see for evangelism in the church today?

7. ACTION HERITAGE: What act or attitude of obedience in this chapter is the most meaningful example to you of following Christ through the power of the Holy Spirit?

FOR GOING DEEPER

Consider again Paul's encounter with the Greek philosophers in verses 16-21 and verse 32. What perspective on that encounter do you gain from Paul's remarks to the Corinthian believers in 1 Corinthians 1:18-25?

ACTS 18

Startup: From what you see in verses 12-17, what kind of a man was Gallio?

SEEING WHAT'S THERE

1. Who are the people playing an important part in this chapter?

2. Make an action list together of all that happens in this chapter.

3. EYE FOR DETAIL— *From what you recall seeing in this chapter, try answering the following question without looking at your Bible:* How long did Paul stay in Corinth, teaching the word of God? (See verse 11.)

CAPTURE THE ESSENCE

4. From what you've seen in Acts, how would you explain *in your own words* what Paul considered to be his calling from God?

5. How would you summarize the *victory* the church achieved in this chapter, through the power of the Holy Spirit? How was it strategically important for the continued growth of the church?

FOR LIFE TODAY

6. Here in chapter 18, what appropriate *patterns* and *principles* do you see for evangelism in the church today?

7. ACTION HERITAGE: What act or attitude of obedience in this chapter is the most meaningful example to you of following Christ through the power of the Holy Spirit?

FOR GOING DEEPER

Apollos burst on the scene in Ephesus with a powerful message about Jesus Christ—that only went so far. Read verses 24-26 along with Luke 3:1-18 for an idea of what Apollos may have been declaring so forcefully in the synagogue.

ACTS 19

Startup: Look closely at verse 17. What do you think it would take for the same spiritual environment to be present in *your* community?

SEEING WHAT'S THERE

1. Who are the people playing an important part in this chapter?

2. Imagine again you were helping to produce a film based on Acts. To film the events in chapter 19, summarize all the scenes to be included, and mention also any special kinds of scenery, background music, lighting effects, etc., that you would use to meaningfully portray the action.

3. EYE FOR DETAIL— *Try answering the following question without looking at your Bible:* In the opening scene in this chapter, how many men in Ephesus did Paul baptize and lay his hands on? (See verse 7.)

CAPTURE THE ESSENCE

4. How would you summarize the *victory* the church achieved in this chapter, through the power of the Holy Spirit? How was it strategically important for the continued growth of the church?

FOR LIFE TODAY

5. ACTION HERITAGE: What act or attitude of obedience in this chapter is the most meaningful example to you of following Christ through the power of the Holy Spirit?

FOR GOING DEEPER

Ephesus, a first-century center for occult activity, was stunned by the incident in verses 11-17. Notice God's stern prohibitions against dabbling with magic in Deuteronomy 18:9-14. Discuss a Christian's appropriate response to modern occultic practices in our culture, in view of the Ephesian believers' reactions in Acts 19:18-20.

Acts 20

you of following Christ through the power of the Holy Spirit?

Startup: When you get to heaven, and you meet Eutychus, what's the first question you'd like to ask him?

FOR GOING DEEPER

SEEING WHAT'S THERE

1. Who are the people playing an important part in this chapter?

2. Once again, take a "walk" together through the incidents of this chapter. Using your imagination, talk about the kinds of sights, smells, sounds, and feelings you might experience.

3. EYE FOR DETAIL— *From what you recall seeing in this chapter, try answering the following question without looking at your Bible:* As Paul speaks to the Ephesian elders, he asks them to *remember* something specific. What was it? (See verse 31.)

CAPTURE THE ESSENCE

4. In your own words, how would you define Paul's basic *mindset* or *attitude* in life as you see it lived out in this chapter?

5. How would you summarize the *victory* the church achieved in this chapter, through the power of the Holy Spirit? How was it strategically important for the continued growth of the church?

FOR LIFE TODAY

6. In chapter 20, what appropriate *patterns* and *principles* do you see for leadership in the church today?

7. Imagine you saw earlier today a message written in fire in the sky. It was addressed to you by name, then continued with these words: *Thus saith the LORD: "Read Acts 20, for I have something for you there."* Which verses in this chapter do you think He most likely would be referring to?

8. ACTION HERITAGE: What act or attitude of obedience in this chapter is the most meaningful example to

Read again Paul's farewell encouragements and warnings to the Ephesian church elders in verses 18-32. Then, turn to the glorified Christ's personal letter to the church at Ephesus in Revelation 2:1-7. In view of the fact that the second passage was written many years later, what can you conclude about what the church learned—or did not learn—from Paul's earlier warnings?

ACTS 21

Startup: Picture yourself being present in the situation described in verses 10-14. In light of your own personality, what thoughts or questions would be in your mind after you heard both Agabus and Paul speak?

SEEING WHAT'S THERE

1. Who are the people playing an important part in this chapter?

2. How would you summarize the *action* in this chapter?

3. EYE FOR DETAIL— *From what you recall seeing in this chapter, try answering the following question without looking at your Bible:* What was the name of the prophet who tied his hands and feet with Paul's belt? (See verses 10-11.)

CAPTURE THE ESSENCE

4. Look again at verse 4, then discuss whether or not you believe it was wrong for Paul to have proceeded on to Jerusalem.

FOR LIFE TODAY

5. What principles for finding guidance from God do you see in Paul's experience in this chapter?

6. ACTION HERITAGE: What act or attitude of obedience in this chapter is the most meaningful example to you of following Christ through the power of the Holy Spirit?

FOR GOING DEEPER

The gift of prophecy was exercised by both women and men. Philip's four daughters were part of an elite company of distinguished female prophets. Look up the following Scriptures for a mural of those who prophesied before them— Exodus 15:20, Judges 4:4, 2 Kings 22:14, Nehemiah 6:14, and Luke 2:36-38.

ACTS 22

Startup: Picture yourself being present in the tense situation described in this chapter. Using your imagination, talk about the kinds of sights, smells, sounds, and feelings you might experience.

SEEING WHAT'S THERE

1. Who are the people playing an important part in this chapter?

2. Imagine you are an editor for the "Jerusalem Journal." What headline would you give to the story about what we see happening here in Acts 22?

3. EYE FOR DETAIL— *From what you recall seeing in this chapter, try answering the following question without looking at your Bible:* Before the crowd in Jerusalem, Paul tells of his encounter with Jesus on the road to Damascus. He mentions two questions that he asked Jesus in this encounter. What were those two questions? (See verses 8 and 10.)

CAPTURE THE ESSENCE

4. Notice at what point Paul's testimony was angrily interrupted by the crowd. How would you explain the cause of this interruption?

FOR LIFE TODAY

5. In chapter 22, what appropriate *patterns* and *principles* do you see for evangelism in the church today?

6. ACTION HERITAGE: What act or attitude of obedience in this chapter is the most meaningful example to you of following Christ through the power of the Holy Spirit?

FOR GOING DEEPER

Scripture does not say if Paul ever saw the Lord Jesus while He walked on earth as the God-man. Yet Paul saw an angel once, and the risen, glorified Christ again and again. Look up the following verses, and discuss what sorts of things Paul learned in these visions and divine encounters: Acts 9:3-7, 18:9-10, 22:17-21, 23:10-11, 26:14-18, 27:21-25, and 2 Corinthians 12:1-4.

Acts 23

Startup: When you get to heaven, and you meet Paul's nephew, what's the first question you'd like to ask him?

SEEING WHAT'S THERE

1. Who are the people playing an important part in this chapter?

2. How would you summarize the *action* in this chapter?

3. Which important details in this chapter do you think might be the easiest to overlook?

4. EYE FOR DETAIL—*From what you recall seeing in this chapter, try answering the following question without looking at your Bible:* What was the name of the Roman commander who sent Paul with a mounted guard to appear before Governor Felix in Caesarea? (See verse 26.)

CAPTURE THE ESSENCE

5. How would you summarize the *victory* the church achieved in this chapter, through the power of the Holy Spirit? How was it strategically important for the continued growth of the church?

FOR LIFE TODAY

6. What do you like most about Paul's example in this chapter?

7. ACTION HERITAGE: What act or attitude of obedience in this chapter is the most meaningful example to you of following Christ through the power of the Holy Spirit?

FOR GOING DEEPER

How does Deuteronomy 19:15-19 expand your understanding of Paul's sharp exchange with Ananias in verses 1-3?

ACTS 24

Startup: Suppose you were a lawyer in Caesarea, and suppose Governor Felix appointed you to be the defense attorney for Paul in another trial session that would follow the one described in this chapter. When you brought Paul to the witness stand, what kind of questions would you ask him?

SEEING WHAT'S THERE

1. Who are the people playing an important part in this chapter?

2. Imagine you are an editor for the "Caesarea Star" newspaper. What headline would you give to the story about what we see happening here in Acts 24?

3. EYE FOR DETAIL— *From what you recall seeing in this chapter, try answering the following question without looking at your Bible:* In the trial before Felix, what was the name of the lawyer who spoke for the Jewish leaders? (See verses 1-2.)

CAPTURE THE ESSENCE

4. Look again at verse 21. Why did Paul emphasize the resurrection in his self-defense?

FOR LIFE TODAY

5. Here in chapter 24, what appropriate *patterns* and *principles* do you see for evangelism in the church today?

6. Look at the standard Paul gives in verse 16. Then imagine God evaluating you on a scale of one to ten, in which ten equals full conformity to Paul's example in this verse, and one equals total nonconformity. What score do you think He would probably assign to you?

7. ACTION HERITAGE: What act or attitude of obedience in this chapter is the most meaningful example to you of following Christ through the power of the Holy Spirit?

FOR GOING DEEPER

What similarities do you see between Governor Felix's relationship with the prisoner Paul (verses 22-27) and Herod's relationship with the prisoner John in Mark 6:14-20?

ACTS 25

Startup: Picture yourself being present in the situation described in the last five verses of this chapter. Using your imagination, talk about the kinds of sights, smells, sounds, and feelings you might experience.

SEEING WHAT'S THERE

1. Who are the people playing an important part in this chapter?

2. Here in Acts, a book of *action,* make an action list of what happens in this chapter.

3. From what you see in the words of Festus in verses 24-27, exactly why was Paul appearing before King Agrippa?

4. EYE FOR DETAIL— *From what you recall seeing in this chapter, try answering the following question without looking at your Bible:* Why did Festus ask Paul if he was willing to stand trial in Jerusalem? (See verses 3 and 9.)

CAPTURE THE ESSENCE

5. How would you summarize the *victory* the church achieved in this chapter, through the power of the Holy Spirit? How was it strategically important for the continued growth of the church?

6. How do you see the *power* of Paul's personality coming through in this chapter? And how would you explain the source of it?

FOR LIFE TODAY

7. How would you compare the force of your own personality with that of Paul's? Does God desire everyone to have the same degree of spiritual power Paul did? Why or why not?

8. ACTION HERITAGE: What act or attitude of obedience in this chapter is the most meaningful example to you of following Christ through the power of the Holy Spirit?

FOR GOING DEEPER

Examine Paul's statement in verse 8 in light of his directive to the Roman believers in Romans 13:1-7.

ACTS 26

Startup: How would you define the structure of Paul's testimony here? Is it a "Before-I-Met-Christ, How-I-Met-Christ, After-I-Met-Christ" approach, or something different?

SEEING WHAT'S THERE

1. Who are the people playing an important part in this chapter?

2. In his testimony before King Agrippa, what is the only question Paul asked the king?

3. Imagine you were one of King Agrippa's officials, and you were present in the situation described in this chapter. What words spoken by Paul here would stand out most to you, and why?

4. EYE FOR DETAIL— *From what you recall seeing in this chapter, try answering the following question without looking at your Bible:* In his testimony before King Agrippa, Paul says what language Jesus used to speak to him on the road to Damascus. What language was it? (See verse 14.)

CAPTURE THE ESSENCE

5. What do you think caused Festus to say what he did in verse 24?

FOR LIFE TODAY

6. Here in chapter 26, what appropriate *patterns* and *principles* do you see for evangelism in the church today?

7. ACTION HERITAGE: What act or attitude of obedience in this chapter is the most meaningful example to you of following Christ through the power of the Holy Spirit?

FOR GOING DEEPER

In what way might the responses of Agrippa and Festus to Paul's message (verses 24-28) have been illustrative of the apostle's words in 1 Corinthians 1:22-24?

ACTS 27

Startup: Picture yourself as one of the sailors on the ship in this chapter. In light of your own personality, what thoughts or questions would be in your mind after you heard Paul's words in verses 21-26?

SEEING WHAT'S THERE

1. Who are the people playing an important part in this chapter?

2. Imagine again you were helping to produce a film based on the book of Acts. To film the events recorded in chapter 27, summarize all the scenes to be included, and mention also any special kinds of scenery, background music, lighting effects, etc., that you would use to meaningfully portray the action.

3. EYE FOR DETAIL— *From what you recall seeing in this chapter, try answering the following question without looking at your Bible:* How many people were on board the ship that was wrecked? (See verse 37.)

CAPTURE THE ESSENCE

4. Look closely at verse 24. What fears do you think Paul might have been experiencing?

FOR LIFE TODAY

5. In chapter 27, what appropriate *patterns* and *principles* do you see for evangelism in the church today?

6. ACTION HERITAGE: What act or attitude of obedience in this chapter is the most meaningful example to you of following Christ through the power of the Holy Spirit?

FOR GOING DEEPER

Compare verses 13-44 with the "sea storm song" in Psalm 107:23-32. Using these two passages, what encouragement could you offer to Christians enduring frightening storms in their lives?

ACTS 28

Startup: Imagine being one of the Romans in verse 15 who went out to meet Paul as he approached the city. After exchanging greetings, and joining Paul in his prayer of thanksgiving, you ask him, "Paul, how was your trip?" How do you think he would answer?

SEEING WHAT'S THERE

1. Who are the people playing an important part in this chapter, and what do they do?

2. EYE FOR DETAIL— *From what you recall seeing in this chapter, try answering the following question without looking at your Bible:* How long did Paul and his companions stay on the island of Malta until continuing their journey to Rome? (See verse 11.)

CAPTURE THE ESSENCE

3. How would you summarize the *victory* the church achieved in this chapter, through the power of the Holy Spirit? How was it strategically important for the continued growth of the church?

FOR LIFE TODAY

4. In chapter 28, what appropriate *patterns* and *principles* do you see for evangelism in the church today?

5. ACTION HERITAGE: What act or attitude of obedience in this chapter is the most meaningful example to you of following Christ through the power of the Holy Spirit?

FOR GOING DEEPER

In what ways did the Lord allow Paul's expressed desire in Romans 1:9-12 (written ten years before his actual visit) to be fulfilled in his ministry among the Romans? (Here in Acts 28, notice verses 14-15, 23-24, and 30).

ACTS:

THE BIG PICTURE

(Discuss again the questions in the "Overview," plus the questions below.)

1. Look together at each of these verses, and discuss which one you believe is the best candidate for "KEY VERSE" in the book of Acts—the one which brings into sharpest focus what this book is most about: 1:8, 2:42-43, 4:32-33, 12:24 or 20:32.

2. What are biggest ways you've seen the Holy Spirit's *power* in this book?

3. Suppose that at the very end of Acts, Luke added this line: "If you remember only one thing from this historical account, let it be this:…" How do you think Luke would complete that sentence?

4. In James 1:23-24 we're told that "anyone who listens to the word but does not do what it says is like a man who looks at his face in a mirror and, after looking at himself, goes away and immediately forgets what he looks like." In what ways has the book of Acts been a "mirror" for you—showing you what you can and should do?

5. If you've decided on a starting point for applying something in this book more effectively to your life, what commitment would you be willing to make to others in your group regarding this?

6. How would you complete the following word of advice to growing Christians? *Explore the book of Acts if you want to learn more about...*

Romans

OVERVIEW

(Discuss these OVERVIEW questions both at the beginning of your study of Romans, and again after you've studied together all sixteen chapters. Your answers may change significantly once you've looked more closely at the entire book.)

Startup: What comes to your mind when you think of the ancient city of Rome?

SEEING WHAT'S THERE

1. Look together at these verses in the book of Acts, and discuss what you see there about Paul's personal attachment to Rome: Acts 19:21, 23:11, 28:14-16, and 28:30-31.

2. What details about Paul and the Romans can be learned from Romans 15:23-24?

3. By looking at the evidence in the following verses in Romans, decide together whether you think the church in Rome consisted mostly of Gentiles, mostly of Jews, or a fairly even mixture of each: 1:13, 2:17, 3:1, 4:1, 7:1, 10:1, 11:13, 11:25-31, 15:5-12, and 15:15-16. (Look also in Acts 2:10-11, and notice that visitors from Rome were among those who heard the first Christian sermon preached by Simon Peter in Jerusalem on the day the Holy Spirit came at Pentecost.)

4. What else do you learn about the church at Rome in these verses— 1:8, and 15:14?

5. Many Bible scholars think Paul wrote the letter to the Romans while he was in Greece for three months near the end of his third missionary journey. Look at the description of this time period in Acts 20:1-6. From what you see in this passage in Acts, what matters might well be occupying Paul's thoughts at this time?

6. Look also at the list of "Questions to Ask as You Begin Your Study of Each Book" on page 393.

CAPTURE THE ESSENCE

7. What have been your previous impressions about the book of Romans, in regard to (a) its content, (b) its level of difficulty, and (c) its importance?

8. Take a quick look together at only the *first three verses* in each chapter in Romans. What impressions and expectations of this book do you get from this partial scan?

9. Imagine you were the person carrying this letter from Paul to Rome. Along the way, you were attacked by a band of robbers who stripped you of all your valuables, including this letter. The leader of the robber band could not read, and when you asked him to return the letter, he replied, "Why? What's in it that's so important?" How would you answer him?

FOR LIFE TODAY

10. At this point in your life, how strong is your desire to study more thoroughly the great Christian doctrines of our salvation, which Paul teaches in the book of Romans? Use a scale of one to ten (one = "extremely

weak," ten = "extremely powerful")
to help you decide.

11. Many great blessings of Christian experience are taught with clarity and power in the book of Romans. Among them are *joy, peace, hope,* and *victory.* On a scale of one to ten (one is low, ten is high), identify how strongly you feel you're experiencing each one of these four qualities at this point in your life.

12. How can you ensure that your study of Romans is not merely theoretical and intellectual, but is instead truly practical and relevant? Talk together about this. What can you do to help keep the process alive and interesting?

FOR GOING DEEPER

Romans 3:10, 3:23, 5:12, 6:23, 5:8, 10:9-10, and 10:13 are often called the "Roman Road" to salvation, because of the help they offer in guiding a person into a saving relationship with Christ. Explore these verses and determine together how clearly they communicate the gospel.

ROMANS 1

Startup: What do you consider the three most important ingredients for being happy in today's world?

SEEING WHAT'S THERE

1. From what you see in verses 1-6, describe as fully as you can Paul's view of himself.

2. From what you see in verses 8-15, what were Paul's deepest motives for wanting to visit Rome?

3. After identifying (in verses 8-15) Paul's reasons for wanting to visit the Romans, do you think he could have accomplished these desires just as well through this letter? (Explain your answer.)

4. Look at the passage beginning with verse 16, and explain in your own words exactly *why* Paul was not ashamed of the gospel.

5. In verse 17, Paul uses the word *righteousness.* Including what you see here in this chapter, what do you know about the meaning of this biblical term?

6. In verse 18, what is "the wrath of God" which Paul says is being revealed from heaven?

7. From what you see in verses 18-20, how would you describe in your own words what God has revealed about Himself to all people everywhere?

8. How would you summarize what verses 21-32 tell us about human nature?

9. How complete would you say is the list of sinful actions in verses 29-31?

10. Paul's letter to the Romans is often considered to be the most orderly and systematic presentation of Christian doctrine in the Bible. With that in mind, how would you summarize the main point or points of this chapter, and how would you say they

fit into what you know of Paul's overall purpose for the book?

11. Look also at the list of "Questions to Ask as You Study Each Chapter" on page 392, which you may want to do for each chapter in Romans.

12. EYE FOR DETAIL—*If everyone in the group has read the entire chapter, try answering the following question without looking at your Bible:* Only one person from the Old Testament is named in this chapter. Who is he? (See verse 3.)

CAPTURE THE ESSENCE

13. Which "side" of God's character would you say comes through most strongly in this chapter—His wrath and holiness, or His love and mercy?

14. From what you see in this chapter, how would you describe Paul's passion for life?

15. What impressions does this chapter give you about Paul's character as a man?

16. Imagine yourself looking over Paul's shoulder as he wrote the words of this chapter, under the direction of the Holy Spirit's inner guidance. What emotions do you think he most likely experienced as he wrote verses 18-32?

17. For what possible reasons do you think Paul included so many specific sins in the last part of this chapter, instead of simply saying that people turned away from God and sinned, then going on to chapter 2?

18. Look in 2 Peter 3:15-16 at what the apostle Peter says about Paul's letters, and their theme of *the Lord's patience.* How do you see this theme coming through in this chapter?

FOR LIFE TODAY

19. How would you summarize what the truth of verse 6 means for you on a practical and personal level?

20. Look in verse 8 at Paul's mention of the "famous faith" of the Roman Christians. What do you think it would take for a church today to become famous for its faith?

21. Paul writes in verses 11-12 about what he wants to happen when he gets together with the Romans. How would you say this compares with what happens when *you* get together as a group of Christians with a pastor or teacher?

22. Looking again at Paul's perspective on fellowship in verses 11-12, what can most easily *prevent* this from happening when Christians get together today?

23. Paul speaks in verse 13 of his own personal "harvest" or "fruit" which he seeks among the Roman Christians. What kind of personal "harvest" or "fruit" do you think would be right for us to seek among our Christian brothers and sisters today?

24. Discuss together the ways in which Christians today can show that they feel exactly as Paul does in verse 16.

25. In what ways would you say verse 32 accurately describes non-Christians today?

FOR GOING DEEPER

Discuss together a definition of *evil,* as you compare the list of sinful deeds and qualities in verses 29-31 with the lists you see in these passages—Mark 7:21-22; 1 Corinthians 6:9-10; Galatians 5:19-21; and Revelation 22:15.

ROMANS 2

Startup: What aspects of reality do you think people today find it hardest to accept and face up to?

1. Paul uses a question-and-answer format throughout the book of Romans as he explores the profound meaning of the gospel for us. Scan this chapter, and together, list aloud the *questions* Paul asks.

2. After reading through this chapter, which words or phrases or sentences here would you most like to understand better?

3. Look together at Matthew 7:1-5. Then discuss together how closely the words of Jesus in this passage fit with what Paul says in the opening verses of Romans 2.

4. What people would you say qualify to be included in the category which Paul describes in verses 7 and 10?

5. What people would you say qualify to be included in the category which Paul describes in verses 8 and 9?

6. Who exactly are the two kinds of people Paul speaks of in verse 12?

7. Focus again on this book's reputation as the most orderly and systematic presentation of Christian doctrine in the Bible. How would you summarize the main point or points of this chapter, and how would you say they fit into what you know of Paul's overall purpose for the book?

8. EYE FOR DETAIL— *From what you recall seeing in this chapter, try answering the following question without looking at your Bible:* Paul says in verse 4 that the riches of God's goodness—His kindness, forbearance, and patience—are meant to lead us toward one thing. What is it?

9. Which "side" of God's character would you say comes through most strongly in this chapter—His wrath and holiness, or His love and mercy?

10. According to Paul's definition of a true Jew in verses 28-29, can a Gentile become one also?

11. What would you say we can learn about our basic human nature, as created by God, in verses 14-15?

12. If a non-Christian friend said to you, "I'm not sure there really is such thing as sin," how could you use Romans 1 and 2 to help you respond to him?

13. Look again in 2 Peter 3:15-16 at what Peter says about Paul's letters, and their theme of *the Lord's patience.* How do you see this theme coming through in this chapter? And why is this theme so important?

Review what Paul says about true circumcision in the last five verses in this chapter. Then discuss the importance of this concept throughout the Bible as you look together at these verses— Deuteronomy 10:16 and 30:6, Jeremiah 4:3-4, and Genesis 17:9-14.

ROMANS 3

Startup: If you were on an isolated island with two other survivors from a shipwreck, both of whom were total strangers to you, what qualities would you most want them to have?

SEEING WHAT'S THERE

1. Noting again Paul's question-and-answer format throughout the book of Romans, what are the *questions* he asks in this chapter?

2. After reading through this chapter, which words or phrases or sentences here would you most like to understand better?

3. With verses 1-2 in mind, look ahead also to 9:4-5. How would you summarize in your own words the benefits of being Jewish?

4. How would you summarize in your own words what verses 10-18 tell us about human nature?

5. What exactly is the "glory of God" which human beings fall short of, as Paul describes in verse 23?

6. In verse 24, Paul writes that we are "justified." Including what you see here in this chapter, what do you know about the meaning of this biblical term?

7. Exactly *how* does verse 24 say that we are "justified"?

8. Another key word in verse 24 is *redemption.* In your own words, how would you explain what this term means?

9. How would you explain verse 24 to a small child?

10. From the evidence you see in verse 25, express in your own words what Paul wants us most to understand about Jesus.

11. From what you've seen so far in Romans, how are Jews and Gentiles alike, and how are they different?

12. From what you've seen so far in the book of Romans, why do we *need* righteousness?

13. Focus again on this book's reputation as the most orderly and systematic presentation of Christian doctrine in the Bible. How would you summarize the main point or points of this chapter, and how do they fit into what you know of Paul's overall purpose for the book?

14. EYE FOR DETAIL— *From what you recall seeing in this chapter, try answering the following question without looking at your Bible:* In the middle of this chapter, Paul quotes a collection of Old Testament passages that show the power of sin over all human beings. One of these quotations compares our *throats* to something. What is it? (See verse 13.)

CAPTURE THE ESSENCE

15. Which "side" of God's character would you say comes through most strongly in this chapter—His wrath and holiness, or His love and mercy?

16. From the evidence in chapters 2 and 3, who would you say Paul considered to be the worst sinners in general—Jews or Gentiles? (Explain your answer.)

17. From what you see in verses 21-26, give a summary explanation of how Jesus takes away the guilt of our sins.

18. Notice how often the word *faith* appears in verses 21-30. From the evidence you see in this chapter, how do you think Paul would define this word?

19. What do you think were Paul's reasons for saying what he does in verse 31?

20. In 1:16, Paul describes the gospel as "the power of God" for our salvation. How do you see that power on display in what Paul teaches in this chapter?

21. Discuss how much you agree or disagree with this statement: As a description of humanity as we know it today, verses 10-18 are primarily an exaggeration intended to make a point.

22. If you had only this chapter in Scripture to refer to, how would you use it to help show someone how to become a Christian?

23. How could you use the last part of this chapter to help an unsaved friend who felt he lived a good enough life already, and didn't need to believe in Christ?

24. How could you use this chapter to help an unsaved friend who felt he was too sinful for God to accept him?

FOR GOING DEEPER

Focus again on the crucial importance in this chapter of the word *faith*. Then look together at the following verses from other letters of Paul, and decide together what you feel is the best way to define this term from Paul's perspective, using your own words—1 Corinthians 2:4-5 and 15:16-17, 2 Corinthians 4:13-14, Galatians 5:5-6, Ephesians 2:8, and 2 Timothy 4:7.

ROMANS 4

Startup: What's the most hopeless situation you can recall ever being in?

SEEING WHAT'S THERE

1. Again with Paul's question-and-answer format in mind, what are the *questions* he asks in this chapter?

2. After reading through this chapter, which words or phrases or sentences here would you most like to understand better?

3. For helpful background on this chapter, look at the narratives about Abraham in Genesis 15 and 17-18. How do you see Abraham demonstrating his faith in those passages?

4. Notice the description of God which Paul gives at the end of verse 17. How would you explain this description to a child?

5. In what ways does the *personality* of Abraham come through in this chapter…and how would you compare it with Paul's personality?

6. Keep in mind again this book's reputation as the most orderly and systematic presentation of Christian doctrine in the Bible. How would you summarize the main point or points of this chapter, and how would you say they fit into Paul's overall purpose for the book?

7. EYE FOR DETAIL—*From what you recall seeing in this chapter, try answering the following question without looking at your Bible:* After describing how Abraham was made strong in his faith and gave glory to God, Paul tells us that Abraham was "fully persuaded" or "fully assured" of something very specific about God. What was it?

CAPTURE THE ESSENCE

8. The word *righteousness* appears often in this chapter, and many Bible teachers consider it the most impor-

tant word in the book of Romans. From the evidence you see in this chapter, how do you think Paul would define this word?

9. If you had only Abraham's example in this chapter to go by, how would you define the word *faith?*

10. Focus your mind on what you've seen so far in the book of Romans about *righteousness* and about *faith.* If you were to look at human beings from God's perspective, what would you say is the relationship between *righteousness* and *faith?*

11. Look at Abraham's example of faith as summarized by Paul in verses 20-21. What do you think were the chief reasons Abraham was able to grow strong in his faith?

12. Recall again how Paul described the gospel as "the power of God" for our salvation (1:16). How do you see that power on display in what Paul teaches in this chapter?

FOR LIFE TODAY

13. How could you use verses 5-8 to offer encouragement to a Christian brother who was afraid of losing his salvation because of a sin he had recently committed?

14. From what you see in this chapter, what are the most important ways in which Christians today are like Abraham? What are the most important ways in which we are different from him?

15. In Philippians 4:8 we're given the following command: "Whatever is true, whatever is noble, whatever is right, whatever is pure, whatever is lovely, whatever is admirable—if anything is excellent or praiseworthy—*think about such things.*" What food for thought can you find in this chapter that especially strikes you as being *true,* or *noble,* or *right,* or *pure,* or *lovely,* or *admirable,* or *excellent,* or *praiseworthy?*

16. Reflect together on verses 16-17. What does it mean to you *personally* to be a son or daughter of Abraham?

FOR GOING DEEPER

Another New Testament passage which focuses on Abraham is found in James 2:14-26. Review the main points James makes there, and compare them with what Paul says here in Romans 4. How do you see these passages as either *conflicting,* or *complementary?*

ROMANS 5

Startup: What is one significant area in which you want to grow personally in the next several months?

SEEING WHAT'S THERE

1. After reading through this chapter, which words or phrases or sentences here would you most like to understand better?

2. Define as fully as you can what Paul means when he speaks of "peace with God" in verse 1.

3. What exactly is our "hope of the glory of God" that Paul mentions in verse 2, and how does this meaning compare with what Paul says in 3:23?

4. Notice together verse 3. Why do you think Paul, for the first time in this book, introduces now the fact of our "sufferings" or "tribulations"?

5. Determine together which one of the following statements you regard as the best paraphrase of what Paul says at the beginning of verse 3—(a) "We rejoice *in spite of* our sufferings"; (b) "We rejoice *because of* our sufferings"; (c) "We rejoice *in the midst of* our sufferings."

6. What kind of *death* is Paul speaking of in verse 12?

7. Compare verses 12, 15, and 18, which together speak of Adam and Jesus, and what each one did. Let the words in these verses form a picture of each man in your mind, then describe that picture.

8. What exactly is "the gift" Paul speaks of in verses 15-17? (Describe it in your own words.)

9. Look carefully at each phrase in verse 17, where Paul says that those who receive God's rich grace and the gift of righteousness will actually "reign in life." Describe as fully as you can what Paul meant by this.

10. Keep in mind again this book's reputation as the most orderly and systematic presentation of Christian doctrine in the Bible. How would you summarize the main point or points of this chapter, and how would you say they fit into Paul's overall purpose for the book?

11. EYE FOR DETAIL— *From what you recall seeing in this chapter, try answering the following question without looking at your Bible:* In verse 5, Paul speaks of something that has been "poured out into our hearts" or "shed abroad in our hearts" by the Holy Spirit. What is it?

CAPTURE THE ESSENCE

12. Look again at the progression described in verses 3-4. Would you agree that this is the *only* pathway to hope?

13. If verse 5 was the only Scripture portion you had, how much could you conclude about who the Holy Spirit is, and what His ministry is?

14. Why do you think God uses the word *enemies* in verse 10?

15. Discuss how much you agree or disagree with this statement: "Although non-Christians are the enemies of God, God is not *their* enemy."

16. Paul mentions our "rejoicing" or "exulting" first in verses 2-3, then again in verse 11. How much importance would you say Paul attaches to this concept, and why?

17. If this chapter was the only Scripture portion you had, what would you conclude from it about how important it was for Jesus Christ to die?

18. Which "side" of God's character would you say comes through most strongly in this chapter—His wrath and holiness, or His love and mercy?

19. Taking the evidence in this chapter alone, summarize in your own words

what Paul wants us most to understand about Jesus.

20. Recall again how Paul described the gospel as "the power of God" for our salvation (1:16). How do you see that power on display in what Paul teaches in this chapter?

FOR LIFE TODAY

21. In Colossians 3:1 we read this command: "Since, then, you have been raised with Christ, set your hearts on things above, where Christ is seated at the right hand of God." What have you personally observed about Jesus Christ in this chapter that would be worthy of setting your heart on?

22. Consider again Paul's words in verse 17 about "reigning in life." What can prevent Christians today from experiencing the kind of life Paul speaks of?

23. Again with verse 17 in mind, what would you identify as the most important areas of life in which you need to "reign" in victory through Christ?

24. Were you ever one of God's "enemies," as Paul puts it in verse 10? Why or why not?

25. If you had only this chapter in Scripture to refer to, how would you use it to help show someone how to become a Christian?

FOR GOING DEEPER

Fix in mind the major points Paul makes in this chapter about Adam and Jesus Christ; then discuss together how they amplify the portrayals of these two men given in these passages—Genesis 2:15-17 and 3:1-20; Mark 10:45 and 14:22-24; and John 3:16-17.

ROMANS 6

Startup: What positive and negative connotations come to your mind when you think of the term *doctrine?*

SEEING WHAT'S THERE

1. Once again, what are the *questions* Paul asks in this chapter?

2. After reading through this chapter, which words or phrases or sentences here would you most like to understand better?

3. If you had only verses 3-4 to go by, how would you explain the meaning of *baptism?*

4. How real is our own burial and death which Paul speaks of in verse 4?

5. Paul speaks in verse 5 of how we are united with Jesus in both His death and His resurrection. Discuss together how *real* this union with Jesus is in each of these areas—*physically, emotionally, mentally,* and *spiritually.*

6. Remember again this book's reputation as the most systematic presentation of Christian doctrine in the Bible. How would you summarize the main point or points of this chapter, and how would you say they fit into Paul's overall purpose for the book?

7. EYE FOR DETAIL—*From what you recall seeing in this chapter, try answering the following question without looking at your Bible:* Paul says that all who were baptized into Christ Jesus were baptized into...*what?* (See verse 3.)

CAPTURE THE ESSENCE

8. From what you see in the first part of this chapter, how would you explain the relationship between *baptism* and *faith?*

9. Picture in your mind two Christians, one who has learned to obey the command we are given in verse 11,

and one who has not learned how to do it. What practical differences do you see in the way these two persons live?

10. Look at all the commands given in verses 11-13. Discuss where you believe successful obedience to these commands actually begins—mostly in your *mind,* mostly in your *habits,* or mostly in your *words?*

11. Look at the two contrasting kinds of slavery Paul speaks of in verses 15-18. Is it possible for a person to be participating in both kinds of slavery at the same time? Explain your answer.

12. What might you conclude about the power of sin—and even about the tactics of Satan—from what you read in this chapter?

13. Paul speaks of "the wages of sin" in verse 23. When he presents the opposite, however, he does not talk about "wages from God," but about a "gift." Discuss why this is so. (Refer also to Romans 4:4 to help you answer.)

14. To what degree can you see both "sides" of God's character in this chapter—His wrath and holiness on one side, and His love and mercy on the other? And which "side" would you say comes through most strongly?

15. Think again about what Paul says in 5:17 about "reigning in life." How would you say this chapter expands and explains the meaning of that phrase?

16. Look once more in 2 Peter 3:15-16 at what Peter says about Paul's letters, and their theme of *the Lord's patience.* How do you see this theme coming through in this chapter?

17. Look at everything Paul says in 2 Corinthians 5:21. Which parts of this verse, if any, are *not* reflected also in what you've seen so far in Paul's letter to the Romans? How well do you think this verse would serve as a summary statement for Romans 1-6?

18. Taking the evidence in this chapter alone, summarize in your own words what Paul wants us most to understand about Jesus.

19. Recall once more how Paul described the gospel as "the power of God" for our salvation (1:16). How do you see that power on display in what Paul teaches in this chapter?

FOR LIFE TODAY

20. Look at the newness of life which Paul speaks of in verse 4. What has been a meaningful example of this newness in your own life?

21. If God had written this chapter only for *you,* which words or phrases do you think He would have underlined?

22. If everyone in your group thoroughly understood this chapter, and you all had a passion for living out its truth in your lives, what kind of practical changes do you think would result?

23. If a Christian friend confessed a recurring sin to you, then asked you, "How can I get free of this sin in my life?" what help could you offer from Romans 6?

FOR GOING DEEPER

Review the content of this chapter once more, and offer as many answers as you can to this question: What has God done about our sin?

ROMANS 7

Startup: Talk together about your greatest frustrations and your greatest "breakthroughs" in the past week.

SEEING WHAT'S THERE

1. Once more, make a list aloud of the *questions* Paul asks in this chapter.

2. After reading through this chapter, which words or phrases or sentences here would you most like to understand better?

3. As this chapter begins, Paul continues the themes he was developing in chapter 6. Notice the death which he speaks of in verse 4 and 6. From Paul's perspective—and from God's—why is this death so important?

4. What kind of "fruit" would you say Paul is speaking of at the end of verse 4?

5. Notice the subject Paul begins to address in verse 7. What might lead some Christians to say that the law is actually sin?

6. Keeping in mind this book's reputation as the most systematic presentation of Christian doctrine in the Bible, how would you summarize the main point or points of this chapter, and how do they fit into Paul's overall purpose for the book?

7. EYE FOR DETAIL— *From what you recall seeing in this chapter, try answering the following question without looking at your Bible:* Near the end of this chapter, after Paul exclaims, "O wretched man that I am!" he asks this question: Who will rescue me (or "deliver me" or "set me free") from…*what?* (See verse 24.)

CAPTURE THE ESSENCE

8. If this chapter was the only Scripture portion you had, what would you conclude from it about how important it was for Jesus Christ to die?

9. As he speaks about sin and breaking the law of God, Paul in verses 7-8 chooses the very last of the Ten Commandments as an example. What significance, if any, do you see in this choice?

10. Look at the perspective on sin that Paul gives at the end of verse 13. Do you think he is speaking primarily of God's viewpoint here, or the viewpoint of Christians? (Explain your answer.)

11. Review the experiences Paul describes in verses 13-25, then discuss together your opinions on each of these interpretations of this passage: (a) These experiences happened *before* Paul became a Christian; (b) These experiences happened *after* Paul became a Christian; (c) These experiences are primarily Paul's illustration of what all Christians would be doomed to if we did not have the power of Christ and the power of the Holy Spirit to help us overcome sin.

12. Imagine yourself looking over Paul's shoulder as he wrote the words of this chapter, under the direction of the Holy Spirit's inner guidance. What emotions do you think he most likely experienced as he wrote verses 14-25?

13. From what you see in this chapter, would you say our most important battle with evil is fought against *specific sins,* or against the *sin nature* in general?

14. Discuss how much you agree or disagree with this statement: From what Paul teaches in the book of Romans, sin can be overcome if we'll only demonstrate the necessary willpower.

FOR LIFE TODAY

15. If a Christian friend confessed a recurring sin to you, then asked you, "How can I get free of this sin in my

life?" what help could you offer from Romans 7?

16. How might you use this chapter in a discussion with a non-Christian friend who believed human nature is inherently good?

FOR GOING DEEPER

Look together at the way Jesus described the ministry of the Holy Spirit in John 16:5-11. How would you compare the words of Jesus with what Paul teaches in Romans 7?

ROMANS 8

Startup: In the way we read and study the Bible, what kind of mental habits can most easily block this book of Romans from coming alive in our minds and hearts?

SEEING WHAT'S THERE

1. After reading through this chapter, which words or phrases or sentences here would you most like to understand better?

2. After seeing in chapter 7 how powerful sin can be, what keys do you see in chapter 8 for breaking sin's power?

3. What are the biggest *promises* which you see God making to us in chapter 8?

4. Picture verses 5-11 in your mind as a before-and-after comparison. What images do you see on the "before" side? And what do you see on the "after" side?

5. In verse 9 Paul speaks of "the Spirit of God" living in you, while in the next verse he speaks of "Christ" being in you. Discuss whether you think Paul means the same thing by these two phrases.

6. Paul begins speaking in verse 12 of an *obligation* we have. Imagine this obligation being expressed in the form of a brief contract agreement. How do you think this contract should be worded?

7. In verse 28 Paul mentions God's *purpose* for us. From what you see in this chapter, describe as fully as possible what this purpose is.

8. How would you explain verse 30 to a child?

9. Go through all the questions Paul asks in verses 31-35, and discuss together what you believe is the correct answer for each one.

10. From all you see in this chapter, how would you summarize the different

aspects of the Holy Spirit's work in our lives?

11. What one-word adjectives would you use to best describe the character and personality of the Holy Spirit as you see Him in this chapter?

12. How would you summarize the main point or points of this chapter, and how do they fit into Paul's overall purpose for the book?

13. From what you've seen in these middle chapters of Romans, what would you say is the key to living a life of righteousness?

14. EYE FOR DETAIL— *From what you recall seeing in this chapter, try answering the following question without looking at your Bible:* In verse 18, Paul says our sufferings at this present time are not worth comparing with…*what?*

CAPTURE THE ESSENCE

15. From what you see especially in verses 17-18, what is the right way for Christians to view the sufferings they experience in their lives?

16. With verse 17 in mind, discuss how much you agree or disagree with this statement: For Christians, there is always a *price* to be paid for following Jesus Christ in their daily lives.

17. From what you know in the Scriptures, how would you describe the glory Paul mentions in verse 18?

18. In verse 22, why do you think Paul enlarges the discussion here to include not just God's redeemed people, but the entire creation? What does this tell us about the right way to view our earthly environment?

19. Notice again the emphasis on *hope* in verses 22-25. How would you explain the relationship between *hope* and *faith*?

20. In verse 29, Paul speaks of our becoming "conformed" to the image or likeness of Christ. From what you've seen here and elsewhere in Scripture, how exactly will we be like Him? And in what ways, if any, will we *not* be like Him?

21. In verse 31, Paul states the assumption that God is "for us." In what ways, exactly, is God "for us"?

22. Paul uses the phrase "all things" at the end of verse 32. Does this refer to exactly the same things as the phrase "all things" in verse 28? Explain your answer.

23. What evidence does this chapter offer us about God's character? What is He like?

24. Think again about what Paul says in 5:17 about "reigning in life." How would you say this chapter expands and explains the meaning of that phrase?

25. Remember again Paul description of the the gospel as "the power of God" for our salvation (1:16). How do you see that power on display in what Paul teaches in this chapter?

26. Taking the evidence in this chapter alone, summarize in your own words what Paul wants us most to understand about Jesus.

27. Now that you're halfway through Romans, how would you summarize the most important teachings in this book?

28. From what you've seen in the first eight chapters of Romans, how would you summarize God's sovereign plan of salvation?

FOR LIFE TODAY

29. Look at the freedom Paul speaks of in verse 2. At this point in your life, how real is this freedom to you, compared with other times in the past? Use a scale of one to ten (one = "less noticeable than ever," ten = "more

powerfully real than ever") to help you decide.

30. How might you use verses 5-9 to help a friend who was worried about whether he or she was truly a Christian?

31. What does verse 8 imply about the amount of *change* we can expect to face in our lives?

32. What practical differences should it make in our prayer life if we truly understand the principles presented in verses 26-27? (See also verse 34.)

33. Though Paul makes it clear in the last part of this chapter that nothing can separate us from God's love for us through Christ, we may sometimes *feel* separated from that love. What causes this feeling—and how would you describe the cure?

34. From all you see in this chapter, how would you summarize the *cooperation* from Christians which is needed before God can accomplish His purpose in us?

35. If a Christian friend confessed a recurring sin to you, then asked you, "How can I get free of this sin in my life?" what help could you offer from Romans 7 and 8?

36. As presented in this chapter alone, what are the most important facts about *you?*

37. If God had written this chapter only for *you,* which words or phrases do you think He would have underlined?

FOR GOING DEEPER

Look again at the majestic words of Paul in the final three verses of this chapter, then compare them together with his words in 1 Corinthians 3:21-23. How are these passages alike, and how are they different?

ROMANS 9

Startup: What's the biggest, most unexpected gift you can recall receiving, when the occasion wasn't your birthday or anniversary or a holiday?

SEEING WHAT'S THERE

1. Once more, make a list together of the *questions* Paul asks in this chapter.

2. After reading through this chapter, which words or phrases or sentences here would you most like to understand better?

3. Paul speaks in verse 2 of his intense sorrow. From what you see later in this chapter, is this sorrow because of what God has done, what the people of Israel have done, or what both have done? Explain your answer.

4. What does the word "it" refer to in verse 16?

5. Who or what is the "stumbling stone" in verses 32-33?

6. How would you summarize the main point or points of this chapter, and how do they fit into Paul's overall purpose for the book?

7. EYE FOR DETAIL— *From what you recall seeing in this chapter, try answering the following question without looking at your Bible:* In verse 15 Paul mentions a certain Old Testament figure to whom God spoke these words: "I will have mercy on whom I have mercy, and I will have compassion on whom I have compassion." Who was the person whom God said this to?

CAPTURE THE ESSENCE

8. From what you see in verses 19-21 (and elsewhere in this chapter), discuss how much you agree or disagree with this statement: Even when we do not agree with or understand God's actions in our lives, we should never ask Him for an explanation.

9. Which "side" of God's character would you say comes through most strongly in this chapter—His wrath and holiness, or His love and mercy?

10. Paul speaks in verse 32 of how Israel stumbled upon "the stumbling stone." Is it possible for Christians today to stumble in the same way? If so, how? If not, why not?

For helpful background on verses 7-18, and the theme of God's sovereign election, explore together these Old Testament passages—Genesis 21:8-21, and 25:19-34; Exodus 9:13-19 and 33:12-23; and Malachi 1:1-5.

ROMANS 10

Startup: In what situations in life have you been most impressed with God's patience?

1. Once again, make a list together of the *questions* Paul asks in this chapter.

2. After reading through this chapter, which words or phrases or sentences here would you most like to understand better?

3. Paul speaks in verse 3 of a specific righteousness that comes from God. What is this righteousness?

4. Exactly *how* is Christ "the end of the law," as Paul says in verse 4?

5. How would you summarize the main point or points of this chapter, and how do they fit into Paul's overall purpose for the book?

6. EYE FOR DETAIL— *From what you recall seeing in this chapter, try answering the following question without looking at your Bible:* This chapter ends with an Old Testament quotation in which God says He has held out His hands "all day long" to Israel. In this quotation, God describes the people of Israel with two words. What are they? (See verse 21.)

7. Paul speaks in verse 9 about confessing Jesus as "Lord." Explain as fully as possible what this means, and why it is important.

8. If this chapter was the only Scripture portion you had, what would you conclude from it about (a) the people of Israel, and (b) the character of Israel's God?

9. From what you see in this chapter, how would you describe Paul's passion for life?

10. How could you use verses 8-12 to help an unbelieving friend who wanted to know how to become a Christian?

11. What motivation for evangelism do you find in this chapter, and how strongly does it appeal to you?

In verses 6-8, Paul quotes from the words of Moses in Deuteronomy 30:11-20. Look up and read together this Old Testament passage in full, and discuss how its message compares with Paul's message.

ROMANS 11

Startup: What's the earliest experience in your childhood in which you can recall learning about how *big* God is?

1. Once more, make a list of the *questions* Paul asks in this chapter.

2. After reading through this chapter, which words or phrases or sentences here would you most like to understand better?

3. Paul mentions in verses 7 and 25 a "hardening" or "blindness" of most of the people of Israel. From your observations in chapters 9-11, what would you state as the cause of this?

4. In your own words, how would you summarize the hope Paul holds out for Israel in verses 11-24 of this chapter?

5. From what you see from Paul's words to the Gentiles in verses 13-24, for what reasons did God bring Gentiles into His redeemed family?

6. How would you restate in your own words the praise for God which Paul expresses in the last four verses of this chapter?

7. Notice Paul's use of the phrase "all things" in verse 36. Does this refer to exactly the same things as the phrase "all things" in 8:28 and 8:32? Explain your answer.

8. From what you've seen in this chapter, and so far in the book of Romans, how would you explain from *God's* perspective the relationship between Jews and Gentiles in the church of Jesus Christ?

9. From what you've seen in chapters 9-11 of Romans, discuss how much you agree or disagree with this statement: The message of salvation is essentially the same in both the Old and New Testaments, because it is rooted in the unchanging nature of

God, whose character is the same throughout the Bible.

10. How would you summarize the main point or points of this chapter, and how do they fit into Paul's overall purpose for the book?

11. EYE FOR DETAIL— *From what you recall seeing in this chapter, try answering the following question without looking at your Bible:* A certain kind of tree—in both its wild and cultivated varieties—gets lots of attention in this chapter. What kind of tree was it? (See verses 17-24.)

CAPTURE THE ESSENCE

12. In verse 20, notice the fear which we are commanded to have. How would you define this fear, and what is the reason for it?

13. Why do you think it is important for non-Jewish Christians to understand what Paul is speaking about in chapters 9, 10, and 11?

14. From what you see in chapters 9, 10, and 11, how would you summarize (a) Israel's past; (b) Israel's present; and (c) Israel's future?

15. In verses 20 and 25 Paul speaks of an attitude we are to avoid, and it is variously translated as "arrogance" or "conceit" or "highmindedness" or "being wise in your own estimation." What kind of wrong assumptions or misinformation would most easily cause this attitude?

16. From what Paul says in verses 28-32, summarize the benefits and blessings that Jews and Gentiles derive from one another.

17. Paul concludes his three-chapter discussion of Israel with the exalted words of praise in verses 33-36. How can you reconcile the tone of this praise passage with the great sorrow Paul expressed at the opening of chapter 9, as he began this discussion of Israel? How is it possible for him to know both the sorrow and the praise?

18. How would you say the content of this chapter relates to what Paul says about true Jews in 2:28-29?

19. Again, look in 2 Peter 3:15-16 at what Peter says about Paul's letters, and their theme of *the Lord's patience.* How do you see this theme coming through in this chapter?

20. From what you've seen in chapters 9-11 of Romans, how would you summarize the way Jews and Gentiles fit into God's sovereign plan of salvation?

FOR LIFE TODAY

21. In verse 22, Paul tells us to consider two "sides" of God's character. In your own view of God, does one side dominate the other? If so, which one? And why do you think this is so?

22. Notice again in verse 20 the fear which Paul tells us to have. In what practical ways would you say God wants to see this command lived out in your life?

FOR GOING DEEPER

Compare what Paul says about Jews and Gentiles here with what he says on the subject in Ephesians 2:11-22. What different emphases do you see in the Ephesians passage?

ROMANS 12

Startup: What would you say are the most important ways in which your patterns of thought have changed in the last five years?

SEEING WHAT'S THERE

1. With chapter 12, we begin a new part of the book of Romans. How would you summarize the most important teachings so far in this book?

2. What have you seen earlier in the book of Romans that helps explain what Paul means in verse 2 when he speaks of "renewing your mind"?

3. Think again about what Paul says in 5:17 about "reigning in life." How would you say this chapter expands and explains the meaning of that phrase?

4. Keeping in mind this book's reputation as the most systematic presentation of Christian doctrine in the Bible, how would you summarize the main point or points of this chapter, and how do they fit into Paul's overall purpose for the book?

5. EYE FOR DETAIL— *From what you recall seeing in this chapter, try answering the following question without looking at your Bible:* In verse 2, Paul describes God's will with three words. What are they?

CAPTURE THE ESSENCE

6. Scan the list of commands in verses 9-21, and for each one decide together whether it is primarily a *choice,* or primarily an *emotion.*

7. If the first eleven chapters of the book of Romans had somehow been lost in history, what difference would that make in regard to the meaning of what you see in chapter 12?

8. In which of the following categories do you think the teachings of this chapter best belong: *Christian Duties;*

Warnings to Christians; Christian Privileges; or *Prophecies of the Future?*

9. Which commands in this chapter would you say are the easiest for most Christians to disobey?

10. Discuss how much you agree or disagree with this statement: The transformation and renewal of mind which Paul speaks of in verse 2 is something that can and should proceed at an increasingly faster pace for a healthy Christian.

11. Picture in your mind two Christians, one who has learned to obey the command we are given in verse 3, and one who has not learned how to do it. What practical differences do you see in the way these two persons live?

FOR LIFE TODAY

12. What insights do you find in verses 1-2 regarding the right way to approach God in worship?

13. At the end of verse 3, Paul speaks of the "measure of faith" God has given each of us. How would you describe the measure of faith God has given you?

14. Paul mentions some specific spiritual gifts in verses 6-8. Which of them, if any, do you believe God has given to you?

15. Get in mind a picture of yourself five years in the future, as a man or woman who is living in true obedience to the commands listed in verses 9-21. As this kind of person, what practical things do you see yourself doing?

16. In verse 11, Paul presents the command to keep up our spiritual fervor in serving the Lord. At this point in your life, how strong is your zeal and fervor for serving God, compared with other times in the past? Use a scale of one to ten (one = "much weaker than ever," ten = "much

stronger than ever") to help you decide.

17. Look again at verse 18. Give an example of a time when it is *not* possible to live in peace with someone.

18. What are some common and dangerous ways in which we can most easily be "overcome by evil," as Paul warns us in the last verse of this chapter?

19. If a Christian friend told you he was tired of the church and other Christians, and was thinking about spending much less time in those relationships, what teachings in Romans 12 would be most helpful in the way you responded to him?

20. If God had written this chapter only for *you,* which words or phrases do you think He would have underlined?

FOR GOING DEEPER

Look again at what Paul says in verses 4-8 about Christian unity and spiritual gifts. Then study together how Paul expands on these subjects in 1 Corinthians 12:12-30. What major points are found in both passages?

ROMANS 13

Startup: Can you recall a time when you felt like rebelling against governmental authority?

SEEING WHAT'S THERE

1. From what Paul says in verses 1-7, discuss together *why* we are to submit to governing authorities, and *how.*

2. From what you see in this chapter, when would it be right in God's eyes to refuse to obey a government law or official?

3. As Paul begins to address the topic of love in verse 8, he speaks of it as a debt or obligation. When and how can this debt finally be repaid?

4. In verse 12, what exactly does Paul mean by the two words *night* and *day?*

5. How would you summarize the main point or points of this chapter, and how do they fit into Paul's overall purpose for the book?

6. EYE FOR DETAIL— *From what you recall seeing in this chapter, try answering the following question without looking at your Bible:* As examples of the full range of Old Testament laws which are summed up in the rule, "Love your neighbor as yourself," Paul quotes four of the Ten Commandments. Which four does he mention? (See verse 9.)

CAPTURE THE ESSENCE

7. What real or potential *problems* among the Roman Christians would you say Paul was trying to solve or prevent by what he says in verses 1-7?

8. Suppose you were living in another nation, and were asked to serve on a committee to write a new constitution for that nation. What principles arising from verses 1-7 would you try to incorporate into the constitution,

and what practical form would they take?

9. Notice the six words included in the list of sinful actions in verse 13. How would you rank these six according to their prevalence in your community?

10. Let the words of verse 14 form a picture in your mind, then describe that picture.

11. Which commands in this chapter would you say are the easiest for most Christians to disobey?

FOR LIFE TODAY

12. To what degree are the statements Paul makes in verses 11-12 still true today?

13. Get in mind a picture of yourself five years in the future, as a man or woman who is truly wearing the armor of light, in obedience to the commands listed in verses 12-14. As this kind of person, what practical things do you see yourself doing?

14. In light of how you're doing spiritually in your life today, which verse in this chapter do you think is the most important at this time—and why?

FOR GOING DEEPER

Look again in verse 14 at what Paul says about clothing ourselves with Jesus Christ. Then discuss the guidelines you find for doing this in Galatians 3:27, Ephesians 4:22—5:2, and Colossians 3:9-17.

ROMANS 14

Startup: What are some important experiences in your life which taught you to be accepting of other people?

SEEING WHAT'S THERE

1. Though Paul had not yet visited the Roman Christians when he wrote this letter, and though he had high praise for them (as in 1:8), this chapter seems to imply Paul's awareness of some shortcomings in the Roman church. How would you describe those shortcomings?

2. Many Bible teachers think that when Paul speaks in verse 1 of the person who is "weak in faith," he has in mind the Jewish Christians in Rome. What evidence do you see of that in the first six verses of this chapter?

3. Discuss whether you think Paul's words in verses 7-8 are about Christians only, or about all people.

4. How would you restate verses 7-8 in your own words?

5. How would you summarize the main point or points of this chapter, and how do they fit into Paul's overall purpose for the book?

6. EYE FOR DETAIL— *From what you recall seeing in this chapter, try answering the following question without looking at your Bible:* In verse 9, Paul mentions a specific reason for which Christ died and then returned to life. What is that reason?

CAPTURE THE ESSENCE

7. From what you've seen in this chapter, how would you define the term *Christian freedom?*

8. Which of these qualities would you say this chapter emphasizes most: liberty, unity, or love? (Explain your answer.)

9. Picture in your mind two Christians, one who has learned to obey the command we are given in verse 19,

and one who has not learned how to do it. What practical differences do you see in the way these two persons live?

FOR LIFE TODAY

10. In your church today what would you say is a good example of the "disputable matters" or "opinions" or "doubtful disputations" which Paul speaks of in verse 1?

11. Paul speaks in verse 1 of the person who is "weak in faith." At this point in your life, how strong is your faith, compared with times in the past? Use a scale of one to ten (one = "much weaker than ever," ten = "much stronger than ever") to help you decide.

12. Look again at the command in verse 13. Practically speaking, what kinds of obstacles or stumbling blocks are easiest for us to put in the way of a Christian brother or sister?

13. If the apostle Paul were alive today, and he visited your church, how do you think he might paraphrase verses 17-18 to best fit your situation?

14. If everyone in your church thoroughly understood this chapter, and they all had a passion for living out its truth in their lives, what kind of practical changes do you think would result?

FOR GOING DEEPER

Look at Paul's words in verses 10-12 about the coming judgment of God. Then compare these words with the following additional passages, and discuss what they together tell us about the judgment to come—Matthew 12:36-37, 2 Corinthians 5:10, Philippians 2:9-11, and Hebrews 4:12-13.

ROMANS 15

Startup: Talk about a particular personal *strength* which you've noticed in the life of someone else in your group.

SEEING WHAT'S THERE

1. According to what Paul says in chapters 14 and 15, would you say the person who is strong in faith has *more* freedom or *less* freedom in his Christian life? Does he also have *more* responsibilities, or *fewer* responsibilities?

2. Review Paul's words in verse 4. In your own words, how would you explain the *purpose* of Scripture, as mentioned here?

3. What does Paul mean by the statement he makes about his work in verse 23? What does this statement imply about how Paul viewed his purpose in life?

4. From the evidence you see in this chapter, how do you think Paul would have worded the job description for his ministry?

5. How would you summarize the main point or points of this chapter, and how do they fit into Paul's overall purpose for the book?

6. EYE FOR DETAIL— *From what you recall seeing in this chapter, try answering the following question without looking at your Bible:* Paul says in this chapter that he plans to visit Rome on his way to somewhere else. What was this other destination? (See verse 24.)

CAPTURE THE ESSENCE

7. What real or potential *problems* among the Roman Christians would you say Paul was trying to solve or prevent by what he says in verses 1-7?

8. What is the key to the Christian unity which Paul teaches in verses 5-6?

9. From what you see in the first seven verses of this chapter, how would Paul describe our highest purpose in life?

10. From what you've seen in this chapter, how would you define the term *Christian freedom?*

11. If everyone in your church thoroughly understood verses 5-7, and they all had a passion for living out these verses in their lives, what kind of practical changes do you think would result?

12. If the words in verse 14 were in a letter written to *your* church, how accurate would they be? If they were written to your Bible study group, how accurate would they be?

13. What appropriate guidelines for pastors and preachers today can you draw from this chapter?

14. If a Christian friend told you he was tired of the church and other Christians, and was thinking about spending much less time in those relationships, what teachings in Romans 14 and 15 would be most helpful in the way you responded to him?

15. From what you see in this chapter, how fully can you describe Paul's relationship with God?

16. From what you've seen in chapters 12-15 of Romans, how would you summarize the way Christians are supposed to live?

17. In light of how you're doing spiritually in your life today, which verse in this chapter do you think is the most important at this time—and why?

Paul mentions the "signs and miracles" or "signs and wonders" that have accompanied his ministry. Explore these together in the following verses from the book of Acts, and discuss together how important you think these were in offering encouragement to Paul—Acts 14:8-10, 16:16-18, 16:25-26, 20:7-12, and 28:7-9.

ROMANS 16

Startup: What to you are the most pleasing qualities to find in another person in your church?

SEEING WHAT'S THERE

1. Since Paul tells the Romans in verses 1- 2 to give a good welcome to Phoebe, it is possible she was the person who carried this letter from Paul to the Romans. If so, imagine you were her, on your way to Rome. Among all the people whose names are listed by Paul in verses 3-15, who do you think you'd most like to meet and talk with first?

2. What conclusions about the church in Rome can you find in the evidence presented in this chapter?

3. The "Gaius" in verse 23 is thought to be the man by that name in Corinth who's mentioned in 1 Corinthians 1:14. From looking at these two verses together, what do you learn about this man and his relationship to Paul?

4. In the last part of verse 23, notice the mention Paul makes of a man named "Erastus." He may be the man by that name who's mentioned in 2 Timothy 4:20 and Acts 19:22. From looking at these verses together, what do you learn about this man and his relationship to Paul?

5. EYE FOR DETAIL— *From what you recall seeing in this chapter, try answering the following question without looking at your Bible:* How many *women* can you recall being singled out by Paul here for greetings or commendation? (See verses 1, 3, 6, 7, 12, and 15.)

CAPTURE THE ESSENCE

6. What real or potential *problems* among the Roman Christians would you say Paul was trying to solve or prevent by what he says in verses 17-18?

7. Look at Paul's stated desire for the Roman Christians in the last part of verse 19. How would you express this in your own words?

8. How do verses 25-27 summarize Paul's key themes in this letter?

9. From what you've seen in this book, what *expectations* would you say Paul had of the Roman Christians?

10. Suppose that at the very end of Romans, Paul added this line: "If you remember only one thing from this letter, let it be this:..." How do you think Paul would complete that sentence?

FOR LIFE TODAY

11. How prepared are you to recognize the kind of people Paul warns us against in verses 17-18?

12. From what you've seen in this book, what *expectations* does God have of you?

FOR GOING DEEPER

Review verses 17-20, then compare Paul's teaching there with the account in Genesis 3 of Adam and Eve's fall into sin.

ROMANS:

THE BIG PICTURE

(Discuss again the questions in the "Overview," plus the questions below.)

1. Look back in 1:8-15 at Paul's expressed desire to come to Rome, and what he hoped to accomplish when he came there. How do you think this letter prepared the way for him to accomplish these things once he finally got to Rome?

2. What would you say are the most important ways in which this book is *unique* in all the Bible?

3. Look together at each of these passages, and discuss which one you believe is the best candidate for "KEY VERSE" in the book of Romans— the one which brings into sharpest focus what this book is most about: 1:16-17, 3:23-24, 5:1-2, 5:17, 6:23, 8:1-2, and 12:1-2.

4. What would you say is the main theme (or themes) in the book of Romans?

5. Which passage or chapter in this book do you think Paul would recognize as the most important?

6. In James 1:23-24 we're told that "anyone who listens to the word but does not do what it says is like a man who looks at his face in a mirror and, after looking at himself, goes away and immediately forgets what he looks like." In what important ways has the book of Romans been a "mirror" for you—showing you what you can and should do?

7. Think about the most important personal decision or concern which has been on your mind during the time you've been studying the book of Romans. What help has this book offered you in facing that concern or decision?

8. How would you complete the following word of advice to growing Christians? *Explore the book of Romans if you want to learn more about...*

1 Corinthians

OVERVIEW

(Discuss these OVERVIEW questions both at the beginning of your study of First Corinthians, and again after you've studied together all sixteen chapters. Your answers may change significantly once you've looked more closely at the entire book.)

Startup: What comes to your mind when you think of ancient Greece?

SEEING WHAT'S THERE

1. Start scanning the book until you come to a verse that brings a question to your mind. What's the question?

2. Begin scanning the book again until you come to a verse that gives you a smile or a sense of gratitude or joy. What is pleasing to you about this verse?

3. What is the first *command* that Paul gives the Corinthians in this letter?

4. What is the first *encouragement* that Paul gives the Corinthians in this letter?

5. What do you know about the location and importance of the city of Corinth at the time of Paul?

6. What do you know about what the world was like at the time this letter was written? What would you guess to be the typical hopes and dreams and concerns of the Corinthians?

7. Look at verses 7:1, 8:1, 12:1, and 16:1. What are the questions the Corinthians had apparently been asking Paul?

8. Look also at the list of "Questions to Ask as You Begin Your Study of Each Book" on page 393.

CAPTURE THE ESSENCE

9. What previous impressions, if any, have you had about the book of First Corinthians in regard to (a) its content, (b) its level of difficulty, and (c) its importance?

10. The book of First Corinthians has been called "The Epistle of Gifts," "The Book of Carnal vs. Spiritual Christian Living," "Living by the Spirit of God," and "The Book for Church Disorders." With that reputation for this book, what answers and guidelines and solutions would you like to gain as you examine it more closely?

11. Take a quick look together at only the *first two or three verses* in each chapter in First Corinthians. What impressions and expectations of this book do you get from this partial scan?

12. Imagine that you were the person carrying this letter from Paul to Corinth. Along the way, you were attacked by a band of robbers who stripped you of all your valuables, including this letter. The leader of the robber band could not read, and when you asked him to return the letter, he replied, "Why? What's in it that's so important?" How would you answer him?

13. As you think about the various situations presented in this book, what parallels do you see with what *has* happened or *is* happening in your family or church, or in your personal life?

14. How can you ensure that your study of First Corinthians is not merely theoretical and intellectual, but is instead truly practical and relevant? Talk together about this. What can you do to help keep the process alive and interesting?

FOR GOING DEEPER

Look again at the praise and encouragement Paul gives the Corinthians in verses 4-9 of chapter 1. Then look together at the way Paul's other letters are begun (see especially Philippians, Colossians, and First Thessalonians), and discuss the patterns you see.

1 CORINTHIANS 1

Startup: What kind of pictures come to your mind when you put these two words together: *wisdom* and *power?*

SEEING WHAT'S THERE

1. Discuss together which verses in this chapter your attention would most likely be drawn to if you were... (a) a person who just earned his second graduate degree from a local university. (b) a Jew who had just become a Christian, and was reading the New Testament for the first time. (c) a language analyst who was doing an investigation of Paul's personality as revealed in his writings. (d) a hardened atheist who was looking for ways to discredit and disprove the Bible. (e) a person who was considering whether to send a large donation to a television evangelist.

2. Look closely at verse 10, then discuss how much you agree or disagree with this statement: Paul is expressing a noble concept here, but in practical terms, this kind of unity is not possible to any lasting degree among Christians here and now.

3. If Paul were reading verses 10-17 aloud to this group right now, which word or words do you think he would emphasize most?

4. How would you explain verse 25 to a young child?

5. Imagine that you were preparing a special audio-visual presentation for your church. As a strong, prerecorded voice read through verses 18-31 word for word, a series of slides would be projected on a screen in front of the people. What kind of photographs would you select to be included in the slide presentation, to best fit this passage?

6. If Satan wrote down some guidelines and commands to get people to do just the opposite of what this chapter

teaches, how do you think his message might be worded?

7. Look also at the list of "Questions to Ask as You Study Each Chapter" on page 392, which you may want to do for each chapter in First Corinthians.

8. EYE FOR DETAIL—*If everyone in the group has read the entire chapter, try answering the following question without looking at your Bible:* In verse 12, as Paul was speaking against the divisions in the Corinthian church, he mentioned four persons with whom different factions of the Corinthians were identifying themselves. Who were these four?

CAPTURE THE ESSENCE

9. From the evidence you see in this chapter, what does Paul want us most to understand about Jesus?

10. From what you see in this chapter alone, what *expectations* can we rightly have of God?

11. Look again at verse 18. What is it about the gospel that seems so foolish to some people?

12. In what ways would you say verse 30 expands the biblical definition of the word *wisdom?*

13. Picture this book of First Corinthians as a fast-moving train. Chapter 1 is the locomotive in front, and the other chapters represent railway cars that follow behind. From what you see here in chapter 1, what is the *energy* in the locomotive—the point or principle or theme that's the driving force for the locomotive and the entire train?

FOR LIFE TODAY

14. In Colossians 3:1 we read this command: "Since, then, you have been raised with Christ, set your hearts on things above, where Christ is seated at the right hand of God." What have you personally observed about Jesus Christ in this chapter that would be worthy of setting your heart on?

15. If the words in verse 26 were in a letter written to your Bible study group, how accurate would they be?

16. In practical terms, what do you think is the best way for a Christian to live out verse 31?

17. If you thought of this chapter as a roadmap for your life, what would be the safest "roads" to take, as taught in this chapter? What would be the unsafe, dangerous roads to avoid?

18. If God had written this chapter only for *you,* which words or phrases do you think He would have underlined?

FOR GOING DEEPER

Look again at the praise and encouragement Paul gives the Corinthians in verses 4-9 of chapter 1. Then look together at the way Paul's other letters are begun (see especially Philippians, Colossians, and First Thessalonians), and discuss the patterns you see.

1 CORINTHIANS 2

Startup: What kinds of things have you tried before to increase your brainpower?

SEEING WHAT'S THERE

1. If you were asked to cut out all the verses except three, and still keep as much of the meaning of this chapter as you could, which three verses would you leave in?

2. After reading through this chapter, which words or phrases or sentences here would you most like to understand better?

3. In verse 12, when Paul speaks of the things God has freely given us, what is he talking about?

4. Look at Paul's brief, final sentence in this chapter. How would you explain this in your own words?

5. In what ways do the words of Jesus in John 3:8 shed light on the meaning of 1 Corinthians 2:11-12?

6. EYE FOR DETAIL— *From what you recall seeing in this chapter, try answering the following question without looking at your Bible:* Paul teaches us in verse 10 that the Spirit searches all things; then Paul mentions something in particular that the Spirit searches. What is it?

CAPTURE THE ESSENCE

7. Suppose a band of armed terrorists stormed into the room where you're now meeting, and took you as hostages in a captivity that was likely to last for days or weeks. Just before they confiscated your Bibles, they allowed you to take one last look at the chapter open before you. Which verse in this chapter would you most try to fix in mind before your Bible was snatched away, and why?

8. From what you see in verses 10-12, what conclusions could you make about the relationship between our *spirit* and our *mind?*

9. How would you summarize what this chapter teaches about a Christian's self-image?

10. If this chapter was the only Scripture you had, how would you use it to help explain to someone else what the Holy Spirit is like?

FOR LIFE TODAY

11. In Philippians 4:8 we're given the following command: "Whatever is true, whatever is noble, whatever is right, whatever is pure, whatever is lovely, whatever is admirable—if anything is excellent or praiseworthy— *think about such things."* What food for thought can you find in this chapter that especially strikes you as being *true,* or *noble,* or *right,* or *pure,* or *lovely,* or *admirable,* or *excellent,* or *praiseworthy?*

12. If a new Christian asked you, "How can I understand the Bible more?" how could you use verses 9-14 to help you give a meaningful reply?

13. What examples can you give of the present-day truth of the principle found in verse 14?

14. If it's true that "you *become* what you *think,"* then what are the most important thoughts from this chapter to plant firmly in your mind?

FOR GOING DEEPER

Look at the following passages to see how they expand or reinforce the meaning of verse 7 in this chapter—Romans 16:25-27 and 1 Peter 1:10-12.

1 Corinthians 3

Startup: What abilities and character qualities do you look for in a leader?

1. In your own words, how would you explain the problem or issue that Paul is dealing with in this chapter?

2. What in this chapter do you think might be most surprising to a new Christian reading it for the first time?

3. With all else being equal, which of these people do you think would have the best chance of uncovering the most meaning in this chapter— a construction foreman, an architect, or a professional mediator? Why?

4. What would you say are the most important *verbs*—the action words —in this chapter?

5. Imagine yourself looking over Paul's shoulder as he wrote the words of this chapter, under the direction of the Holy Spirit's inner guidance. What emotions, or longings, or re-membrances do you think he most likely experienced as he wrote each portion of this chapter?

6. What do you think Paul means in verse 18 about "becoming a fool"? How does a person do this?

7. From what you've seen so far in this letter, how would you describe Paul's relationship with the Corinthians?

8. EYE FOR DETAIL— *From what you recall seeing in this chapter, try answering the following question without looking at your Bible:* As he talks about how we can build on the foundation of Jesus Christ, Paul mentions six types of "building materials." What are they? (See verse 12.)

9. Looking back on the first three chapters in this letter, how would you summarize their most important principles and guidelines on how to have unity in the church?

10. Look again at the command Paul gives at the end of verse 10, then look together at the related *reward* mentioned in verse 14. What do you think this reward is?

11. Think carefully about Paul's teaching in the last three verses of this chapter. Is there anything of value that does *not* belong to you? If so, what is it?

12. How would you summarize what this chapter teaches about a Christian's self-image?

13. From what you see in this chapter, do you think God is grieved that there are so many different Christian denominations today? Why or why not?

14. Choose one of these sentences, and complete it as fully and candidly as you can:
    > *What I see and understand in this chapter is important to my life because...*
    > *What I see and understand in this chapter does NOT seem important to my life at this time, because...*

15. If the words in verse 3 were in a letter written to the Christians in your community, how accurate would they be?

16. Look again at verses 10 and 14. How would you summarize what it is that you're building with *your* life?

17. How susceptible do you think Christians in general are today to the deception which Paul warns against in verse 18?

18. If everyone in your group thoroughly understood verses 21-23, and you all had a passion for living out its truth

in your lives, what kind of practical changes do you think would result?

Look again at the majestic words of Paul in verses 21-23, then compare them with his words in the last three verses of Romans 8. How are these passages alike, and how are they different?

1 CORINTHIANS 4

Startup: If the governments of all the nations got together and decided to give you ownership of the entire world, what would you do first with your new responsibilities and possessions?

SEEING WHAT'S THERE

1. If you were asked to cut out all the verses except three, and yet still keep as much of the meaning of this chapter as you could, which three verses would you leave in?

2. From what you see in this chapter, how would you describe Paul's relationship with the Corinthians? And how would you describe his relationship with God?

3. Which important details in this chapter do you think might be the easiest to overlook?

4. EYE FOR DETAIL— *From what you recall seeing in this chapter, try answering the following question without looking at your Bible:* Near the end of the chapter, Paul says God's kingdom is not a matter of mere words or talk, but of something else. What is it? (See verse 20.)

CAPTURE THE ESSENCE

5. If you were responsible for giving the apostle Paul a job performance review, what comments would you make to him, based on his ministry as you see it revealed in this chapter?

6. How would you summarize what this chapter teaches about pride?

7. From what you've seen so far in this letter, what kind of *power* is Paul speaking of in verses 19-20? How does it show itself in our lives?

FOR LIFE TODAY

8. How would you answer personally the first two questions in verse 7?

9. If God had written this chapter only for *you,* which words or phrases do

you think He would have under-lined?

FOR GOING DEEPER

Look again at verse 16. Then look up together the following passages, and discuss what you see in common in all of them, and what they say about the apostle Paul's life and character—1 Corinthians 11:1; Philippians 3:17 and 4:9; 2 Thessalonians 3:7-9; and 1 Timothy 1:16.

1 CORINTHIANS 5

Startup: What was one of the most memorable doses of discipline which you received as a child?

SEEING WHAT'S THERE

1. In your own words, how would you explain the problem or issue that Paul is dealing with in this chapter?

2. If Paul were reading verses 1-5 aloud to this group right now, which word or words do you think he would emphasize most?

3. Imagine the Corinthians writing back to Paul and quoting his words in verse 5, then adding this question: "What exactly do you mean by this?" How do you think Paul would explain it?

4. How would you explain verse 12 to a young child?

5. Again, imagine yourself looking over Paul's shoulder as he wrote the words of this chapter, under the direction of the Holy Spirit's inner guidance. What emotions, or longings, or remembrances do you think he most likely experienced as he wrote each portion of this chapter?

6. EYE FOR DETAIL—*From what you recall seeing in this chapter, try answering the following question without looking at your Bible:* Paul presents a contrast in this chapter: On one side is the "old leaven" or "old yeast," which we're to get rid of; on the other side is the new "unleavened bread"—bread without yeast—which we are to become. Paul explains his meaning by using two nouns to describe the old leaven, and two other nouns to describe the new unleavened bread. Can you remember each of these four words? (See verse 8.)

7. In verses 2-3, Paul reveals a drastic difference in attitude between himself and the Corinthians toward the situation described in verse 1. What would you say were the *values* and the *assumptions* that caused both Paul and the Corinthians to respond as they did?

8. *How,* exactly, does a person go about obeying the command given in verse 7?

9. From what you see in this chapter, what is the right way to take a stand against sin?

10. From the evidence you've seen so far in this letter, what are the most important *expectations* Paul has of the Corinthians?

11. If this chapter was the only Scripture portion you had ever known, what would you conclude from it about God's purity and holiness?

FOR LIFE TODAY

12. Look again at the command in verse 11, and discuss how fully you think Christians are obeying this teaching today.

FOR GOING DEEPER

For helpful background on verses 7-8, explore together Exodus 12:14-15 and 13:6-7, and Isaiah 53:7.

1 CORINTHIANS 6

Startup: What kind of pictures come to your mind when you think of the word *honor?*

SEEING WHAT'S THERE

1. In your own words, how would you explain the problem or issue that Paul is dealing with in this chapter?

2. If Satan wrote down some guidelines and commands to get people to do just the opposite of what this chapter teaches, how do you think his message might be worded?

3. Looking back on chapters 5 and 6, how would you summarize their most important principles and guidelines on how Christians should cultivate purity in their church?

4. EYE FOR DETAIL— *From what you recall seeing in this chapter, try answering the following question without looking at your Bible:* In this chapter Paul uses two phrases to describe our bodies; what are they? (See verses 15 and 19.)

CAPTURE THE ESSENCE

5. Try to "read between the lines" as you think about Paul's words in verses 1-8. What foundational principles would you say are the source of Paul's teaching here?

6. In Psalm 119:45, the psalmist says to God, "I will walk at liberty, for I seek Thy precepts." As you think about the "precept" or command given at the beginning of verse 18, in what ways can you see it offering true freedom and liberty to a Christian?

7. Look at the command in the last verse of this chapter. If you asked Paul, "How exactly does a person bring glory or honor to God with his body?"—how do you think Paul would answer?

8. If you were asked to write a discussion question to help your Bible

study group examine and understand something in this chapter, how would you word the question?

9. If the words in verse 8 were in a letter written to *your* church, how accurate would they be?

10. How susceptible do you think Christians in general are today to the deception which Paul warns against in verses 9-10?

11. If it's true that "you *become* what you *think*," then what are the most important thoughts from this chapter to plant firmly in your mind?

12. As you think about the situation presented in this chapter, what parallels do you see with what *has* happened or *is* happening in your family or church, or in your personal life?

FOR GOING DEEPER

For helpful background on verse 2, explore together Matthew 19:28, John 5:22, 2 Timothy 2:12, and Revelation 3:21 and 20:4.

1 CORINTHIANS 7

Startup: If you ever married, what are some of the biggest surprises that marriage brought to you?

SEEING WHAT'S THERE

1. Again in your own words, how would you explain the problem or issue that Paul is dealing with in this chapter?

2. What in this chapter do you think might be most surprising to a new Christian reading it for the first time?

3. Making a mental list together of the principles and guidelines Paul offers in this chapter concerning (a) whether or not to get married, and (b) how to live if you're already married.

4. Imagine the Corinthians writing back to Paul and quoting his words in verses 29-31, then adding this question: "What exactly did you mean by this?" How do you think Paul would answer?

5. EYE FOR DETAIL—*From what you recall seeing in this chapter, try answering the following question without looking at your Bible:* How does Paul complete the following sentence? "It is better to marry than to…" (See verse 9.)

CAPTURE THE ESSENCE

6. Which of the following statements do you think is most accurate? (a) In this chapter, Paul clearly supports the concept of commitment to one another in marriage. (b) In this chapter, Paul does not address the concept of commitment to one another in marriage. (c) In this chapter, Paul raises questions about the concept of commitment to one another in marriage.

7. If this chapter was the only Scripture portion you had ever known, what would you conclude from it about God's design for marriage?

8. Regarding the subjects you've seen addressed so far in this book, what questions do you have that remain unanswered?

FOR LIFE TODAY

9. How would you explain and relate the principles in this chapter to a new Christian who was trying to decide whether or not to get married?

10. Look at the common theme in verses 17, 20, and 24. How would you say this teaching applies to *your* life now?

FOR GOING DEEPER

Compare what Paul says about marriage in this chapter with what he says in the following passages, then discuss how these teachings fit together—Ephesians 5:22-33, Colossians 3:18-19, and 1 Timothy 3:2 and 3:12, and 5:14.

1 CORINTHIANS 8

Startup: Describe a time in your life when you felt especially *free.*

SEEING WHAT'S THERE

1. Again in your own words, how would you explain the problem or issue that Paul is dealing with in this chapter?

2. From what you see in this chapter, how do you think Paul would define *Christian liberty* or *Christian freedom?*

3. EYE FOR DETAIL— *From what you recall seeing in this chapter, try answering the following question without looking at your Bible:* What brief statement does Paul give in verse 3 about the person who loves God?

CAPTURE THE ESSENCE

4. Would you say this is a chapter that especially requires *patience* as you read and study it, in order to understand it? If so, why?

5. Would you say the main point in verse 2 is more about *knowledge,* more about *pride,* or more about *spiritual growth?* Explain your answer.

6. Now that you're halfway through 1 Corinthians, how would you summarize the most important teachings in this book?

FOR LIFE TODAY

7. Consider carefully the major teachings in this chapter. Which do you think is harder for Christians—understanding what this chapter says, or putting it into practice?

8. The older you get, in what ways does it get easier to obey the command in verse 9? In what ways does it get harder?

FOR GOING DEEPER

Is your view of God big enough? Look again in verse 6 at the descriptions of God and Jesus Christ, and their relationship to "all things." Then compare this verse with the following passages which also explore the theme of "all things," and discuss together the greater perspective on God these verses can give us—Romans 11:36, Ephesians 1:9-10, Colossians 1:16-17 and 1:20, Hebrews 1:3, and Revelation 4:11.

1 CORINTHIANS 9

Startup: Can you recall a time in life when you declined the use of something you were entitled to, for the sake of a higher purpose?

SEEING WHAT'S THERE

1. As you read this chapter, what's the strongest impression or image it leaves in your mind?

2. Once again, if you were responsible for giving the apostle Paul a job performance review, what comments would you make to him, based on his ministry as you see it in this chapter?

3. What are the answers to all of Paul's questions in verse 1? How would you support each answer?

4. If Paul were reading verses 19-23 aloud to this group right now, which word or words do you think he would emphasize most?

5. Again, imagine yourself looking over Paul's shoulder as he wrote the words of this chapter, under the direction of the Holy Spirit's inner guidance. What emotions, or longings, or remembrances do you think he most likely experienced as he wrote verses 15-27?

6. EYE FOR DETAIL—*From what you recall seeing in this chapter, try answering the following question without looking at your Bible:* What did Paul say was his *reward* for willingly preaching the gospel? (See verse 17-18.)

7. Remember to look also at the list of "Questions to Ask as You Study Each Chapter" on page 392, which can help you explore each chapter in First Corinthians.

CAPTURE THE ESSENCE

8. Suppose that at the end of this chapter, Paul added this line: "If you remember only one thing from this

chapter, let it be this:…" How do you think he would complete that sentence?

9. Look at Paul's example as stated in verse 19. Are there some areas of life in which this example is *not* necessarily a good one for Christians to follow? If so, what are they?

10. How do you think the principles and guidelines in this chapter should be applied to Christian ministers today?

11. Look at the *reward* Paul mentions in verses 17-18. How satisfying would this reward be to you in your life today?

12. Review verses 24-27, especially keeping in mind verse 24. What do you feel are the most important factors for you personally that will determine whether or not you'll be a *winner* in life?

Run for the prize! With the challenge in verses 24-27 in mind, look also at the following passages that teach endurance, then discuss some workable ways to put them into practice—Galatians 6:9-10, Ephesians 6:10-20, Philippians 3:12-14, and 2 Timothy 2:1-13.

1 CORINTHIANS 10

Startup: What comes to mind when you think of the word *idolatry?*

1. What *commands* does Paul give the Corinthians in this chapter? As a group, list them all aloud.

2. After reading through this chapter, which words or phrases or sentences here would you most like to understand better?

3. Look together at verse 12, then discuss how much you agree or disagree with this statement: This verse tells us there is no room in the Christian life for certainty or contentment about our spiritual growth.

4. How would you explain verse 13 to a young child?

5. EYE FOR DETAIL— *From what you recall seeing in this chapter, try answering the following question without looking at your Bible:* How did Paul complete the following sentence? "Whether you eat or drink or whatever you do,…" (See verse 31.)

6. What fundamental misunderstandings about sin and temptation can be corrected by a full and true understanding of what Paul says in verses 12-13?

7. James 1:22 tells us that when we merely listen to the Word without putting it into practice, we deceive ourselves. What kind of self-deceiving excuses or rationalization do you think could most easily keep Christians from actually *doing* what verse 24 says?

8. If you thought of this chapter as a roadmap for a Christian's life, what would be the safest "roads" to take, as taught in this chapter? And what would be the unsafe, dangerous roads to avoid?

9. A 3-step question: (a) Think of someone you know who doesn't spend much time reading the Bible. (b) Select a verse or brief passage in this chapter which you think this person would probably find boring. (c) Now decide how you could clarify or open up this passage in a way that might appeal to this person.

10. If this chapter was a good answer to a question that began with the word *Why...* then what would the rest of the question say?

FOR LIFE TODAY

11. In verse 7-10, notice again all the things Paul tells us *not* to do. Take each one, and discuss the ways in which Christians today are most in danger of doing it.

12. Look again at the command in verse 10 about "grumbling" or "murmuring." In the last 24 hours, what are the biggest things (if any) that you've grumbled about?

13. Look again at verse 13. At this point in your life, how quick is your typical reaction time in finding and taking the "way of escape" from temptation, as compared with times in your past? To help you decide, use a scale of one to ten (one = "much slower than ever," ten = "much faster than ever").

14. Reflect on Paul's teaching in verses 23-33, then put together a helpful list of guidelines for deciding whether an action is right or wrong for you as an individual.

15. If everyone in your group thoroughly understood verse 31, and you all had a new passion for living out its truth in your lives, what kind of practical changes do you think would result?

16. If God had written this chapter only for *you,* which words or phrases do you think He would have underlined?

17. If you were asked to write a discussion question to help your Bible study group apply something in this chapter to their lives, how would you word the question?

FOR GOING DEEPER

Look up the following Old Testament passages, and see if you can match each one to something Paul mentions in verses 7-10—Exodus 12:23 and 32:5-7, and Numbers 14:2, 14:36-37, 16:41-50, 21:4-6, and 25:1-9.

1 CORINTHIANS 11

Startup: In what ways has celebrating the Lord's Supper been particularly meaningful to you?

SEEING WHAT'S THERE

1. If you were asked to cut out all the verses except three, and yet still keep as much of the meaning of this chapter as you could, which three verses would you leave in?

2. Discuss how much you agree or disagree with this statement: Verse 1 in this chapter assures us that the values and standards of the apostle Paul's life are achievable for all Christians.

3. Try to "read between the lines" as you think about Paul's words in verses 2-16. What foundational principles would you say are the source of Paul's teaching here?

4. How would you explain in your own words the statements Paul makes in verses 11-12?

5. If Satan wrote down some guidelines and commands to get people to do just the opposite of what this chapter teaches, how do you think his message might be worded?

6. Which important details in this chapter do you think might be the easiest to overlook?

7. EYE FOR DETAIL— *From what you recall seeing in this chapter, try answering the following question without looking at your Bible:* As Paul quotes in this chapter the words of Jesus on the night of the Lord's Supper, how did Jesus describe the cup as He took it in in His hands? (See verse 25.)

CAPTURE THE ESSENCE

8. How would you summarize what this chapter says about the right way to approach God in worship?

9. How would you explain the meaning of what Jesus did and said in verses 23-25 to someone who had never seen or heard this passage?

10. From the evidence in this chapter, how would you state the importance of observing the Lord's Supper?

11. To carry out the "examination" which Paul commands in verse 28, what are some good, practical questions a Christian should ask himself or herself?

12. If this chapter was the only Scripture portion you had, what would you conclude from it about how important it was for Jesus Christ to die?

FOR LIFE TODAY

13. Think again of Philippians 4:8, where we're given the following command: "Whatever is true, whatever is noble, whatever is right, whatever is pure, whatever is lovely, whatever is admirable—if anything is excellent or praiseworthy— *think about such things.*" What food for thought can you find in this chapter that especially strikes you as being *true,* or *noble,* or *right,* or *pure,* or *lovely,* or *admirable,* or *excellent,* or *praiseworthy?*

14. If someone wrote the words in verse 17 in a letter to *your* church, how much truth would there be in it?

FOR GOING DEEPER

Look again at Paul's bold statement in verse 1. Then discuss how the following passages reinforce what Paul says— Galatians 4:12, Philippians 3:17, 1 Thessalonians 1:6, and 2 Thessalonians 3:7-9.

1 CORINTHIANS 12

Startup: Talk about any experiences you've had when an injury or illness caused you to do without a particular part of your body.

SEEING WHAT'S THERE

1. If this chapter was a good answer to a question that began with the word *How…* then what might the rest of the question say?

2. What is the only command that Paul gives the Corinthians in this chapter?

3. How would you summarize what this chapter teaches about the *purpose* of spiritual gifts?

4. How would you explain verse 12 to a young child?

5. What are the "greater" or "best" gifts which Paul tells us to desire in verse 31?

6. From what you see in this chapter alone, what *expectations* can we rightly have of God?

7. EYE FOR DETAIL— *From what you recall seeing in this chapter, try answering the following question without looking at your Bible:* Which of these body parts is *not* named in this chapter: eye, ear, nose, mouth, hand, foot, head, and shoulder? (See verses 14-21.)

CAPTURE THE ESSENCE

8. With all else being equal, which of these people do you think would have the best chance of uncovering the most meaning in this chapter— an owner of a gift shop, a physical therapist, or a football coach?

9. Keep in mind what Paul teaches about the different "parts of the body" beginning in verse 12, then discuss how much you agree or disagree with this statement: "When Paul speaks of the 'parts of the body' in this passage, he is primarily referring to the different denominations and churches which have become an established part of Christianity."

10. What guidelines do you see in this chapter for helping Christians discover their spiritual gifts?

11. From what you see in this chapter, how would you define and describe a *spiritually healthy Christian?*

12. If this chapter was the only Scripture portion you had ever known, what would you conclude from it about how a local church should behave and operate?

FOR LIFE TODAY

13. Suppose a new Christian asked you, "How can I *know* that the Holy Spirit lives in me?" How could you use verses 1-11 to help you give a meaningful answer?

14. Choose one of these sentences, and complete it as fully and candidly as you can:
    What I see and understand in this chapter is important to my life because…
    What I see and understand in this chapter does NOT seem important to my life at this time, because…

15. If it's true that "you *become* what you *think,*" then what are the most important thoughts from this chapter to plant firmly in your mind?

FOR GOING DEEPER

Keep in mind what you see in this chapter regarding spiritual gifts. Then compare the following passages, and summarize what you see as the most important biblical principles on this subject— Romans 12:3-8; Ephesians 4:3-13, and 1 Peter 4:10-11.

1 CORINTHIANS 13

Startup: If you were given the opportunity to instantly and permanently achieve perfection in *one* of the aspects of love presented in verses 4-7 in this chapter, which one of these aspects would you choose?

SEEING WHAT'S THERE

1. SMALL, BUT IMPORTANT: Discuss together the significance of the little words *if* and *but* in verses 1-3.

2. Try restating the passage in verses 4-7 in completely different language, without using any words from the original (except those that are three letters or less). You may want to go around the group and have each person restate one phrase from the passage.

3. Paul speaks in verse 10 of the coming of "perfection," or "that which is perfect." What do you think he means by this?

4. Imagine once more that you are preparing a special audio-visual presentation for your church. A strong, prerecorded voice will read through this chapter word for word as a series of slides is projected on a screen in front of the people. What kind of photographs would you select to be included in the slide presentation, to best fit this chapter?

5. What things in this chapter do you think non-Christians would find hardest to understand?

6. EYE FOR DETAIL— *From what you recall seeing in this chapter, try answering the following question without looking at your Bible:* How does Paul complete the following sentence? "When I became a man..." (See verse 11.)

CAPTURE THE ESSENCE

7. In verse 8, Paul says love does not rejoice or delight in *evil* (or *iniquity* or *unrighteousness,* as some translations put it). What would you say are the *reasons* love does not do this?

8. Practically speaking, what do you think is the strongest motivation for people to be more *loving?*

FOR LIFE TODAY

9. Imagine that you saw earlier today a message written in fire in the sky. It was addressed to you by name, then continued with these words: *Thus saith the Lord: "Read 1 Corinthians 13, for I have something for you there."* Which verse or verses in this chapter do you think He most likely would be referring to?

10. What kind of mental habits do you think could most easily block the words in this chapter from staying alive in your mind and heart?

11. If God had written this chapter only for *you,* which words or phrases do you think He would have underlined?

FOR GOING DEEPER

Notice Paul's grouping of faith, hope, and love in verse 13. Look at the following verses, and discuss the differences between faith, hope, and love, and how they work together—Galatians 5:5-6, Colossians 1:4-5, 1 Thessalonians 1:3 and 5:8, and Hebrews 10:22-24.

1 CORINTHIANS 14

Startup: How would you describe the ideal church?

SEEING WHAT'S THERE

1. If chapters 12 and 13 of this letter had somehow been lost in history, what difference would that make in regard to the meaning of what you see in verse 1 of chapter 14?

2. What *commands* does Paul give the Corinthians in this chapter? Together, list them all aloud.

3. From what you see in this chapter, how would you define the New Testament spiritual gift of *prophecy?*

4. Imagine the Corinthians writing back to Paul and quoting his words in verse 20, then adding this question: "What exactly did you mean by this?" How do you think Paul would explain it?

5. EYE FOR DETAIL— *From what you recall seeing in this chapter, try answering the following question without looking at your Bible:* In this chapter the apostle Paul gives guidelines for how many people should speak in tongues at a worship meeting, and how many should prophesy. What are the numbers he gives for each one? (See verses 26-27.)

CAPTURE THE ESSENCE

6. From what Paul says in this chapter, especially verses 1 and 14, discuss how much you agree or disagree with this statement: A Christian may have whatever spiritual gift he desires.

7. As a guideline for Christians in worship, how would you express in your own words what Paul says in verse 15?

8. Compare verses 12 and 26. From these verses, what conclusions would you make about the *purpose* of our church involvement? Would you say this is the *most important reason* for our church involvement? Why or why not?

9. Notice what Paul says about God at the beginning of verse 33. What evidence for this truth have you seen yourself?

10. Look again at the commands in verse 39, and discuss how fully you think Christians are obeying this teaching today.

11. Suppose that at the end of this chapter, Paul added this line: "If you remember only one thing from this chapter, let it be this:…" How do you think he would complete that sentence?

12. If this chapter was the only Scripture portion you had ever known, what would you conclude from it about what should happen in a church worship service?

13. From what you've seen in chapters 12-14 of First Corinthians, what would you state as the most important principles to remember about using our spiritual gifts?

FOR LIFE TODAY

14. Using the teachings in this chapter as a guideline, discuss this question: If the apostle Paul could visit your church, how do you think he would evaluate the worship services there?

15. Consider carefully the major teachings in this chapter. Which do you think is harder for Christians—understanding what this chapter says, or putting it into practice?

FOR GOING DEEPER

Look again at the picture of worship Paul presents in verses 15-17, then compare it with what you see in these passages—1 Chronicles 16:36, Nehemiah 8:6, and Psalms 13:6 and 150:6.

1 CORINTHIANS 15

Startup: What do you consider the three most important ingredients allowing a church today to reach out successfully to the community around it?

SEEING WHAT'S THERE

1. Discuss how much you agree or disagree with this statement: In this chapter, God clearly promises a literal, bodily resurrection for every Christian.

2. After reading through this chapter, which words or phrases or sentences would you most like to understand better?

3. Discuss which verses in this chapter your attention would most likely be drawn to if you were… (a) a convicted criminal who was due to be executed tomorrow. (b) a hardened atheist who was looking for ways to discredit and disprove the Bible. (c) a discouraged missionary living among a tribe of people who were starving both spiritually and physically. (d) a person serving on a jury in a murder case.

4. If Satan wrote down some guidelines and commands to get people to do just the opposite of what this chapter teaches, how do you think his message might be worded?

5. From what you see in this chapter, what can we truly rely on God to do as we obey Him?

6. SMALL, BUT IMPORTANT: How many times does the little word *if* appear in verses 12-19? What important condition or supposition does it highlight each time?

7. If Paul were reading verses 50-57 aloud to this group right now, which word or words do you think he would emphasize most?

8. How fully can you explain what Paul means by "the work of the Lord" in verse 58?

9. EYE FOR DETAIL— *From what you recall seeing in this chapter, try answering the following question without looking at your Bible:* In the span of four verses near the beginning of this chapter, Paul mentions six separate appearances of Jesus after His resurrection. Who did Jesus appear to in each of these instances? (See verses 5-8.)

CAPTURE THE ESSENCE

10. From what you've seen so far in this book, why do you think Paul felt the need to remind the Corinthians of the gospel message, as he does beginning in verse 1?

11. In verse 2, look at the conditional statement that begins with the word *if.* What do you think this statement means? How is it possible for someone to "believe in vain," as Paul says?

12. If this chapter was the only Scripture portion you had ever known, what would you conclude from it about God's power?

13. If this chapter was a good answer to a question that began with the word *What…* then what would the rest of the question say?

FOR LIFE TODAY

14. If you had only this chapter in Scripture to refer to, how would you use it to help show someone how to become a Christian?

15. In Colossians 3:1 we read this command: "Since you have been raised with Christ, set your hearts on things above, where Christ is seated at the right hand of God." What have you personally observed about Jesus Christ in this chapter that would be worthy of setting your heart on?

16. Get in mind a picture of yourself five years in the future, as a man or woman who truly follows the commands in verse 58. As this kind of person, what kinds of things do you see yourself doing?

17. What kind of mental habits do you think could most easily block the words in verse 58 from staying alive in your mind and heart?

Look again at the conditional statement in verse 2. Compare it with the following list of Scriptures, then discuss your findings together—Matthew 10:22 and 24:12-13; and Hebrews 3:6 and 3:14.

1 CORINTHIANS 16

Startup: Talk about a time in life when you especially benefitted from words of challenge spoken by someone in authority over you?

SEEING WHAT'S THERE

1. What *commands* does Paul give the Corinthians in this chapter? Together, make a list of all of them.

2. From what you've seen by now in this letter, how would you describe Paul's relationship with the Corinthians?

3. EYE FOR DETAIL—*From what you recall seeing in this chapter, try answering the following question without looking at your Bible:* Paul said in this chapter that before visiting the Corinthians again, he was first traveling somewhere else. What was this place? (See verse 5.)

CAPTURE THE ESSENCE

4. A 3-step question: (a) Think of someone you know who doesn't spend much time reading the Bible. (b) Select a verse or brief passage in this chapter which you think this person would probably find boring. (c) Now decide how you could clarify or open up this passage in a way that might appeal to this person.

5. What principles or guidelines regarding church leadership and Christian service can you draw from verses 15-18?

6. In verse 24, Paul makes his final statement of this letter. What would you say are the most important ways Paul has shown his love for the Corinthians throughout this letter?

FOR LIFE TODAY

7. Think carefully again about verse 13. Then imagine God evaluating the strength and durability of your faith on a scale of one to ten, in which ten equals full obedience to the com-

mands in this verse, and one equals total disregard of these commands. What score do you think He would assign to you?

8. Now look at verse 14, and this time imagine God evaluating the consistency of your love on a scale of one to ten, in which ten equals full obedience to the command in this verse, and one equals total disregard of this command. What score do you think He would assign to you?

FOR GOING DEEPER

For more information about the collection Paul was taking for God's people (as mentioned in verse 1), explore together Romans 15:25-29 and 2 Corinthians 8:1-7 and 9:1-5.

1 CORINTHIANS:

THE BIG PICTURE

(Discuss again the questions in the "Overview," plus the questions below.)

1. Suppose you were visiting the church in Corinth on the day this letter from Paul was first read aloud. After the church meeting, you walked out in the street with others who had been in attendance. As you did so, some of them asked you the following questions. How would you answer each one? (a) "With all our problems that he pointed out, how can Paul really say he loves us?" (b) "How in the world can we go about doing everything Paul told us to do in that letter?" (c) "There's the meat-market across the street, and I know they're selling some good steaks that come from the temple sacrifices offered to idols; should I buy some for Sunday dinner, or not?"

2. Look together at each of these verses, and discuss which one you believe is the best candidate for "KEY VERSE" in the book of First Corinthians—the one which brings into sharpest focus what this book is most about: 1:10, 2:7-8; 3:10-11, 9:24, 14:1, 14:20, and 15:58.

3. If you've decided on a starting point for applying something in this book more effectively to your life, what commitment would you be willing to make to others in your group regarding this?

4. How would you complete the following word of advice to growing Christians? *Explore the book of First Corinthians if you want to learn more about...*

2 Corinthians

OVERVIEW

(Discuss these OVERVIEW questions both at the beginning of your study of Second Corinthians, and again after you've studied together all thirteen chapters. Your answers may change significantly once you've looked more closely at the entire book.)

Startup: What comes to your mind when you think of the phrase *love letter?*

SEEING WHAT'S THERE

1. From what you see in 1:8 and 13:8-10, what conclusions would you make about Paul's overall purpose in writing this letter?

2. What do you know about the location and importance of the city of Corinth at the time of Paul?

3. What do you know about what the world was like at the time this letter was written? What would you guess were the typical hopes and dreams and concerns of the Corinthians?

4. Start scanning the book until you come to a verse that brings a question to your mind. What's the question?

5. Begin scanning the book again until you come to a verse that gives you a smile or a sense of gratitude or joy. What is pleasing to you about this verse?

6. Look also at the list of "Questions to Ask as You Begin Your Study of Each Book" on page 393.

CAPTURE THE ESSENCE

7. What previous impressions, if any, have you had about the book of Second Corinthians in regard to (a) its content, (b) its level of difficulty, and (c) its importance?

8. The book of Second Corinthians has been called "The Book of a Minister's Heart," "The Glory of the Christian Ministry," "The Great Privilege of Being One of God's Workers," and "Paul's Vindication of His Apostleship." With that reputation for this book, what answers and guidelines and solutions would you like to gain as you examine it more closely?

9. Take a quick look together at only the *first two or three verses* in each chapter in Second Corinthians. What impressions and expectations of this book do you get from this partial scan?

10. Imagine that you were the person carrying this letter from Paul to Corinth. Along the way, you were attacked by a band of robbers who stripped you of all your valuables, including this letter. The leader of the robber band could not read, and when you asked him to return the letter, he replied, "Why? What's in it that's so important?" How would you answer him?

FOR LIFE TODAY

11. Since Second Corinthians is a book that deals especially with ministry, how would you evaluate the strength of your ministry involvement and skills at this point in your life, compared with other times in the past? Use a scale of one to ten (one = "much weaker than ever," ten =

"much stronger than ever") to help you decide.

12. How can you ensure that your study of Second Corinthians is not merely theoretical and intellectual, but is instead truly practical and relevant? Talk together about this. What can you do to help keep the process alive and interesting?

FOR GOING DEEPER

How many letters did Paul write to the Corinthians? Use the following passages to help you form an answer—1 Corinthians 5:9-11 and 16:21, and 2 Corinthians 2:3-9, 7:12, and 13:10.

2 CORINTHIANS 1

Startup: Are you the kind of person who generally likes to stick with the original plan, or the kind who prefers to change and adapt as you go along?

SEEING WHAT'S THERE

1. After reading through this chapter, which words or phrases or sentences here would you most like to understand better?

2. What in this chapter do you think might be most surprising to a new Christian reading it for the first time?

3. Discuss which verses in this chapter your attention would most likely be drawn to if you were… (a) a discouraged missionary living among a tribe of people who were starving both spiritually and physically. (b) a popular but personally insecure entertainer who was beginning to see how empty and unsatisfying fame can be. (c) a young mother whose husband had recently abandoned her and their children. (d) a person wrestling with a major decision.

4. How would you explain verse 4 to a young child?

5. What *risks* would you say Paul is taking by what he says in this chapter?

6. From what you see in this chapter, what *expectations* can we rightly have of God?

7. Look again at 13:8-10, where Paul discusses his purpose for writing this letter, and his desire for the Corinthians. How does he begin accomplishing that purpose in chapter 1?

8. Look also at the list of "Questions to Ask as You Study Each Chapter" on page 392, which you may want to do for each chapter in Second Corinthians.

9. EYE FOR DETAIL—*If everyone in the group has read the entire chapter, try answering the following question*

without looking at your Bible: Paul mentions two of his ministry assistants who helped him preach the gospel to the Corinthians. Who were these two men? (See verse 19.)

CAPTURE THE ESSENCE

10. From what you see in this chapter, what are the essential requirements for being able to offer true comfort to others who are troubled?

11. From what you see in verses 18-22, explain in your own words the relationship Jesus Christ has to God's promises to His people. Then explain the relationship that the Holy Spirit has to these promises.

12. Picture Second Corinthians as a fast-moving train. Chapter 1 is the locomotive in front, and the other chapters represent railway cars that follow behind. From what you see here in chapter 1, what is the *energy* in the locomotive—the point or principle or theme that's the driving force for the locomotive and the entire train?

FOR LIFE TODAY

13. Notice the *process* Paul describes in verse 5. To what degree would you say this process is going on in your life at the present time?

14. If it's true that "you *become* what you *think*," then what are the most important thoughts from this chapter to plant firmly in your mind?

15. If God had written this chapter only for *you,* which words or phrases do you think He would have underlined?

FOR GOING DEEPER

In verse 14, notice Paul's reference to the "day of the Lord Jesus." Look together at the following passages to help you form a good understanding of what will happen on that day—1 Corinthians 5:5, Philippians 1:6, and 1 Thessalonians 2:19-20 and 5:1-3.

2 CORINTHIANS 2

Startup: What are some aromas that for you have a strong connection with memories of past experiences?

SEEING WHAT'S THERE

1. If you were asked to cut out all the verses except three, and yet still keep as much of the meaning of this chapter as you could, which three verses would you leave in?

2. Imagine that you are one of the Corinthians listening to this letter being read for the first time in one of your church meetings. As verses 5-11 are being read, the person next to you taps your shoulder and says, "I'm new here; what is Paul talking about?" How would you answer?

3. Let the words of verse 14 form a picture in your mind, and then describe that picture.

4. If Paul were reading verses 14-17 aloud to this group right now, which word or words do you think he would emphasize most?

5. Look once more at Paul's words in 13:8-10. How would you say this chapter helps Paul fulfill his stated purpose for writing this letter, and his desire for the Corinthians?

6. EYE FOR DETAIL— *From what you recall seeing in this chapter, try answering the following question without looking at your Bible:* While he was in Troas, Paul was waiting for the arrival of one of his ministry helpers, but he never showed up. Who was this man? (See verse 13.)

CAPTURE THE ESSENCE

7. What principles and guidelines for restoration can you draw from verses 5-11?

FOR LIFE TODAY

8. How much ownership can you claim to the statement Paul makes in verse

14? Is this a picture of your life as well?

Notice again Paul's comparison of himself with others in the last verse of this chapter. Look together at the following passages, and discuss how they support Paul's statement—1 Corinthians 9:7-18 and 2 Corinthians 11:7-12.

2 CORINTHIANS 3

Startup: In what areas in life have you most recently grown in your level of confidence?

SEEING WHAT'S THERE

1. Paul speaks of something *new* in verse 6. How would you explain what this is?

2. How does Paul demonstrate in this chapter that he isn't boasting?

3. Which important details in this chapter do you think might be the easiest to overlook?

4. Imagine yourself looking over Paul's shoulder as he wrote the words of this chapter, under the direction of the Holy Spirit's inner guidance. What emotions, longings, or remembrances do you think he most likely experienced as he wrote verses 1-6?

5. Consider again Paul's discussion in 13:8-10 about his purpose for writing this letter, and his desire for the Corinthians. How would you say this chapter helps Paul fulfill that purpose?

6. EYE FOR DETAIL—*From what you recall seeing in this chapter, try answering the following question without looking at your Bible:* How did Paul complete the following sentence? "The letter _____, but the Spirit _____." (See verse 6.)

CAPTURE THE ESSENCE

7. In practical terms, what kind of *freedom* or *liberty* do you think Paul is speaking of in 17? Explain it as fully as you can.

8. In verse 18, notice what Paul says is happening to us. How would you explain this process?

FOR LIFE TODAY

9. Imagine that you saw earlier today a message written in fire in the sky. It was addressed to you by name, then

continued with these words: *Thus saith the LORD: "Read 2 Corinthians 3, for I have something for you there."* Which verses in this chapter do you think He most likely would be referring to?

FOR GOING DEEPER

Look again at Paul's imagery in verse 3, then look together at the following Old Testament passages, and discuss how they relate to Paul's message here—Jeremiah 31:33, and Ezekiel 11:19-21 and 36:26-27.

2 CORINTHIANS 4

Startup: If you were blinded, what are some of the things you would most miss seeing?

SEEING WHAT'S THERE

1. If this chapter was the only Scripture portion you had ever known, what would you conclude from it about how to preach the gospel?

2. Look closely at verses 3-6. What do these verses tell us about *Satan's* strategy and about *God's* strategy in their dealings with human beings?

3. How would you explain verse 6 to a young child?

4. SMALL, BUT IMPORTANT: The word *but* signals a contrast, or a change in direction. What important contrast or change in direction does this word highlight in verse 7?

5. In your own words, how would you describe the *process* that Paul mentions in verse 17?

6. How fully can you explain what Paul means in verse 18 when he speaks of what is "unseen"?

7. From what you see in this chapter, what can we truly rely on God to do as we obey Him?

8. Focus again on 13:8-10, where Paul discusses his purpose for writing this letter, and his desire for the Corinthians. How does this chapter help him accomplish that purpose?

9. EYE FOR DETAIL—*From what you recall seeing in this chapter, try answering the following question without looking at your Bible:* In this chapter, what phrase does Paul use to describe the one who has blinded the minds of unbelievers? (See verse 4.)

CAPTURE THE ESSENCE

10. With all else being equal, which of these people do you think would have the best chance of uncovering

the most meaning in this chapter—
an optometrist, a weightlifter, or a
potter?

11. If you thought of this chapter as a
roadmap for a Christian's life, what
would be the safest "roads" to take, as
taught in this chapter? And what
would be the unsafe, dangerous
roads to avoid?

12. What things in this chapter do you
think non-Christians would find
hardest to understand?

13. Suppose that at the end of this chapter, Paul added this line: "If you remember only one thing from this
chapter, let it be this:…" How do
you think he would complete that
sentence?

14. If you were asked to write a discussion question to help your Bible
study group examine and understand
something in this chapter, how
would you word the question?

15. Compare verse 7 in this chapter with
verse 7 of chapter 4 in *First* Corinthians. How do these two verses complement each other?

FOR LIFE TODAY

16. What mental habits do you think
could most easily block the words in
verses 16-18 from staying alive in
your mind and heart?

FOR GOING DEEPER

Reflect further on Paul's words in verse 6
as you also explore together Genesis 1:1-
4, John 1:3-4 and 8:12, and 1 John 1:5.

2 CORINTHIANS 5

Startup: What do you consider the three
most important ingredients for allowing
a church today to reach out successfully
to the community around it?

SEEING WHAT'S THERE

1. What is the only command that Paul
gives the Corinthians in this chapter?

2. Imagine that you were preparing a
special audio-visual presentation for
your church. As a strong, prerecorded voice read through verses 1-10
word for word, a series of slides
would be projected on a screen in
front of the people. What kind of
photographs would you select to be
included in the slide presentation, to
best fit this passage?

3. Once again, look together at 13:8-
10, where Paul discusses his purpose
for writing this letter. How does this
chapter help him accomplish that
purpose?

4. EYE FOR DETAIL—*From what
you recall seeing in this chapter, try answering the following question without
looking at your Bible:* The *shortest*
verse in this chapter is a concise principle about faith. What is this principle? (It's found in verse 7.)

CAPTURE THE ESSENCE

5. How would you summarize what
this chapter gives as the right *motiva-
tions* for our ministry?

6. If this chapter was a good answer to a
question that began with the word
How… then what would the rest of
the question say?

7. If this chapter was the only Scripture
portion you had, what would you
conclude from it about how important it was for Jesus Christ to die?

FOR LIFE TODAY

8. In Colossians 3:1 we read this command: "Since you have been raised
with Christ, set your hearts on things

above, where Christ is seated at the right hand of God." What have you personally observed about Jesus Christ in this chapter that would be worthy of setting your heart on?

9. With the words of verses 14-21 in mind, identify together the kinds of people in your community whom you would say probably know the least about the living Lord Jesus Christ. What else are these people like? What do they do in daily life? Where do they live? Now imagine that God has brought you together with a small group of these people, and in this meeting they indicate a genuine desire to understand who Jesus is and what He has done. From what you have seen in this chapter, what are the most important things you would want to communicate to them?

FOR GOING DEEPER

Compare the picture Paul gives in verse 4 with the following passages, then discuss what they mean for us—Psalm 69:15, Isaiah 25:7-8, Hosea 13:14, and 1 Corinthians 15:53-57.

2 CORINTHIANS 6

Startup: What have been the most severe physical challenges or physical trials that you have faced in life?

SEEING WHAT'S THERE

1. What *commands* does Paul give the Corinthians in this chapter? Together, list them all aloud.

2. After reading through this chapter, which words or phrases or sentences here would you most like to understand better?

3. In verses 1 and 16, Paul tells the Corinthians what *not* to do. For each verse, how fully can you explain what Paul means?

4. Again, imagine yourself looking over Paul's shoulder as he wrote the words of this chapter, under the direction of the Holy Spirit's inner guidance. What emotions, longings, or remembrances do you think he most likely experienced as he wrote verses 3-13?

5. If Paul were reading verses 14-16 aloud to this group right now, which word or words do you think he would emphasize most?

6. Let the words of verse 14 form a picture in your mind, and then describe that picture.

7. From what you see in this chapter, what *expectations* can we rightly have of God?

8. If you were responsible for giving the apostle Paul a job performance review, what comments would you make to him, based on what you've observed about his ministry so far in this letter?

9. Suppose a band of armed terrorists stormed into the room where you're now meeting, and took you as hostages in a captivity that was likely to last for days or weeks. Just before they confiscated your Bibles, they allowed you to take one last look at the

chapter open before you. Which verse in this chapter would you most try to fix in mind before your Bible was snatched away, and why?

10. Examine once more Paul's words in 13:8-10. How would you say this chapter helps Paul fulfill his purpose for writing this letter?

11. EYE FOR DETAIL—*From what you recall seeing in this chapter, try answering the following question without looking at your Bible:* Early in the chapter, Paul quotes an Old Testament verse and says, "Now is the day of…"—what? (See verse 2.)

CAPTURE THE ESSENCE

12. From what you see in this chapter and elsewhere in Scripture, what do you think is the right definition—both practical and biblical—for the idea of Christians being separate from the world?

13. From the evidence you've seen so far in this letter, what are the most important *expectations* Paul has of the Corinthians?

14. In Psalm 119:45, the psalmist says to God, "I will walk at liberty, for I seek Thy precepts." As you think about the "precept" or command given in verse 14, in what ways can you see it offering true freedom and liberty to a Christian?

15. Regarding the subjects you've seen addressed so far in this book, what questions do you have that remain unanswered?

FOR LIFE TODAY

16. Look again at verse 1 and also verse 16. In what ways would you say Christians are most in danger of doing what Paul urges us *not* to do in each of these verses?

17. Choose one of these sentences, and complete it as fully and candidly as you can:

What I see and understand in this chapter is important to my life because…

What I see and understand in this chapter does NOT seem important to my life at this time, because…

FOR GOING DEEPER

Look again at the command in verse 17 to be "separate." Look together at the following passages, and discuss how they expand and clarify the meaning of this concept—1 Thessalonians 5:22, Titus 2:11-15, 1 Peter 2:12, and 1 John 2:15.

2 CORINTHIANS 7

Startup: What do you feel are the most important things you've learned in life about *grief?*

SEEING WHAT'S THERE

1. What are "these promises" which Paul refers to in verse 1?

2. Would you say that verse 1 teaches us that we can become perfect in this life? If not, what *does* it teach?

3. SMALL, BUT IMPORTANT: How many times do you see the little word *but* in verses 5-14? What important contrast or change in direction does this word highlight in each verse?

4. In your own words, how would you describe the two processes that Paul mentions in verse 10?

5. From what you've seen so far in this letter, how would you describe Paul's relationship with the Corinthians?

6. How would you say this chapter fits in with Paul's purpose for this letter, as expressed in 13:8-10?

7. EYE FOR DETAIL— *From what you recall seeing in this chapter, try answering the following question without looking at your Bible:* Titus told Paul something about the Corinthians, and his news brought joy to Paul. What was it? (See verses 6-7.)

8. Remember to look also at the list of "Questions to Ask as You Study Each Chapter" on page 392, which can help you explore each chapter in Second Corinthians.

CAPTURE THE ESSENCE

9. A 3-step question: (a) Think of someone you know who doesn't spend much time reading the Bible. (b) Select a verse or brief passage in this chapter which you think this person would probably find boring. (c) Now decide how you could clari- fy or open up this passage in a way that might appeal to this person.

10. Now that you're halfway through 2 Corinthians, how would you summarize the most important lessons to learn in this book?

FOR LIFE TODAY

11. Consider again the commands in verse 1, and recall the words of Jesus in John 15:5—"Apart from me you can do nothing." Picture in your mind something good that could happen in your life in this area, something that could clearly be ac- complished only by the Lord's super- natural power. What would this be?

12. Look again at the words of Paul in the first half of verse 4, and also in verse 16. Do you think the Lord Himself could make this same per- sonal assessment of *your* church? If not, what would need to change so that He could?

FOR GOING DEEPER

Look again in verse 1 at Paul's teaching on holiness. Then discuss together how this command is strengthened and clari- fied in these passages—1 Thessalonians 4:3 and 4:7, 1 Peter 1:15-16, and 1 John 3:3.

2 Corinthians 8

Startup: What is something in your life that you've started and then set aside for a while, but want to finish when you can?

SEEING WHAT'S THERE

1. If you were asked to cut out all the verses except three, and yet still keep as much of the meaning of this chapter as you could, which three verses would you leave in?

2. Paul mentions in verse 5 how the Christians in Macedonia had given themselves to the Lord. In practical terms, what do you think Paul means by this?

3. SMALL, BUT IMPORTANT: Again in this chapter, as in chapter 7, the little word *but* plays a major role. How many times do you see it occurring here? And what important contrast or change in direction does it highlight in each verse?

4. If Satan wrote down some guidelines and commands to get people to do just the opposite of what this chapter teaches, how do you think his message might be worded?

5. From the evidence you see in this chapter, what is it that Paul wants us most to understand about Jesus?

6. What part would you say this chapter plays in helping to fulfill Paul's purpose for this letter, as expressed in 13:8-10?

7. EYE FOR DETAIL— *From what you recall seeing in this chapter, try answering the following question without looking at your Bible:* In verse 7, Paul says that the Corinthians "excel" or "abound" in everything; he then mentioned five specific ways in which they did this. How many of these five can you recall?

CAPTURE THE ESSENCE

8. As Paul encourages generosity on the part of the Corinthians, how would you compare his message in this chapter with the fundraising letters and appeals of today which you have received?

FOR LIFE TODAY

9. Notice again the commendation Paul gives to the Corinthian church in verse 7. How accurate would those comments be if someone wrote them in a letter to *your* church?

10. What kind of mental habits do you think could most easily block the words in verse 9 from staying alive in your mind and heart?

11. In verse 11, notice again Paul's urging of the Corinthians to finish what they had started. How big a problem is this kind of "unfinished business" in the church today?

FOR GOING DEEPER

Look again in verse 9 at Paul's picture of what Jesus did when He came to earth. Search together in the following passages for word-pictures and statements that deepen our understanding of this miracle of love—John 1:1 and 1:10-14, Philippians 2:6-11, 1 Timothy 3:16, Hebrews 2:14-17, and 1 John 1:1-2.

2 CORINTHIANS 9

Startup: Practically speaking, what do you think is the strongest motivation for people to be more *generous?*

SEEING WHAT'S THERE

1. Which important details in this chapter do you think might be the easiest to overlook?

2. In your own words, how would you describe the *process* that Paul speaks of in verses 10-15?

3. From what you see in this chapter, what *expectations* can we rightly have of God?

4. With all else being equal, which of these people do you think would have the best chance of uncovering the most meaning in this chapter— a gardener, a cheerleader, or a banker?

5. EYE FOR DETAIL— *From what you recall seeing in this chapter, try answering the following question without looking at your Bible:* Paul mentions something that God specifically loves in this chapter. What is it? (See verse 7.)

CAPTURE THE ESSENCE

6. Looking back on chapters 8—9, how would you summarize their most important principles and guidelines on Christian giving?

FOR LIFE TODAY

7. In Philippians 4:8 we're given the following command: "Whatever is true, whatever is noble, whatever is right, whatever is pure, whatever is lovely, whatever is admirable—if anything is excellent or praiseworthy— *think about such things.*" What food for thought can you find in this chapter that especially strikes you as being *true,* or *noble,* or *right,* or *pure,* or *lovely,* or *admirable,* or *excellent,* or *praiseworthy?*

8. For Christians in general today, what would you say is the hardest thing about obeying the guidelines presented in verse 7?

9. If you were asked to write a discussion question to help your Bible study group apply something in this chapter to their lives, how would you word the question?

FOR GOING DEEPER

Look again at verse 7. How do the words of Jesus in Mark 12:41-44 expand and reinforce what Paul is teaching here?

2 CORINTHIANS 10

Startup: What pictures come to your mind when you think of the word *boast?*

SEEING WHAT'S THERE

1. Again, if you were responsible for giving the apostle Paul a job performance review, what comments would you make to him, based on his ministry as you see it in this chapter?

2. Let the words of verse 4 form a picture in your mind, and then describe that picture.

3. How would you say this chapter fits in with Paul's purpose for this letter and his desire for the Corinthians, as expressed in 13:8-10?

4. EYE FOR DETAIL— *From what you recall seeing in this chapter, try answering the following question without looking at your Bible:* In the first verse of this chapter, Paul mentions two qualities of Christ. One is meekness. What is the other one?

CAPTURE THE ESSENCE

5. How would you say the tone of this chapter compares with that of the previous nine chapters in this letter?

6. What would you say Paul is trying to accomplish among the Corinthians in this part of his letter?

FOR LIFE TODAY

7. Think again about the principles Paul states in verses 3-4. In what ways, if any, do you think this verse relates to involvement by Christians in political causes?

FOR GOING DEEPER

Notice Paul's claim about himself at the end of verse 7. Look together at the following passages to see how this claim is reinforced—Acts 26:12-18 and Galatians 1:11-12.

2 CORINTHIANS 11

Startup: Discuss which you think is harder to do: To try to look better than you are, or to try to look worse than you are?

SEEING WHAT'S THERE

1. As you read this chapter, what's the strongest impression or image it leaves in your mind?

2. What in this chapter do you think might be most surprising to a new Christian reading it for the first time?

3. What *risks* would you say Paul is taking by what he says in this chapter?

4. SMALL, BUT IMPORTANT: What important contrast or change in direction does the little word *but* highlight in verse 3?

5. If Paul were reading verses 11-14 aloud to this group right now, which word or words do you think he would emphasize most?

6. Take another look at 13:8-10. How would you say this chapter helps Paul fulfill his purpose for writing this letter, as expressed in those verses?

7. EYE FOR DETAIL— *From what you recall seeing in this chapter, try answering the following question without looking at your Bible:* As you recall Paul's account of his sufferings as an apostle, how many times did he receive the thirty-nine lashes? How many times was he beaten with rods? How many times was he stoned? How many times was he shipwrecked? (See verses 24-25.)

CAPTURE THE ESSENCE

8. Paul speaks in verse 4 of a different Jesus, a different spirit, and a different gospel. How would you explain these in your own words?

9. Would you say this is a chapter that especially requires *patience* as you read and study it, in order to understand it? If so, why?

10. Suppose that at the end of this chapter, Paul added this line: "If you remember only one thing from this chapter, let it be this:…" How do you think he would complete that sentence?

11. How susceptible do you think Christians in general are today to the deception which Paul warns against in verses 3-4?

12. In what situations do you think it would be easiest for you to see through the kind of deceptions Paul describes in verses 13-15? In what situations would it be the most difficult?

FOR GOING DEEPER

Look at the picture Paul gives of Christ and the church in verse 2. Look together at each of the following passages, and allow this image be enhanced by what you see—Matthew 9:15, John 3:29, 1 Corinthians 6:15, Ephesians 5:24-32, and Revelation 19:7-9 and 21:2.

2 CORINTHIANS 12

Startup: Recall a time in life when you felt particularly weak, either physically, emotionally, or spiritually.

SEEING WHAT'S THERE

1. As you read this chapter, what's the strongest impression or image it leaves in your mind?

2. After reading through this chapter, which words or phrases or sentences here would you most like to understand better?

3. What *risks* would you say Paul is taking by what he says in this chapter?

4. Discuss how much you agree or disagree with this statement: In this letter Paul reveals his minister's heart and motivation; therefore his principles and personal examples apply primarily to pastors and teachers only.

5. Let the words of verses 7-9 form a series of pictures in your mind, and then describe those pictures.

6. What part would you say this chapter plays in helping to fulfill Paul's purpose for this letter, as expressed in 13:8-10?

7. EYE FOR DETAIL—*From what you recall seeing in this chapter, try answering the following question without looking at your Bible:* How did Paul complete the following sentence? "For when I am weak,…" (See verse 10.)

CAPTURE THE ESSENCE

8. If this chapter was a good answer to a question that began with the word *Why…* then what would the rest of the question say?

FOR LIFE TODAY

9. Suppose someone said to you, "I like what Jesus teaches better than what Paul teaches, and I ignore a lot of what Paul says. But that's no problem because Paul's letters don't have

the same authority that the Gospels have." How could you use what you've seen in this chapter or elsewhere in Second Corinthians to help you in your response?

10. How could you use Paul's example and God's dealings with him in verses 7-10 to help a young Christian who felt defeated by his personal limitations?

FOR GOING DEEPER

Look again at what Paul says about weakness and strength in verses 9-10. Then look at the following passages, and discuss the picture they give us of how God deals with our weakness—Psalms 18:1-2, 18:32-33, 46:1, and 118:14; Ephesians 3:16; and Philippians 4:13.

2 CORINTHIANS 13

Startup: What are some of the hardest questions for a person to ask himself?

SEEING WHAT'S THERE

1. Discuss which verses in this chapter your attention would most likely be drawn to if you were… (a) a person who had to give testimony tomorrow in a trial in which a close friend was the defendant. (b) a hardened atheist who was looking for ways to discredit and disprove the Bible. (c) a person wrestling with a major decision.

2. What *commands* does Paul give the Corinthians in this chapter? As a group, list them all aloud.

3. What would you say are the most important *verbs*—the action words —in this chapter?

4. If Satan wrote down some guidelines and commands to get people to do just the opposite of what this chapter teaches, how do you think his message might be worded?

5. To carry out the "examination" Paul commands in verse 5, what are some good, practical questions a Christian should ask himself or herself?

6. Keep in mind again verses 8-10. How would you say this chapter helps Paul accomplish his purpose for this letter, and his desire for the Corinthians?

7. From what you've seen now throughout this letter, how would you describe Paul's relationship with the Corinthians?

8. EYE FOR DETAIL—*From what you recall seeing in this chapter, try answering the following question without looking at your Bible:* What kind of *kiss* does Paul speak of near the end of this chapter? (See verse 12.)

CAPTURE THE ESSENCE

9. Which commands in verse 11 would you say are the easiest for most

Christians to obey? Which are the easiest to *dis*obey?

10. Notice in verse 14 how Paul closes this letter with a reference to the Trinity—God in three Persons. From what you see in this passage and elsewhere in Scripture, what is to be our *experience* and practical understanding of the Trinity?

FOR LIFE TODAY

11. If God had written this chapter only for *you,* which words or phrases do you think He would have underlined?

FOR GOING DEEPER

Notice again Paul's reference in verse 14 to the Trinity. Look at the following passages, and discuss how each one promotes our proper understanding of this foundational concept—Matthew 3:16-17 and 28:18-19, John 14:15-17, 1 Corinthians 12:3-6, 2 Thessalonians 2:13, and 1 Peter 1:1-2.

2 CORINTHIANS:

THE BIG PICTURE

(Discuss again the questions in the "Overview," plus the questions below.)

1. Suppose you were visiting the church in Corinth on the day this letter from Paul was first read aloud. After the church meeting, you walked out in the street with others who had been in attendance. As you did so, some of them asked you the following questions. How would you answer each one? (a) "Do you think Paul was too touchy and defensive in that letter?" (b) "As Paul grows older, is he also growing arrogant and boastful?" (c) "Do you think Paul still cares for us?"

2. Look at each of these verses, and discuss which one you believe is the best candidate for "KEY VERSE" in the book of Second Corinthians—the one which brings into sharpest focus what this book is most about: 2:14, 4:5, 5:17, 5:20, or 12:9.

3. In James 1:23-24 we're told that "anyone who listens to the word but does not do what it says is like a man who looks at his face in a mirror and, after looking at himself, goes away and immediately forgets what he looks like." In what important ways has the book of Second Corinthians been a "mirror" for you—showing you what you can and should do?

4. If you've decided on a starting point for applying something in this book more effectively to your life, what commitment would you be willing to make to others in your group regarding this?

5. How would you complete the following word of advice to growing Christians? *Explore the book of Second Corinthians if you want to learn more about…*

Galatians

OVERVIEW

(Discuss these OVERVIEW questions both at the beginning of your study of Galatians, and again after you've studied together all six chapters. Your answers may change significantly once you've looked more closely at the entire book.)

Startup: What to you are the most important kinds of freedom?

SEEING WHAT'S THERE

1. Start scanning the book until you come to a verse that brings a question to your mind. What's the question?

2. Begin scanning the book again until you come to a verse that gives you a smile or a sense of gratitude or joy. What is pleasing to you about this verse?

3. What important events from Paul's life do we learn about in this letter, and why do they seem to be important?

4. Which parts of this letter do you find most difficult?

5. Which parts of this letter do you find most encouraging?

6. What do you know about what the world was like at the time this letter was written? What would you guess to be the typical hopes and dreams and concerns of the Galatians?

7. Look also at the list of "Questions to Ask as You Begin Your Study of Each Book" on page 393.

CAPTURE THE ESSENCE

8. What previous impressions, if any, have you had about the book of Galatians in regard to (a) its content, (b) its level of difficulty, and (c) its importance?

9. The book of Galatians has been called "The Book of Christian Liberty," "Our Freedom in Christ," and "By Grace, Not by Law." With that reputation for this book, what answers and guidelines and solutions would you like to gain as you examine it more closely?

10. What impressions of Paul's personality do you get from this letter?

11. Take a quick look together at only the *first two or three verses* in each chapter in Galatians. What impressions and expectations of this book do you get from this partial scan?

12. Imagine you were the person carrying this letter from Paul to the churches in Galatia. Along the way, you were attacked by a band of robbers who stripped you of all your valuables, including this letter. The leader of the robber band couldn't read, and when you asked him to return the letter, he replied, "Why? What's in it that's so important?" How would you answer him?

FOR LIFE TODAY

13. When you get to heaven, if you have a long talk with the apostle Paul and he asks you, "What was most helpful to you in my letter to the Galatians?" —how would you like to be able to answer him?

14. From what you see in this book, discuss together how you would com-

plete this sentence: *What God really wants from me is...*

15. How can you ensure that your study of Galatians is not merely theoretical and intellectual, but is instead truly practical and relevant? Talk together about this. What can you do to help keep the process alive and interesting?

FOR GOING DEEPER

Look in Acts 16:6 for Luke's account of Paul's visit to Galatia. Then explore together Acts 15 and 16 to see what issues and events were important to Paul at this time in his life.

GALATIANS 1

Startup: What are the hardest things to communicate to someone you love?

SEEING WHAT'S THERE

1. As you read this chapter, what's the strongest impression or image it leaves in your mind?

2. What in this chapter do you think might be most surprising to a new Christian reading it for the first time?

3. How many times do you see the word *grace* in this chapter? Which verse do you think gives the best illustration of grace?

4. How many times do you see the word *gospel* in this chapter? Which verse in this chapter do you think gives the best definition of the gospel (even if it doesn't include the exact word)?

5. SMALL, BUT IMPORTANT: The word *but* signals a contrast, or a change in direction. What important contrast or change in direction does this word highlight in verse 15?

6. From what you've seen so far in this letter, how would you describe Paul's relationship with the Galatians?

7. Look also at the list of "Questions to Ask as You Study Each Chapter" on page 392, which you may want to do for each chapter in Galatians.

8. EYE FOR DETAIL—*If everyone in the group has read the entire chapter, try answering the following question without looking at your Bible:* In the following list of places, which one is *not* mentioned in this chapter as a place Paul had visited? Arabia, Damascus, Jerusalem, Rome, or Syria? (See verses 17-18 and 21.)

CAPTURE THE ESSENCE

9. Picture this book of Galatians as a fast-moving train. Chapter 1 is the locomotive in front, and the other chapters represent railway cars that

follow behind. From what you see here in chapter 1, what is the *energy* in the locomotive—the point or principle or theme that's the driving force for the locomotive and the entire train?

10. Look closely at verses 11-12. When Christians share the gospel message with non-Christians today, how can they be certain it is the gospel from Jesus Christ, and not merely a gospel that comes from man?

FOR GOING DEEPER

Look again at Paul's statement of cursing or condemnation in verses 8-9, then discuss together how the following passages shed light on the meaning of this —Romans 9:3, and 1 Corinthians 12:2-3 and 16:22.

GALATIANS 2

Startup: What images come to your mind when you think of the contrast between death and life?

SEEING WHAT'S THERE

1. Suppose the telegraph had been invented back in New Testament times, and Paul decided to send the Galatians a brief telegram of this chapter, in advance of the delivery of the full letter. In order to save money, he decided to send only the three most important verses from the chapter. Which three verses do you think Paul would have chosen?

2. From what you see in this chapter, how would you describe Paul's priorities in life?

3. How many times do you see the word *law* in this chapter? How would you define what Paul means by this word, as he uses it here?

4. How does what you learn in this chapter about Simon Peter (also called Cephas) compare with what you know about him from the gospels and Acts?

5. SMALL, BUT IMPORTANT: What important contrast or change in direction does the little word *but* highlight in verse 20?

6. Look again at verse 20. In your own words, what would you say are the marks of someone who truly understands and believes the gospel?

7. EYE FOR DETAIL—*From what you recall seeing in this chapter, try answering the following question without looking at your Bible:* In the following list of names, which one is *not* someone mentioned by Paul in this chapter? Barnabas, Titus, Timothy, Peter, James, or John? (See verses 1 and 7-9.)

8. Notice how often the crucial word *faith* appears in verse 16. From the evidence you see in this chapter, how do you think Paul would define this word?

9. Looking together at verses 19-20, how would you explain what Paul means when he speaks of *living* and *dying?*

10. Review verse 6, then look together at 1 Samuel 16:7. From these verses, what conclusions can you make about God's *character*, and about God's *judgment* of human beings?

11. If you were asked to write a discussion question to help your Bible study group examine and understand something in this chapter, how would you word the question?

FOR LIFE TODAY

12. Look again at Paul's example in verse 20. What kind of mental habits do you think could most easily block the words in this verse from staying alive in your mind and heart?

13. The older you get, in what ways does it get easier to live out what Paul teaches by example and word in verse 20? In what ways does it get harder?

14. As you think about the situation presented in this chapter, what parallels do you see with what *has* happened or *is* happening in your family or church, or in your personal life?

FOR GOING DEEPER

Keep in mind what Paul says about the law in this chapter, as you look together at the following passages and explore what they say on this topic—Romans 7:7-12, 1 Timothy 1:8-11, and Hebrews 7:11-12.

GALATIANS 3

Startup: When you think of the word *law,* what visual images or synonyms come to your mind?

SEEING WHAT'S THERE

1. Imagine you are one of the Galatians listening to this letter being read for the first time in one of your church meetings. As the reader begins reading this chapter, the person next to you taps your shoulder and says, "I'm new here; what is Paul talking about?" How would you answer?

2. After reading through this chapter, which words or phrases or sentences here would you most like to understand better?

3. For useful background on verses 6-18, look over the landmark events in Abraham's life recorded in Genesis 12:1-8, 13:11-18, 15:1-6, 18:16-19, and 22:9-19.

4. Notice again in this chapter the crucial word *faith,* and how often it appears in verses 22-26. If this chapter was the only Scripture portion you had, what biblical definition would you give for this word?

5. From what you see in this chapter, what is the relationship between *law* and *life,* using these words in the same way Paul uses them?

6. In the way Paul describes the *law* in this chapter, what does he identify as the biggest limitations to the law's effectiveness?

7. Regarding the subjects you've seen addressed so far in this book, what questions do you have that remain unanswered?

8. EYE FOR DETAIL—*From what you recall seeing in this chapter, try answering the following question without looking at your Bible:* Near the end of this chapter, Paul tells the Galatian Christians that they are "all one in

Christ Jesus." He also gives three pairs of examples of the kind of human divisions that are overcome by unity in Christ. The first pair is "Jew and Greek." What were the other two pairs of examples? (See verse 28.)

CAPTURE THE ESSENCE

9. Suppose that at the end of this chapter, Paul added this line: "If you remember only one thing from this chapter, let it be this:…" How do you think he would complete that sentence?

10. *How* exactly has Scripture done what Paul says it has in verse 22?

11. Now that you're halfway through the book of Galatians, how would you summarize the most important teachings you've seen in this letter?

FOR LIFE TODAY

12. Look again at the truths expressed in verses 26-29. What practical difference could these truths make in a Christian's self-image? What practical difference could they make in the way a Christian views other Christians?

13. Suppose you were discussing the gospel with a non-Christian friend, and he said to you, "What does the death of Jesus really have to do with it? Can't God save people without having to kill someone on a cross?" In your response, how could you use what Paul teaches in this chapter?

FOR GOING DEEPER

Look together again at verses 19-20, and compare them with 1 Timothy 2:5-6, and Acts 7:38 and 7:53.

GALATIANS 4

Startup: When do you feel most like God's child?

SEEING WHAT'S THERE

1. What is the only command Paul gives the Galatians in this chapter?

2. What does Paul mean by the word *law,* as he uses it in this chapter?

3. Describe as fully as you can, in your own words, the before-and-after picture which Paul is giving us in verses 3-8.

4. SMALL, BUT IMPORTANT: What important contrast or change in direction does the little word *but* highlight in verse 4?

5. When Paul says in verse 16 that he had told the truth to the Galatians, what "truth" do you think he is speaking of?

6. EYE FOR DETAIL—*From what you recall seeing in this chapter, try answering the following question without looking at your Bible:* Paul says that because we are God's children, God sent His Spirit into our hearts. Paul also talks about what the Spirit "cries" within us. What is this cry? (See verse 6.)

CAPTURE THE ESSENCE

7. Would you say this is a chapter that especially requires *patience* as you read and study it, in order to understand it? If so, why?

8. Look again at verses 8-10. How does truly knowing God—and being known by God—take away any need for legalistic rules and principles?

9. If you asked the apostle Paul, "What's the worst form of slavery?" how do you think he might answer, based on what you see in this chapter?

10. From the evidence you've seen so far in this letter, what are the most important *expectations* Paul has of the Galatians?

FOR LIFE TODAY

11. Look again at verse 28. What does it mean to you to be a "child of promise"? How often do you think of yourself that way?

FOR GOING DEEPER

In verse 4, notice again Paul's use of the phrase "in the fullness of time" or "when the time had fully come." Then discuss together how the following verses illuminate his meaning—Mark 1:14-15, Romans 5:6, and Ephesians 1:9-10.

GALATIANS 5

Startup: Look together at the "fruit of the Spirit" listed in verses 22-23. If you were making a poster to illustrate this passage, and you wanted to show a different kind of fruit for each of the qualities listed there, which fruit would you choose for each one?

SEEING WHAT'S THERE

1. What kind of questions or difficulties or doubts in a Christian's daily life do you think this chapter answers best?

2. What *commands* does Paul give the Galatians in this chapter? As a group, list them all aloud.

3. Suppose a band of armed terrorists stormed into the room where you're now meeting, then took you as hostages in a captivity that was likely to last for days or weeks. Just before they confiscated your Bibles, they allowed you to take one last look at the chapter open before you. Which verse in this chapter would you most try to fix in mind before your Bible was snatched away, and why?

4. How would you summarize what the book of Galatians says about *slavery* and *freedom?*

5. What is Paul's chief concern for the Galatians, as expressed in this chapter?

6. If Paul were reading verses 13-15 aloud to this group right now, which word or words do you think he would emphasize most?

7. SMALL, BUT IMPORTANT: Notice the little word *but* in verses 18 and 22, and identify the important contrast or the change in direction that this word highlights in each verse.

8. EYE FOR DETAIL— *From what you recall seeing in this chapter, try answering the following question without*

looking at your Bible: In verse 14, Paul sums up the law in a single command. What is this command?

9. Many times we rob ourselves of the discovery of deeper truths in Scripture because we see a passage and say to ourselves, "I already know that." For which teachings in this chapter might it be easiest for Christians to fall into that trap?

10. Why does a Christian have to stand firm and strong (verse 1) in order to keep out of legalism?

11. How would you compare what Paul says about the Holy Spirit in verses 16-26 with what he said in 4:6?

12. How does the Holy Spirit handle the conflict with evil which Paul speaks of in verse 17?

13. If this chapter was a good answer to a question that began with the word *How…* then what would the rest of the question say?

14. How would you describe the *freedom* God wants us to have in our lives, as you see it expressed in this letter?

15. What can keep us from experiencing the freedom in life that this letter talks about?

16. Look again at verse 13. What are the most important things we have to serve others *with?*

17. Suppose a new Christian asked you, "How can I *know* that the Holy Spirit lives in me?" How could you use verses 22-23 to help you give a meaningful answer?

18. How would you describe your own personal progress in living out the truth expressed in verse 24?

19. In verse 26, notice again what Paul tells us *not* to do. In what ways would you say Christians are most in danger of doing this?

20. Of all that you see in this chapter, what one truth are you most *thankful* for, because of its personal significance to you?

21. If God had written this chapter only for *you,* which words or phrases do you think He would have underlined?

Notice again the description of the fruit of the Spirit in verses 22-23, then discuss how closely this list corresponds to the lists of qualities and virtues in 2 Corinthians 6:6, Ephesians 5:9, and Colossians 3:12-15.

GALATIANS 6

Startup: What kinds of experiences make you the most tired—either mentally or physically—and what kinds of experiences help you most to alleviate that tiredness?

SEEING WHAT'S THERE

1. Describe the kind of person whom you think would gain the most out of this chapter. What would be his or her questions and struggles and concerns?

2. What do you think is the "law of Christ" mentioned in verse 2?

3. Look again at verse 17. For background on the scars on Paul's body, look at Acts 14:19 and 16:22-23, and 2 Corinthians 11:23-25. In what ways do you think these incidents in Paul's life might have influenced what Paul wrote in this letter?

4. What *commands* does Paul give the Galatians in this chapter? Together, make a list of all of them.

5. Which important details in this chapter do you think might be the easiest to overlook?

6. EYE FOR DETAIL— *From what you recall seeing in this chapter, try answering the following question without looking at your Bible:* What does Paul says we fulfill by bearing one another's burdens? (See verse 2.)

CAPTURE THE ESSENCE

7. How would you explain in your own words what the cross of Jesus Christ meant to Paul?

8. Look again at the principles Paul gives in verse 7. How have you seen the truth of these principles in your own life, or in the lives of those around you?

FOR LIFE TODAY

9. How susceptible do you think Christians in general are today to the de-

ception which Paul warns against in verse 7?

10. Imagine you saw earlier today a message written in fire in the sky. It was addressed to you by name, then continued with these words: *Thus saith the LORD: "Read Galatians 6, for I have something for you there."* Which verse or verses in this chapter do you think He most likely would be referring to?

11. In Philippians 4:8 we're given the following command: "Whatever is true, whatever is noble, whatever is right, whatever is pure, whatever is lovely, whatever is admirable—if anything is excellent or praiseworthy— *think about such things."* What food for thought can you find in this chapter that especially strikes you as being *true,* or *noble,* or *right,* or *pure,* or *lovely,* or *admirable,* or *excellent,* or *praiseworthy?*

12. If you were talking with a non-Christian friend who was thinking seriously about the gospel, and who asked you, "But why do so many Christians seem to do wrong things?"— what verses could you use in this chapter (or from elsewhere in Galatians) to help you give a meaningful reply, and how would you use them?

13. If you were asked to write a discussion question to help your Bible study group apply something in this chapter to their lives, how would you word the question?

FOR GOING DEEPER

Don't grow weary! With the challenge in verses 9-10 in mind, look also at the following passages that teach endurance, then discuss some workable ways to put them into practice— 1 Corinthians 9:24-27, Ephesians 6:10-20, Philippians 3:12-14, and 2 Timothy 2:1-13.

GALATIANS:

THE BIG PICTURE

(Discuss again the questions in the "Overview," plus the questions below.)

1. Suppose you were attending a citizens' meeting called by local school officials who were considering the removal of the Bible from the shelves of all school libraries in your community. You spoke up in favor of keeping the Bible available to students. Then another citizen rose to his feet and said, "I see no reason to keep it around. It's a forgotten book anyway. Even most Christians have no idea what's in it. For example," he said, then turned directly to you and asked, "Tell me what the book of Galatians is all about." In that situation, how would you respond?

2. Look together at each of these verses, and discuss which one you believe is the best candidate for "KEY VERSE" in the book of Galatians— the one which brings into sharpest focus what this book is most about: 2:16, 2:20, 3:13, 3:26, 4:6, 5:1, or 5:25.

3. From what you see in the book of Galatians, how would you describe Paul's relationship with God?

4. How would you summarize what this letter says about *faith?*

5. In James 1:23-24 we're told that "anyone who listens to the word but does not do what it says is like a man who looks at his face in a mirror and, after looking at himself, goes away and immediately forgets what he looks like." In what important ways has the book of Galatians been a "mirror" for you—showing you what you can and should do?

6. Suppose you heard a voice from heaven saying to you, "Don't get over-ambitious and try to apply too much from this book to your life right now. Just pick one thing to focus on, and do it well." What one thing would you choose?

7. If you've decided on a starting point for applying something in this book more effectively to your life, what commitment would you be willing to make to others in your group regarding this?

8. How would you complete the following word of advice to growing Christians? *Explore the book of Galatians if you want to learn more about...*

Ephesians

❖

OVERVIEW

(Discuss these OVERVIEW questions both at the beginning of your study of Ephesians, and again after you've studied together all six chapters. Your answers may change significantly once you've looked more closely at the entire book.)

Startup: If an extremely wealthy man promised to make a gift to you of anything you wanted—except a cash payment—what would you want to receive?

SEEING WHAT'S THERE

1. Start scanning the book until you come to a verse that brings a question to your mind. What's the question?

2. Begin scanning the book again until you come to a verse that gives you a smile or a sense of gratitude or joy. What is pleasing to you about this verse?

3. How many times in this letter do you find the word *rich* or *riches?*

4. How many chapters in this book appear to focus most on what *God* has done? How many focus on what *we* should do as a result?

5. What do you know about the location and importance of the city of Ephesus at the time of Paul?

6. What do you know about what the world was like at the time this letter was written? What would you guess to be the typical hopes and dreams and concerns of the Ephesians?

7. What do we find out about the Ephesian church in Revelation 2:1-7?

8. Look also at the list of "Questions to Ask as You Begin Your Study of Each Book" on page 393.

CAPTURE THE ESSENCE

9. What previous impressions, if any, have you had about the book of Ephesians in regard to (a) its content, (b) its level of difficulty, and (c) its importance?

10. The book of Ephesians has been called "The Epistle of Fullness," "Heavenly Blessings in Christ," "Our Riches in Christ," and "The Book of Church Unity." With that reputation for this book, what answers and guidelines and solutions would you like to gain as you examine it more closely?

11. Take a quick look together at only the *first two or three verses* in each chapter in Ephesians. What impressions and expectations of this book do you get from this partial scan?

12. Imagine you were the person carrying this letter from Paul to Ephesus. Along the way, you were attacked by a band of robbers who stripped you of all your valuables, including this letter. The leader of the robber band couldn't read, and when you asked him to return the letter, he replied, "Why? What's in it that's so important?" How would you answer him?

FOR LIFE TODAY

13. What kind of mental habits do you think could most easily block the principles and promises and com-

mands in this book from staying alive in your mind and heart?

14. When you get to heaven, if you have a long talk with the apostle Paul and he asks you, "What was most helpful to you in my letter to the Ephesians?"—how would you like to be able to answer him?

15. Suppose you heard a voice from heaven saying to you, "Don't get over-ambitious and try to apply too much from this book to your life right now. Just pick one thing to focus on, and do it well." What one thing would you choose?

16. How can you ensure that your study of Ephesians is not merely theoretical and intellectual, but is instead truly practical and relevant? Talk together about this. What can you do to help keep the process alive and interesting?

FOR GOING DEEPER

For helpful background on Paul's experiences with the Ephesians, look together at Acts 19 and 20, especially 20:17-38. How would you describe Paul's relationship with the Ephesians?

EPHESIANS 1

Startup: Talk about an especially memorable position or team or honor for which you were once chosen.

SEEING WHAT'S THERE

1. Point out everything you see in this chapter that shows a *decision* or *purpose* on God's part.

2. From what you see in verse 3, what is your relationship to heaven *right now?*

3. Look closely at verses 3-14. Then together, list aloud everything this passage says that we have *in Christ.*

4. Looking again at verses 3-14, which of these verses are mostly about God the Father? Which are mostly about His Son, Jesus Christ? Which are mostly about the Holy Spirit?

5. What happens in the relationship between God and Jesus Christ in this chapter?

6. What do verses 9-10 tell us to expect in the future?

7. In verse 18, Paul uses the term "the eyes of your heart," or "the eyes of your understanding." What do you think he means by this phrase, and why do you think he worded it this way?

8. Consider carefully verses 19-20, then discuss how much you agree or disagree with this sentence: The force and energy available to us from God as an everyday experience is just as great and godly as the power with which Jesus rose up from the dead and then ascended into heaven.

9. What does Paul mean by the word *fullness* in verse 23?

10. Look also at the list of "Questions to Ask as You Study Each Chapter" on page 392, which you may want to do for each chapter in Ephesians.

11. EYE FOR DETAIL—*If everyone in the group has read the entire chapter, try answering the following question without looking at your Bible:* As Paul repeats his prayer for the Ephesians, what is the first thing he asks God to give them? (See verse 17.)

12. What picture is Paul giving us in verses 22-23? Describe what it looks like to you.

13. Look again at verses 22-23. If there were no church, what loss would that mean for Jesus?

14. From what you see in this chapter, complete this sentence: *God saved us because…*

15. If this chapter was the only Scripture you had, how would you use it to help explain to someone else what the Holy Spirit is like?

16. Picture this book of Ephesians as a fast-moving train. Chapter 1 is the locomotive in front, and the other chapters represent railway cars following behind. From what you see here in chapter 1, what is the *energy* in the locomotive—the point or principle or theme that's the driving force for the locomotive and the entire train?

17. If this chapter was a good answer to a question that began with the word *Why…* then what would the rest of the question say?

18. If this chapter was the only Scripture portion you had access to, what could you still discover about God's personality?

19. If it's true that "you *become* what you *think,*" then what are the most important thoughts from this chapter to plant firmly in your mind?

20. Look again at Paul's prayer for the Ephesians in verses 16-19. Suppose you and God were looking over a written transcript of all your prayers in the past year. Which elements of Paul's prayer do you think God might encourage you to add more often in your prayers for yourself? Which elements do you think He might encourage you to add more often in your prayers for other people?

21. In Colossians 3:1 we read this command: "Since you have been raised with Christ, set your hearts on things above, where Christ is seated at the right hand of God." What have you personally observed about Jesus Christ in this chapter that would be worthy of setting your heart on?

22. Notice the places in this chapter in which Paul mentions God's *will.* Suppose a new Christian asked you, "How can I discover God's will for my life?" How could you use this chapter to help you give a meaningful answer?

23. If this chapter were the only portion of Scripture you had access to, how could you use it to help answer this question: *What is the most powerful and effective way to improve my life?*

24. Of all that you see in this chapter, what one truth are you most *thankful* for, because of its personal significance to you?

Look again at Paul's mention of the "heavenly realms" or "heavenly places" in verses 3 and 20. Look also at how this term is used in 2:6, 3:10, and 6:12. Taking all these verses together, define as fully as you can what Paul means by this term.

EPHESIANS 2

Startup: Can you recall being in a situation in which two groups of people were very hostile to one another?

SEEING WHAT'S THERE

1. Suppose the telegraph had been invented back in New Testament times, and Paul decided to send the Ephesians a brief telegram of this chapter, in advance of the delivery of the full letter. To save money, he decided for now to send only the three most important verses from the chapter. Which three verses do you think Paul would have chosen?

2. After reading through this chapter, which words or phrases or sentences here would you most like to understand better?

3. What in this chapter do you think might be most surprising to a new Christian reading it for the first time?

4. In a single sentence, summarize what God has accomplished through Christ in our individual lives, as described in verses 1-10. Then, in another sentence, summarize what God accomplished through Christ in the life of the church, as described in verses 11-22.

5. What happens in the relationship between God and Jesus Christ in this chapter?

6. Picture verses 1-10 in your mind as a before-and-after comparison. What images do you see on the "before" side? What do you see on the "after" side?

7. How would you explain verses 4-5 to a young child?

8. From what you see in verse 6, what is your relationship to heaven *right now?*

9. From what you see in verses 8-10, discuss how much you agree or disagree with this statement: Faith is not so much something we must develop before we can be saved, but more a gift God gives us *because* He is saving us.

10. Discuss together which verses in this chapter your attention would most likely be drawn to if you were... (a) a person who had just been released from prison. (b) a convicted criminal who was due to be executed tomorrow. (c) a Jew who had just become a Christian, and was reading the New Testament for the first time. (d) a language analyst who was doing an investigation of Paul's personality as revealed in his writings. (e) a hardened atheist who was looking for ways to discredit and disprove the Bible. (f) a counselor who was working with someone having suicidal tendencies. (g) a person serving on a jury in a murder case. (h) a person wrestling with a major decision.

11. EYE FOR DETAIL— *From what you recall seeing in this chapter, try answering the following question without looking at your Bible:* Paul mentions a specific way in which God is rich. What is it? (See verse 4.)

CAPTURE THE ESSENCE

12. From what you see in this chapter, what *expectations* can we rightly have of God?

13. If you were not yet a Christian, what teachings about Jesus Christ in this chapter do you think would be most intriguing to you, and why?

14. Many times we rob ourselves of the discovery of deeper truths in Scripture because we see a passage and say to ourselves, "I already know that." For which teachings in this chapter might it be easiest for Christians to fall into that trap?

15. Suppose that at the end of this chapter, Paul added this line: "If you remember only one thing from this

chapter, let it be this:..." How do you think he would complete that sentence?

16. Explain as fully as you can what *response* you think God expects for the gift mentioned in verse 8.

17. Review Paul's statement in verse 10. *Why* would you say God wants us to know this?

18. Look at the building Paul describes in verses 19-22, and imagine a picture of it in your mind. What does this building look like, and what happens inside it?

19. If this chapter was the only Scripture you had, how would you use it to help explain to someone else what the Holy Spirit is like?

FOR LIFE TODAY

20. In Philippians 4:8 we're given the following command: "Whatever is true, whatever is noble, whatever is right, whatever is pure, whatever is lovely, whatever is admirable—if anything is excellent or praiseworthy—*think about such things.*" What food for thought can you find in this chapter that especially strikes you as being *true,* or *noble,* or *right,* or *pure,* or *lovely,* or *admirable,* or *excellent,* or *praiseworthy?*

21. If you had only this chapter in Scripture to refer to, how would you use verses 8-10 to help show someone how to become a Christian?

22. In light of how you're doing spiritually in your life today, which verse in this chapter do you think is the most important at this time—and why?

FOR GOING DEEPER

What is the church supposed to *be* and to *do?* To answer, look together at what Paul says in verses 19-22, and in the following verses elsewhere in Ephesians— 1:11, 1:22, 3:18-19, 3:21, 4:3, 4:11-13, and 4:16.

EPHESIANS 3

Startup: Talk about a time when you had knowledge of something important but had to keep it secret for a while.

SEEING WHAT'S THERE

1. What is the only command Paul gives the Ephesians in this chapter?

2. What would you say are the most important *verbs*—the action words —in this chapter?

3. How many times do you see the word *mystery* in this chapter? What is this mystery, and what is Paul's relationship to it?

4. From what you read in verses 1-13, state in your own words Paul's job description for his ministry.

5. From what you see in verse 10, what is your present relationship to heaven and the entire spiritual universe?

6. From what you see in verses 10-11 and 20-21, state in your own words the *church's* job description.

7. If Paul came to this meeting of your group and read aloud his prayer in verses 14-21, which word or words do you think he would emphasize most?

8. From what you've seen so far in this book, how would you define the most important *goals* which God has for the church?

9. EYE FOR DETAIL—*From what you recall seeing in this chapter, try answering the following question without looking at your Bible:* What brief phrase did Paul use to describe the message of Christ which he had been given to preach to the Gentiles? (See verse 8.)

CAPTURE THE ESSENCE

10. If you were asked to write a discussion question to help your Bible study group examine and understand

something in this chapter, how would you word the question?

11. In verse 13, Paul talks about the process of his sufferings resulting in glory for the Ephesians. How does that process work?

12. What insights do you find in verses 20-21 regarding the right way to approach God in worship?

13. A 3-step question: (a) Think of someone you know who doesn't spend much time reading the Bible. (b) Select a verse or brief passage in this chapter which you think this person would probably find boring. (c) Now, how could you clarify or open up this passage in a way that might appeal to this person?

14. If this chapter was the only Scripture you had, how would you use it to help explain to someone else what the Holy Spirit is like?

15. Imagine yourself looking over Paul's shoulder as he wrote the words of this chapter, under the direction of the Holy Spirit's inner guidance. What emotions, or longings, or remembrances do you think he most likely experienced as he wrote the different parts of this chapter?

16. Regarding the subjects you've seen addressed so far in this book, what questions do you have that remain unanswered?

17. From the evidence you've seen so far in this letter, what are the most important *expectations* Paul has of the Ephesians?

FOR LIFE TODAY

18. As you consider your own life, how much ownership can you claim to the statement Paul makes in verse 7? Is this a picture of your life as well?

19. Notice again verse 13, where Paul says that his sufferings or tribulations were for the "glory" of the Ephesians.

Explain whether or not you believe his sufferings were for *your* glory too. Discuss also whether there are others today whose sufferings are for your glory.

20. In verses 14-19, look at Paul's second prayer for the Ephesians recorded in this letter. Imagine again that you and God are looking over a written transcript of all your prayers in the past year. Which elements of this prayer of Paul's do you think God might encourage you to add more often in your prayers for yourself? Which elements do you think He might encourage you to add more often in your prayers for other people?

FOR GOING DEEPER

Notice again Paul's use of the word *mystery* in this chapter. Is that word a mystery to you? Look at Romans 11:25 and 16:25-26, Colossians 1:25-27, and Revelation 10:5-7 to understand more of how this word is used in the Bible.

EPHESIANS 4

Startup: If you've traveled at sea, what's the worst storm you can recall experiencing?

SEEING WHAT'S THERE

1. With chapter 4, we begin a new part of the book of Ephesians. In only a few sentences, how would you summarize the most important teachings so far in this book?

2. What kind of questions or difficulties or doubts in a Christian's daily life do you think this chapter answers best?

3. What *commands* does Paul give the Ephesians in chapter 4? Together, list them all aloud.

4. If you had never heard anything else about Christianity, what would you say were the most important features of the Christian *lifestyle,* based only on what you see in this chapter?

5. From what you see in verses 1-16, *why* has God offered us spiritual gifts?

6. Let the words of verse 14 form a picture in your mind, and then describe that picture.

7. How would you explain verses 15-16 to a young child?

8. Picture verses 13-32 in your mind as a before-and-after comparison. Depict as fully as you can what you see on both the "before" side, and the "after" side?

9. From what you see in this chapter alone, what would you say are the most important moral standards for Christians?

10. EYE FOR DETAIL— *From what you recall seeing in this chapter, try answering the following question without looking at your Bible:* Paul provides in this chapter a long list of things of which there is only "one" for Christians. Which of the following things is *not* included on Paul's list? One Spirit, one hope, one Lord, one faith, one love, one baptism, one God and Father. (See verses 4-6.)

CAPTURE THE ESSENCE

11. If the first three chapters of this letter to the Ephesians had somehow been lost in history, what difference would that make in regard to the meaning of what you see in chapter 4?

12. If you thought of this chapter as a roadmap for a Christian's life, what would be the safest "roads" to take, as taught in this chapter? What would be the unsafe, dangerous roads to avoid?

13. From what you see in this chapter, what can we truly rely on God to do as we obey Him?

14. In Psalm 119:45, the psalmist says to God, "I will walk at liberty, for I seek Thy precepts." As you think about the "precepts" or commands given in verses 1-3, in what ways can you see it offering true freedom and liberty to a Christian?

15. Paul uses the word *neighbor* in verse 25. Does he mean "everyone" when he says this? If not, who exactly does he mean?

16. In Proverbs 13:13 we're told, "He who respects a command is rewarded," or in another translation, "He that feareth the commandment shall be rewarded." Look at the command in verse 29. What would you say is the likely *reward* for respecting and keeping this command?

17. If this chapter was the only Scripture you had, how would you use it to help explain to someone else what the Holy Spirit is like?

FOR LIFE TODAY

18. Imagine you saw earlier today a message written in fire in the sky. It was addressed to you by name, then con-

tinued with these words: *Thus saith the LORD: "Read Ephesians 4, for I have something for you there."* Which verse or verses in this chapter do you think He most likely would be referring to?

19. Practically speaking, what do you think is the strongest motivation for Christians to find and experience more *unity* with other Christians?

20. Imagine some new neighbors moved in next door to you, and that their lives were perfect examples of what Paul speaks about in verse 2. In practical terms, how would you describe what their relationship with *you* would be like?

21. In verse 17, notice again what Paul tells us *not* to do. In what ways would you say Christians are most in danger of doing this?

22. Consider again verse 25. What kind of people in your life are the hardest to be honest with?

23. If everyone in your church thoroughly understood this chapter, and had a passion for living out its truth, what kind of practical changes do you think might result?

24. Express in your own words a prayer any Christian could confidently offer to God, based on both the *promises* you found in this chapter, and God's *character* as it's revealed here.

FOR GOING DEEPER

Keep in mind what you see in verses 8-13 regarding spiritual gifts. Then compare the following passages, and summarize what you see as the most important biblical principles on this subject—Romans 12:3-8; 1 Corinthians 12:1-31, and 1 Peter 4:10-11.

EPHESIANS 5

Startup: What's the darkest place you've ever been?

SEEING WHAT'S THERE

1. Describe the kind of person whom you think would gain the most out of this chapter. What would be his or her questions and struggles and concerns?

2. Suppose a band of armed terrorists stormed into the room where you're now meeting, then took you as hostages in a captivity that was likely to last for days or weeks. Just before they confiscated your Bibles, they allowed you to take one last look at the chapter open before you. Which verse in this chapter would you most try to fix in mind before your Bible was snatched away, and why?

3. What *commands* does Paul give the Ephesians in chapter 5? Together, list them all aloud.

4. Again, if you had never heard anything else about Christianity, what would you say were the most important features of the Christian *lifestyle,* based only on what you see in this chapter?

5. From what you see in this chapter alone, what would you say are the most important moral standards for Christians?

6. Look again at verses 22-23. From God's point of view, what are the most important *results* that should come out of a marriage?

7. Which important details in this chapter do you think might be the easiest to overlook?

8. EYE FOR DETAIL—*From what you recall seeing in this chapter, try answering the following question without looking at your Bible:* Paul gives two standards or measures for how hus-

bands are to love their wives. What are they? (See verses 25 and 28.)

9. If Satan wrote down some guidelines and commands to get people to do just the opposite of what this chapter teaches, how do you think his message might be worded?

10. Which commands in this chapter would you say are the easiest for most Christians to obey? Which are the easiest to *dis*obey?

11. Look at the commands given in verses 1-2. Discuss where you believe successful obedience to these commands actually begins—mostly in our *mind,* mostly in our *habits,* or mostly in our *words?*

12. James 1:22 tells us that when we merely listen to the Word without putting it into practice, we deceive ourselves. What kind of self-deceiving excuses or rationalization do you think could most easily keep Christians from actually *doing* what we see in Ephesians 5:3-7?

13. Picture in your mind two Christians, one who has learned to obey the command we are given in verses 15-17, and one who has *not* learned how to do it. What practical differences do you see in the way these two people live?

14. *How,* exactly, does a person go about obeying the command given in verse 17?

15. At the end of verse 18, Paul tells us to be filled with the Spirit. If this chapter was the only Scripture portion you had access to, how would you describe what it means to be "filled with the Spirit"?

16. Think carefully about verses 18-20. Then imagine God evaluating your spirituality on a scale of one to ten, in which ten equals perfect obedience to the commands in this passage, and one equals total disregard of those commands. What score do you think He would probably assign to you?

17. From the evidence you see in this chapter alone, how do you think Paul would define the terms *success* and *true significance?*

18. It's been said that "the human heart resists nothing more than change." What truths in this chapter—truths that could require some changes in your life—cause some degree of hesitation and resistance inside you?

19. Consider again verses 29-31, and recall the words of Jesus in John 15:5 —"Apart from me you can do nothing." Picture in your mind something good that could happen in your life in this area, something that could clearly be accomplished only by the Lord's supernatural power. What would this be?

20. When it comes to obeying the commands given in verse 4, what practical guidelines would you offer to one another?

21. Look again at the command in verse 20. In the last 24 hours, what are the biggest things (if any) that you've thanked God for? How do you really decide what is right to say, and what isn't?

22. In Psalm 119:47, these words are spoken to God: "I will *delight* myself in thy commandments, which I have *loved.*" At this point in your life, which commands in this chapter would be the quickest to bring you fulfillment and pleasure?

23. Of all that you see in this chapter, what one truth are you most *thankful* for, because of its personal significance to you?

Look at the picture Paul gives of Christ and the church in verses 24-32. Look together at each of the following passages, and allow this image to be enhanced by what you see—Matthew 9:15, John 3:29, 1 Corinthians 6:15, 2 Corinthians 11:2, and Revelation 19:7-9 and 21:2.

EPHESIANS 6

Startup: If you were asked to go back in history, and become a warrior in a particular war or time of battle what war or time period would you choose?

SEEING WHAT'S THERE

1. What *commands* does Paul give the Ephesians in chapter 6? Make a list of them together.

2. Compare the main verb in verse 1 with the main verb in verse 2. Is there a difference in the meaning of these two words? If so, what is it?

3. How would you explain verses 1-3 to a young child?

4. Notice that verse 4 has both a negative command and a positive command. How do these two work together for effective fathering?

5. If every life is a battle, then how would you outline our correct military strategy, according to verses 10-18?

6. In your own words, how would you describe our enemy, according to what you see in verse 12?

7. Looking again at verse 12, how would you describe your present relationship to heaven and the entire spiritual universe?

8. From what you see in this chapter alone, what would you say are the most important moral standards for Christians?

9. With all else being equal, which of these people do you think would have the best chance of uncovering the most meaning in this chapter— an army general, a professional football player, or a weapons manufacturer?

10. From what you've seen in this letter, how would you describe Paul's relationship with the Ephesians?

11. EYE FOR DETAIL—*From what you recall seeing in this chapter, try answering the following question without looking at your Bible:* As he begins speaking about our spiritual armor, how does Paul complete the following sentence? "Be strong in the Lord…" (See verse 10.)

CAPTURE THE ESSENCE

12. If you were asked to summarize the most important "marks of Christian maturity" as taught in this chapter, which ones would you mention first?

13. From what you see in this chapter, what can we truly rely on God to do as we obey Him?

14. Review the statement in verse 12. *Why* would you say God wants us to know this?

15. If you wanted to capture the essence of this chapter in a brief prayer for yourself or someone else, how would you say it in your own words?

FOR LIFE TODAY

16. From what you see in this chapter and elsewhere in Scripture, what can you reasonably expect in life if you do *not* obey the command in verse 10?

17. How could you use verses 10-18 to help an unsaved friend who was afraid he was too enslaved by the power of sin to become a Christian?

18. What would you say is an especially good *starting point* for applying verses 10-18 more effectively to your life?

19. Look again at verse 18. In the last 24 hours, what are the biggest things you've prayed for?

20. Notice again what Paul asks the Ephesians to pray for him in verses 19-20. Although none of us today are apostles, what parts of this prayer would be appropriate to pray for one another in your group?

21. If you were asked to write a discussion question to help your Bible study group apply something in this chapter to their lives, how would you word the question?

22. If God had written this chapter only for *you,* which words or phrases do you think He would have underlined?

FOR GOING DEEPER

Be strong! With the challenge in verses 10-20 in mind, look also at the following passages that teach endurance, then discuss some workable ways to put them into practice—1 Corinthians 9:24-27, Galatians 6:9-10, Philippians 3:12-14, and 2 Timothy 2:1-13.

EPHESIANS:

THE BIG PICTURE

(Discuss again the questions in the "Overview," plus the questions below.)

1. Suppose you were attending a citizens' meeting called by local school officials who were considering the removal of the Bible from the shelves of all school libraries in your community. You spoke up in favor of keeping the Bible available to students. Then another citizen rose to his feet and said, "I see no reason to keep it around. It's a forgotten book anyway. Even most Christians have no idea what's in it. For example," he said, then turned directly to you and asked, "Tell me what the book of Ephesians is all about." In that situation, how would you respond?

2. Look together at each of these verses, and discuss which one you believe is the best candidate for "KEY VERSE" in the book of Ephesians— the one which brings into sharpest focus what this book is most about: 1:3, 1:11, 1:22, 2:21, 3:19, 4:3, 4:4-6, 4:16, or 4:24.

3. In James 1:23-24 we're told that "anyone who listens to the word but does not do what it says is like a man who looks at his face in a mirror and, after looking at himself, goes away and immediately forgets what he looks like." In what important ways has the book of Ephesians been a "mirror" for you—showing you what you can and should do?

4. If you've decided on a starting point for applying something in this book more effectively to your life, what commitment would you be willing to make to others in your group regarding this?

5. How would you complete the following word of advice to growing Christians? *Explore the book of Ephesians if you want to learn more about...*

Philippians

OVERVIEW

(Discuss these OVERVIEW questions both at the beginning of your study of Philippians, and again after you've studied together all four chapters. Your answers may change significantly once you've looked more closely at the entire book.)

Startup: In your opinion, what's the difference, if any, between *joy* and *happiness?*

SEEING WHAT'S THERE

1. What does Paul reveal in 1:12-13 about his situation and condition as he writes this letter?

2. What does Paul reveal in 4:10, 4:14, and 4:18 about his occasion for writing this letter to the Philippian Christians?

3. What do you know about the location and importance of the city of Philippi at the time of Paul?

4. What do you know about what the world was like when this letter was written? What would you guess were the typical hopes and dreams and concerns of the Philippians?

5. To find out more about Paul's experiences with the Philippians, discuss what you see in Acts 16:9-40.

6. Start scanning the book until you come to a verse that brings a question to your mind. What's the question?

7. Begin scanning the book again until you come to a verse that gives you a smile or a sense of gratitude or joy. What is pleasing to you about this verse?

8. Look together at the following verses in Philippians, and discuss what you see as the source of true joy—1:4-5, 1:18-19, 2:2, 3:1, and 4:1.

9. What in this book do you think might be most refreshing to someone who was learning about God for the first time?

10. Look also at the list of "Questions to Ask as You Begin Your Study of Each Book" on page 393.

CAPTURE THE ESSENCE

11. What previous impressions, if any, have you had about the book of Philippians in regard to (a) its content, (b) its level of difficulty, and (c) its importance?

12. The book of Philippians has been called "Paul's Joy Letter," "The Joy of Knowing Christ," and "The Missionary Book." With that reputation for this book, what answers and guidelines and solutions would you like to gain as you examine it more closely?

13. Take a quick look together at only the *first two or three verses* in each chapter in Philippians. What impressions and expectations of this book do you get from this partial scan?

14. Imagine you were the person carrying this letter from Paul to Philippi. Along the way, you were attacked by a band of robbers who stripped you of all your valuables, including this letter. The leader of the robber band couldn't read, and when you asked him to return the letter, he replied,

"Why? What's in it that's so important?" How would you answer him?

FOR LIFE TODAY

15. When you get to heaven, if you have a long talk with the apostle Paul and he asks you, "What was most helpful to you in my letter to the Philippians?"—how would you like to be able to answer him?

16. Suppose you heard a voice from heaven saying to you, "Don't get over-ambitious and try to apply too much from this book to your life right now. Just pick one thing to focus on, and do it well." What one thing would you choose?

17. How can you ensure that your study of Philippians is not merely theoretical and intellectual, but is instead truly practical and relevant? Talk together about this. What can you do to help keep the process alive and interesting?

FOR GOING DEEPER

Notice Paul's mention of Timothy in the first verse of this book. Then look together at the opening verses of First Corinthians, Second Corinthians, Colossians, First Thessalonians, Second Thessalonians, and Philemon (see also Galatians 1:1-2). Notice how often Paul includes the name of one of his ministry associates, along with his own identification. What might this say about Paul's view of himself and his apostleship?

PHILIPPIANS 1

Startup: What images come to your mind when you think of the word *partnership?*

SEEING WHAT'S THERE

1. In verse 1, look at who Paul addresses this letter to. What reason might Paul have had in mind for singling out the two groups of church leaders, and including them in the heading of this letter?

2. In verse 11, Paul speaks of the "fruit of righteousness." How would you explain what Paul means by this?

3. Which statements in this chapter clearly show Paul's *confidence?*

4. What is the only *command* Paul gives the Philippians in chapter 1?

5. Paul writes in this chapter of a particular gift, a gift that is perhaps unexpected and unusual, and at first glance maybe even unwanted. What is that gift?

6. What do verses 27-30 tell us about the right way to view our circumstances in life?

7. From the evidence you see in this chapter, describe as fully as you can Paul's circumstances in prison. What is he doing with his time and his thoughts?

8. Suppose the telegraph had been invented back in New Testament times, and Paul decided to send the Philippians a brief telegram of this chapter, in advance of the delivery of the full letter. To save money, he decided for now to send only the three most important verses from the chapter. Which three verses do you think Paul would have chosen?

9. What in this chapter do you think might be most surprising to a new Christian reading it for the first time?

10. Look also at the list of "Questions to Ask as You Study Each Chapter" on

page 392, which you may want to do for each chapter in Philippians.

11. EYE FOR DETAIL— *If everyone in the group has read the entire chapter, try answering the following question without looking at your Bible:* How does Paul complete the following sentence? "For to me, to live is Christ…" (See verse 21.)

CAPTURE THE ESSENCE

12. Imagine yourself looking over Paul's shoulder as he wrote this letter, under the direction of the Holy Spirit's inner guidance. What emotions, or longings, or remembrances do you think he most likely experienced as he wrote the words of this chapter?

13. Imagine you are one of the Philippians listening to this letter being read for the first time in one of your church meetings. While the last half of this chapter is being read, the person next to you taps your shoulder and says, "I'm new here; who is this Paul guy?" How would you answer?

14. In regard to Paul's relationship with the Philippians, how would you explain in your own words what he says in verse 8?

15. With verse 9 in mind, discuss how much you agree or disagree with this statement: Love has its own natural increase, and it's safe to say that if your love isn't growing, it isn't really biblical love.

16. Review the statement in verse 13. *Why* would you say God wants us to know this?

17. In verse 19, look at what Paul says he *knows.* How would you describe the process by which he came to know this?

18. Suppose that at the end of this chapter, Paul added this line: "If you remember only one thing from this chapter, let it be this:…" How do you think he would complete that sentence?

19. A 3-step question: (a) Think of someone you know who doesn't spend much time reading the Bible. (b) Select a verse or brief passage in this chapter which you think this person would probably find boring. (c) Now, how could you clarify or open up this passage in a way that might appeal to this person?

20. What impressions of Paul's prayer life do you gain from this chapter?

21. Picture this book of Philippians as a fast-moving train. Chapter 1 is the locomotive in front, and the other chapters represent railway cars following behind. From what you see here in chapter 1, what is the *energy* in the locomotive—the point or principle or theme that's the driving force for the locomotive and the entire train?

FOR LIFE TODAY

22. Consider again verse 5, in which Paul tells the Philippians how glad he is for their "partnership in the gospel" or "participation in the gospel" or "fellowship in the gospel." What do you think Paul means by this phrase? And in what important ways would you say that *you* now have this same partnership or fellowship?

23. Notice again Paul's statement of confidence in verse 6. Then define as fully and personally as you can the "good work" that God has begun in you (and will complete on the day of Christ Jesus!).

24. Look again at Paul's prayer for the Philippians in verses 9-11. Suppose you and God were looking over a written transcript of all your prayers in the past year. Which elements of Paul's prayer do you think God might encourage you to add more

often in your prayers for yourself? Which elements do you think He might encourage you to add more often in your prayers for other people?

25. To what degree would you say verse 12 could also serve as a statement about *your* life?

26. Focus your mind for a moment on the basic facts of the gospel. Think of *what* Jesus did…and *how* He did it…and *why* He did it. Then think about verse 27 in this chapter. What guidelines will help you decide whether an action or thought is truly worthy of the gospel of Christ?

27. If God had written this chapter only for *you,* which words or phrases do you think He would have underlined?

FOR GOING DEEPER

Paul speaks in verse 29 about the gift of suffering for the sake of Christ. Look also at the following passages, and identify together the genuine blessings that come from suffering—Matthew 5:11-12, Acts 5:40-42, James 1:2-4, and 1 Peter 4:12-14.

PHILIPPIANS 2

Startup: Can you recall a time when you especially enjoyed watching the stars?

SEEING WHAT'S THERE

1. What *commands* does Paul give the Philippians in this chapter? As a group, list them all aloud.

2. Suppose a band of armed terrorists stormed into the room where you're now meeting, then took you as hostages in a captivity that was likely to last for days or weeks. Just before they confiscated your Bibles, they allowed you to take one last look at the chapter open before you. Which verse in this chapter would you most try to fix in mind before your Bible was snatched away, and why?

3. Try restating the description of Jesus in verses 6-11 in completely different language, without using any words from the original (except those that are three letters or less, and the names of God and Jesus). You may want to go around the group and have each person paraphrase one sentence from the passage.

4. If Paul came to this meeting of your group and read aloud verses 12-16, which word or words do you think he would emphasize most?

5. How would you explain verse 13 to a young child?

6. Let the words of verses 14-16 form a picture in your mind, and then describe that picture.

7. Make a summary list together of all the evidence you see in this chapter concerning the character of the two men Timothy and Epaphroditus.

8. From what you see in this chapter alone, what would you say are the most important moral standards for Christians?

9. From what you've learned in this chapter, how would you define true *humility?*

10. Which important details in this chapter do you think might be the easiest to overlook?

11. Describe the kind of person whom you think would gain the most out of this chapter. What might be his or her questions and struggles and concerns?

12. Imagine you were preparing a special audio-visual presentation for your church. As a strong, pre-recorded voice read through verses 3-13 word for word, a series of photographic slides would be projected on a screen in front of the people. What kind of photographs would you select to be included in the slide presentation, to best fit this passage?

13. EYE FOR DETAIL— *From what you recall seeing in this chapter, try answering the following question without looking at your Bible:* Paul mentions two of his fellow workers in this chapter. Who are they? (See verses 19 and 25.)

CAPTURE THE ESSENCE

14. From the evidence you see in this chapter, what does Paul want most for the Philippians to understand about Jesus?

15. If you thought of this chapter as a roadmap for a Christian's life, what would be the safest "roads" to take, as taught in this chapter? What would be the unsafe, dangerous roads to avoid?

16. Think carefully about verses 12-13. In your own words, tell what it is exactly that we are to do, and what it is that God will do.

17. In what ways do you think it might be easy for Christians to misinterpret and misapply verse 12?

18. James 1:22 tells us that when we merely listen to the Word without putting it into practice, we deceive ourselves. What kind of self-deceiving excuses or rationalization do you think could most easily keep Christians from actually *doing* what verse 14 teaches us to do?

19. When the Philippian Christians first read or heard the words in this chapter, what kind of emotions, thoughts, or questions do you think it may have produced in them?

20. If this chapter was a good answer to a question that began with the word *How...* then what would the rest of the question say?

21. Many times we rob ourselves of the discovery of deeper truths in Scripture because we see a passage and say to ourselves, "I already know that." For which teachings in this chapter might it be easiest for Christians to fall into that trap?

22. If you were not yet a Christian, what teachings about Jesus Christ in this chapter do you think would be most intriguing to you, and why?

23. If this chapter was the only Scripture portion you had, what would you conclude from it about how important it was for Jesus Christ to die?

24. If you were asked to write a discussion question to help your Bible study group examine and understand something in this chapter, how would you word the question?

FOR LIFE TODAY

25. If it's true that "you *become* what you *think,*" then what are the most important thoughts from this chapter to plant firmly in your mind?

26. If everyone in your church thoroughly understood this chapter, and had a passion for living out its truth, what kind of practical changes do you think might result?

27. In Colossians 3:1 we read this command: "Since you have been raised with Christ, set your hearts on things above, where Christ is seated at the right hand of God." What have you personally observed about Jesus Christ in this chapter that would be worthy of setting your heart on?

28. In a typical day, how often would the commands in verse 3 offer useful and timely guidelines for your immediate situation?

29. Focus your mind on what you consider to be your two or three most important responsibilities in life. In what ways could verses 12-13 help you carry out any or all of these responsibilities?

30. Look again at the command in verse 14. In the last 24 hours, what are the biggest things (if any) that you've complained or grumbled about?

31. Notice what Paul says in verse 13 about the *will* and the *work* of God. Suppose a new Christian asked you, "How can I discover God's will for my life?" How could you use this verse to help you give a meaningful answer?

32. Consider again verses 3-8. Get in mind a picture of yourself five years in the future, as a man or woman who is truly unselfish in a Christlike way. As this kind of person, what kinds of things do you see yourself doing?

FOR GOING DEEPER

Look again in verses 6-11 at Paul's picture of what Jesus did when He came to earth. Search together also in the following passages for word-pictures and statements that deepen our understanding of this miracle of love—John 1:1 and 1:10-14, 2 Corinthians 8:9, 1 Timothy 3:16, Hebrews 2:14-17, and 1 John 1:1-2.

PHILIPPIANS 3

Startup: What is the best prize you've ever won?

SEEING WHAT'S THERE

1. From the evidence you see in this chapter, what does Paul want most for the Philippians to understand about himself?

2. After reading through this chapter, which words or phrases or sentences would you most like to understand better?

3. With verse 1 in mind, what keys can you find in this chapter to the secret of true joy?

4. Look at Paul's warning about the "dogs" in verse 2. From what you see in this chapter, what wrong actions or teachings were these men guilty of?

5. Picture verses 4-11 in your mind as a before-and-after comparison. What images do you see on the "before" side? What do you see on the "after" side?

6. How would you explain in your own words the "prize" which Paul speaks of in verse 14?

7. Paul speaks in verse 18 of "many" who are "enemies of the cross of Christ." From what you see in this chapter, who are these people?

8. How would you explain verses 20-21 to a young child?

9. With all else being equal, which of these people do you think would have the best chance of uncovering the most meaning in this chapter—a surgeon, an athlete, or a ship's captain?

10. What *commands* does Paul give the Philippians in this chapter? Together, list them all aloud.

11. EYE FOR DETAIL— *From what you recall seeing in this chapter, try an-*

swering the following question without looking at your Bible: Early in this chapter, Paul speaks of a specific way in which we worship. What is it? (See verse 3.)

CAPTURE THE ESSENCE

12. From the evidence you've seen so far in this letter, what are the most important *expectations* Paul has of the Philippians?

13. From what you see in the last half of this chapter, what expectations can we rightly have of God?

14. If Satan wrote down some guidelines and commands to get people to do just the opposite of what this chapter teaches, how do you think his message might be worded?

15. Review what Paul says in verse 12. At what point can a Christian truly say, "I have already been made perfect."

16. From what you see in verses 15-21, what *expectations* can we rightly have of God?

17. Review what Paul says in verses 18-19. *Why* would you say God wants us to know this?

18. Look again at verse 20. As a citizen of heaven, what are (a) your rights and privileges, and (b) your duties and responsibilities?

19. Regarding the subjects you've seen addressed so far in this book, what questions do you have that remain unanswered?

FOR LIFE TODAY

20. If this chapter were the only portion of Scripture you had access to, how could you use it to help answer this question: *What is the most powerful and effective way to improve my life?*

21. Imagine you saw earlier today a message written in fire in the sky. It was addressed to you by name, then continued with these words: *Thus saith the LORD: "Read Philippians 3, for I have something for you there."* Which verse or verses in this chapter do you think He most likely would be referring to?

22. What is it in our lives that most often makes it hard to see the supreme value of knowing Christ, which Paul describes in verse 8?

23. As you consider your own life, how much ownership can you claim to what Paul says in verse 12-14? Is this a picture of your life as well?

24. Are the kind of people Paul talks about in verses 18-19 still around today? If so, from what you know in Scripture, what should be our response to them?

25. In what ways, if any, would you say this chapter gives guidelines for the right mental perspective to have when we fall short of what we know God wants us to do or be?

FOR GOING DEEPER

Press on for the prize! With the challenge in verses 12-14 in mind, look also at the following passages that teach endurance, then discuss some workable ways to put them into practice — 1 Corinthians 9:24-27, Galatians 6:9-10, Ephesians 6:10-20, and 2 Timothy 2:1-13.

PHILIPPIANS 4

Startup: What images come to your mind when you think of the word *peace*?

SEEING WHAT'S THERE

1. What are the biggest *promises* which you see God making to us in this chapter?

2. What kind of questions or difficulties or doubts in a Christian's daily life do you think this chapter answers best?

3. What *commands* does Paul give the Philippians in this chapter? Together, make a list of all of them.

4. What would you say are the most important *verbs*—the action words—in this chapter?

5. From the evidence you see in this chapter, describe as fully as you can Paul's circumstances in prison. What is he doing with his time and his thoughts?

6. Let the words of verse 19 form a picture in your mind, and then describe that picture.

7. From what you've seen in this letter, how would you describe Paul's relationship with the Philippians?

8. EYE FOR DETAIL— *From what you recall seeing in this chapter, try answering the following question without looking at your Bible:* In verse 8, Paul gives eight descriptions of the right things for us to think about. Three of the adjectives on this list are "true," "pure," and "lovely." How many of the other five qualities can you name?

CAPTURE THE ESSENCE

9. If the first three chapters of this letter had somehow been lost in history, what difference would that make in regard to the meaning of what you see in chapter 4?

10. Discuss together which verses in this chapter your attention would most likely be drawn to if you were… (a) a young mother whose husband had recently abandoned her and their children. (b) someone who had an increasing dislike for someone else in your Bible study group. (c) a language analyst who was doing an investigation of Paul's personality as revealed in his writings. (d) a hardened atheist who was looking for ways to discredit and disprove the Bible. (e) a person wrestling with a major decision.

11. In Proverbs 13:13 we're told, "He who respects a command is rewarded," or in another translation, "He that feareth the commandment shall be rewarded." Look at the command in verse 3. What would you say is the likely *reward* for respecting and keeping this command?

12. *How,* exactly, does a person go about obeying the command given in verse 4?

13. Look again at the command in verse 5, and discuss how fully you think Christians are obeying this teaching today.

14. In Psalm 119:45, the psalmist says to God, "I will walk at liberty, for I seek Thy precepts." As you think about the "precept" or command given in verse 6, in what ways can you see it offering true freedom and liberty to a Christian?

15. Look again closely at Paul's statements in verse 7 and at the end of verse 9. Then express in your own words what we can truly rely on God to do as we obey Him.

16. Picture in your mind two Christians, one who has learned to obey the command we are given in verse 8, and one who has *not* learned how to do it. What practical differences do

you see in the way these two people live?

17. If you were responsible for giving the apostle Paul a job performance review, what comments would you make to him, based on his ministry as you've seen it in this letter?

FOR LIFE TODAY

18. In Psalm 119:47, these words are spoken to God: "I will *delight* myself in thy commandments, which I have *loved.*" At this point in your life, which commands in this chapter would be the quickest to bring you fulfillment and pleasure?

19. Look at verse 4, and remember again where Paul was when he wrote this letter. Then discuss whether you think the *rejoicing* which Paul speaks of begins in your *intellect,* in your *emotions,* in your *will,* or in all three.

20. With verse 4 in mind, what do you think is the strongest motivation for people to be more *joyful?*

21. Think again about verse 4. At this point in your life, how much *joy* is there in your life, compared with other times in the past? Use a scale of one to ten (one = "much less than ever," ten = "much more than ever") to help you decide.

22. In a typical day, how often would the commands in verse 6 offer useful and timely guidelines for your immediate situation?

23. From what you see in this chapter and elsewhere in Scripture, what can you reasonably expect in life if you do *not* obey the commands in verse 6?

24. What for you are the greatest hindrances to obeying the command in verse 8?

25. Consider again verses 6-8, and recall the words of Jesus in John 15:5— "Apart from me you can do nothing." Picture in your mind something good that could happen in your life in response to the commands in this passage, something that could clearly be accomplished only by the Lord's supernatural power. What would this be?

26. If you were asked to write a discussion question to help your Bible study group apply something in this chapter to their lives, how would you word the question?

27. In light of how you're doing spiritually in your life today, which verse in this chapter do you think is the most important at this time—and why?

FOR GOING DEEPER

Look again at verse 9. Then look up the following passages, and discuss what you see in common in all of them, and what they say about the apostle Paul's life and character—1 Corinthians 4:16 and 11:1; Philippians 3:17; 2 Thessalonians 3:7-9; and 1 Timothy 1:16.

PHILIPPIANS:

THE BIG PICTURE

(Discuss again the questions in the "Overview," plus the questions below.)

1. If you were a member of the Philippian church, and decided to write a letter back to Paul after receiving this one, what would you include in the letter—what questions, comments, words of appreciation, etc.?

2. Suppose you were attending a citizens' meeting called by local school officials who were considering the removal of the Bible from the shelves of all school libraries in your community. You spoke up in favor of keeping the Bible available to students. Then another citizen rose to his feet and said, "I see no reason to keep it around. It's a forgotten book anyway. Even most Christians have no idea what's in it. For example," he said, then turned directly to you and asked, "Tell me what the book of Philippians is all about." In that situation, how would you respond?

3. Look together at each of these verses, and discuss which one you believe is the best candidate for "KEY VERSE" in the book of Philippians —the one which brings into sharpest focus what this book is most about: 1:5, 1:18, 2:2, or 3:1.

4. If you've decided on a starting point for applying something in this book more effectively to your life, what commitment would you be willing to make to others in your group regarding this?

5. In James 1:23-24 we're told that "anyone who listens to the word but does not do what it says is like a man who looks at his face in a mirror and, after looking at himself, goes away and immediately forgets what he looks like." In what important ways has the book of Philippians been a "mirror" for you—showing you what you can and should do?

6. How would you complete the following word of advice to growing Christians? *Explore the book of Philippians if you want to learn more about...*

Colossians

OVERVIEW

(Discuss these OVERVIEW questions both at the beginning of your study of Colossians, and again after you've studied together all four chapters. Your answers may change significantly once you've looked more closely at the entire book.)

Startup: What to you are the most important qualities to look for in a leader?

SEEING WHAT'S THERE

1. Start scanning the book until you come to a verse that brings a question to your mind. What's the question?

2. Begin scanning the book again until you come to a verse that gives you a smile or a sense of gratitude or joy. What is pleasing to you about this verse?

3. What is the first *command* Paul gives the Colossians in this letter?

4. What is the first *encouragement* Paul gives the Colossians in this letter?

5. What do you know about what the world was like at the time this letter was written? What would you guess to be the typical hopes and dreams and concerns of the Colossians?

6. What information do you have about the location and importance of the city of Colosse at the time of Paul?

7. Look also at the list of "Questions to Ask as You Begin Your Study of Each Book" on page 393.

CAPTURE THE ESSENCE

8. What in this book do you think might be most interesting to some-

one who was learning about Jesus Christ for the first time?

9. What previous impressions, if any, have you had about the book of Colossians in regard to (a) its content, (b) its level of difficulty, and (c) its importance?

10. The book of Colossians has been called "The Book of Christ Preeminent," "The Completeness of Christ," "The Supreme Glory of Christ," "Jesus Christ: Our Perfect Leader," and "The Godhood and All-Sufficiency of Christ." With that reputation for this book, what answers and guidelines and solutions would you like to gain as you examine it more closely?

11. Take a quick look together at only the *first two or three verses* in each chapter in Colossians. What impressions and expectations of this book do you get from this partial scan?

12. Imagine you were the person carrying this letter from Paul to Colosse. Along the way, you were attacked by a band of robbers who stripped you of all your valuables, including this letter. The leader of the robber band couldn't read, and when you asked him to return the letter, he replied, "Why? What's in it that's so important?" How would you answer him?

FOR LIFE TODAY

13. When you get to heaven, if you have a long talk with the apostle Paul and he asks you, "What was most helpful to you in my letter to the Colos-

sians?"—how would you like to be able to answer him?

14. Suppose you heard a voice from heaven saying to you, "Don't get over-ambitious and try to apply too much from this book to your life right now. Just pick one thing to focus on, and do it well." What one thing would you choose?

15. How can you ensure that your study of Colossians is not merely theoretical and intellectual, but is instead truly practical and relevant? Talk together about this. What can you do to help keep the process alive and interesting?

FOR GOING DEEPER

How much of God is expressed or revealed in Jesus? To best answer this question, look first at Colossians 1:15, 1:19, and 2:9. Then look together at the following verses, and discuss how they reinforce or expand what Paul teaches in Colossians—John 1:1 and 1:18, Hebrews 1:3, and 2 Corinthians 4:4.

COLOSSIANS 1

Startup: What are some of the questions you can recall having had in your mind about Jesus?

SEEING WHAT'S THERE

1. What is the most convincing evidence you see in this chapter for the fact that Jesus is God?

2. Notice Paul's positive mention of Epaphras in verses 7-8. What else do you learn about this man from Colossians 4:12-13 and Philemon 23?

3. Picture in your mind the before-and-after comparison Paul makes in verses 13-14. What images do you see on the "before" side? What do you see on the "after" side?

4. How would you explain verse 15 to a child?

5. How could you use verses 15-20 in response to a false teacher who said everything physical was evil, and only the spiritual realm was good?

6. From what you see in verse 22, why did Jesus have to die?

7. How could you use the same passage —verses 15-20—in response to a false teacher who said Christ could not be both human and divine?

8. Notice the word *mystery* in verse 26. How would you define this word in the way Paul uses it here?

9. After reading through this chapter, which words or phrases or sentences here would you most like to understand better?

10. Discuss together which verses in this chapter your attention would most likely be drawn to if you were... (a) a person who had just been told he was dying of cancer. (b) a hardened atheist who was looking for ways to discredit and disprove the Bible. (c) a popular but personally insecure entertainer who was beginning to see

how empty and unsatisfying fame can be. (d) an astronomer who had just discovered a strange and beautiful star cluster in outer space. (e) a married couple who had been separated by mutual consent for some time, but were now ready to come back together. (f) a person wrestling with a major decision.

11. Imagine you were preparing a special audio-visual presentation for your church. As a strong, prerecorded voice read through verses 15-19 word for word, a series of slides would be projected on a screen in front of the people. What kind of photographs would you select to be included in the slide presentation, to best fit this passage?

12. Look also at the list of "Questions to Ask as You Study Each Chapter" on page 392, which you may want to do for each chapter in Colossians.

13. EYE FOR DETAIL— *If everyone in the group has read the entire chapter, try answering the following question without looking at your Bible:* Paul mentioned his fellow servant who taught the gospel to the Colossians. What was his name? (See verse 7.)

CAPTURE THE ESSENCE

14. From the evidence you see in this chapter, what does Paul want most for the Colossians to understand about Jesus?

15. Look at verses 24-29. What does Paul want most for the Colossians to understand about himself?

16. Many times we rob ourselves of the discovery of deeper truths in Scripture because we see a passage and say to ourselves, "I already know that." For which teachings in this chapter might it be easiest for Christians to fall into that trap?

17. From what you see in verses 21-23, express in your own words what we can truly rely on God to do as we obey Him.

18. In verse 24, notice what Paul says he does in regard to the afflictions of Christ. How would you explain the *process* which he speaks of?

19. If you were not yet a Christian, what teachings about Jesus Christ in this chapter do you think would be most intriguing to you, and why?

20. If this chapter was the only Scripture portion you had, what would you conclude from it about how important it was for Jesus Christ to die?

21. Picture this book of Colossians as a fast-moving train. Chapter 1 is the locomotive in front, and the other chapters represent railway cars following behind. From what you see here in chapter 1, what is the *energy* in the locomotive—the point or principle or theme that's the driving force for the locomotive and the entire train?

FOR LIFE TODAY

22. Look again at Paul's prayer for the Colossians in verses 3 and 9-12. Suppose you and God were looking over a written transcript of all your prayers in the past year. Which elements of Paul's prayer do you think God might encourage you to add more often in your prayers for yourself? Which elements do you think He might encourage you to add more often in your prayers for other people?

23. Notice what Paul says about God's *will* in verse 9. Suppose a new Christian asked you, "How can I discover God's will for my life?" How could you use verses 9-14 to help you give a meaningful answer?

24. What principles or guidelines for teachers in the church today would you draw from verses 28-29?

25. As you consider your own life, how much ownership can you claim to Paul's words in verses 28-29? Is this a picture of your life as well?

26. In Colossians 3:1 we read this command: "Since you have been raised with Christ, set your hearts on things above, where Christ is seated at the right hand of God." What have you personally observed about Jesus Christ in this chapter that would be worthy of setting your heart on?

27. In Philippians 4:8 we're given the following command: "Whatever is true, whatever is noble, whatever is right, whatever is pure, whatever is lovely, whatever is admirable—if anything is excellent or praiseworthy—*think about such things.*" What food for thought can you find in this chapter that especially strikes you as being *true,* or *noble,* or *right,* or *pure,* or *lovely,* or *admirable,* or *excellent,* or *praiseworthy?*

28. Which verse in this chapter do you think God wants you to understand best?

FOR GOING DEEPER

Is your view of the Lord big enough? Look again in verses 16-17 and 19-20 at the descriptions of Jesus Christ, and His relationship to "all things." Then compare this verse with the following passages which also explore the theme of "all things," and discuss together the greater perspective these verses can give us—1 Corinthians 8:6, Ephesians 1:9-10, Hebrews 1:3, and Revelation 4:11.

COLOSSIANS 2

Startup: What do you consider the most important *freedoms* you have?

SEEING WHAT'S THERE

1. Suppose the telegraph had been invented back in New Testament times, and Paul decided to send the Colossians a brief telegram of this chapter, in advance of the delivery of the full letter. To save money, he decided for now to send only the three most important verses from the chapter. Which three verses do you think Paul would have chosen?

2. What kind of questions or difficulties or doubts in a Christian's daily life do you think this chapter answers best?

3. What *commands* does Paul give the Colossians in this chapter? As a group, list them all aloud.

4. What would you say are the most important *verbs*—the action words—in this chapter?

5. What in this chapter do you think might be most surprising to a new Christian reading it for the first time?

6. Paul writes in this chapter of a particular gift God has given us. What is that gift? How would you describe it?

7. How could you use verses 13-15 in response to a false teacher who said we do not need to be reconciled to God, because our basic nature is good?

8. Discuss which of the following statements you think best reflect what Paul is teaching in verses 20-23: (a) Rules are evil, and no Christian should ever get caught up in them. (b) Negative rules are not the right pathway to living a new life; they may aim for the right thing, but they don't really have the power to help you accomplish it. (c) Look to human religion, and you'll see a mass

of rules and regulations; look to Christ and you'll see something very different—you'll see real life.

9. With all else being equal, which of these people do you think would have the best chance of uncovering the most meaning in this chapter—a lawyer, a college professor in philosophy, or a professional treasure hunter?

10. From what you've seen so far in this letter, how would you describe Paul's relationship with the Colossians?

11. EYE FOR DETAIL— *From what you recall seeing in this chapter, try answering the following question without looking at your Bible:* In this chapter's shortest verse, Paul says that in Christ are hidden all the treasures of...*what?* (See verse 3.)

CAPTURE THE ESSENCE

12. Would you say this is a chapter that especially requires *patience* as you read and study it, in order to understand it? If so, why?

13. If Satan wrote down some guidelines and commands to get people to do just the opposite of what this chapter teaches, how do you think his message might be worded?

14. If this chapter was a good answer to a question that began with the word *Why...* then what would the rest of the question say?

15. Look closely at verse 8. From what you know of human nature, how can what is hollow and empty appear so attractive and satisfying to people?

16. From what you see in verses 9-12, explain in your own words what Paul most wants us to understand about ourselves.

17. Read over together verses 13-15, and let them form a picture or pictures in your mind. Then discuss the images you see.

18. Try to "read between the lines" as you think about Paul's words in verses 16-19. What foundational principles would you say are the source of Paul's teaching here?

19. Suppose that at the end of this chapter, Paul added this line: "If you remember only one thing from this chapter, let it be this:..." How do you think he would complete that sentence?

20. If you were asked to write a discussion question to help your Bible study group examine and understand something in this chapter, how would you word the question?

21. Regarding the subjects you've seen addressed so far in this book, what questions do you have that remain unanswered?

FOR LIFE TODAY

22. Consider again verses 6-7, and recall the words of Jesus in John 15:5— "Apart from me you can do nothing." Picture in your mind something good that could happen in your life in response to the commands in this passage, something that could clearly be accomplished only by the Lord's supernatural power. What would this be?

23. Notice the phrase at the end of verse 7. In the last 24 hours, what are the biggest things (if any) that you've thanked God for?

24. How susceptible do you think Christians in general are today to the deception which Paul warns against in verse 8?

25. If this chapter were the only portion of Scripture you had access to, how could you use it to help answer this question: *What is the most powerful and effective way to improve my life?*

26. Of all that you see in this chapter, what one truth are you most *thankful*

for, because of its personal significance to you?

FOR GOING DEEPER

With verses 9-10 in mind, discuss what the following passages say about our *perfection* or *fullness* or *completeness*—2 Corinthians 12:9, Ephesians 1:22-23, Philippians 3:12, and Hebrews 10:10-14.

COLOSSIANS 3

Startup: It's been said that "you *become* what you *think.*" Discuss how much you agree or disagree with that statement.

SEEING WHAT'S THERE

1. How do the first four verses in chapter 3 relate to the last four verses in chapter 2?

2. If Paul came to this meeting of your group and read aloud verses 1-4, which word or words do you think he would emphasize most?

3. What *commands* does Paul give the Colossians in this chapter? Together, list them all aloud.

4. What do verses 1-4 tell us about Jesus?

5. From what you see in verses 9-15, what are the right *reasons* for *doing* good and *being* good?

6. How would you explain verse 20 to a young child?

7. From what you see in this chapter alone, what would you say are the most important moral standards for Christians?

8. Which important details in this chapter do you think might be the easiest to overlook?

9. EYE FOR DETAIL— *From what you recall seeing in this chapter, try answering the following question without looking at your Bible:* Paul says in verse 12 that we are God's elect and chosen people, and should therefore put on (or clothe ourselves with) five qualities. One of them is kindness. How many of the other four can you name?

CAPTURE THE ESSENCE

10. If the first two chapters of this letter had somehow been lost in history, what difference would that make in regard to the meaning of what you see in chapter 3?

11. If you thought of this chapter as a roadmap for a Christian's life, what would be the safest "roads" to take, as taught in this chapter? What would be the unsafe, dangerous roads to avoid?

12. In Psalm 119:45, the psalmist says to God, "I will walk at liberty, for I seek Thy precepts." As you think about the "precepts" or commands in verses 1-2, in what ways can you see them offering true freedom and liberty to a Christian?

13. In order to accomplish what Paul tells us to do in verse 5, is it enough to simply obey the command in verse 2? Why or why not?

14. Look at the list of sins in verses 5-8. Which of them might be the hardest to think of as being sinful?

15. What fundamental principles for right relationships can you find in verses 16-25 (and also in verse 1 of chapter 4)?

16. In Proverbs 13:13 we're told, "He who respects a command is rewarded," or in another translation, "He that feareth the commandment shall be rewarded." Look at the command in verse 16. What would you say is the likely *reward* for respecting and keeping this command?

17. Focus your mind on what you consider to be your two or three most important responsibilities in life. In what ways could verse 17 help you carry out any or all of these responsibilities?

18. Look at the reward Paul mentions in verse 24. What ideas do you have about what this reward will be?

19. What insights do you find in this chapter regarding the right way to approach God in worship?

20. If you were not yet a Christian, which teachings about Jesus Christ in this chapter do you think would be most intriguing to you, and why?

21. From the evidence you've seen so far in this letter, what are the most important *expectations* Paul has of the Colossians?

FOR LIFE TODAY

22. In Psalm 119:47, these words are spoken to God: "I will *delight* myself in thy commandments, which I have *loved*." At this point in your life, which commands in this chapter would be the quickest to bring you fulfillment and pleasure?

23. If everyone in your church thoroughly understood this chapter, and had a passion for living out its truth, what kind of practical changes do you think would result?

24. It's been said that "the human heart resists nothing more than change." What truths in this chapter—truths that could require some changes in your life—cause some degree of hesitation and resistance inside you?

25. Consider again verses 1-4. Get in mind a picture of yourself five years in the future, as a man or woman whose heart is truly and consistently focused on Christ. As this kind of person, what kinds of things do you see yourself doing?

26. Review the commands and teachings in verses 5-10. In a typical day, how often would these verses offer useful and timely guidelines for your immediate situation?

27. Think carefully about verses 12-14. Then imagine God evaluating you on a scale of one to ten, in which ten equals perfect obedience to the commands in this passage, and one equals total disregard of those commands. What score do you think He would probably assign to you?

28. Look at the end of verses 15, 16 and 17, to see what these three verses

have in common. In the last 24 hours, what are the biggest things (if any) that you've thanked God for?

29. Practically speaking, what do you think is the strongest motivation for people to be more *thankful*?

30. If you were asked to write a discussion question to help your Bible study group apply something in this chapter to their lives, how would you word the question?

31. Imagine you saw earlier today a message written in fire in the sky. It was addressed to you by name, then continued with these words: *Thus saith the LORD: "Read Colossians 3, for I have something for you there."* Which verse or verses in this chapter do you think He most likely would be referring to?

FOR GOING DEEPER

Notice again the list of qualities and virtues in verses 12-14, then discuss how closely this list corresponds to those in 2 Corinthians 6:6, Galatians 5:22-23, and Ephesians 5:9. Taking them all together, what conclusions would you make about how best to please God?

COLOSSIANS 4

Startup: On what kinds of foods do you generally like to add salt?

SEEING WHAT'S THERE

1. Describe the kind of person whom you think would gain the most out of this chapter. What would be his or her questions and struggles and concerns?

2. What *commands* does Paul give the Colossians in this chapter? Together, make a list of all of them.

3. Who are the outsiders whom Paul mentions in verse 5?

4. Notice Paul's mention of the church in Laodicea in verse 16. What do you discover about this church in Revelation 3:14-22?

5. Suppose you were a Bible translator for a remote tribe on a faraway continent, and this tribe did not have any experience or knowledge of salt. How would you explain what salt is, so they could understand the meaning of verse 6?

6. EYE FOR DETAIL— *From what you recall seeing in this chapter, try answering the following question without looking at your Bible:* Just before he ends this letter, Paul passes along a specific message to someone named Archippus. Can you remember what the message is? (See verse 17.)

CAPTURE THE ESSENCE

7. A 3-step question: (a) Think of someone you know who doesn't spend much time reading the Bible. (b) Select a verse or brief passage in this chapter which you think this person would probably find boring. (c) Now, how could you clarify or open up this passage in a way that might appeal to this person?

FOR LIFE TODAY

8. Look at the *reason* Paul gives in verse 1 for masters to be right and fair. In

what relationships of *your* life is this reason an especially important factor in how you treat others?

9. Look again at the command in verse 2. In the last 24 hours, what are the biggest things you've prayed for?

10. From what you see in this chapter and elsewhere in Scripture, what can you reasonably expect in life if you do *not* obey the command in verse 2?

11. Notice again what Paul asks the Colossians to pray for him in verses 3-4. Although none of us today are apostles, what parts of this prayer would be appropriate to pray for one another in your group?

12. In a typical day, how often would the commands in verses 5-6 offer useful and timely guidelines for your immediate situation?

13. If God had written this chapter only for *you,* which words or phrases do you think He would have underlined?

FOR GOING DEEPER

Do you possess the wisdom Paul speaks of in verse 5? In the following verses, explore together what this wisdom means in practical terms—Proverbs 10:19, 11:2, 13:20, 19:20, and 28:26, and James 3:13 and 3:17.

COLOSSIANS:

THE BIG PICTURE

(Discuss again the questions in the "Overview," plus the questions below.)

1. Suppose you were attending a citizens' meeting called by local school officials who were considering the removal of the Bible from the shelves of all school libraries in your community. You spoke up in favor of keeping the Bible available to students. Then another citizen rose to his feet and said, "I see no reason to keep it around. It's a forgotten book anyway. Even most Christians have no idea what's in it. For example," he said, then turned directly to you and asked, "Tell me what the book of Colossians is all about." In that situation, how would you respond?

2. Look at each of these verses, and discuss which one you believe is the best candidate for "KEY VERSE" in the book of Colossians—the one which brings into sharpest focus what this book is most about: 1:16, 1:19, 1:21-22, 2:13, or 2:17.

3. If you've decided on a starting point for applying something in this book more effectively to your life, what commitment would you be willing to make to others in your group regarding this?

4. How would you complete the following word of advice to growing Christians? *Explore the book of Colossians if you want to learn more about…*

1 Thessalonians

OVERVIEW

(Discuss these OVERVIEW questions both at the beginning of your study of First Thessalonians, and again after you've studied together all five chapters. Your answers may change significantly once you've looked more closely at the entire book.)

Startup: Of all that you've been taught about the Lord's second coming, what has made the strongest impression?

SEEING WHAT'S THERE

1. As you scan together this letter, how often do you see Paul making mention of the coming of the Lord Jesus?

2. What is the first *command* Paul gives the Thessalonians in this letter?

3. What is the first *encouragement* Paul gives the Thessalonians in this letter?

4. Look at the last two or three verses in each chapter, and at verse 23 in the last chapter. What single topic is on Paul's mind throughout this book?

5. What do you know about the location and importance of the city of Thessalonica at the time of Paul?

6. What do you know about what the world was like when this letter was written? What would you guess to be the typical hopes and dreams and concerns of the people to whom Paul was writing?

7. Look together at Acts 17:1-9 to learn more of Paul's experiences in Thessalonica. How do you think these events might have affected Paul's later view of the believers in this city?

8. Start scanning the book until you come to a verse that brings a question to your mind. What's the question?

9. Begin scanning the book again until you come to a verse that gives you a smile or a sense of gratitude or joy. What is pleasing to you about this verse?

10. How often do you see the word *brothers* (or *brethren*) in this book?

11. At the end of this letter, notice verse 27. What do these words of Paul communicate about the purpose and importance of this letter?

12. Look also at the list of "Questions to Ask as You Begin Your Study of Each Book" on page 393.

CAPTURE THE ESSENCE

13. What previous impressions, if any, have you had about the book of First Thessalonians in regard to (a) its content, (b) its level of difficulty, and (c) its importance?

14. The book of First Thessalonians has been called "A Model Church," "The Epistle of the Rapture," "A Look to the Lord's Second Coming." With that reputation for this book, what answers and guidelines and solutions would you like to gain as you examine it more closely?

FOR LIFE TODAY

15. When you get to heaven, if you have a long talk with the apostle Paul and he asks you, "What was most helpful to you in my first letter to the Thessalonians?" how would you like to be able to answer him?

16. Suppose you heard a voice from heaven saying to you, "Don't get over-ambitious and try to apply too much from this book to your life right now. Just pick one thing to focus on, and do it well." What one thing would you choose?

17. How can you ensure that your study of First Thessalonians is not merely theoretical and intellectual, but is instead truly practical and relevant? Talk together about this. What can you do to help keep the process alive and interesting?

FOR GOING DEEPER

Concentrate your focus on the second coming of Christ as you look together at the following passages. How would you summarize what Paul most wanted the Christians in Thessalonica to understand about this subject?—1 Thessalonians 1:10, 2:19, 3:13, and 4:13-18; and 2 Thessalonians 1:7-10 and 2:1-3.

1 THESSALONIANS 1

Startup: What is the most encouraging thing to happen to you in the last week?

SEEING WHAT'S THERE

1. Suppose the telegraph had been invented back in New Testament times, and Paul decided to send the Thessalonians a brief telegram of this chapter, in advance of the delivery of the full letter. To save money, he decided for now to send only the three most important verses from the chapter. Which three verses do you think Paul would have chosen?

2. In this chapter, what does Paul teach the Thessalonians about God? What does he teach them about Jesus Christ? What does he teach them about the Holy Spirit?

3. What kind of *power* do you think Paul is speaking of in verse 5?

4. Look also at the list of "Questions to Ask as You Study Each Chapter" on page 392, which you may want to do for each chapter in First Thessalonians.

5. EYE FOR DETAIL— *If everyone in the group has read the entire chapter, try answering the following question without looking at your Bible:* In the last verse of this chapter, Paul says the Thessalonians are known to be waiting for something. What are they waiting for?

CAPTURE THE ESSENCE

6. If verses 5 and 6 were the only Scriptures you knew that mentioned the Holy Spirit, what conclusions could you draw from them about the Spirit's work?

7. If you were asked to summarize the most important "marks of Christian maturity" as taught in this chapter, which ones would you mention first?

8. Picture this book of First Thessalonians as a fast-moving train. Chapter 1

is the locomotive in front, and the other chapters represent railway cars following behind. From what you see here in chapter 1, what is the *energy* in the locomotive—the point or principle or theme that's the driving force for the locomotive and the entire train?

9. From what you've seen so far in this letter, what is Paul's main reason for writing it? Is it to offer encouragement, to offer instruction, or something else?

10. When the Thessalonian Christians first read or heard the words in this chapter, what kind of emotions, thoughts, or questions do you think it may have produced in them?

FOR LIFE TODAY

11. Look again at Paul's prayer for the Thessalonians in verses 2-3. Suppose you and God were looking over a written transcript of all your prayers in the past year. Which elements of Paul's prayer do you think God might encourage you to add more often in your prayers for other people?

12. In verses 9-10, notice the report which Paul had heard about the Thessalonians. How accurate would these statements be if they were made about *you?*

13. Which verse in this chapter do you think God wants you to understand best?

14. Suppose Paul was writing a letter to *your* church today, and he referred to a copy of this Thessalonian letter as a model for writing yours. How many of the words and phrases in chapter 1 could also be used accurately in such a letter to your church?

FOR GOING DEEPER

What does Paul teach the Thessalonians about the Holy Spirit? Look again at verses 5-6, and compare what you see there with what Paul says in 1 Thessalonians 4:8 and 5:19, and 2 Thessalonians 2:13. How would you summarize the perspective Paul gives the church at Thessalonica on this subject?

1 THESSALONIANS 2

Startup: How would you describe the ideal pastor of a church?

1. As you read this chapter, what's the strongest impression or image it leaves in your mind?

2. What are Paul's strongest memories of his time with the Thessalonians?

3. What would you say are the most important *verbs*—the action words—in this chapter?

4. What in this chapter do you think might be most surprising to a new Christian reading it for the first time?

5. With all else being equal, which of these people do you think would have the best chance of uncovering the most meaning in this chapter— a mother at home with young children, a government ambassador to a foreign capital, or a school bus driver?

6. Let the words of verses 19-20 form a picture in your mind, and then describe that picture.

7. From what you've seen so far in this letter, how would you describe Paul's relationship with the Thessalonians?

8. EYE FOR DETAIL— *From what you recall seeing in this chapter, try answering the following question without looking at your Bible:* Paul commends the Thessalonians for following or imitating the churches in another place. What place was this? (See verse 14.)

CAPTURE THE ESSENCE

9. Imagine yourself looking over Paul's shoulder as he wrote this letter, under the direction of the Holy Spirit's inner guidance. What emotions, or longings, or remembrances do you think he most likely experienced as he wrote the words of this chapter?

10. From the evidence you see in this chapter, what does Paul want most for the Thessalonians to understand about his ministry?

11. If you were responsible for giving the apostle Paul a job performance review, what comments would you make to him, based on his ministry as you see it in this chapter?

12. If this chapter was the only Scripture portion you had ever known, what would you conclude from it about how to help new believers grow into Christian maturity?

13. A 3-step question: (a) Think of someone you know who doesn't spend much time reading the Bible. (b) Select a verse or brief passage in this chapter which you think this person would probably find boring. (c) Now, how could you clarify or open up this passage in a way that might appeal to this person?

14. If you were asked to write a discussion question to help your Bible study group examine and understand something in this chapter, how would you word the question?

15. From what you've seen so far in this letter, what is Paul's main reason for writing it? Is it to offer encouragement, to offer instruction, or something else?

FOR LIFE TODAY

16. In verses 1-12, what principles or guidelines can you find for pastors and teachers and preachers today?

17. As you consider your own life, how much ownership can you claim to the statement Paul makes in verse 4? Is this a picture of your life as well?

18. Look at the question Paul asks in verse 19. How would you answer this question for yourself?

19. In light of how you're doing spiritually in your life today, which verse in

this chapter do you think is the most important at this time—and why?

FOR GOING DEEPER

Notice Paul's use of the word *crown* in verse 19. Enjoy together the imagery of this term as you explore these verses— Proverbs 4:7-9, 14:24 and 16:31; Isaiah 62:2-3; and Revelation 2:10.

1 THESSALONIANS 3

Startup: What's the best news you've received in the past week?

SEEING WHAT'S THERE

1. What does this chapter reveal about Paul's relationship with the Thessalonians?

2. If this chapter was a good answer to a question that began with the word *Why...* then what would the rest of the question say?

3. EYE FOR DETAIL— *From what you recall seeing in this chapter, try answering the following question without looking at your Bible:* Where was Paul when he sent Timothy to the Thessalonians? (See verse 1.)

CAPTURE THE ESSENCE

4. From the evidence you've seen so far in this letter, what are the most important *expectations* Paul has of the Thessalonians?

5. Suppose that at the end of this chapter, Paul added this line: "If you remember only one thing from this chapter, let it be this:..." How do you think he would complete that sentence?

6. From what you've seen so far in this letter, what is Paul's main reason for writing it? Is it to offer encouragement, to offer instruction, or something else?

FOR LIFE TODAY

7. Notice Paul's reminder in verse 4 of his previous prediction to the Thessalonians. If someone had made this prediction about *you* a year or two ago, how accurate would it have been?

8. Look at Paul's prayer for the Thessalonians as recorded in verses 11-13. Imagine again that you and God are looking over a written transcript of all your prayers in the past year. Which elements of this prayer of

Paul's do you think God might encourage you to add more often in your prayers for yourself? Which elements do you think He might encourage you to add more often in your prayers for others?

9. If God had written this chapter only for *you*, which words or phrases do you think He would have underlined?

Does Paul make clear to the Thessalonians the fact that Jesus is God? Look again at verse 11, and compare what you see there with what Paul says in 1 Thessalonians 1:1 and 2 Thessalonians 1:2 and 2:16-17. How would you summarize the viewpoint that Paul gives the church at Thessalonica on this subject?

1 THESSALONIANS 4

Startup: What kind of signals can most quickly tell you whether someone is pleased or displeased with you?

SEEING WHAT'S THERE

1. What kind of questions or difficulties or doubts in a Christian's daily life do you think this chapter answers best?

2. After reading through this chapter, which words, phrases, or sentences here would you most like to understand better?

3. From what you see in verses 1-8, what are the right *reasons* for living a godly life?

4. From what you see in verses 14-17, what *expectations* can we rightly have of God?

5. How would you explain verses 16-17 to a young child?

6. Suppose a band of armed terrorists stormed into the room where you're now meeting, then took you as hostages in a captivity that was likely to last for days or weeks. Just before they confiscated your Bibles, they allowed you to take one last look at the chapter open before you. Which verse in this chapter would you most try to fix in mind before your Bible was snatched away, and why?

7. Which important details in this chapter do you think might be the easiest to overlook?

8. EYE FOR DETAIL— *From what you recall seeing in this chapter, try answering the following question without looking at your Bible:* Paul says that when Jesus comes down from heaven, he will be accompanied by three sounds. What are these three sounds? (See verse 16.)

CAPTURE THE ESSENCE

9. Many times we rob ourselves of the discovery of deeper truths in Scrip-

ture because we see a passage and say to ourselves, "I already know that." For which teachings in this chapter might it be easiest for Christians to fall into that trap?

10. From the evidence you see in this chapter, what does Paul want most for the Thessalonians to understand about the coming of the Lord?

11. Picture in your mind two Christians, one who has learned to obey the commands we are given in verses 11-12, and one who has *not* learned how to do it. What practical differences do you see in the way these two people live?

12. At the end of the chapter, Paul says that his words in verses 13-17 should be encouraging and comforting to us. Why should they be?

13. From what you've seen so far in this letter, what is Paul's main reason for writing it? Is it to offer encouragement, to offer instruction, or something else?

FOR LIFE TODAY

14. If it's true that "you *become* what you *think*," then what are the most important thoughts from this chapter to plant firmly in your mind?

15. If hope is defined as our "eager and confident expectation of what God has promised," then what in this chapter do you eagerly and confidently expect from God?

16. If everyone in your church thoroughly understood this chapter, and had a passion for living out its truth, what kind of practical changes do you think would result?

17. How well would verses 11-12 work for you as a *statement of purpose* for your life?

18. Imagine you saw earlier today a message written in fire in the sky. It was addressed to you by name, then continued with these words: *Thus saith the LORD: "Read 1 Thessalonians 4, for I have something for you there."* Which verse or verses in this chapter do you think He most likely would be referring to?

19. In Philippians 4:8 we're given the following command: "Whatever is true, whatever is noble, whatever is right, whatever is pure, whatever is lovely, whatever is admirable—if anything is excellent or praiseworthy—*think about such things.*" What food for thought can you find in this chapter that especially strikes you as being *true,* or *noble,* or *right,* or *pure,* or *lovely,* or *admirable,* or *excellent,* or *praiseworthy?*

FOR GOING DEEPER

What gospel did Paul teach to the Thessalonians? Look again at verse 14, and compare what you see there with what Paul says in 1 Thessalonians 5:9-10 and 2 Thessalonians 2:13-14. How would you summarize the perspective Paul gives the church at Thessalonica on this subject?

1 THESSALONIANS 5

Startup: What kinds of things are you most looking forward to at this time in your life?

SEEING WHAT'S THERE

1. Describe the kind of person whom you think would gain the most out of this chapter. What would be his or her questions and struggles and concerns?

2. What is "the day of the Lord" which Paul speaks of in verse 2?

3. What *promises* regarding the day of the Lord are made in verses 2-4?

4. Notice again verse 4. If a Christian is not to be surprised at the coming of the day of the Lord, what needs to be happening in his or her life, according to what you see in this chapter?

5. Notice Paul's command in verse 11. What principles and guidelines for obeying this command do you see throughout the rest of this chapter?

6. From what you see in this chapter and elsewhere in Scripture, what can you reasonably expect in life if you do *not* obey the command in verse 18?

7. From what you see in verses 23-24, what *expectations* can we rightly have of God?

8. EYE FOR DETAIL— *From what you recall seeing in this chapter, try answering the following question without looking at your Bible:* Near the end of this chapter, Paul uses a brief phrase to describe God. What is that phrase? (See verse 23.)

CAPTURE THE ESSENCE

9. If you thought of this chapter as a roadmap for a Christian's life, what would be the safest "roads" to take, as taught in this chapter? And what would be the unsafe, dangerous roads to avoid?

10. If Satan wrote down some guidelines and commands to get people to do just the opposite of what this chapter teaches, how do you think his message might be worded?

11. Imagine the Thessalonians writing back to Paul and quoting his words in verses 6-8, then adding this question: "What exactly did you mean by this?" How do you think Paul would explain it?

12. In Proverbs 13:13 we're told, "He who respects a command is rewarded," or in another translation, "He that feareth the commandment shall be rewarded." Look at the command in verse 8. What would you say is the likely *reward* for respecting and keeping this command?

13. Try to "read between the lines" as you think about Paul's words in verses 19-21. What foundational principles would you say are the source of Paul's teaching here?

14. From what you see in this chapter alone, what would you say are the most important moral standards for Christians?

FOR LIFE TODAY

15. Suppose a new Christian asked you, "How can I discover God's will for my life?" How could you use chapters 4 and 5 in this book to help you give a meaningful answer?

16. It's been said that "the human heart resists nothing more than change." What truths here in chapter 5— truths that could require some changes in your life—cause some degree of hesitation and resistance inside you?

17. In Psalm 119:47, these words are spoken to God: "I will *delight* myself in thy commandments, which I have *loved.*" At this point in your life, which commands in this chapter

would be the quickest to bring you fulfillment and pleasure?

18. In a typical day, how often would the commands in verses 6-8 offer useful and timely guidelines for your immediate situation?

19. Imagine some new neighbors moved in next door to you, and that their lives were perfect examples of what Paul speaks about in verse 11. In practical terms, how would you describe what their relationship with *you* would be like? What would they do *for* you and *with* you?

20. Who is Paul referring to in verses 12-13, and how does this passage relate to us today?

21. In Psalm 119:45, the psalmist says to God, "I will walk at liberty, for I seek Thy precepts." As you think about the "precept" or command given in verse 15, in what ways can you see it offering true freedom and liberty to a Christian?

22. Look again at the command in verse 16. In the last 24 hours, what has given you the greatest joy?

23. Look again at the command in verse 17. In the last 24 hours, what are the biggest things (if any) you've prayed about?

24. Look again at the command in verse 18. In the last 24 hours, what are the biggest things (if any) you've thanked God for?

25. If this chapter were the only portion of Scripture you had access to, how could you use it to help answer this question: *What is the most powerful and effective way to improve my life?*

26. If you were asked to write a discussion question to help your Bible study group apply something in this chapter to their lives, how would you word the question?

FOR GOING DEEPER

How does Paul teach the Thessalonians to view our relationship with Christ? Look again at verses 9-10, and compare what you see there with what Paul says in 1 Thessalonians 1:1, and in 2 Thessalonians 1:12 and 2:16-17. How would you summarize the perspective Paul gives the church at Thessalonica on this subject?

1 THESSALONIANS:

THE BIG PICTURE

(Discuss again the questions in the "Overview," plus the questions below.)

1. From what you've seen in this book, how would you summarize our future destiny as Christians?

2. Look together at each of these verses, and discuss which one you believe is the best candidate for "KEY VERSE" in the book of First Thessalonians—the one which brings into sharpest focus what this book is most about: 1:9-10, 4:1, or 4:14.

3. Of all that you see in this book, what one truth are you most *thankful* for, because of its personal significance to you?

4. In James 1:23-24 we're told that "anyone who listens to the word but does not do what it says is like a man who looks at his face in a mirror and, after looking at himself, goes away and immediately forgets what he looks like." In what important ways has the book of First Thessalonians been a "mirror" for you—showing you what you can and should do?

5. If you've decided on a starting point for applying something in this book more effectively to your life, what commitment would you be willing to make to others in your group regarding this?

6. How would you complete the following word of advice to growing Christians? *Explore the book of First Thessalonians if you want to learn more about...*

2 Thessalonians

OVERVIEW

(Discuss these OVERVIEW questions both at the beginning of your study of Second Thessalonians, and again after you've studied together all three chapters. Your answers may change significantly once you've looked more closely at the entire book.)

Startup: What are the hardest things for you to *wait* for?

SEEING WHAT'S THERE

1. What is the first *command* Paul gives the Thessalonians in this letter?

2. What is the first *encouragement* Paul gives the Thessalonians in this letter?

3. What do you know about the location and importance of the city of Thessalonica at the time of Paul?

4. What do you know about what the world was like when this letter was written? What would you guess to be the typical hopes and dreams and concerns of the Thessalonians?

5. Look together at Acts 17:1-9 to learn more of Paul's experiences in Thessalonica. How do you think these events might have affected Paul's later view of the believers in this city?

6. Start scanning the book until you come to a verse that brings a question to your mind. What's the question?

7. Begin scanning the book again until you come to a verse that gives you a smile or a sense of gratitude or joy. What is pleasing to you about this verse?

8. How often do you see the word *brothers* (or *brethren)* in this book?

9. Look also at the list of "Questions to Ask as You Begin Your Study of Each Book" on page 393.

CAPTURE THE ESSENCE

10. What previous impressions, if any, have you had about the book of Second Thessalonians in regard to (a) its content, (b) its level of difficulty, and (c) its importance?

11. The book of Second Thessalonians has been called "Comfort in Persecution," and "More about the Lord's Second Coming." With that reputation for this book, what answers, guidelines, and solutions would you like to gain as you examine it more closely?

FOR LIFE TODAY

12. When you get to heaven, if you have a long talk with the apostle Paul and he asks you, "What was most helpful to you in my second letter to the Thessalonians?" how would you like to be able to answer him?

13. Suppose you heard a voice from heaven saying to you, "Don't get over-ambitious and try to apply too much from this book to your life right now. Just pick one thing to focus on, and do it well." What one thing would you choose?

14. How can you ensure that your study of Second Thessalonians is not merely theoretical and intellectual, but is instead truly practical and relevant? Talk together about this. What can you do to help keep the process alive and interesting?

How fully do we understand the destiny of those who will not believe in Christ, and who do not look forward to His coming again? Look together at 2 Thessalonians 1:6-10, and compare that passage with what you discover in the following verses—Matthew 8:11-12, John 3:18 and 3:36, Romans 2:8, and 2 Peter 3:7.

2 THESSALONIANS 1

Startup: What images come to your mind when you think of the term *Judgment Day?*

SEEING WHAT'S THERE

1. As you read this chapter, what's the strongest impression or image which it leaves in your mind?

2. From what you see in this chapter, what good reasons do the Thessalonians have for being encouraged?

3. What would you say are the most important *verbs*—the action words —in this chapter?

4. From what you see in verses 5-10, what *expectations* can we rightly have of God?

5. How would you explain verses 8-9 to a young child?

6. Look also at the list of "Questions to Ask as You Study Each Chapter" on page 392, which you may want to do for each chapter in Second Thessalonians.

7. EYE FOR DETAIL— *If everyone in the group has read the entire chapter, try answering the following question without looking at your Bible:* As Paul repeats his prayer for the Thessalonians, what is the first thing he asks God to do for them? (See verse 11.)

CAPTURE THE ESSENCE

8. If you were not yet a Christian, what teachings about Jesus Christ in this chapter do you think would be most intriguing to you, and why?

9. A 3-step question: (a) Think of someone you know who doesn't spend much time reading the Bible. (b) Select a verse or brief passage in this chapter which you think this person would probably find boring. (c) Now, how could you clarify or open up this passage in a way that might appeal to this person?

10. Review what Paul says in verses 8-9. *Why* would you say God wants us to know this?

11. From what you've seen so far in this letter, what is Paul's main reason for writing it? Is it to offer encouragement, to offer instruction, or something else?

FOR LIFE TODAY

12. Look again at Paul's prayer for the Thessalonians in verses 11-12. Suppose you and God were looking over a written transcript of all your prayers in the past year. Which elements of Paul's prayer do you think God might encourage you to add more often in your prayers for yourself? Which elements do you think He might encourage you to add more often in your prayers for other people?

13. In Philippians 4:8 we're given this command: "Whatever is true, whatever is noble, whatever is right, whatever is pure, whatever is lovely, whatever is admirable—if anything is excellent or praiseworthy— *think about such things.*" What food for thought can you find in this chapter that especially strikes you as being *true,* or *noble,* or *right,* or *pure,* or *lovely,* or *admirable,* or *excellent,* or *praiseworthy?*

14. Of all that you see in this chapter, what one truth are you most *thankful* for, because of its personal significance to you?

FOR GOING DEEPER

What does Paul tell the Thessalonians about God's judgment upon sin? Look again at verses 5-10, and compare what you see there with what Paul says in 1 Thessalonians 1:10 and 2:16. How would you summarize the perspective Paul gives the church at Thessalonica on this subject?

2 THESSALONIANS 2

Startup: Who's the worst fictional villain you can recall reading about or seeing in a book or motion picture?

SEEING WHAT'S THERE

1. What *commands* do you see Paul giving the Thessalonians in this chapter?

2. After reading through this chapter, which words or phrases or sentences here would you most like to understand better?

3. From what you see in verses 1-12, what misunderstanding about the Lord's coming was Paul trying to correct, and how did he try to correct it?

4. If this chapter was a good answer to a question that began with the word *When…* then what would the rest of the question say?

5. Look in verses 3-10 at the details which Paul uses to describe a certain man. What does Paul most wants the Thessalonians to understand about this man?

6. What are the most important conclusions to make about the unbelievers mentioned in verses 10-12?

7. What conclusions can you make from verses 13-17 about what we should *be* and what we should *have* as Christians?

8. If Paul came to this meeting of your group and read aloud verses 13-17, which word or words do you think he would emphasize most?

9. From what you've seen so far in this letter, how would you describe Paul's relationship with the Thessalonians?

10. EYE FOR DETAIL— *From what you recall seeing in this chapter, try answering the following question without looking at your Bible:* When Paul speaks of those who are "perishing," he mentions something which they would neither love nor believe. What is it? (See verses 10 and 12.)

11. *Who* is this chapter most about?

12. Many times we rob ourselves of the discovery of deeper truths in Scripture because we see a passage and say to ourselves, "I already know that." For which teachings in this chapter might it be easiest for Christians to fall into that trap?

13. Would you say this is a chapter that especially requires *patience* as you read and study it, in order to understand it? If so, why?

14. If you were asked to write a discussion question to help your Bible study group examine and understand something in this chapter, how would you word the question?

FOR LIFE TODAY

15. In verses 16-17, look at Paul's second prayer for the Thessalonians recorded in this letter. Imagine again that you and God are looking over a written transcript of all your prayers in the past year. Which elements of this prayer of Paul's do you think God might encourage you to add more often in your prayers for yourself? Which elements do you think He might encourage you to add more often in your prayers for other people?

16. Which verse in this chapter do you think God wants you to understand best?

FOR GOING DEEPER

Notice again Paul's reference in verses 13-16 to members of the Trinity. Look at the following passages, and discuss what they tell us about our proper understanding of this concept—Matthew 3:16-17 and 28:18-19, John 14:15-18, 1 Corinthians 12:3-6, 2 Corinthians 13:14, and 1 Peter 1:1-2.

2 THESSALONIANS 3

Startup: What's the hardest labor you've ever done?

SEEING WHAT'S THERE

1. Describe the kind of person whom you think would gain the most from a study of this chapter. What would be his or her questions and struggles and concerns?

2. Suppose a band of armed terrorists stormed into the room where you're now meeting, then took you as hostages in a captivity that was likely to last for days or weeks. Just before they confiscated your Bibles, they allowed you to take one last look at the chapter open before you. Which verse in this chapter would you most try to fix in mind before your Bible was snatched away, and why?

3. What in this chapter do you think might be most surprising to a new Christian reading it for the first time?

4. What *commands* do you see Paul giving the Thessalonians in this chapter?

5. How would you explain verse 3 to a young child?

6. Look at Paul's words in verse 5. How would you rephrase this prayer in your own words?

7. If you could ask Paul, "Why did you include verse 17 in this letter?" how do you think he might answer?

8. Which important details in this chapter do you think might be the easiest to overlook?

9. EYE FOR DETAIL— *From what you recall seeing in this chapter, try answering the following question without looking at your Bible:* As he begins closing down this letter, what does Paul pray for the Thessalonians? (See verse 16.)

CAPTURE THE ESSENCE

10. If Satan wrote down some guidelines and commands to get people to do

just the opposite of what this chapter teaches, how do you think his message might be worded?

11. Think carefully about what Paul says concerning idleness in verses 6-13. Based on this chapter, how would you explain the difference between the sin of idle laziness on one hand, and the proper enjoyment of leisure and recreation on the other?

12. In Proverbs 13:13 we're told, "He who respects a command is rewarded," or in another translation, "He that feareth the commandment shall be rewarded." Look at the command in verse 13. What would you say is the likely *reward* for respecting and keeping this command?

13. Try to "read between the lines" as you think about Paul's words in verses 14-15. What foundational principles would you say are the source of Paul's teaching here?

14. From the evidence you've seen in this letter, what are the most important *expectations* Paul has of the Thessalonians?

15. Notice again what Paul asks the Thessalonians to pray for him in verses 1-2. Although none of us today are apostles, what parts of this prayer would be appropriate to pray for one another in your group?

16. Think again about Paul's warnings concerning idleness in verses 6-13. How serious would you say is this problem today among Christians, and what forms does it take?

17. In a typical day, how often would the command in verse 13 offer useful and timely guidelines for your immediate situation?

18. If you were asked to write a discussion question to help your Bible study group apply something in this chapter to their lives, how would you word the question?

19. In light of how you're doing spiritually in your life today, which verse in this chapter do you think is the most important at this time—and why?

Look again at verses 7 and 9. Then look up together the following passages, and discuss what you see in common in all of them, and what they say about the apostle Paul's life and character—1 Corinthians 4:16 and 11:1; Philippians 3:17 and 4:9; and 1 Timothy 1:16.

2 THESSALONIANS:

THE BIG PICTURE

(Discuss again the questions in the "Overview," plus the questions below.)

1. From what you've seen in Second Thessalonians, discuss how accurately you think the content of this letter is reflected in each of the following statements: (a) Since the day of the Lord is coming, we should work hard and well at what God has given us to do. (b) Since Christ is coming back any moment now, it's time to relax and enjoy life. (c) The world will continue to get better and better, and when it is finally perfect, Christ will return.

2. From what you've seen in this book, how would you summarize our future destiny as Christians?

3. Look together at each of these verses, and discuss which one you believe is the best candidate for "KEY VERSE" in the book of Second Thessalonians—the one which brings into sharpest focus what this book is most about: 2:13-14, 2:15, or 3:5.

4. Suppose that at the very end of this book, Paul added this line: "If you remember only one thing from this letter, let it be this:..." How do you think Paul would complete that sentence?

5. In James 1:23-24 we're told that "anyone who listens to the word but does not do what it says is like a man who looks at his face in a mirror and, after looking at himself, goes away and immediately forgets what he looks like." In what important ways has the book of Second Thessalonians been a "mirror" for you—showing you what you can and should do?

6. Of all that you see in this book, what one truth are you most *thankful* for, because of its personal significance to you?

7. If you've decided on a starting point for applying something in this book more effectively to your life, what commitment would you be willing to make to others in your group regarding this?

8. How would you complete the following word of advice to growing Christians? *Explore the book of Second Thessalonians if you want to learn more about...*

1 Timothy

❖

OVERVIEW

(Discuss these OVERVIEW questions both at the beginning of your study of First Timothy, and again after you've studied together all six chapters. Your answers may change significantly once you've looked more closely at the entire book.)

Startup: What is your favorite kind of work?

SEEING WHAT'S THERE

1. Look at 3:14-15, where Paul tells Timothy his purpose for this letter. With those words in mind, what kinds of expectations would you say Paul has for the *church,* and for *leaders* in the church?

2. Look together at Philippians 2:19-23. Discuss together what you learn in that passage about Timothy's character, and about Paul's esteem for Timothy.

3. Look also at Acts 16:1-5 and 2 Timothy 1:5-6 and 3:14-15, then summarize what you learn there about Timothy's background and ministry.

4. What exactly was Timothy's position? Was he another apostle? Was he an elder or overseer? To help you find an answer, look together at the following passages, noticing especially how Paul describes him: Romans 16:21; 1 Corinthians 4:16-17; 2 Corinthians 1:1; and Philippians 1:1.

5. Start scanning the book until you come to a verse that brings a question to your mind. What's the question?

6. Begin scanning the book again until you come to a verse that gives you a smile or a sense of gratitude or joy. What is pleasing to you about this verse?

7. What is the first *command* that Paul gives Timothy in this letter?

8. What is the first *encouragement* that Paul gives Timothy in this letter?

9. How many times do you see the words *godly* and *godliness* in this letter?

10. Look also at the list of "Questions to Ask as You Begin Your Study of Each Book" on page 393.

CAPTURE THE ESSENCE

11. What previous impressions, if any, have you had about the book of First Timothy in regard to (a) its content, (b) its level of difficulty, and (c) its importance?

12. The book of First Timothy has been called "The Handbook of Church Administration and Discipline," "Directions for Church Order," "Taking Care of God's People," and "Advice to Church Leaders." With that reputation for this book, what answers, guidelines, and solutions would you like to gain as you examine it more closely?

13. From the evidence you see in this letter, how would you describe Paul's relationship with Timothy?

14. Imagine that you were the person carrying this letter from Paul to Timothy. Along the way, you were attacked by a band of robbers who

stripped you of all your valuables, including this letter. The leader of the robber band couldn't read, and when you asked him to return the letter, he replied, "Why? What's in it that's so important?" How would you answer him?

15. When you get to heaven, if you have a long talk with the apostle Paul and he asks you, "What was most helpful to you in my first letter to Timothy?" how would you like to be able to answer him?

16. Suppose you heard a voice from heaven saying to you, "Don't get over-ambitious and try to apply too much from this book to your life right now. Just pick one thing to focus on, and do it well." What one thing would you choose?

17. What kind of perspectives and mental habits do you think could most easily block the principles and promises and commands in this book from staying alive in your mind and heart?

18. How can you ensure that your study of First Timothy is not merely theoretical and intellectual, but is instead truly practical and relevant? Talk together about this. What can you do to help keep the process alive and interesting?

FOR GOING DEEPER

To learn more about Timothy's ministry experience, look at the following verses and discuss how Timothy might have viewed each situation—Acts 17:14-15, 18:5, 19:21-22, and 20:1-6, 1 Corinthians 16:10-11, 2 Corinthians 1:19, Philippians 1:1, 1 Thessalonians 3:2-6, and Hebrews 13:23.

1 TIMOTHY 1

Startup: When you're given a job to do, would you rather have every detail spelled out for you as to how to do it, or would you rather discover and improvise on your own?

SEEING WHAT'S THERE

1. Look again at 3:14-15, where Paul writes about his purpose for this letter. How does he begin accomplishing that purpose in chapter 1?

2. If you were Timothy receiving this letter from your leader Paul, what additional understanding would you have about your job after you finished reading this first chapter?

3. As Paul speaks about himself in this chapter, what is it that he most wants Timothy to understand?

4. From Paul's words of praise in verse 17, how would you describe his relationship with God?

5. From what you see in verses 18-19, what does Timothy need to understand about himself?

6. Suppose the telegraph had been invented back in New Testament times, and Paul decided to send Timothy a brief telegram of this chapter, in advance of the delivery of the full letter. To save money, he decided for now to send only the three most important verses from the chapter. Which three verses do you think Paul would have chosen?

7. What in this chapter do you think might be most surprising to a new Christian reading it for the first time?

8. What in your opinion is the most important word or phrase in this chapter?

9. Look also at the list of "Questions to Ask as You Study Each Chapter" on page 392, which you may want to do for each chapter in First Timothy.

10. EYE FOR DETAIL— *If everyone in the group has read the entire chapter, try answering the following question without looking at your Bible:* Paul uses three terms to describe what he was like before he came to Christ. The first is "blasphemer." What are the other two terms? (See verse 13.)

CAPTURE THE ESSENCE

11. Look again at verse 5. In your own words, how would you describe the relationship of love to purity, sincerity, and faith?

12. If you wanted to adapt verse 5 as a useful guideline to test something, what could you test with it?

13. Imagine yourself looking over Paul's shoulder as he wrote the words of this chapter, under the direction of the Holy Spirit's inner guidance. What emotions, or longings, or re-membrances do you think he most likely experienced as he wrote verses 12-17?

14. From what you see in this chapter, what *expectations* would you say Paul has of Timothy?

15. Picture this book of First Timothy as a fast-moving train. Chapter 1 is the locomotive in front, and the other chapters represent railway cars that follow behind. From what you see here in chapter 1, what is the *energy* in the locomotive—the point or principle or theme that's the driving force for the locomotive and the entire train?

FOR LIFE TODAY

16. If it's true that "you *become* what you *think,*" then what are the most important thoughts from this chapter to plant firmly in your mind?

17. Suppose a new Christian asked you, "Why doesn't the Lord show Himself in person to me, and speak to me, just as he did to Paul?" How could you use verse 16 to help you give a meaningful answer?

18. Which verse in this chapter do you think God wants you to understand best?

FOR GOING DEEPER

Look again at verse 16. Then look up together the following passages, and discuss what you see in common in all of them, and what they say about the apostle Paul's life and character.—1 Corinthians 4:16 and 11:1; Philippians 3:17 and 4:9; and 2 Thessalonians 3:7-9.

1 TIMOTHY 2

Startup: When is prayer in a group most meaningful to you?

SEEING WHAT'S THERE

1. What evidence does this chapter offer about God's personality?

2. What would you say are the most important *verbs*—the action words —in this chapter?

3. What does Paul say about *prayer* in this chapter?

4. Look again at 3:14-15, where Paul gives his purpose for this letter. How does he help accomplish that purpose in chapter 2?

5. If you were Timothy receiving this letter from your leader Paul, what additional understanding would you have about your job after you finished reading this second chapter?

6. EYE FOR DETAIL— *From what you recall seeing in this chapter, try answering the following question without looking at your Bible:* In verse 5, how does Paul complete the following statement? "For there is one God…"

CAPTURE THE ESSENCE

7. What insights do you find in this chapter regarding the right way to approach God in worship?

8. Look at what Paul says in verse 4 about God's desire. Then discuss together how much you agree or disagree with this statement: Since other Scriptures make it clear that not all people are going to heaven, there must be something that God wants even *more* than for everyone to be saved.

9. Try to "read between the lines" as you think about Paul's words in this chapter. What foundational principles would you say are the source of Paul's teaching here?

10. In Proverbs 13:13 we're told, "He who respects a command is rewarded," or in another translation, "He that feareth the commandment shall be rewarded." What would you say is the likely *reward* for Christians who respect and follow the commands and guidelines in this chapter?

11. Review Paul's statement in verse 5. From God's point of view, *why* do you think this is important for us to know?

12. If you were asked to write a discussion question to help your Bible study group examine and understand something in this chapter, how would you word the question?

FOR LIFE TODAY

13. Consider carefully the major teachings in this chapter. Which do you think is harder for Christians—understanding what this chapter says, or putting it into practice?

14. What response would you make to someone who read verses 3-4 to you and then said, "This verse clearly says that everyone will go to heaven"?

15. If God had written this chapter only for *you,* which words or phrases do you think He would have underlined?

FOR GOING DEEPER

Will everyone be saved? In verse 4, look again at what Paul tells us about God's desire. Then look at the following passages, and summarize what they together teach us—2 Peter 3:8-9, 1 Peter 1:1-2, Hebrews 10:26-29, and Matthew 25:41-46.

1 TIMOTHY 3

Startup: Suppose a first-time visitor to a church made this remark: "This church must really have good leaders." What kind of observations do you think would cause the visitor to say that?

SEEING WHAT'S THERE

1. After reading through this chapter, which words or phrases or sentences here would you most like to understand better?

2. In verses 2-13, look closely at the stated requirements for church leadership. Which of these requirements relate more to *ability,* which relate more to *character,* and which relate to neither?

3. From what you see in verse 5, what was the basic responsibility of a person chosen as an "overseer" or "bishop"?

4. Look once more at verse 14-15. How would you say this chapter helps Paul fulfill his stated purpose for writing this letter?

5. If you were Timothy receiving this letter from your leader Paul, what additional understanding about your job would you gain from this third chapter?

6. EYE FOR DETAIL— *From what you recall seeing in this chapter, try answering the following question without looking at your Bible:* At the end of this chapter, Paul mentions "the church of the living God." What else does he say in describing the church? (See verse 15.)

CAPTURE THE ESSENCE

7. If this chapter was the only Scripture portion you had ever known, what would you conclude from it about how churches should be governed?

8. Review again each of criteria for church leaders in this chapter. For each requirement, discuss *why* it is important. For each one, ask this question: What could easily happen in a church if the leaders were very weak in this area?

FOR LIFE TODAY

9. Think carefully about Paul's statement in verse 1. How much do you desire to have leadership in your church? Use a scale of one to ten (one = "no desire at all," ten = "extreme desire") to help you decide.

10. In your own opinion, which leadership qualifications mentioned in this chapter are the most urgently needed in the church's leadership today?

11. Of all that you see in this chapter, what one truth are you most *thankful* for, because of its personal significance to you?

FOR GOING DEEPER

Look again in verse 16 at Paul's picture of what Jesus did when He came to earth. Search together also in the following passages for word-pictures and statements that deepen our understanding of this miracle of love—John 1:1 and 1:10-14, 2 Corinthians 8:9, Philippians 2:6-11, Hebrews 2:14-17, and 1 John 1:1-2.

1 TIMOTHY 4

Startup: What images come to your mind as you think of these words together: *training, discipline, conditioning.*

SEEING WHAT'S THERE

1. What kind of questions come to mind as you get into this chapter?

2. Look back again at Paul's statement of purpose for this letter in 3:14-15. How does he help accomplish that purpose in chapter 4?

3. If you were Timothy receiving this letter from your leader Paul, what additional understanding would you have about your job after you finished reading this fourth chapter?

4. Suppose a band of armed terrorists stormed into the room where you're now meeting, then took you as hostages in a captivity that was likely to last for days or weeks. Just before they confiscated your Bibles, they allowed you to take one last look at the chapter open before you. Which verse in this chapter would you most try to fix in mind before your Bible was snatched away, and why?

5. What *commands* does Paul give to Timothy in this chapter? As a group, list them all aloud.

6. Which important details in this chapter do you think might be the easiest to overlook?

7. EYE FOR DETAIL— *From what you recall seeing in this chapter, try answering the following question without looking at your Bible:* Paul mentions a number of ways in which Timothy should set an example for the believers. How many of them can you name? (See verse 12.)

CAPTURE THE ESSENCE

8. From what you've seen so far in this letter, how would you describe the *lifestyle* that God wanted Timothy to have?

9. If Satan wrote down some guidelines and commands to get Timothy to do just the opposite of what this chapter teaches, how do you think his message might be worded?

10. Notice what Paul says in verses 3 and 4 about the importance of our gratitude or thanksgiving in receiving gifts from God. From God's point of view, why do you think this is so important?

11. In verse 16, Paul tells Timothy to "watch closely" or "take heed" or "pay attention" to two things. Assuming that the order in which he gives them is significant, how would you explain that significance?

12. If you had only this chapter to go by, what would you say is the difference between a false teacher and a true teacher?

13. If you were Timothy and had just received this letter, what thoughts and feelings and questions would you have after reading verses 11-16?

14. Picture in your mind two young Christian leaders, one who has learned to obey the commands in verses 12-16, and one who has *not* learned how to do it. What practical differences do you see in the way these two persons live and work?

15. Regarding the subjects that you've seen addressed so far in this book, what questions do you have that remain unanswered?

FOR LIFE TODAY

16. Are the kind of people Paul talks about in verses 1-3 still around today? If so, from what you know in Scripture, what should be our response to them?

17. In verses 7-8, Paul mentions the need for godly "discipline" or "training" or "exercise." If you were to set up a spiritual "exercise" program based es-

pecially on what you've seen in this book, what would it include?

18. Look again at the gratitude or thanksgiving mentioned in verses 3-4. In the last 24 hours, what are the biggest things (if any) that you've received from God and thanked Him for?

19. Which verse in this chapter do you think God wants you to understand best?

Notice again how this chapter begins. If the Spirit has spoken something so clearly—how clearly have we listened and understood? Look together at the following passages, and discuss how they support what Paul says here—Matthew 24:9-12, Mark 13:22, and Acts 20:29-31.

1 TIMOTHY 5

Startup: Besides the obvious physical changes, what would you say are the most important things that happen to a person as he or she matures into old age?

SEEING WHAT'S THERE

1. Return once more to Paul's statement of purpose for this letter in 3:14-15. How does he help accomplish that purpose in chapter 5?

2. If you were Timothy receiving this letter from your leader Paul, what additional understanding about your job would you gain from this fifth chapter?

3. With all else being equal, which of these people do you think would have the best chance of uncovering the most meaning in verses 3-16— a woman who had been widowed for several years, or a woman whose husband died only a month ago?

4. Try to "read between the lines" as you think about Paul's words in this chapter. What foundational principles would you say are the source of Paul's teaching here?

5. In your own words, how would you summarize the guidelines in verses 17-20 about church leadership?

6. If you could ask Paul, "Why did you include verse 23 in this letter?" how do you think he might answer?

7. EYE FOR DETAIL— *From what you recall seeing in this chapter, try answering the following question without looking at your Bible:* Paul mentions something to Timothy about water and wine in this chapter. What is it? (See verse 23.)

CAPTURE THE ESSENCE

8. A 3-step question: (a) Think of someone you know who doesn't spend much time reading the Bible. (b) Select a verse or brief passage in this chapter which you think this

person would probably find boring. (c) Now, how could you clarify or open up this passage in a way that might appeal to this person?

FOR LIFE TODAY

9. If everyone in your church thoroughly understood this chapter, and had a passion for living out its truth, what kind of practical changes do you think would result?

10. Choose one of these sentences, and complete it as fully and candidly as you can:

> *What I see and understand in this chapter is important to my life because…*
>
> *What I see and understand in this chapter does NOT seem important to my life at this time, because…*

FOR GOING DEEPER

How should the church help needy groups of people? Review again the principles you see in this chapter for providing help to widows, and compare those principles with what you see in the following passages—Acts 2:44-47 and 6:1-6, 1 Corinthians 16:1-4, and 2 Corinthians 8:13-15.

1 TIMOTHY 6

Startup: What images come to your mind when you think of the word *contentment?*

SEEING WHAT'S THERE

1. What *commands* does Paul give to Timothy in this chapter? Together, list them all aloud.

2. In your own words, how would you express the main point that Paul makes about *godliness* in this chapter?

3. In your own words, how would you express the main point that Paul makes about *wealth* in this chapter?

4. Notice the word *fight* in verse 12. How would you define this word in the way Paul uses it here?

5. As you read this chapter, what's the strongest impression or image which it leaves in your mind?

6. What kind of questions or difficulties or doubts in a Christian's daily life do you think this chapter answers best?

7. Discuss together which verses in this chapter your attention would most likely be drawn to if you were… (a) a person serving on a jury in an embezzlement case. (b) a store owner who recently caught one of his employees stealing merchandise. (c) a person wrestling with a major decision. (d) a business owner who found out today from his personal accountant that his net worth has now surpassed the two million dollar mark.

8. Once again, notice Paul's statement of purpose for this letter in 3:14-15. How does he help accomplish that purpose in this final chapter?

9. If this chapter was a good answer to a question that began with the word *How…* then what would the rest of the question say?

10. EYE FOR DETAIL— *From what you recall seeing in this chapter, try answering the following question without looking at your Bible:* Paul speaks of something that leads to "great gain." What is it? (See verse 6.)

CAPTURE THE ESSENCE

11. Many times we rob ourselves of the discovery of deeper truths in Scripture because we see a passage and say to ourselves, "I already know that." For which teachings in this chapter might it be easiest for Christians to fall into that trap?

12. If you thought of this chapter as a roadmap for a Christian's life, what would be the safest "roads" to take, as taught in this chapter? And what would be the unsafe, dangerous roads to avoid?

13. If Satan wrote down some guidelines and commands to get Timothy to do just the opposite of what this chapter teaches, how do you think his message might be worded?

14. In Psalm 119:45, the psalmist says to God, "I will walk at liberty, for I seek Thy precepts." As you think about the "precepts" or commands given in verses 11-12, in what ways can you see it offering true freedom and liberty to a Christian?

15. Look again at verse 17. Practically speaking, how can rich people show that their trust and hope is in God, and not in their money?

16. James 1:22 tells us that when we merely listen to the Word without putting it into practice, we deceive ourselves. What kind of self-deceiving excuses or rationalization do you think could most easily keep Christians from actually *doing* what is taught in verses 17-18?

FOR LIFE TODAY

17. If this chapter were the only portion of Scripture you had access to, how could you use it to help answer this question: *What is the most powerful and effective way to improve my life?*

18. Imagine that you saw earlier today a message written in fire in the sky. It was addressed to you by name, then continued with these words: *Thus saith the LORD: "Read 1 Timothy 6, for I have something for you there."* Which verse or verses in this chapter do you think He most likely would be referring to?

19. In Philippians 4:8 we're given the following command: "Whatever is true, whatever is noble, whatever is right, whatever is pure, whatever is lovely, whatever is admirable—if anything is excellent or praiseworthy—*think about such things."* What food for thought can you find in this chapter that especially strikes you as being *true,* or *noble,* or *right,* or *pure,* or *lovely,* or *admirable,* or *excellent,* or *praiseworthy?*

20. From what you see in this chapter and elsewhere in Scripture, what can a Christian reasonably expect in life if he or she does *not* obey the command in verse 18?

21. If you were asked to write a discussion question to help your Bible study group apply something in this chapter to their lives, how would you word the question?

FOR GOING DEEPER

With verses 3-5 in mind, look together at the following verses and discuss how they reinforce or expand Paul's teaching here—1 Timothy 1:4, 2 Timothy 2:14-17 and 2:23-26, and Titus 1:10-16.

1 TIMOTHY:

THE BIG PICTURE

(Discuss again the questions in the "Overview," plus the questions below.)

1. If you were Timothy, and decided to write a letter back to Paul after receiving this one, what would you include in the letter—what questions, comments, words of appreciation, etc.?

2. If you were responsible for giving the apostle Paul a job performance review, what comments would you make to him, based on his ministry as you see it in this letter?

3. Look together at each of these verses, and discuss which one you believe is the best candidate for "KEY VERSE" in the book of First Timothy—the one which brings into sharpest focus what this book is most about: 3:14-15, 3:16, 4:12, or 6:11-12.

4. Suppose that at the very end of chapter 6, Paul added this line: "Timothy, if you remember only one thing from this letter, let it be this:..." How do you think Paul would complete that sentence?

5. In James 1:23-24 we're told that "anyone who listens to the word but does not do what it says is like a man who looks at his face in a mirror and, after looking at himself, goes away and immediately forgets what he looks like." In what important ways has the book of First Timothy been a "mirror" for you—showing you what you can and should do?

6. If you've decided on a starting point for applying something in this book more effectively to your life, what commitment would you be willing to make to others in your group regarding this?

7. How would you complete the following word of advice to growing Christians? *Explore the book of First Timothy if you want to learn more about...*

2 Timothy

❖

OVERVIEW

(Discuss these OVERVIEW questions both at the beginning of your study of Second Timothy, and again after you've studied together all four chapters. Your answers may change significantly once you've looked more closely at the entire book.)

Startup: Think of someone important to you who is no longer on this earth. What's an example of the good heritage which this person left to you?

SEEING WHAT'S THERE

1. What do you learn about Timothy's spiritual heritage in 1:5-6 and 3:14-15?

2. Look together at Philippians 2:19-23. Discuss together what you learn in that passage about Timothy's character, and about Paul's esteem for Timothy.

3. Look also at Acts 16:1-5 and summarize what you learn there about Timothy's background and ministry.

4. What exactly was Timothy's position? Was he another apostle? Was he an elder or overseer? To help you find an answer, look together at the following passages, noticing especially how Paul describes him: Romans 16:21; 1 Corinthians 4:16-17; 2 Corinthians 1:1; and Philippians 1:1.

5. Start scanning the book until you come to a verse that brings a question to your mind. What's the question?

6. Begin scanning the book again until you come to a verse that gives you a smile or a sense of gratitude or joy.

What is pleasing to you about this verse?

7. Look also at the list of "Questions to Ask as You Begin Your Study of Each Book" on page 393.

CAPTURE THE ESSENCE

8. What previous impressions, if any, have you had about the book of Second Timothy in regard to (a) its content, (b) its level of difficulty, and (c) its importance?

9. The book of Second Timothy has been called "Paul's Final Message," "Being a Good Soldier of Jesus Christ," and "A Dying Shout of Victory." With that reputation for this book, what answers, guidelines, and solutions would you like to gain as you examine it more closely?

10. What one-word adjectives best describe the *tone* of this letter?

11. From the evidence you see in this letter, how would you describe Paul's relationship with Timothy?

12. Imagine that you were the person carrying this letter from Paul to Timothy. Along the way, you were attacked by a band of robbers who stripped you of all your valuables, including this letter. The leader of the robber band couldn't read, and when you asked him to return the letter, he replied, "Why? What's in it that's so important?" How would you answer him?

FOR LIFE TODAY

13. When you get to heaven, if you have a long talk with the apostle Paul and

he asks you, "What was most helpful to you in my second letter to Timothy?" how would you like to be able to answer him?

14. What kind of perspectives and mental habits do you think could most easily block the principles and promises and commands in this book from staying alive in your mind and heart?

15. How can you ensure that your study of Second Timothy is not merely theoretical and intellectual, but is instead truly practical and relevant? Talk together about this. What can you do to help keep the process alive and interesting?

FOR GOING DEEPER

To learn more about Timothy's ministry experience, look at the following verses and discuss how Timothy might have viewed each situation—Acts 17:14-15, 18:5, 19:21-22, and 20:1-6; 1 Corinthians 16:10-11; 2 Corinthians 1:19; Philippians 1:1; 1 Thessalonians 3:2-6; and Hebrews 13:23.

2 TIMOTHY 1

Startup: What are some typical moments in life when you especially appreciate a word of encouragement from someone?

SEEING WHAT'S THERE

1. If you were Timothy receiving this letter from Paul—your faithful friend, leader, and spiritual father—what emotions and thoughts and questions would you experience after reading this first chapter?

2. What *commands* does Paul give to Timothy in this chapter?

3. From what you see in this chapter, what does Timothy need to understand about himself?

4. According to various translations, Paul speaks to Timothy in verse 14 about the "good deposit" or "treasure" or "good thing" that was entrusted Timothy. What was this treasure or deposit?

5. If you could ask Paul, "Why did you include verses 16-18 in this letter?" how do you think he might answer?

6. What does this chapter tell us about (a) Paul's desires and affections, and (b) Paul's priorities in life?

7. What in your opinion is the most important word or phrase in this chapter?

8. Look also at the list of "Questions to Ask as You Study Each Chapter" on page 392, which you may want to do for each chapter in Second Timothy.

9. EYE FOR DETAIL— *If everyone in the group has read the entire chapter, try answering the following question without looking at your Bible:* Paul asks for God's mercy for a man named Onesiphorus, because of the service he rendered to Paul. In what two cities does Paul say this man helped him? (See verses 16-18.)

10. If Satan wrote down some guidelines and commands to get Timothy to do just the opposite of what this chapter teaches, how do you think his message might be worded?

11. In order to obey the command Paul gave him in verse 6, what exactly do you think Timothy did?

12. Imagine yourself looking over Paul's shoulder as he wrote the words of this chapter, under the direction of the Holy Spirit's inner guidance. What emotions, or longings, or remembrances do you think he most likely experienced as he wrote verses 8-12?

13. At the end of verse 12, notice what Paul says he is convinced or persuaded of. How would you describe the process by which he came to this confident knowledge?

14. Paul's language in 4:6-8 indicates that he is nearing death. In that case, from what you see here in chapter 1, what is it that Paul most wants Timothy to remember about him?

15. Picture this book of Second Timothy as a fast-moving train. Chapter 1 is the locomotive in front, and the other chapters represent railway cars that follow behind. From what you see here in chapter 1, what is the *energy* in the locomotive—the point or principle or theme that's the driving force for the locomotive and the entire train?

16. If you were responsible for giving the apostle Paul a job performance review, what comments would you make to him, based on his ministry as you see it in this chapter?

17. A 3-step question: (a) Think of someone you know who doesn't spend much time reading the Bible. (b) Select a verse or brief passage in this chapter which you think this person would probably find boring. (c) Now, how could you clarify or open up this passage in a way that might appeal to this person?

FOR LIFE TODAY

18. Look again at Paul's command to Timothy in verse 6. If your spiritual life needed a fresh rekindling or stirring up, how would you do it?

19. Focus your mind on what you consider to be your two or three most important responsibilities in life. In what ways could verse 7 help you carry out any or all of these responsibilities?

20. Look again at Paul's words in verse 14 about the "good deposit" or "treasure" or "good thing" that Timothy needed to guard. What is it in *your* life that could be described in the same way?

21. If it's true that "you *become* what you *think,*" then what are the most important thoughts from this chapter to plant firmly in your mind?

22. Suppose you heard a voice from heaven saying to you, "Don't get over-ambitious and try to apply too much from this chapter to your life right now. Just pick one thing to focus on, and do it well." What one thing would you choose?

FOR GOING DEEPER

Look again at Paul's statement in verse 10 about what Jesus did. How did Jesus "destroy" or "abolish" death, as this verse says? Answer this question together as you look at the following passages— Romans 6:8-10, 1 Corinthians 15:24-26 and 15:54-57, 1 John 3:8, and Revelation 20:14.

2 Timothy 2

Startup: What images come to your mind when you think of the word *endure?*

SEEING WHAT'S THERE

1. If you were Timothy receiving this letter from Paul, what emotions and thoughts and questions would you experience after reading this second chapter?

2. How do you think a soldier would elaborate on the meaning of verses 3-4?

3. How do you think an athlete would elaborate on the meaning of verse 5?

4. How do you think a farmer would elaborate on the meaning of verse 6?

5. How would you explain verses 20-21 in your own words?

6. What does this chapter tell us about (a) Paul's desires and affections, and (b) Paul's priorities in life?

7. Suppose the telegraph had been invented back in New Testament times, and Paul decided to send Timothy a brief telegram of this chapter, in advance of the delivery of the full letter. To save money, he decided for now to send only the three most important verses from the chapter. Which three verses do you think Paul would have chosen?

8. If this letter was the only Scripture portion you had ever known, what would you conclude from it about *who Jesus is,* and what it means to *follow Him?*

9. What in this chapter do you think might be most surprising to a new Christian reading it for the first time?

10. What kind of questions or difficulties or doubts in a Christian's daily life do you think this chapter answers best?

11. What *commands* does Paul give to Timothy in this chapter? As a group, list them all aloud.

12. Which important details in this chapter do you think might be the easiest to overlook?

13. In the final verse of this chapter, Paul refers to the will of the devil. From what you understand in this chapter and elsewhere in Scripture, what is the devil's will?

14. EYE FOR DETAIL— *From what you recall seeing in this chapter, try answering the following question without looking at your Bible:* Paul tells Timothy in this chapter to remember something specific. What was it? (See verse 8.)

CAPTURE THE ESSENCE

15. If you thought of this chapter as a roadmap for a Christian's life, what would be the safest "roads" to take, as taught in this chapter? What would be the unsafe, dangerous roads to avoid?

16. Many times we rob ourselves of the discovery of deeper truths in Scripture because we see a passage and say to ourselves, "I already know that." For which teachings in this chapter might it be easiest for Christians to fall into that trap?

17. If this chapter was your only source of such information, how would you describe the right qualities and actions for a person involved in Christian ministry?

18. Picture in your mind two young Christian leaders, one who has learned to obey the commands in verses 2-7, and one who has *not* learned how to do it. What practical differences do you see in the way these two persons live and work?

19. In Proverbs 13:13 we're told, "He who respects a command is rewarded," or in another translation, "He

that feareth the commandment shall be rewarded." Look at the command in verse 15. What would you say is the likely *reward* for respecting and keeping this command?

20. Imagine that you wrote a song based on verse 16. What title would you give the song?

21. Look at Paul's mention of a "firm foundation" in verse 19. What is this a firm foundation *for?*

22. If you were asked to write a discussion question to help your Bible study group examine and understand something in this chapter, how would you word the question?

23. In practical terms, what would it take for a person today to live up to the guidelines given in verse 15?

24. Look again at verses 20-21. Then focus your mind on what you consider to be your two or three most important responsibilities in life. In what ways could verse 21 help you carry out any or all of these responsibilities?

25. In a typical day, how often would the command in verse 22 offer useful and timely guidelines for your immediate situation?

26. If this chapter were the only portion of Scripture you had access to, how could you use it to help answer this question: *What is the most powerful and effective way to improve my life?*

27. In Colossians 3:1 we read this command: "Since you have been raised with Christ, set your hearts on things above, where Christ is seated at the right hand of God." What have you personally observed about Jesus Christ in this chapter that would be worthy of setting your heart on?

28. Of all that you see in this chapter, what one truth are you most *thankful* for, because of its personal significance to you?

Be strong! Endure! With the challenge in verses 1-13 in mind, look also at the following passages that teach endurance, then discuss some workable ways to put them into practice—1 Corinthians 9:24-27, Galatians 6:9-10, Ephesians 6:10-20, and Philippians 3:12-14.

2 TIMOTHY 3

Startup: What's the earliest point in life when you can remember learning about something in the Bible?

SEEING WHAT'S THERE

1. As you read this chapter, what's the strongest impression or image which it leaves in your mind?

2. After reading through this chapter, which words or phrases or sentences here would you most like to understand better?

3. If you were Timothy receiving this letter from Paul, what emotions and thoughts and questions would you experience after reading this third chapter?

4. What would you say are the most important *verbs*—the action words—in this chapter?

5. What *commands* does Paul give to Timothy in this chapter? Together, list them all aloud.

6. What does this chapter tell us about (a) Paul's desires and affections, and (b) Paul's priorities in life?

7. Recall again Paul's words in 4:6-8, indicating that he is nearing death. From what you see here in chapter 3, what is it that Paul most wants Timothy to remember about him?

8. EYE FOR DETAIL— *From what you recall seeing in this chapter, try answering the following question without looking at your Bible:* Paul says that persecution will come to a certain group of people. How does he describe these people? (See verse 12.)

CAPTURE THE ESSENCE

9. If this chapter was your only source of such information, how would you describe the right qualities and actions for a person involved in Christian ministry?

10. From what you see in this chapter, what *expectations* would you say Paul has of Timothy?

11. Look together at 2 Peter 1:20-21, and compare what you see there with 2 Timothy 3:16. Taking both passages together, answer this question: When we say that the Scriptures are *inspired,* what does that mean?

FOR LIFE TODAY

12. Go through the list of descriptions Paul gives in verses 1-5. Are there people around today who fit each one? If so, do the words of Paul at the end of verse 5 mean that we should not try to oppose these people? (Explain your answer.)

13. Review the list at the end of verse 16 of the four things for which the Scriptures are useful or profitable. Which of these four has the most value or importance in your life right now?

14. Which verse in this chapter do you think God wants you to understand best?

FOR GOING DEEPER

Is persecution a guaranteed promise from God? Look together at verse 12 again, and compare it with what you see in the following passages—Matthew 10:22, Acts 14:21-22, Philippians 1:29, and 1 Peter 4:12-14.

2 TIMOTHY 4

Startup: What would you like to be said about you at your funeral?

SEEING WHAT'S THERE

1. What one-word adjectives best describe the *tone* of this chapter?

2. If you were Timothy receiving this letter from Paul, what emotions and thoughts and questions would you experience after reading this final chapter?

3. What does this chapter tell us about (a) Paul's desires and affections, and (b) Paul's priorities in life?

4. As you read this chapter, what's the strongest impression or image which it leaves in your mind?

5. Describe the kind of person whom you think would gain the most out of this chapter. What would be his or her questions and struggles and concerns?

6. Suppose a band of armed terrorists stormed into the room where you're now meeting, then took you as hostages in a captivity that was likely to last for days or weeks. Just before they confiscated your Bibles, they allowed you to take one last look at the chapter open before you. Which verse in this chapter would you most try to fix in mind before your Bible was snatched away, and why?

7. What *commands* does Paul give to Timothy in this chapter? Together, make a list of all of them.

8. EYE FOR DETAIL— *From what you recall seeing in this chapter, try answering the following question without looking at your Bible:* As he writes this letter, Paul says that only one of his friends and co-workers is with him. Who is it? (See verse 11.)

CAPTURE THE ESSENCE

9. What one-word adjectives would you use to best describe Paul as you see him in this chapter?

10. What would you say is Paul's strongest motive in this chapter?

11. If Satan wrote down some guidelines and commands to get Timothy to do just the opposite of what this chapter teaches, how do you think his message might be worded?

12. Picture in your mind two young Christian leaders, one who has learned to obey the commands in verses 2-5, and one who has *not* learned how to do it. What practical differences do you see in the way these two persons live and work?

13. From the evidence you see in this chapter alone, how do you think Paul would define the terms *success* and *true significance?*

14. If this chapter was a good answer to a question that began with the word *How...* then what would the rest of the question say?

FOR LIFE TODAY

15. In Philippians 4:8 we're given the following command: "Whatever is true, whatever is noble, whatever is right, whatever is pure, whatever is lovely, whatever is admirable—if anything is excellent or praiseworthy—*think about such things.*" What food for thought can you find in this chapter that especially strikes you as being *true,* or *noble,* or *right,* or *pure,* or *lovely,* or *admirable,* or *excellent,* or *praiseworthy?*

16. Imagine that you saw earlier today a message written in fire in the sky. It was addressed to you by name, then continued with these words: *Thus saith the LORD: "Read 2 Timothy 4, for I have something for you there."* Which verse or verses in this chapter

do you think He most likely would be referring to?

17. If you were asked to write a discussion question to help your Bible study group apply something in this chapter to their lives, how would you word the question?

The "crown of righteousness" which Paul mentions in verse 8 is one of three kinds of crowns which the Bible says God will award to His faithful servants. Look together for the names of the other two crowns in James 1:12 and 1 Peter 5:4.

2 TIMOTHY:

THE BIG PICTURE

(Discuss again the questions in the "Overview," plus the questions below.)

1. If you were Timothy, and decided to write a letter back to Paul after receiving this one, what would you include in the letter—what questions, comments, words of appreciation, etc.?

2. Look together at each of these verses, and discuss which one you believe is the best candidate for "KEY VERSE" in the book of Second Timothy—the one which brings into sharpest focus what this book is most about: 1:8, 2:15, 3:14, or 4:2.

3. Suppose that at the very end of this book, Paul added this line: "Timothy, if you remember only one thing from this letter, let it be this:..." How do you think Paul would complete that sentence?

4. In James 1:23-24 we're told that "anyone who listens to the word but does not do what it says is like a man who looks at his face in a mirror and, after looking at himself, goes away and immediately forgets what he looks like." In what important ways has the book of Second Timothy been a "mirror" for you—showing you what you can and should do?

5. If you've decided on a starting point for applying something in this book more effectively to your life, what commitment would you be willing to make to others in your group regarding this?

6. How would you complete the following word of advice to growing Christians? *Explore the book of Second Timothy if you want to learn more about...*

Titus

OVERVIEW

(Discuss these OVERVIEW questions both at the beginning of your study of Titus, and again after you've studied together all three chapters. Your answers may change significantly once you've looked more closely at the entire book.)

Startup: Which of these would you rather be called, and why—a good person, a do-gooder, or a good-timer?

SEEING WHAT'S THERE

1. From what you see in 1:5 and 2:15, what would you say is Paul's overall purpose for this letter to Titus?

2. Start scanning this letter until you come to a verse that brings a question to your mind. What's the question?

3. Begin scanning the letter again until you come to a verse that gives you a smile or a sense of gratitude or joy. What is pleasing to you about this verse?

4. Discuss what you you learn about Titus from these verses: 2 Corinthians 2:13, 7:6-7, 7:13-15, 8:16-17, and 8:23, and Galatians 2:1-3.

5. In this brief letter, Paul frequently uses a term that is translated in our various English Bibles as "doing good," "good deeds," or "good works." Look together at the following occurrences of this phrase in Titus, and decide together how you would define it in your own words —2:7 and 2:14, and 3:1, 3:8, and 3:14.

6. Look also at the list of "Questions to Ask as You Begin Your Study of Each Book" on page 393.

CAPTURE THE ESSENCE

7. What previous impressions, if any, have you had about the book of Titus in regard to (a) its content, (b) its level of difficulty, and (c) its importance?

8. The book of Titus has been called "The Order of God's House," and "God's People Are Called to Be Good People." With that reputation for this book, what answers, guidelines, and solutions would you like to gain as you examine it more closely?

9. From the evidence you see in this letter, how would you describe Paul's relationship with Titus?

10. Imagine that you were the person carrying this letter from Paul to Titus. Along the way, you were attacked by a band of robbers who stripped you of all your valuables, including this letter. The leader of the robber band could not read, and when you asked him to return the letter, he replied, "Why? What's in it that's so important?" How would you answer him?

FOR LIFE TODAY

11. Suppose you heard a voice from heaven saying to you, "Don't get over-ambitious and try to apply too much from this book to your life right now. Just pick one thing to focus on, and do it well." What one thing would you choose?

12. When you get to heaven, if you have a long talk with the apostle Paul and he asks you, "What was most helpful to you in my letter to Titus?" how would you like to be able to answer him?

13. What kind of perspectives and mental habits do you think could most easily block the principles and promises and commands in this book from staying alive in your mind and heart?

14. How can you ensure that your study of Titus is not merely theoretical and intellectual, but is instead truly practical and relevant? Talk together about this. What can you do to help keep the process alive and interesting?

FOR GOING DEEPER

Paul's letters to his young helpers Titus and Timothy are known as the "pastoral" epistles. What did an aging apostle feel was most important to pass on to his ministry partners who would live on after him? Look up together the following verses to see the important themes that are found in Paul's words to both men. Compare Titus 1:6-7 with 1 Timothy 3:2-3; compare Titus 2:7-8 with 1 Timothy 4:12; compare Titus 2:1 with 2 Timothy 1:13; and compare Titus 3:9 with 2 Timothy 2:16.

TITUS 1

Startup: In your opinion, what are the most important ingredients for a healthy church?

SEEING WHAT'S THERE

1. In verses 6-9, look closely at the stated requirements for church leadership. Which of these requirements relate more to *ability,* which relate more to *character,* and which relate to neither?

2. Notice Paul's words about "rebellious" or "unruly" people in verse 10. What are the main points he makes about these people in the rest of this chapter?

3. Suppose the telegraph had been invented back in New Testament times, and Paul decided to send Titus a brief telegram of this chapter, in advance of the delivery of the full letter. To save money, he decided for now to send only the three most important verses from the chapter. Which three verses do you think Paul would have chosen?

4. What in this chapter do you think might be most surprising to a new Christian reading it for the first time?

5. Look also at the list of "Questions to Ask as You Study Each Chapter" on page 392, which you may want to do for each chapter in Titus.

6. EYE FOR DETAIL— *If everyone in the group has read the entire chapter, try answering the following question without looking at your Bible:* Paul quoted a saying about the people of Crete. What three things did it say about them? (See verse 12.)

CAPTURE THE ESSENCE

7. A 3-step question: (a) Think of someone you know who doesn't spend much time reading the Bible. (b) Select a verse or brief passage in this chapter which you think this

person would probably find boring. (c) Now decide how you could clarify or open up this passage in a way that might appeal to this person.

8. Imagine Titus writing back to Paul and quoting his words in verse 15, then adding this question: "What exactly did you mean by this?" How do you think Paul would explain it?

9. From what you see in this chapter, what *expectations* would you say Paul has of Titus?

FOR LIFE TODAY

10. In your own opinion, which leadership qualifications mentioned in verses 6-9 are the most urgently needed in the church's leadership today?

11. Which verse in this chapter do you think God wants you to understand best?

FOR GOING DEEPER

Look again at verse 15. Does Paul mean here that there is no such thing as impurity for the Christian? Look together at the following verses to help you answer —1 Timothy 4:3-5 and Matthew 15:16-20.

TITUS 2

Startup: What are the qualities you like best in a good teacher?

SEEING WHAT'S THERE

1. What *commands* does Paul give Titus in this chapter?

2. How would you summarize what this chapter says about the right things to be taught by Christian teachers?

3. What kind of questions or difficulties or doubts in a Christian's daily life do you think this chapter answers best?

4. If this letter was the only Scripture portion you had ever known, what would you conclude from it about how Christians should relate to one another?

5. Suppose a band of armed terrorists stormed into the room where you're now meeting, then took you as hostages in a captivity that was likely to last for days or weeks. Just before they confiscated your Bibles, they allowed you to take one last look at the chapter open before you. Which verse in this chapter would you most try to fix in mind before your Bible was snatched away, and why?

6. What would you say are the most important *verbs*—the action words —in this chapter?

7. Which important details in this chapter do you think might be the easiest to overlook?

8. With all else being equal, which of these two persons do you think would have the best chance of uncovering the most meaning in this chapter— a young pastor in his first church, or an older pastor with years of church experience?

9. What in your opinion is the most important word or phrase in this chapter?

10. EYE FOR DETAIL— *From what you recall seeing in this chapter, try answering the following question without looking at your Bible:* Paul emphasizes one thing for Titus to teach to young men. What was it? (See verse 6.)

CAPTURE THE ESSENCE

11. Many times we rob ourselves of the discovery of deeper truths in Scripture because we see a passage and say to ourselves, "I already know that." For which teachings in this chapter might it be easiest for Christians to fall into that trap?

12. If Satan wrote down some guidelines and commands to get Titus to do just the opposite of what this chapter teaches, how do you think his message might be worded?

13. In verses 1-10, look at the things which Titus is commanded to teach various groups. Taking them as a whole, would you say they involve mostly inward attitudes, mostly outward practices, or an even mixture of both?

14. Consider again the guidelines for good teaching in verses 7-8. In your own words, how would you explain each of these criteria?

15. If you were not yet a Christian, what teachings in this chapter do you think would be most intriguing to you, and why?

16. If you were asked to write a discussion question to help your Bible study group examine and understand something in this chapter, how would you word the question?

FOR LIFE TODAY

17. Look again at verse 1. Suppose you were listening to a preacher or teacher and he said something which to you was questionable in its biblical accuracy. How would you go about deciding whether or not his message was "sound doctrine"?

18. In verses 2-6, notice the four categories of people for whom Titus received instructions to pass on. For the category that you belong to, how important in your life are these instructions?

19. Consider again verse 12, and recall the words of Jesus in John 15:5— "Apart from me you can do nothing." Picture in your mind something good that could happen in your life in conformity to this verse, something that could clearly be accomplished only by the Lord's supernatural power. What would this be?

20. If everyone in your church thoroughly understood this chapter, and had a passion for living out its truth, what kind of practical changes do you think would result?

21. If this chapter were the only portion of Scripture you had access to, how could you use it to help answer this question: *What is the most powerful and effective way to improve my life?*

22. Imagine that you saw earlier today a message written in fire in the sky. It was addressed to you by name, then continued with these words: *Thus saith the LORD: "Read Titus 2, for I have something for you there."* Which verse or verses in this chapter do you think He most likely would be referring to?

23. Suppose a new Christian asked you, "How can I discover God's will for my life?" How could you use this chapter to help you give a meaningful answer?

24. In Colossians 3:1 we read this command: "Since you have been raised with Christ, set your hearts on things above, where Christ is seated at the right hand of God." What have you personally observed about Jesus Christ in this chapter that would be worthy of setting your heart on?

With verse 1 in mind, look at these other passages to help you know the right way for determining what is "sound doctrine"—John 14:26, 1 Timothy 1:10-11 and 6:3, and 2 Timothy 1:13-14.

TITUS 3

Startup: What qualities in someone else would most quickly lead you to think of that person as a *good* person?

SEEING WHAT'S THERE

1. What *commands* does Paul give Titus in this chapter?

2. How would you summarize what this chapter says about the right things to be taught by Christian teachers?

3. From what you see in this chapter alone, how many important *purposes* can you find for Christians to have in living their lives for God?

4. After reading through this chapter, which words or phrases or sentences here would you most like to understand better?

5. Try to "read between the lines" as you think about Paul's words in verses 10-11. What foundational principles would you say are the source of Paul's teaching here?

6. If you could ask Paul, "Why did you include verse 14 in this letter?" how do you think he might answer?

7. If this chapter was a good answer to a question that began with the word *Why…* then what would the rest of the question say?

8. EYE FOR DETAIL— *From what you recall seeing in this chapter, try answering the following question without looking at your Bible:* After mentioning the mercy and grace God has given us through Jesus Christ, Paul said he wanted Titus to teach those things so that people who trust in God will be careful to do something. What is it that they are to be careful to do? (See verse 8.)

CAPTURE THE ESSENCE

9. From what you see in this chapter alone, how would you describe the

lifestyle that God wants His people to have?

10. If Satan wrote down some guidelines and commands to get Titus to do just the opposite of what this chapter teaches, how do you think his message might be worded?

11. James 1:22 tells us that when we merely listen to the Word without putting it into practice, we deceive ourselves. What kind of self-deceiving excuses or rationalization do you think could most easily keep Christians from actually *doing* what is taught in verses 1-2?

12. In Psalm 119:45, the psalmist says to God, "I will walk at liberty, for I seek Thy precepts." As you think about the "precept" given in verse 14, in what ways can you see it offering true freedom and liberty to a Christian?

FOR LIFE TODAY

13. From what you see in this chapter alone, what *desires* does God have for you? And what *expectations* does He have of you?

14. Think carefully again about verses 1-2. Then imagine God evaluating you on a scale of one to ten, in which ten equals perfect obedience to the commands in this passage, and one equals total disregard of those commands. What score do you think He would probably assign to you?

15. From what you see in this chapter and elsewhere in Scripture, what can you reasonably expect in life if you do *not* obey the command in verse 9?

16. If it's true that "you *become* what you *think*," then what are the most important thoughts from this chapter to plant firmly in your mind?

17. If you were asked to write a discussion question to help your Bible study group apply something in this chapter to their lives, how would you word the question?

18. If God had written this chapter only for *you,* which words or phrases do you think He would have underlined?

FOR GOING DEEPER

When there's foolish, divisive talk—how should it be handled? Keep in mind Paul's teaching in verses 9-10 as you look together at the following passages—1 Timothy 1:4 and 6:3-5, 2 Timothy 2:14-17 and 2:23-26, and Titus 1:10-16.

TITUS:

THE BIG PICTURE

(Discuss again the questions in the "Overview," plus the questions below.)

1. If you were Titus, and decided to write a letter back to Paul after receiving this one, what would you include in the letter—what questions, comments, words of appreciation, etc.?

2. If you were responsible for giving the apostle Paul a job performance review, what comments would you make to him, based on his ministry as you see it in this letter?

3. If you thought of this letter to Titus as a roadmap for a Christian's life, what would be the safest "roads" to take, as taught in this chapter? And what would be the unsafe, dangerous roads to avoid?

4. Suppose you were attending a citizens' meeting called by local school officials who were considering the removal of the Bible from the shelves of all school libraries in your community. You spoke up in favor of keeping the Bible available to students. Then another citizen rose to his feet and said, "I see no reason to keep it around. It's a forgotten book anyway. Even most Christians have no idea what's in it. For example," he said, then turned directly to you and asked, "Tell me what the book of Titus is all about." In that situation, how would you respond?

5. Look together at each of these verses, and discuss which one you believe is the best candidate for "KEY VERSE" in the book of Titus—the one which brings into sharpest focus what this book is most about: 1:5, 2:11-12, 3:1, or 3:5.

6. Suppose that at the very end of this book, Paul added this line: "Titus, if you remember only one thing from this letter, let it be this:…" How do you think Paul would complete that sentence?

7. In James 1:23-24 we're told that "anyone who listens to the word but does not do what it says is like a man who looks at his face in a mirror and, after looking at himself, goes away and immediately forgets what he looks like." In what important ways has the book of Titus been a "mirror" for you—showing you what you can and should do?

8. If you've decided on a starting point for applying something in this book more effectively to your life, what commitment would you be willing to make to others in your group regarding this?

9. How would you complete the following word of advice to growing Christians? *Explore the book of Titus if you want to learn more about…*

Philemon

Startup: Imagine that you were a slave in an earlier century. What do you think would have been the hardest part of your existence?

SEEING WHAT'S THERE

1. As you read this brief letter, what's the strongest impression or image which it leaves in your mind?

2. Start scanning this letter until you come to a verse that brings a question to your mind. What's the question?

3. Begin scanning the letter again until you come to a verse that gives you a smile or a sense of gratitude or joy. What is pleasing to you about this verse?

4. From what you see in this letter, what kind of feelings toward one another do you think Paul, Onesimus, and Philemon might have experienced in the developments described in this chapter?

5. Discuss together which verses in this book your attention would most likely be drawn to if you were... (a) a person who had just been released from prison. (b) a store owner who recently caught one of his employees stealing merchandise. (c) a married couple who had been separated by mutual consent for some time, but were now ready to come back together.

6. Look also at the list of "Questions to Ask as You Begin Your Study of Each Book" on page 393, and the list of "Questions to Ask as You Study Each Chapter" on page 392.

7. EYE FOR DETAIL— *If everyone in the group has read all of Philemon, try answering the following question without looking at your Bible:* In the first verse, what does Paul call Philemon?

8. If you were Philemon, and had just read this letter for the first time, what kinds of thoughts and questions would likely be occurring in your mind?

CAPTURE THE ESSENCE

9. The book of Philemon has been called "The Original Emancipation Proclamation," "Christian Fellowship in Action," and "A Slave's Salvation Story." With that reputation for this book, what kinds of answers, guidelines, and solutions would you like to gain as you examine it more closely?

10. Why do you think Paul didn't ask Onesimus to simply enjoy his freedom, and to stay away from Philemon forever?

11. If this letter was the only Scripture portion you had ever known, what would you conclude from it about Paul's personality?

12. If you were asked to write a discussion question to help your Bible study group examine and understand something in this book, how would you word the question? (And how you would you answer it as well?)

13. If you could ask Paul, "Why did you include verse 19 in this letter?" how do you think he might answer?

14. In the example of what Paul did for Onesimus, many Bible teachers have seen a picture of what Jesus does for us. Scan the book to see how you would develop this parallel.

15. Would you say this epistle is an endorsement of slavery? Why or why not?

16. Suppose that at the very end of Philemon, Paul added this line: "Onesimus, if you remember only one thing from this letter, let it be this:..." How do you think Paul would complete that sentence?

FOR LIFE TODAY

17. For each of the following areas, discuss what examples and guidelines and principles can you draw from this letter for Christians today : (a) Christian unity; (b) humility; (c) sensitivity; (d) generosity; (e) forgiveness.

18. Who are some people in *your* life to whom you could easily repeat the words of verse 7?

19. If you've decided on a starting point for applying something in this book more effectively to your life, what commitment would you be willing to make to others in your group regarding this?

20. How would you complete the following word of advice to growing Christians? *Explore the book of Philemon if you want to learn more about...*

FOR GOING DEEPER

Discuss together how you would compare Paul's instructions in this letter with his general instructions to slaves and masters in the following verses — 1 Corinthians 7:20-24, Ephesians 6:5-9, and Colossians 3:22—4:1.

Hebrews

OVERVIEW

(Discuss these OVERVIEW questions both at the be-ginning of your study of Hebrews, and again after you've studied together all thirteen chapters. Your answers may change significantly once you've looked more closely at the entire book.)

Startup: In practical terms, what do you think is the best reason for a Christian to have a good understanding of Jesus' death on the cross, and what it means?

SEEING WHAT'S THERE

1. Start scanning this book until you come to a verse that brings a ques-tion to your mind. What's the ques-tion?

2. Begin scanning the book again until you come to a verse that gives you a smile or a sense of gratitude or joy. What is pleasing to you about this verse?

3. If this book of Hebrews were not in-cluded in the Bible, how would you describe what would be missing in the total picture of the Bible's mes-sage?

4. Suppose you were attending a citi-zens' meeting called by local school officials, who were considering the removal of the Bible from the shelves of all school libraries in your com-munity. You spoke up in favor of keeping the Bible available to stu-dents. Then another citizen rose to his feet and said, "I see no reason to keep it around. It's a forgotten book anyway. Even most Christians have no idea what's in it. For example," he said, then turned directly to you and

asked, "Tell me what the book of Hebrews is all about." In that situa-tion, how would you respond?

5. How does the author describe this book in Hebrews 13:22?

6. From what you see in Hebrews 2:3, what conclusions could you make about the author of this letter (who is not named in the text), and about his *source* for the teaching in this book?

7. Throughout history, Paul has been suggested as the possible author of this anonymous letter. Among other possibilities mentioned are Barnabas and Apollos. Discuss what you learn about these last two men in these verses—Acts 4:36-37, 11:22-26, and 13:1-4 (for Barnabas); and Acts 18:24-28 (Apollos).

8. Look also at the list of "Questions to Ask as You Begin Your Study of Each Book" on page 393.

CAPTURE THE ESSENCE

9. Look especially at these verses— 2:18, 5:7-8, and 12:2—and summa-rize what you think the author of Hebrews wants us most to under-stand about the *suffering* of Jesus.

10. What previous impressions, if any, have you had about the book of He-brews in regard to (a) its content, (b) its level of difficulty, and (c) its im-portance?

11. The book of Hebrews has been called "The Book of Shadows and Substance," "The Superiority of Christ," "The Book of Better Things," and "The Glorious Destiny

of Man." With that reputation for this book, what answers, guidelines, and solutions would you like to gain as you examine it more closely?

FOR LIFE TODAY

12. FIXED ON JESUS: Look at the commands given in 3:1 and 12:2. For Christians today, what would you say are the worst obstacles to having a Christ-centered thought life?

13. How can you ensure that your study of Hebrews is not merely theoretical and intellectual, but is instead truly practical and relevant? Talk together about this. What can you do to help keep the process alive and interesting?

14. Imagine yourself in heaven, where you discover for sure who the author of this book is. As you have a talk with him, he asks you, "By the way, what was most helpful to you in my book?" How would you like to be able to answer him?

FOR GOING DEEPER

Often in this book the author introduces a command or encouragement with the words "Let us…" Look together at the following verses, and consider carefully together the picture they give of what our lives should be like—4:1, 4:11, 4:16, 6:1, 10:22-25, 12:1-2, and 13:15.

HEBREWS 1

Startup: When you think of *angels,* what comes to your mind?

SEEING WHAT'S THERE

1. As this book gets started, what does the author seem to most want us to understand about Jesus?

2. Of all the descriptive statements about Jesus in verses 2-3, which phrase is the most significant to you, and why?

3. Hebrews is a book of many *comparisons.* Explain in your own words the comparison being made in verse 4.

4. FIXED ON JESUS: Remember again the commands in 3:1 and 12:2. Then think carefully about verses 8-9 in this chapter. What do these words *really* say about Jesus, and why is this message important?

5. *Why* is Jesus greater than the angels? Summarize the main points made in this chapter concerning His superiority to angels.

6. Look also at the list of "Questions to Ask as You Study Each Chapter" on page 392, which you may want to do for each chapter in Hebrews.

7. EYE FOR DETAIL— *If everyone in the group has read the entire chapter, try answering the following question without looking at your Bible:* The last verse in this chapter speaks of those who will inherit something. What is it that they will inherit?

CAPTURE THE ESSENCE

8. If you decided to make a list of "Names and Titles of Jesus," what names and titles would you add from verses 2-5?

9. If you were asked to cut out all the verses except three, and yet still keep as much of the meaning of this chapter as you could, which three verses would you leave in?

10. If the Old Testament Scriptures did not exist, and therefore couldn't be quoted or referred to in the New Testament, which verses in this chapter would disappear?

11. If this chapter was the only Scripture portion you had ever known, what would you conclude from it about angels?

12. Picture this book of Hebrews as a fast-moving train. Chapter 1 is the locomotive in front, and the other chapters represent railway cars that follow behind. From what you see here in chapter 1, what is the *energy* in the locomotive—the point or principle or theme that's the driving force for the locomotive and the entire train?

FOR LIFE TODAY

13. If a non-Christian friend said to you, "I don't really see how the man Jesus could also be God," how could you use this chapter to help you give a good answer?

14. In Colossians 3:1 we read this command: "Since you have been raised with Christ, set your hearts on things above, where Christ is seated at the right hand of God." What have you personally observed about Jesus Christ in this chapter that would be worthy of setting your heart on?

15. Which verse in this chapter do you think God wants you to understand best?

FOR GOING DEEPER

Compare verses 1-3 with the opening verses of the fourth gospel (John 1:1-5 and 1:14-18). What similarities do you see in the way the two writers present God's Son?

HEBREWS 2

Startup: Imagine yourself in heaven, and you and an angel are approaching a doorway at the same time. To be proper, which of you should let the other enter first?

SEEING WHAT'S THERE

1. How would you summarize in your own words the *warning* given in verses 1-3?

2. FIXED ON JESUS: Remember again the commands in 3:1 and 12:2. Then think carefully about verses 9-18 in this chapter. What do these verses *really* say about Jesus, and why is their message important?

3. From what you see in this chapter, what did *God* do for *Jesus,* and what did *Jesus* do for *us?*

4. From what this chapter teaches in verses 11-18, what are the most important facts about who *you* are?

5. Let the words of verses 14-15 form a picture in your mind, and then describe that picture.

6. Keeping verses 14-18 in mind, think of as many things as you can which you have in common with Jesus.

7. EYE FOR DETAIL— *From what you recall seeing in this chapter, try answering the following question without looking at your Bible:* In the opening verse, the author of Hebrews tells us why we must pay more careful attention to what we have heard. What was this reason?

CAPTURE THE ESSENCE

8. Look at the author's mention in verse 3 of our "great salvation." What exactly is so "great" about it? Look together at Ephesians 1:19 and 2:4 as you form an answer together.

9. If you were keeping a list of "Names and Titles of Jesus," what names and titles would you add from verses 10-11 and 17?

10. From what you see in this chapter, what does the author of Hebrews want us most to understand about our relationship to Christ?

11. If you were not yet a Christian, what teachings about Jesus Christ in this chapter do you think would be most intriguing to you, and why?

12. Suppose a band of armed terrorists stormed into the room where you're now meeting, then took you as hostages in a captivity that was likely to last for days or weeks. Just before they confiscated your Bibles, they allowed you to take one last look at the chapter open before you. Which verse in this chapter would you most try to fix in mind before your Bible was snatched away, and why?

FOR LIFE TODAY

13. How susceptible do you think Christians in general are today to what the author of Hebrews warns against in verses 1-3?

14. Choose one of these sentences, and complete it as fully and candidly as you can:

> *What I see and understand in this chapter is important to my life because…*
> *What I see and understand in this chapter does NOT seem important to my life at this time, because…*

15. If it's true that "you *become* what you *think,*" then what are the most important thoughts from this chapter to plant firmly in your mind?

16. If God had written this chapter only for *you,* which words or phrases do you think He would have underlined?

FOR GOING DEEPER

After presenting a strong case for Christ's deity, the author goes on to highlight His humanity in verses 14-18. Search together also in the following passages for word-pictures and statements that deepen our understanding of this miracle of love—John 1:1 and 1:10-14, 2 Corinthians 8:9, Philippians 2:6-11, 1 Timothy 3:16, and 1 John 1:1-2.

HEBREWS 3

Startup: When you hear the phrase *hardened heart,* who or what do you think of?

SEEING WHAT'S THERE

1. As you read this chapter, what's the strongest impression or image which it leaves in your mind?

2. What in this chapter do you think might be most surprising to a new Christian reading it for the first time?

3. What is the first *command* given in this chapter?

4. How does the author appear to be using the word *house* in verses 2-6? How does he want us to understand it?

5. Summarize in your own words the *warning* given in verse 12.

6. SMALL, BUT IMPORTANT: The word *but* signals a contrast, or a change in direction. What important contrast or change in direction does this word highlight in verse 13?

7. What would you say are the most important *verbs*—the action words —in this chapter?

8. If the Old Testament Scriptures did not exist, and therefore couldn't be quoted or referred to in the New Testament, which verses in this chapter would disappear?

9. *Why* is Jesus greater than Moses? Summarize the main points made in this chapter concerning the superiority of Jesus to Moses.

10. EYE FOR DETAIL— *From what you recall seeing in this chapter, try answering the following question without looking at your Bible:* This chapter quotes an oath which God spoke in anger. What was that oath? (See verse 11.)

CAPTURE THE ESSENCE

11. *How,* exactly, does a person go about obeying the command given in verse 1?

12. If you were keeping a list of "Names and Titles of Jesus," what names and titles would you add from verses 1 and 6?

13. If this chapter was the only Scripture portion you had ever known, what would you conclude from it about Moses?

14. Suppose that at the end of this chapter, the author added this line: "If you remember only one thing from this chapter, let it be this:..." How do you think he would complete that sentence?

15. If you were asked to write a discussion question to help your Bible study group examine and understand something in this chapter, how would you word the question?

16. From what you see in this chapter, what can we truly rely on God to do as we obey Him?

FOR LIFE TODAY

17. Consider carefully the major teachings in this chapter. Which do you think is harder for Christians—understanding what this chapter says, or putting it into practice?

18. How susceptible do you think Christians in general are today to what the author of Hebrews warns against in verse 12?

19. Look again at verse 13. What would you say are sin's most powerful deceptions today... (a) in our world? (b) in your church? (c) in your home?

20. From what you see in this chapter, discuss together how you would complete this sentence: *What God really wants from me is...*

21. In light of how you're doing spiritually in your life today, which verse in this chapter do you think is the most important at this time—and why?

FOR GOING DEEPER

Look ahead to 10:24-25, and lay those verses alongside verses 12-13 in this chapter. Then discuss possible reasons for the author's strong emphasis on mutual encouragement.

HEBREWS 4

Startup: Recall these words from the creation account in the opening pages of Genesis: "God rested on the seventh day from all his work which he had made." When you think of God resting like this, what do you think of?

SEEING WHAT'S THERE

1. After reading through this chapter, which words or phrases or sentences here would you most like to understand better?

2. How would you summarize in your own words the *warning* given in verses 1-2?

3. SMALL, BUT IMPORTANT: Notice the "little" word *but* in verse 2, and identify the important contrast or the change in direction that this word highlights in this verse.

4. How would you describe in your own words the *rest* which the author speaks of in this chapter?

5. FIXED ON JESUS: Remember again the commands in 3:1 and 12:2. Then think carefully about verse 15 in this chapter. What do these words *really* say about Jesus, and why is this message important?

6. How would you explain verse 16 to a young child?

7. From what you see in verses 12-13, what does the author of Hebrews want us most to understand about God and His Word?

8. From what you see in verse 16, what *expectations* can we rightly have of God?

9. If the Old Testament Scriptures did not exist, and therefore couldn't be quoted or referred to in the New Testament, which verses in this chapter would disappear?

10. EYE FOR DETAIL— *From what you recall seeing in this chapter, try answering the following question without*

looking at your Bible: The author of Hebrews says that the word of God is "sharper" than something. What is it? (See verse 12.)

CAPTURE THE ESSENCE

11. Imagine that you were preparing a special audio-visual presentation for your church. As a strong, pre-recorded voice read through verses 9-16 word for word, a series of photographic slides would be projected on a screen in front of the people. What kind of photographs would you select to be included in the slide presentation, to best fit this passage?

12. If you were asked to cut out all the verses except three, and yet still keep as much of the meaning of this chapter as you could, which three verses would you leave in?

13. A 3-step question: (a) Think of someone you know who doesn't spend much time reading the Bible. (b) Select a verse or brief passage in this chapter that you think this person would probably find boring. (c) Now decide how you could clarify or open up this passage in a way that might appeal to this person.

14. If this chapter was a good answer to a question that began with the word *How...* then what would the rest of the question say?

FOR LIFE TODAY

15. What parts of this chapter would you say are probably the easiest for most Christians today to understand?

16. How susceptible do you think Christians in general are today to what the author of Hebrews warns against in verses 1-2?

17. Think carefully again about the command at the end of verse 14. Then imagine God evaluating you on a scale of one to ten, in which ten equals perfect obedience to this command, and one equals total disregard of that command. What score do you think He would probably assign to you?

18. Look again at the command in verse 16. In the last 24 hours, what are the biggest things (if any) for which you've asked God's help?

19. In Philippians 4:8 we're given the following command: "Whatever is true, whatever is noble, whatever is right, whatever is pure, whatever is lovely, whatever is admirable—if anything is excellent or praiseworthy—*think about such things.*" What food for thought can you find in this chapter that especially strikes you as being *true,* or *noble,* or *right,* or *pure,* or *lovely,* or *admirable,* or *excellent,* or *praiseworthy?*

20. Of all that you see in this chapter, what one truth are you most *thankful* for, because of its personal significance to you?

FOR GOING DEEPER

Add the word picture in verse 12 to the one in Jeremiah 23:29. In your own words, describe how the Word of God is like a fire, a rock, and a sword.

Hebrews 5

Startup: Focus your thoughts on verse 7 in this chapter, and get a picture in your mind of Jesus praying. What do you see, and hear, and feel?

SEEING WHAT'S THERE

1. After reading through this chapter, which words or phrases or sentences here would you most like to understand better?

2. FIXED ON JESUS: Remember again the commands in 3:1 and 12:2. Then think carefully about verses 7-10 in this chapter. What do these verses *really* say about Jesus, and why is their message important?

3. SMALL, BUT IMPORTANT: What important contrast or change in direction does the little word *but* highlight in verse 14?

4. For helpful background on the "Melchizedek" mentioned in this chapter, look together at Genesis 14:17-20 and Psalm 110:4. What is clear about this man, and what is mysterious about him?

5. If the Old Testament Scriptures did not exist, and therefore couldn't be quoted or referred to in the New Testament, which verses in this chapter would disappear?

6. EYE FOR DETAIL— *From what you recall seeing in this chapter, try answering the following question without looking at your Bible:* What two men from the Old Testament are mentioned in this chapter? (See verses 4 and 6.)

CAPTURE THE ESSENCE

7. If you were keeping a list of "Names and Titles of Jesus," what names and titles would you add from verses 9-10?

8. In verse 11, look at the reason the author gives for why some spiritual teaching is "hard to explain." From what you see in the rest of the chapter, what is the solution to this problem?

9. In verses 11-14, look for each of these words: *time, teach,* and *good.* Then decide which one you think is the most important word in this passage, and tell why you think so.

FOR LIFE TODAY

10. What parts of this chapter would you say are probably the easiest for most Christians today to understand?

11. Think through the meaning of verses 11-14. Does this passage give you *discomfort* or *encouragement*—or some of both?

12. Which verse in this chapter do you think God wants you to understand best?

FOR GOING DEEPER

Consider verses 11-14 along with Paul's words to the Corinthian believers in 1 Corinthians 3:1-4. What reasons does each author give for addressing his audience as "baby Christians"?

HEBREWS 6

Startup: In the way we read and study the Bible, what kind of mental habits can most easily block this book of Hebrews from coming alive in our minds and hearts?

SEEING WHAT'S THERE

1. As you read this chapter, what's the strongest impression or image which it leaves in your mind?

2. After reading through this chapter, which words or phrases or sentences here would you most like to understand better?

3. What does God *offer* or *promise* to do for us in this chapter?

4. In the difficult passage in verses 4-6, which things are easiest to understand?

5. Hebrews is a book of many *comparisons.* In the context of what you see in this chapter, explain the comparison being made in verse 9.

6. Who do you think the author is speaking of in verse 12? Who are we supposed to "imitate" or "follow"?

7. Which important details in this chapter do you think might be the easiest to overlook?

8. EYE FOR DETAIL— *From what you recall seeing in this chapter, try answering the following question without looking at your Bible:* What four-letter word is described here as the "anchor" for our souls? (See verse 19.)

CAPTURE THE ESSENCE

9. Picture in your mind the images presented in the parable in verses 7-8. How would you explain the meaning of this parable?

10. Suppose that at the end of this chapter, the author added this line: "If you remember only one thing from this chapter, let it be this:..." How do you think he would complete that sentence?

11. From what you see in this chapter, what can we truly rely on God to do as we obey Him?

FOR LIFE TODAY

12. If the words in verses 11-12 were in a letter written to *your* church, how accurate would they be?

13. Look again in verse 12, where we're told not to become "lazy" or "sluggish" or "slothful." What's the most tempting form of laziness in *your* life?

14. From what you see in this chapter, discuss together how you would complete this sentence: *What God really wants from me is...*

15. If God had written this chapter only for *you,* which words or phrases do you think He would have underlined?

FOR GOING DEEPER

In verses 7-8, the author uses a word picture of professing Christians who are like unproductive land in danger of rejection. What similarities do you see in the picture God used to warn Israel in Isaiah 5:1-7?

Hebrews 7

help you explore each chapter in Hebrews.

Startup: If you were producing a motion picture on the life of Abraham, and were including the scene in Genesis in which Abraham and Melchizedek meet, what kind of person would you want to cast in the role of Melchizedek?

SEEING WHAT'S THERE

1. After reading through this chapter, which words or phrases or sentences here would you most like to understand better?

2. SMALL, BUT IMPORTANT: What important contrast or change in direction does the little word *but* highlight in verse 24?

3. FIXED ON JESUS: Remember again the commands in 3:1 and 12:2. Then think carefully about verses 24-28 in this chapter. What do these verses *really* say about Jesus, and why is their message important?

4. Refer again to Genesis 14:17-20 and Psalm 110:4 to keep in mind the Old Testament account of King Melchizedek. What would you say is the biggest lesson to learn from his life?

5. If the Old Testament Scriptures did not exist, and therefore couldn't be quoted or referred to in the New Testament, which verses in this chapter would disappear?

6. EYE FOR DETAIL— *From what you recall seeing in this chapter, try answering the following question without looking at your Bible:* Which of the following pairs of Old Testament characters is *not* mentioned in this chapter? Abraham and Melchizedek; Levi and Judah; Moses and Aaron; David and Solomon. (See verses 1, 9, 11, and 14.)

7. Remember to look also at the list of "Questions to Ask as You Study Each Chapter" on page 392, which can

CAPTURE THE ESSENCE

8. Would you say this is a chapter that especially requires *patience* as you read and study it, in order to understand it? If so, why?

9. If you were asked to cut out all the verses except three, and yet still keep as much of the meaning of this chapter as you could, which three verses would you leave in?

10. Now that you're halfway through Hebrews, how would you summarize the most important lessons to learn in this book?

FOR LIFE TODAY

11. What parts of this chapter would you say are probably the easiest for most Christians today to understand?

12. Which verse in this chapter do you think God wants you to understand best?

FOR GOING DEEPER

Link verse 25 with Hebrews 9:24, Romans 8:34, 1 Timothy 2:5, and 1 John 2:1. What do each of these passages contribute to your understanding of Jesus Christ's *present activities* on behalf of those who have placed faith in Him?

Hebrews 8

Startup: Imagine yourself being suddenly transported back to Old Testament times, and watching the priests offer sacrifices in the tabernacle or temple. What do you think would be your strongest sensations or perceptions when you first arrived on the scene?

SEEING WHAT'S THERE

1. After reading through this chapter, which words or phrases or sentences here would you most like to understand better?

2. From what you see in this chapter, what is it that the author most wants us to understand about the "new covenant"?

3. FIXED ON JESUS: Remember again the commands in 3:1 and 12:2. Then think carefully about verses 1-2 in this chapter. What do these words *really* say about Jesus, and why is their message important?

4. Hebrews is a book of many *comparisons.* Explain in your own words the comparison being made in verse 6, in light of what you see in the rest of the chapter.

5. If the Old Testament Scriptures did not exist, and therefore couldn't be quoted or referred to in the New Testament, which verses in this chapter would disappear?

6. EYE FOR DETAIL— *From what you recall seeing in this chapter, try answering the following question without looking at your Bible:* How is God described in the opening verse of this chapter?

CAPTURE THE ESSENCE

7. Would you say this is a chapter that especially requires *patience* as you read and study it, in order to understand it? If so, why?

8. If you were asked to write a discussion question to help your Bible study group examine and understand something in this chapter, how would you word the question?

FOR LIFE TODAY

9. Suppose you met someone from your Bible study group for lunch tomorrow, who said to you, "That book we're studying is for Hebrews, all right. It's so obviously written to first-century Jews who understood all about the temple and the priesthood and so on, I doubt it could really be practical and relevant for anybody today." How would you answer this person?

10. If God had written this chapter only for *you,* which words or phrases do you think He would have underlined?

FOR GOING DEEPER

In what way does Philippians 2:12-13 expand your understanding of how the New Covenant described in verse 10 actually works?

HEBREWS 9

Startup: From what you know of the Old Testament, name the first fact that comes to mind regarding the layout of the temple, or the kinds of sacrifices that took place there.

SEEING WHAT'S THERE

1. After reading through this chapter, which words or phrases or sentences here would you most like to understand better?

2. How many times do you see the word *once* in this chapter, and what is it referring to each time?

3. FIXED ON JESUS: Remember again the commands in 3:1 and 12:2. Then take time to review carefully in this chapter verses 11-12, 14-15, and 24-28. What do these passages *really* say about Jesus, and why is their message important?

4. SMALL, BUT IMPORTANT: What important contrast or change in direction does the little word *but* highlight in verse 12?

5. From what you see in verse 14, what *expectations* can we rightly have of God?

6. What *comparison* is being made in verse 23? Explain it in your own words, in light of what you see in the rest of the chapter.

7. In verses 24-28, find and discuss the things that have happened only *once,* or will happen only *once.*

8. Regarding the subjects that you've seen addressed so far in this book, what questions do you have that remain unanswered?

9. EYE FOR DETAIL— *From what you recall seeing in this chapter, try answering the following question without looking at your Bible:* In the original tabernacle, what three items are mentioned as being inside the ark of the covenant? (See verse 4.)

CAPTURE THE ESSENCE

10. Would you say this is a chapter that especially requires *patience* as you read and study it, in order to understand it? If so, why?

11. Suppose that at the end of this chapter, the author added this line: "If you remember only one thing from this chapter, let it be this:…" How do you think he would complete that sentence?

12. If this chapter was the only Scripture portion you had, what would you conclude from it about how important it was for Jesus Christ to die?

13. Which verse in this chapter do you think God wants you to understand best?

FOR LIFE TODAY

14. Suppose you were talking with a non-Christian friend who had been considering the gospel, and he said to you, "But how can we know for sure there's life after death? Maybe we simply stop existing once our heart and our breathing stops." How could you use verses 27-28 to help give a meaningful reply?

FOR GOING DEEPER

Verses 12-14 make a vital point about how Christ offered Himself to God as a sacrifice *without blemish.* In what way does that help explain God's burning anger and grief over the actions of the priesthood back in Malachi 1:6-14?

Hebrews 10

SEEING WHAT'S THERE

1. As you read this chapter, what's the strongest impression or image which it leaves in your mind?

2. How would you summarize the *comparison* that the writer of Hebrews is making in verses 1-10?

3. With the teachings of verses 1-4 in mind, discuss how much you agree or disagree with this statement: Even in the Old Testament, salvation from God was given only by His grace, and not as a reward for sacrifices or good deeds.

4. FIXED ON JESUS: Remember again the commands in 3:1 and 12:2. Then think carefully about verses 5-10 in this chapter. What do these words *really* say about Jesus, and why is their message important?

5. How would you summarize in your own words the *warning* given in verses 26-31?

6. Explain in your own words the comparison being made in verse 34.

7. What do you think is the reward which the author speaks of in verses 35-36?

8. SMALL, BUT IMPORTANT: What important contrast or change in direction does the little word *but* highlight in verse 39?

9. EYE FOR DETAIL— *From what you recall seeing in this chapter, try answering the following question without looking at your Bible:* Near the end of this chapter, God speaks of the kind of person who does not please Him, or give Him pleasure. What kind of person is this? (See verse 38.)

CAPTURE THE ESSENCE

10. If you thought of this chapter as a roadmap for a Christian's life, what would be the safest "roads" to take, as taught in this chapter? What would be the unsafe, dangerous roads to avoid?

11. How would you summarize the most important differences between the sacrifices of the Old Testament priests, and Jesus' sacrifice of His life on the cross?

12. In verses 7-10 there is frequent reference to God's *will.* In the context of this passage, what is God's will as it relates to Jesus and to us?

13. James 1:22 tells us that when we merely listen to the Word without putting it into practice, we deceive ourselves. What kind of self-deceiving excuses or rationalization do you think could most easily keep Christians from actually *doing* what we're told in verses 24-25?

14. From what you've seen so far in the book of Hebrews, how would you say that God's *holiness* and His *love* come together in His character?

FOR LIFE TODAY

15. How susceptible do you think Christians in general are today to what the author of Hebrews warns against in verses 26-31?

16. In verses 25 and 35, notice again what the author tells us *not* to do. In what ways would you say Christians are most in danger of doing each one of them?

17. From what you see in this chapter, discuss together how you would complete this sentence: *What God really wants from me is...*

18. If it's true that "you *become* what you *think,*" then what are the most important thoughts from this chapter to plant firmly in your mind?

19. If you were asked to write a discussion question to help your Bible study group apply something in this chapter to their lives, how would you word the question?

20. Suppose you heard a voice from heaven saying to you, "Don't get over-ambitious and try to apply too much from this chapter to your life right now. Just pick one thing to focus on, and do it well." What one thing would you choose?

FOR GOING DEEPER

Relate verses 23-25 to Paul's admonitions in Colossians 3:15-17. What key elements do these passages have in common?

HEBREWS 11

Startup: Which of the people mentioned in this chapter would you most like to talk to in heaven, and why?

SEEING WHAT'S THERE

1. Count the number of times that the word *faith* appears in this chapter.

2. How many times do you see the word *better* in this chapter?

3. Go through the list of people mentioned in this chapter, and for each one, discuss what other important facts you know about him, apart from those mentioned in this chapter.

4. Look again at the comments about faith in verse 6, especially the mention of a reward from God. Scan through the other verses here and discuss what rewards from God the people in this chapter were looking for.

5. What *comparisons* are made in verses 16, 35, and 40? Summarize them in your own words.

6. If the Old Testament Scriptures did not exist, and therefore couldn't be quoted or referred to in the New Testament, which verses in this chapter would disappear?

7. EYE FOR DETAIL— *From what you recall seeing in this chapter, try answering the following question without looking at your Bible:* Which one of these *places* is not mentioned in this chapter? Egypt, the Red Sea, Jericho, and Jerusalem. (See verses 22, 29, and 30.)

CAPTURE THE ESSENCE

8. What kind of questions or difficulties or doubts in a Christian's daily life do you think this chapter answers best?

9. From what you see in this chapter, what is the relationship between Old Testament faith, and our faith in

Jesus Christ today? Are they one and the same? If not, what are the differences?

10. What things in this chapter do you think non-Christians would find hardest to understand?

11. Read this chapter aloud in your group, with everyone taking turns reading. Switch to a different reader each time you come to the words "by faith."

12. How would you explain verse 6 to a young child?

13. Which person named in this chapter would you say is most like you?

14. Look again at the definition of faith in verse 1, thinking about it again in light of all the illustrations of faith given in this chapter. At this point in your life, how strong in general is your faith in God, compared with other times in the past? To help you give a valid answer, use a scale of one to ten (one = "much weaker than ever," ten = "much stronger than ever").

15. Suppose once more that you met someone from your Bible study group for lunch tomorrow. As you discussed your study of Hebrews 11, this person said to you, "I get the message, all right—faith, faith, faith. But what I'd like to know is, *faith in what?*" How would you answer this person?

16. Think again of Philippians 4:8, where we're given this command: "Whatever is true, whatever is noble, whatever is right, whatever is pure, whatever is lovely, whatever is admirable—if anything is excellent or praiseworthy—*think about such things.*" What food for thought can you find in this chapter that especially strikes you as being *true,* or *noble,* or *right,* or *pure,* or *lovely,* or *admirable,* or *excellent,* or *praiseworthy?*

17. If God had written this chapter only for *you,* which words or phrases do you think He would have underlined?

Both verse 6 and James 2:18-20 speak of an *active* faith in God. What does each passage teach about the distinctives of that active faith?

Hebrews 12

Startup: In what areas of your life would you say you most often have a need for *encouragement* and *endurance?*

SEEING WHAT'S THERE

1. What *commands* are given in this chapter? As a group, list them all aloud.

2. Let the words of verses 1-2 form a picture in your mind, and then describe that picture.

3. From what you see in this chapter, what does the author of Hebrews want us most to understand about *discipline?*

4. What in this chapter do you think might be most surprising to a new Christian reading it for the first time?

5. SMALL, BUT IMPORTANT: What important contrast or change in direction does the little word *but* highlight in verse 22?

6. What *comparison* is being made in verse 24? Explain it in your own words.

7. How would you summarize in your own words the *warning* given in verse 25?

8. Which important details in this chapter do you think might be the easiest to overlook?

9. EYE FOR DETAIL— *From what you recall seeing in this chapter, try answering the following question without looking at your Bible:* In this chapter, how does the author of Hebrews complete the following sentence? *"For our God is..."* (See verse 29.)

CAPTURE THE ESSENCE

10. Which commands in this chapter would you say are the easiest for most Christians to obey? Which are the easiest to *dis*obey?

11. As you review verses 1-2, discuss where you believe successful obedience to these commands actually begins—mostly in our *mind,* mostly in our *habits,* or mostly in our *words?*

12. Think again about verse 3. How would you describe the worst treatment Jesus received from His persecutors? When Christians keep this in focus, how can that help them practically to stay encouraged?

13. Let the words of verses 22-24 form a picture in your mind, and then describe that picture.

14. From what you see in verses 22-24, what does the author of Hebrews want us most to understand about heaven?

15. Review again the contrast given in verses 18-24. *Why* would you say God wants us to understand this?

16. Look again at verse 29. What mental process do you think the author went through to arrive at this conclusion?

17. If the first eleven chapters of this book had somehow been lost in history, what difference would that make in regard to the meaning of what you see in chapter 12?

18. If you thought of this chapter as a roadmap for a Christian's life, what would be the safest "roads" to take, as taught in this chapter? What would be the unsafe, dangerous roads to avoid?

FOR LIFE TODAY

19. Many times we rob ourselves of the discovery of deeper truths in Scripture because we see a passage and say to ourselves, "I already know that." For which teachings in this chapter might it be easiest for Christians to fall into that trap?

20. In verse 1, look again at the author's reference to a race we must run. How would you describe the particular race that's marked out for *you?*

21. The older you get, in what ways does it get easier to obey the teachings in verses 1-3? In what ways does it get harder?

22. From what you see in this chapter and elsewhere in Scripture, what can you reasonably expect in life if you do *not* obey the command in verse 7?

23. In a typical day, how often would the commands in verses 14-15 offer useful and timely guidelines for your immediate situation?

24. Look again at the command in verse 28. In the last 24 hours, what are the biggest things (if any) that you've thanked God for?

25. In practical terms, how would you say verses 28-29 should be applied to the way you worship God in your church?

26. It's been said that "the human heart resists nothing more than change." What truths in this chapter—truths that could require some changes in your life—cause some degree of hesitation and resistance inside you?

27. Suppose you heard a voice from heaven saying to you, "Don't get over-ambitious and try to apply too much from this chapter to your life right now. Just pick one thing to focus on, and do it well." What one thing would you choose?

FOR GOING DEEPER

What more do you learn about Christ's "joy" in verse 2 from reading Isaiah 53:10-11?

HEBREWS 13

Startup: Has there ever been a time when you thought (either during or after the fact) that you were in an angel's presence? If so, talk about it.

SEEING WHAT'S THERE

1. Together, list aloud all the *commands* you see in this chapter.

2. FIXED ON JESUS: Remember again the commands in 3:1 and 12:2. Then think carefully about verse 8 in this chapter. What does this verse *really* say about Jesus, and why is its message important?

3. How would you explain verse 8 to a young child?

4. From what you see in this chapter alone, what would you say are the most important moral standards for Christians?

5. SMALL, BUT IMPORTANT: What important contrast or change in direction does the little word *but* highlight in verse 14?

6. EYE FOR DETAIL— *From what you recall seeing in this chapter, try answering the following question without looking at your Bible:* In this chapter the author tells his readers to remember three specific categories of people. What were they? (See verses 3 and 7.)

CAPTURE THE ESSENCE

7. Which commands in this chapter would you say are the easiest for most Christians to obey? Which are the easiest to *dis*obey?

8. In Proverbs 13:13 we're told, "He who respects a command is rewarded," or in another translation, "He that feareth the commandment shall be rewarded." Look at the command in verse 3. What would you say is the likely *reward* for respecting and keeping this command?

9. Picture in your mind two Christians, one who has learned to obey the command we are given in verse 5, and one who has *not* learned how to do it. What practical differences do you see in the way these two persons live?

10. From what you see in verses 7 and 17 alone, what conclusions could you make about the job of church leaders?

11. Look again at the commands in verses 7 and 17, and discuss how fully you think Christians are obeying these teachings today.

12. In Psalm 119:45, the psalmist says to God, "I will walk at liberty, for I seek Thy precepts." As you think about the "precepts" or commands in verses 15-16, in what ways can you see them offering true freedom and liberty to a Christian?

FOR LIFE TODAY

13. Focus your mind on what you consider to be your two or three most important responsibilities in life. Which teachings in this chapter could best help you carry out any or all of these responsibilities?

14. In Psalm 119:47, these words are spoken to God: "I will *delight* myself in thy commandments, which I have *loved*." At this point in your life, which commands in this chapter would be the quickest to bring you fulfillment and pleasure?

15. Imagine that you saw earlier today a message written in fire in the sky. It was addressed to you by name, then continued with these words: *Thus saith the* LORD: *"Read Hebrews 13, for I have something for you there."* Which verses in this chapter do you think He most likely would be referring to?

16. Look again at the command in verse 1. At this point in your life, how strong in general is your love for other Christians, compared with other times in the past? To help you give a valid answer, use a scale of one to ten (one = "much weaker than ever," ten = "much stronger than ever").

17. Think carefully again about the command concerning hospitality to strangers in verse 2. Then imagine God evaluating you on a scale of one to ten, in which ten equals perfect obedience to this command, and one equals total disregard of those commands. What score do you think He would probably assign to you?

18. In verses 2 and 16, notice again what the author tells us *not* to do. In what ways would you say Christians are most in danger of doing each of them?

19. Look again at the command in verse 4. At this point in your life, how much honor do you give to marriage, compared with other times in the past? To help you give a valid answer, use a scale of one to ten (one = "much less than ever," ten = "much more than ever").

20. Look again at the first command in verse 5. At this point in your life, how free are you from the love of money, compared with other times in the past? To help you give a valid answer, use a scale of one to ten (one = "much more enslaved than ever," ten = "much freer than ever").

21. Look also at the second command in verse 5. At this point in your life, how *contented* are you, compared with other times in the past? To help you give a valid answer, use a scale of one to ten (one = "far less contented than ever," ten = "much more contented than ever").

22. Look again at the command in verse 15. In the last 24 hours, what are the

biggest things (if any) that you've praised God for?

23. Suppose a new Christian asked you, "How can I discover God's will for my life?" How could you use verses 15-16 to help you give a meaningful answer?

24. What would you say is an especially good *starting point* for applying verse 17 more effectively to your life?

25. If everyone in your church thoroughly understood this chapter, and had a passion for living out its truth in their lives, what kind of practical changes do you think would result?

FOR GOING DEEPER

Take time to consider three Bible characters who, as in verse 2, entertained angels without (at first) knowing it. See Genesis 18:1-8; Judges 6:11-23; and Judges 13:2-21.

HEBREWS:

THE BIG PICTURE

(Discuss again the questions in the "Overview," plus the questions below.)

1. If you were asked to summarize the most important "marks of Christian maturity" as taught in this book, which ones would you mention first?

2. If this book were the only portion of Scripture you had access to, how could you use it to help answer this question: *What is the most powerful and effective way to improve my life?*

3. Look at each of these verses, and discuss which one you believe is the best candidate for "KEY VERSE" in the book of Hebrews—the one which brings into sharpest focus what this book is most about: 1:3, 4:14-16, 6:1, 11:1, 11:39-40, or 12:1-2.

4. Think once more about the commands in 3:1 and 12:2 to fix our thoughts on Jesus. After completing this study of Hebrews, how strong would you say is your _desire_ to think more about Jesus, as compared with times in the past? To help you give a valid answer, use a scale of one to ten (one = "much weaker than ever," ten = "much stronger than ever").

5. Again with the commands in 3:1 and 12:2 in mind, how strong is your _ability_ now to focus your mindset more on Jesus, as compared with times in the past? Once more, use a scale of one to ten (one = "much weaker than ever," ten = "much stronger than ever").

6. In James 1:23-24 we're told that "anyone who listens to the word but does not do what it says is like a man who looks at his face in a mirror and, after looking at himself, goes away and immediately forgets what he looks like." In what important ways has the book of Hebrews been a

"mirror" for you—showing you what you can and should do?

7. If you've decided on a starting point for applying something in this book more effectively to your life, what commitment would you be willing to make to others in your group regarding this?

8. How would you complete the following sentence as a word of advice to growing Christians? *Explore the book of Hebrews if you want to learn more about...*

James

OVERVIEW

(Discuss these OVERVIEW questions both at the beginning of your study of James, and again after you've studied together all five chapters. Your answers may change significantly once you've looked more closely at the entire book.)

Startup: What is the most recent "how-to" book you've read?

SEEING WHAT'S THERE

1. Start scanning this letter until you come to a verse that brings a question to your mind. What's the question?

2. Begin scanning the letter again until you come to a verse that gives you a smile or a sense of gratitude or joy. What is pleasing to you about this verse?

3. Look for each sentence in the book in which James addresses his readers as "brothers." What is the general tone of these passages?

4. James, the younger half-brother of Jesus, is considered by many scholars to be the author of this book. Learn more about this man by looking together at these passages: Matthew 13:55; John 7:2-5; Acts 1:14, 12:17, 15:13, and 21:18; 1 Corinthians 15:7; and Galatians 1:19 and 2:9.

5. Look also at the list of "Questions to Ask as You Begin Your Study of Each Book" on page 393.

CAPTURE THE ESSENCE

6. What previous impressions, if any, have you had about the book of James in regard to (a) its content, (b) its level of difficulty, and (c) its importance?

7. The book of James has been called "The Book of Practical Christianity," "Why Faith Must Be Alive and Working," "The Book of Christian Wisdom." With that reputation for this book, what kinds of answers, guidelines, and solutions would you like to gain as examine it more closely?

8. From what you see in this book, how would you define the term "strong faith"?

9. From the evidence you see in this book, how would you define the word *wisdom?*

10. Since James is often thought of as a "how-to book" on Christian living, are there any practical areas of Christian living which you do *not* see addressed in this book?

FOR LIFE TODAY

11. If faith means "depending on God," can a person have strong faith in God and still be an "independent" person? Why or why not?

12. Many Bible teachers say that James is above all a book about faith. On a scale of one to ten (one = "not at all," ten = "very intensely"), how would you rate the *reality* of your faith—how useful and personal and meaningful is it?

13. How can you ensure that your study of James is not merely theoretical and intellectual, but is instead truly practical and relevant? Talk together

about this. What can you do to help keep the process alive and interesting?

The book of James is sometimes likened to the Old Testament writings of the prophet Amos. Scan together the book of Amos to look for themes and teachings that correspond to what you see in James.

JAMES 1

Startup: Talk together about some of the most difficult circumstances or conditions which you can recall experiencing in the past year.

SEEING WHAT'S THERE

1. What differences do you see, if any, between the *trials* or *testings* of verses 2-3, and the *temptations* of verses 13-14?

2. Which character qualities of God would you say are emphasized in this chapter?

3. Review verses 5-7, and explain in your own words the *requirements* for answered prayer that are taught here.

4. How would you explain verse 12 to a young child?

5. Let the words of verse 17 form a picture in your mind, and then describe that picture.

6. Notice the word *religion* in verse 27. How would you define this word in the way that James uses it?

7. Look also at the list of "Questions to Ask as You Study Each Chapter" on page 392, which you may want to do for each chapter in James.

8. EYE FOR DETAIL— *If everyone in the group has read the entire chapter, try answering the following question without looking at your Bible:* In this chapter, James mentions something specific which we are *not* to say; what is it? (See verse 13.)

CAPTURE THE ESSENCE

9. In what ways does God's "perfect law" (verse 25) give us freedom? (See also 2:12.)

10. From what you see in this chapter, what is the most important thing to know about *trials?* What is the most important thing for us to know about *temptations?*

11. What in this chapter do you think might be most refreshing to someone who was learning about God for the first time?

12. Which commands in this chapter would you say are the easiest for most Christians to obey? And which are the easiest to *disobey*?

13. Look again at what James says about God in verse 17. *Why* would you say God wants us to know this?

14. From what you see in this chapter, what *expectations* would you say James has of the Christians he is writing to?

15. Picture this book of James as a fast-moving train. Chapter 1 is the locomotive in front, and the other chapters represent railway cars that follow behind. From what you see here in chapter 1, what is the *energy* in the locomotive—the point or principle or theme that's the driving force for the locomotive and the entire train?

16. What kind of mental habits do you think could most easily block the words in this chapter from staying alive in our minds and hearts?

17. According to what you see in this chapter, how can a person find true stability in life?

18. Look again at verses 9 and 10. Which of these two verses applies most to you? In what ways might they *both* apply to you?

19. What would you say is your *typical* response when you face trials from the outside, and what is it when you face temptations from the inside?

20. Notice again verse 26. Do you consider yourself "religious"? If so, why? And if not— how would you like that word to be defined so that it *would* describe you?

21. If God had written this chapter only for *you,* which words or phrases do you think He would have underlined?

Look again in verse 27 at the kind of religion God sees as pure and faultless. Explore the following passages to see how they amplify this verse: Exodus 22:22-24; Deuteronomy 10:18 and 14:28-29; Psalms 68:5 and 146:9; Isaiah 1:17; and 1 Timothy 5:3-4.

Also: look again at verse 12, and compare its message with other verses of blessing in Scripture...such as Psalm 1:1, Psalm 40:4, Psalm 94:12, Proverbs 3:11-14, and Matthew 5:3-12.

JAMES 2

Startup: When you meet a stranger, what things about that person's manner or appearance are most likely to give you a favorable impression?

SEEING WHAT'S THERE

1. How would you define the favoritism that James speaks against in verses 1-13?

2. Discuss how much you agree or disagree with this statement: It is impossible to demonstrate faith without deeds.

3. James calls our attention to Abraham in Genesis 15 and 22. How did Abraham demonstrate his faith in these passages? (See also Hebrews 11:17-19.)

4. James also reminds us of Rahab. How did she demonstrate her faith in Joshua 2? (See also Hebrews 11:30-31.)

5. EYE FOR DETAIL— *From what you recall seeing in this chapter, try answering the following question without looking at your Bible:* In his opening illustration in this chapter, James speaks of two men who enter a meeting of the Christians. What is each man wearing? (See verse 2.)

CAPTURE THE ESSENCE

6. Together, list aloud all the *questions* which you see James asking in this chapter.

7. In what ways has God chosen the poor (verse 5) to receive his blessings? (See also Luke 6:20 and 1 Corinthians 1:26-31.)

8. Think carefully together about the meaning of verse 10. What is the "why" behind this verse? What is it about God and the way He created us that makes this statement true?

9. How would you explain in your own words the last part of verse 13—about mercy triumphing over judgment?

10. From the evidence you see in this chapter, how would you define true, saving faith?

11. James says in verse 17 that faith without works is dead. Discuss together your answers to this question: Which is worse—to have no faith at all, or to have a dead faith?

12. Discuss which of the following sentences you think is the most accurate: (a) Faith *requires* action. (b) Faith *inspires* action. (c) Faith *desires* action.

13. If this chapter was the only Scripture you had, how would you use it to explain to someone else what God is like?

14. How does the message in 1 John 3:17 reflect the message in this chapter? Are *faith in God* and *love for God* the same thing?

15. How would you say James 2:24 relates to Ephesians 2:8-9?

16. Explain how much you agree or disagree with this statement: James is more interested in how we *define* our faith than he is in how we *express* our faith.

FOR LIFE TODAY

17. How is favoritism towards the rich sometimes manifested in our lives and churches today?

18. What guidance does this chapter give you about our public responsibility as Christians to the society around us?

19. Think through the meaning of verses 12-13. Does this passage give you discomfort, or encouragement—or some of both?

20. Are we saved by faith, by good deeds, or by a combination of both?

21. Look again at Abraham's example (verse 23). How would you define

what friendship with God means today?

22. What actions can you say took place in your life today which would *not* have taken place if you did not have faith in God?

FOR GOING DEEPER

Review the main points James makes in verses 14-26, and compare them with what Paul says in Romans 3:27-28 and 4:9-22, and Galatians 2:15-16. How do these passages fit together?

JAMES 3

Startup: What were some of the most lasting and influential things that were said to you as a child— words you've never forgotten? (The effect these words had may have been either positive or negative— or perhaps both.)

SEEING WHAT'S THERE

1. What visual images does James bring to our minds in this chapter?

2. Look at each of the descriptions of godly wisdom in verse 17. In what ways do these descriptions fit with the general idea of wisdom that most people today have? In what ways do they clash?

3. How does James describe a peacemaker (verse 18)? What do you think this description means?

4. EYE FOR DETAIL— *From what you recall seeing in this chapter, try answering the following question without looking at your Bible:* In verse 3, what mark of a perfect man does James tells us about?

CAPTURE THE ESSENCE

5. If the apostle James were here in this room, what thoughts and feelings do you think he would like us to have while we look at verses 1-12 in this chapter of his letter?

6. Jesus says in Mark 7 that the words from our mouth are actually flowing from our hearts (Matthew 12:34 and 15:18). With that truth in mind, what does this chapter imply about our hearts?

7. Why do you think teachers will be judged more strictly?

8. How does the message of this chapter compare with what Jesus says in Mark 7:14-23?

9. Although this chapter does not use the word *faith,* what insights about faith can you find here?

10. Chapter 2 speaks of the relationship between faith and *works*. Now, from chapter 3, what would you say is the right relationship between faith and *words?*

11. How would you describe the relationship between true faith (see chapter 2) and true wisdom? Is it possible to be a person of strong faith, and yet not be wise?

12. In verse 13 James speaks of the *humility* or *gentleness* or *meekness* that comes with wisdom. In your opinion, what is it about wisdom that produces such a quality, and what is the process like?

13. For each of the words used to describe heavenly wisdom in verse 17, come up with as many synonyms or word-pictures or examples as you can.

14. What in this chapter do you think might be most surprising to a new Christian reading it for the first time?

FOR LIFE TODAY

15. Since our words have so much potential for harm, as described in verses 3-12—what should we do about it?

16. As you think of yourself and the people around you, where are peacemakers needed today?

17. Think of someone whom you consider to be a wise person. How does he or she demonstrate the qualities in verse 17?

18. Get in mind a picture of yourself five years in the future, as a man or woman who is truly wise, in the way mentioned by James in verses 13 and 17. As this kind of person, what kinds of things do you see yourself doing?

19. In Philippians 4:8 we're given the following command: "Whatever is true, whatever is noble, whatever is right, whatever is pure, whatever is lovely, whatever is admirable—if anything is excellent or praiseworthy—*think about such things.*" What food for thought can you find in this chapter that especially strikes you as being *true,* or *noble,* or *right,* or *pure,* or *lovely,* or *admirable,* or *excellent,* or *praiseworthy?*

FOR GOING DEEPER

As you scan together through the book of Proverbs, find at least one verse there for each of the descriptions of godly wisdom in James 3:17.

JAMES 4

Startup: If you knew you had only one more month to live, how would you live that month?

SEEING WHAT'S THERE

1. Summarize what James presents as the basic cause of interpersonal conflicts.

2. Discuss how much you agree or disagree with this statement: All interpersonal conflicts are caused by an inadequate view of God.

3. In your own words, how would you describe what James means in verse 4 by friendship with the world and hatred toward God?

4. How would you explain verse 7 to a young child?

5. What does this chapter tell us about God's values and character?

6. What does this chapter tell us about the degree of Satan's power?

7. What should be our motive and motivation for not speaking derogatory words about others?

8. Which important details in this chapter do you think might be the easiest to overlook?

9. What things in this chapter do you think non-Christians would find hardest to understand?

10. EYE FOR DETAIL— *From what you recall seeing in this chapter, try answering the following question without looking at your Bible:* Near the end of the chapter, what picture does James give of what everyone's life is like? (See verse 14.)

CAPTURE THE ESSENCE

11. From what you've seen so far in the book of James, would you say that a life of faith is easy or hard? Do you think God wants us to think of it that way?

12. If verse 3 tells us the *wrong* way to pray, then what is the *right* way to pray?

13. Would you say verses 7-10 are more about *emotions,* more about *actions,* equally about both, or about something else entirely?

14. Picture in your mind two Christians, one who has learned to obey the commands we are given in verses 7-10, and one who has *not* learned how to obey them. What practical differences do you see in the way these two persons live?

15. How exactly do we clean ourselves from sin and pride, as James tells us to do in verse 8?

16. Look again at verses 10-11. How do we submit humbly to God in the way we speak about others?

17. How do we submit humbly to God in the way we plan our future?

18. Think about verses 13-17 as you discuss how much you agree or disagree with this statement: God does not want us to place any confidence in our future plans here on earth.

19. "Pride goes before destruction," we read in Proverbs 16:18. Discuss how much you think James would agree or disagree with this statement: The only way to get rid of pride is to destroy something.

20. From what you see in this chapter, how would you define the word *humility?*

21. Although chapter 4 does not use the word *faith,* what insights about faith can you find here?

FOR LIFE TODAY

22. Look again at verse 4. What part can faith play in moving us away from "friendship with the world"?

23. Discuss how much you agree or disagree with this statement: Without faith, it is impossible to have friend-

ship with God. (You may want to look back at verse 23 in chapter 2.)

24. What makes it difficult for most people to submit to God (verse 7), and to humble themselves before Him (verse 10)?

25. What kind of plans do you have for the future, and how do they fit with what James says in verses 13-16?

26. Choose one of these sentences, and complete it as fully and candidly as you can:

> *What I see and understand in this chapter is important to my life because…*
> *What I see and understand in this chapter does NOT seem important to my life at this time, because…*

27. Discuss how much you agree or disagree with this statement: Faith is a requirement for Christian living, but it does make decision-making in life more difficult.

FOR GOING DEEPER

What examples can you give from Scripture of how God opposes the proud? What examples can you give of how God gives grace to the humble?

JAMES 5

Startup: Give an example of something you were eagerly expecting, but had to wait a long time to get.

SEEING WHAT'S THERE

1. How would you state in your own words the message James has for the rich in verses 1-6? And how does this message fit with what James said about the rich in 1:10?

2. Let the words of verse 7 form a picture in your mind, and then describe that picture.

3. What reason does James give us in this chapter for not complaining against one another? How does this reason compare with what James said in 4:11-12?

4. James asks us to consider the patient example of the prophets in the face of suffering. What examples of this in the Old Testament can you think of?

5. How did Job persevere? Look especially at Job 1:13-22 and 2:7-10.

6. EYE FOR DETAIL— *From what you recall seeing in this chapter, try answering the following question without looking at your Bible:* As James describes the coming misery of the rich, what does he say will happen to their clothing, and what will happen to their gold and silver? (See verses 2-3.)

CAPTURE THE ESSENCE

7. In verse 7, God commands us to be patient. Why is patience so important in the Christian life?

8. What does this chapter tell us about God's values and character?

9. What do the last two verses in this book tell us about what is important to the apostle James…and to God?

10. In chapter 5, James uses the word *faith* only once (in verse 15). What

insights about faith can you find in other parts of the chapter?

11. Imagine yourself looking over the shoulder of James as he wrote the words of this chapter, under the direction of the Holy Spirit's inner guidance. What emotions do you think he most likely experienced as he wrote the different parts of this chapter?

FOR LIFE TODAY

12. What things make it difficult for us to wait patiently for the Lord's coming?

13. How often do you think about the Lord's coming?

14. What does it mean to let your yes be yes, and your no be no, as James says in verse 12?

15. Think carefully again about verses 13-18. Then imagine God evaluating your personal prayer and praise on a scale of one to ten, in which ten equals perfect obedience to the commands in this passage, and one equals total disregard of those commands. What score do you think He would probably assign to you?

16. How can the guidelines in verses 14-16 be followed today in our care for those in the church who are sick?

17. If God had written this chapter only for *you,* which words or phrases do you think He would have underlined?

18. If everyone in your group thoroughly understood this chapter, and you all had a passion for living out its truth in your lives, what kind of practical changes do you think would result?

FOR GOING DEEPER

To see how closely the thinking of James reflected the teachings of Jesus, compare the following verses in James with the words of Jesus in the Sermon on the Mount:

JAMES:	MATTHEW:
1:2	5:11-12
2:5	5:3
2:13	5:7, and 6:14-15
3:10	7:16-20
4:11	7:1-2
5:2	6:19-20

JAMES:

THE BIG PICTURE

(Discuss again the questions in the "Overview," plus the questions below.)

1. Suppose you were attending a citizens' meeting called by local school officials who were considering the removal of the Bible from the shelves of all school libraries in your community. You spoke up in favor of keeping the Bible available to students. Then another citizen rose to his feet and said, "I see no reason to keep it around. It's a forgotten book anyway. Even most Christians have no idea what's in it. For example," he said, then turned directly to you and asked, "Tell me what the book of James is all about." In that situation, how would you respond?

2. Look together at each of these verses, and discuss which one you believe is the best candidate for "KEY VERSE" in the book of James—the one which brings into sharpest focus what this book is most about: 1:19, 1:22; 2:14, 2:17, 2:18, or 4:17.

3. What are the biggest *promises* which you see God making to us in this letter from James?

4. In 1 John 5:4, John says, "This is the victory that has overcome the world, even our faith." How do you see this same "winning power" in the book of James?

5. Is James focusing more on how our faith appears in the eyes of God, or how it appears in the eyes of men? (Explain your answer.)

6. The book of James has been called "the Proverbs of the New Testament." From what you know of both James and Proverbs, what reasons can you give for that comparison?

7. As you consider the teachings in James about true faith, what proof is there in your life that you believe in the Lord?

8. If you've decided on a starting point for applying something in this book more effectively to your life, what commitment would you be willing to make to others in your group regarding this?

9. How would you complete the following sentence as a word of advice to growing Christians? *Explore the book of James if you want to learn more about...*

1 Peter

OVERVIEW

(Discuss these OVERVIEW questions both at the beginning of your study of First Peter, and again after you've studied together all five chapters. Your answers may change significantly once you've looked more closely at the entire book.)

Startup: When you think of the word *hope,* what images come to your mind?

SEEING WHAT'S THERE

1. Look in *Second* Peter, at the first two verses in chapter three, where Peter writes about his purpose for both of these epistles. From what you see in that passage, what importance does Peter place on *the way we think?* What would he view as the best way to *change* the way we think?

2. Start scanning First Peter until you come to a verse that brings a question to your mind. What's the question?

3. Begin scanning the letter again until you come to a verse that gives you a smile or a sense of gratitude or joy. What is pleasing to you about this verse?

4. What is the first *command* that Peter gives in this letter?

5. What is the first *encouragement* Peter gives in this letter?

6. What do you know about what the world was like at the time this letter was written? What would you guess to be the typical hopes and dreams and concerns of the people to whom Peter was writing?

7. Look also at the list of "Questions to Ask as You Begin Your Study of Each Book" on page 393.

CAPTURE THE ESSENCE

8. What previous impressions, if any, have you had about the book of First Peter in regard to (a) its content, (b) its level of difficulty, and (c) its importance?

9. The book of First Peter has been called "The Book of Christian Discipline," "Staying True to Christ in the Face of Suffering," and "Living in the Light of Future Glory." With that reputation for this book, what answers, guidelines, and solutions would you like to gain as you examine it more closely?

10. While Paul has been called "the Apostle of Faith," and John "the Apostle of Love," Peter has been known as "the Apostle of Hope." Where in this letter do you see the theme of *hope* coming through?

11. Summarize what Peter has to say about *our calling as Christians* in the following verses—1:15, 2:9, 2:21, 3:9, and 5:10.

12. Imagine that you were the person carrying copies of this letter from Peter to the churches in the locations mentioned in verse 1. Along the way, you were attacked by a band of robbers who stripped you of all your valuables, including this letter. The leader of the robber band could not read, and when you asked him to return the letter, he replied, "Why?

What's in it that's so important?" How would you answer him?

13. When you get to heaven, if you have a long talk with the apostle Peter and he says to you, "By the way, what was most helpful to you in my first letter?" how would you like to be able to answer him?

14. How can you ensure that your study of First Peter is not merely theoretical and intellectual, but is instead truly practical and relevant? Talk together about this. What can you do to help keep the process alive and interesting?

15. Suppose you heard a voice from heaven saying to you, "Don't get over-ambitious and try to apply too much from First Peter to your life right now. Just pick one thing to focus on, and do it well." What one thing would you choose?

FOR GOING DEEPER

In the first two verses of this letter, notice Peter's reference to the Trinity—God in three Persons. Look at the following passages, and discuss what they also tell us about this concept—Matthew 3:16-17 and 28:18-19, John 14:15-18, 1 Corinthians 12:3-6, 2 Corinthians 13:14, and 2 Thessalonians 2:13-14.

1 PETER 1

Startup: What are the most important lessons you've learned—either in your own life, or from the example of others—about *suffering?*

SEEING WHAT'S THERE

1. Look again at 2 Peter 3:1-2, where Peter gives his purpose for writing both his epistles. How does he begin accomplishing that purpose in chapter 1?

2. Suppose that at the end of this chapter, Peter added this line: "If you remember only one thing from this chapter, let it be this:…" How do you think he would complete that sentence?

3. Look also at the list of "Questions to Ask as You Study Each Chapter" on page 392, which you may want to do for each chapter in First Peter.

4. EYE FOR DETAIL— *If everyone in the group has read the entire chapter, try answering the following question without looking at your Bible:* Which of these substances are *not* mentioned in this chapter—*blood, gold, grass, silver,* or *water?* (See verses 18, 19, and 24.)

CAPTURE THE ESSENCE

5. In Psalm 119:45, the psalmist says to God, "I will walk at liberty, for I seek Thy precepts." As you think about the "precepts" or commands given in verse 13, in what ways can you see it offering true freedom and liberty to a Christian?

6. Picture in your mind two Christians, one who has learned to obey the command we are given in verse 17, and one who has *not* learned how to do it. What practical differences do you see in the way these two persons live?

7. If this chapter was the only Scripture portion you had, what biblical defin-

ition would you give for each of these words: *holiness, faith,* and *hope?*

8. In John 21, the resurrected Jesus said to Peter, "Feed my sheep." How would you describe the food that the sheep are getting from Peter in this chapter?

9. From what you see in this chapter, what *expectations* can we rightly have of God?

10. Picture this book of First Peter as a fast-moving train. Chapter 1 is the locomotive in front, and the other chapters represent railway cars that follow behind. From what you see here in chapter 1, what is the *energy* in the locomotive—the point or principle or theme that's the driving force for the locomotive and the entire train?

FOR LIFE TODAY

11. From what you see in this chapter, discuss together how you would complete this sentence: *What God really wants from me is...*

12. If it's true that "you *become* what you *think,*" then what are the most important thoughts from this chapter to plant firmly in your mind?

13. Consider carefully the major teachings in this chapter. Which do you think is harder for Christians—understanding what this chapter says, or putting it into practice?

14. Focus your mind on what you consider to be your two or three most important responsibilities in life. In what ways could verse 13 help you carry out any or all of these responsibilities?

15. In verse 14, notice again what Peter tells us *not* to do. In what ways would you say Christians are most in danger of doing this?

16. Consider again verses 15-17, and recall the words of Jesus in John 15:5

—"Apart from me you can do nothing." Picture in your mind something good that could happen in your life in response to the guidelines and commands in this passage, something that could clearly be accomplished only by the Lord's supernatural power. What would this be?

17. From what you see in this chapter and elsewhere in Scripture, what can you reasonably expect in life if you do *not* obey the command in verse 22?

18. In Philippians 4:8 we're given the following command: "Whatever is true, whatever is noble, whatever is right, whatever is pure, whatever is lovely, whatever is admirable—if anything is excellent or praiseworthy—*think about such things.*" What food for thought can you find in this chapter that especially strikes you as being *true,* or *noble,* or *right,* or *pure,* or *lovely,* or *admirable,* or *excellent,* or *praiseworthy?*

19. In light of how you're doing spiritually in your life today, which verse in this chapter do you think is the most important at this time—and why?

FOR GOING DEEPER

In verses 6-7, Peter likens the testing of the believer's faith to the refining of precious metal. Three Old Testament writers— in Job 23:10; Psalm 66:10-12, and Proverbs 17:3— had the same idea. How do their words enhance your understanding of Peter's message to suffering Christians?

1 Peter 2

Startup: What comes to your mind when you think of each of these words: *aliens, strangers, pilgrims?*

SEEING WHAT'S THERE

1. If you were not yet a Christian, what teachings about Jesus Christ in this chapter do you think would be most intriguing to you, and why?

2. How would you explain verses 4-5 to a young child?

3. Look once more at 2 Peter 3:1-2, where Peter gives his purpose for his two epistles. How does he help accomplish that purpose here in chapter 2 of First Peter?

4. Suppose the telegraph had been invented back in New Testament times, and Peter decided to send his readers a brief telegram of this chapter, in advance of the delivery of the full letter. In order to save money, he decided to send only the three most important verses from the chapter. Which three verses do you think Peter would have chosen?

5. EYE FOR DETAIL— *From what you recall seeing in this chapter, try answering the following question without looking at your Bible:* In the last verse of this chapter, Peter speaks of our being like sheep gone astray, but who have now returned to the Lord. What title or name does Peter use for the Lord in this verse?

CAPTURE THE ESSENCE

6. Which commands in this chapter would you say are the easiest for most Christians to obey? And which are the easiest to *dis*obey?

7. If you thought of this chapter as a roadmap for a Christian's life, what would be the safest "roads" to take, as taught in this chapter? And what would be the unsafe, dangerous roads to avoid?

8. Review verse 2. Would you say Peter is talking more about an *attitude,* an *action,* a *technique*—or all three?

9. In verse 12, look at the command given, and at the result we're to aim for. Since this result is set in the future, how can we know how well we're obeying this command?

10. Look again at the command in verse 13, and discuss how fully you think Christians are obeying this teaching today.

11. Recall again the words of the resurrected Jesus to Peter in John 21— "Feed my sheep." How would you describe the food that the sheep are getting from Peter in this chapter?

FOR LIFE TODAY

12. In a typical day, how often would the command in verse 1 offer useful and timely guidelines for your immediate situation?

13. Imagine that some new neighbors moved in next door to you, and that their lives were perfect examples of what Peter speaks about in verse 12. In practical terms, how would you describe what their relationship with *you* would be like? What would they do *for* you and *with* you?

14. In verse 16, notice again what Peter tells us *not* to do. In what ways would you say Christians are most in danger of doing this?

15. Look again at verse 17. What would you say is an especially good *starting point* for applying any of these commands more effectively to your life?

16. Describe the kind of person whom you think would gain the most out of this chapter. What would be his or her questions and struggles and concerns?

17. What kind of mental habits do you think could most easily block the truth of this chapter from staying

alive in the minds and hearts of Christians today?

18. In Colossians 3:1 we read this command: "Since you have been raised with Christ, set your hearts on things above, where Christ is seated at the right hand of God." What have you personally observed about Jesus Christ in this chapter that would be worthy of setting your heart on?

19. Which verse in this chapter do you think God wants you to understand best?

FOR GOING DEEPER

How might Paul have enlarged on Peter's exhortation in verse 11, based on what you read in Romans 12:1-2 and 13:14?

1 PETER 3

Startup: If today you could change instantly and permanently some area of your inner life—some attitude or mental tendency or thought pattern—what would you change?

SEEING WHAT'S THERE

1. If this chapter was the only Scripture portion you had ever known, what would you conclude from it about the biblical guidelines for marriage?

2. Consider again 2 Peter 3:1-2, and Peter's stated purpose for his two letters. How does he help accomplish that purpose here in chapter 3 of First Peter?

3. EYE FOR DETAIL— *From what you recall seeing in this chapter, try answering the following question without looking at your Bible:* Which one of these Old Testament characters is *not* mentioned in this chapter—Abraham, Hagar, Noah, or Sarah? (See verses 6 and 20.)

CAPTURE THE ESSENCE

4. Many times we rob ourselves of the discovery of deeper truths in Scripture because we see a passage and say to ourselves, "I already know that." For which teachings in this chapter might it be easiest for Christians to fall into that trap?

5. In Proverbs 13:13 we're told, "He who respects a command is rewarded," or in another translation, "He that feareth the commandment shall be rewarded." Look at the commands in verses 1 and 7. What would you say are the likely *rewards* for respecting and keeping these commands?

6. James 1:22 tells us that when we merely listen to the Word without putting it into practice, we deceive ourselves. What kind of self-deceiving excuses or rationalization do you

think could most easily keep Christians from actually *doing* what we're told in verse 9?

7. In the guideline about suffering given in verse 17, notice the statement about which kind of suffering is *better*. From what you see in this chapter and elsewhere in Scripture, exactly *why* is this kind of suffering better than the other kind?

8. If Satan wrote down some guidelines and commands to get people to do just the opposite of what this chapter teaches, how do you think his message might be worded?

9. From what you see in this chapter, what can we truly rely on God to do as we obey Him?

10. Recall again the words of the resurrected Jesus to Peter in John 21 — "Feed my sheep." How would you describe the food that the sheep are getting from Peter in this chapter?

FOR LIFE TODAY

11. If you're married, think carefully again about verses 1-7, especially the commands for wives in verse 1 and for husbands in verse 7. Then imagine God evaluating you on a scale of one to ten, in which ten equals perfect obedience to whichever command applies to you in this passage, and one equals total disregard of that command. What score do you think He would probably assign to you?

12. What kind of questions or difficulties or doubts in a Christian's daily life do you think this chapter answers best?

13. If everyone in your church thoroughly understood verse 8, and had a passion for living out its truth, what kind of practical changes do you think would result?

14. From what you see in this chapter and elsewhere in Scripture, what can

you reasonably expect in life if you do *not* obey the command in verse 9?

15. If God had written this chapter only for *you*, which words or phrases do you think He would have underlined?

FOR GOING DEEPER

What parallel principle do you find both in Peter's exhortation to husbands in verse 7 and the Lord's directive in Matthew 5:23-24?

1 PETER 4

Startup: Who is the most *hospitable* person you know?

SEEING WHAT'S THERE

1. As you look at verses 1-2, how would you explain the meaning of Peter's statement in the last half of verse 1?

2. Which important details in this chapter do you think might be the easiest to overlook?

3. Suppose a band of armed terrorists stormed into the room where you're now meeting, then took you as hostages in a captivity that was likely to last for days or weeks. Just before they confiscated your Bibles, they allowed you to take one last look at the chapter open before you. Which verse in 1 Peter 4 would you most try to fix in mind before your Bible was snatched away, and why?

4. Review again Peter's statement of purpose for his letters in 2 Peter 3:1-2. How do you think he helps accomplish that purpose here in chapter 4 of First Peter?

5. EYE FOR DETAIL— *From what you recall seeing in this chapter, try answering the following question without looking at your Bible:* In the opening verse of this chapter, what attitude or purpose does Peter tell us to arm ourselves with?

CAPTURE THE ESSENCE

6. Which commands in this chapter would you say are the easiest for most Christians to obey? And which are the easiest to *dis*obey?

7. Regarding the subjects that you've seen addressed so far in this book, what questions do you have that remain unanswered?

8. Recall again the words of the resurrected Jesus to Peter in John 21— "Feed my sheep." How would you describe the food that the sheep are getting from Peter in this chapter?

FOR LIFE TODAY

9. In Psalm 119:47, these words are spoken to God: "I will *delight* myself in thy commandments, which I have *loved.*" At this point in your life, which commands in this chapter would be the quickest to bring you fulfillment and pleasure?

10. It's been said that "the human heart resists nothing more than change." What truths in this chapter—truths that could require some changes in your life—cause some degree of hesitation and resistance inside you?

11. *How,* exactly, does a person go about obeying the command given in verse 1?

12. If verses 7 and 8 were the only Scripture portion you had access to, what conclusions would you draw about your priorities in life? *Prayer is priority, result from love.*

13. Consider again verse 8. Practically speaking, what do you think is the strongest motivation for people today to be more *loving?* *-Covers our sin*

14. Look again at the command about hospitality in verse 9. Can you give an example of when you offered hospitality to someone, but not quite in the way that we're told to here? *No grumbling*

15. What would you say is an especially good *starting point* for applying verse 10 more effectively to your life? *Christ love for me.*

16. In verses 12-19, consider carefully how Peter tells his readers what their situation is like, and what to do about it. To what degree does this description match your own situation at the present time? And to what degree do you think it could match your situation sometime in the future?

Keep in mind what you see in verses 10-11 regarding spiritual gifts. Then compare the following passages, and summarize what you see as the most important biblical principles on this subject—Romans 12:3-8; 1 Corinthians 12:1-31, and Ephesians 4:3-13.

1 PETER 5

Startup: What's the closest you've ever been to a lion?

SEEING WHAT'S THERE

1. In your own words, how would you summarize the guidelines for church leadership given in verses 1-3?

2. In verse 4, notice the promise made to faithful church leaders. How would you explain it in your own words?

3. Once more, take a look in 2 Peter 3:1-2 at Peter's statement of purpose for his two letters. Here in chapter 5, how do you think he fulfills that purpose for this first letter?

4. EYE FOR DETAIL— *From what you recall seeing in this chapter, try answering the following question without looking at your Bible:* What kind of *crown* does Peter mention in this chapter? (See verse 4.)

CAPTURE THE ESSENCE

5. From what you see in this chapter, what *expectations* can we rightly have of God?

6. If you were asked to summarize the most important "marks of Christian maturity" as taught in this chapter, which ones would you mention first?

7. Recall again the words of the resurrected Jesus to Peter in John 21— "Feed my sheep." How would you describe the food that the sheep are getting from Peter in this chapter?

FOR LIFE TODAY

8. In a typical day, how often would the command in verse 7 offer useful and timely guidelines for your immediate situation?

9. Imagine that you saw earlier today a message written in fire in the sky. It was addressed to you by name, then continued with these words: *Thus saith the LORD: "Read 1 Peter 5, for I*

have something for you there." Which verses in this chapter do you think He most likely would be referring to?

10. If everyone in your church thoroughly understood this chapter, and had a passion for living out its truth, what kind of practical changes do you think would result?

FOR GOING DEEPER

If you were to put together a handbook called *Resisting the Devil,* and wanted to base it on verses 6-10 and James 4:6-10 . . . what would your chapter titles be?

1 PETER:

THE BIG PICTURE

(Discuss again the questions in the "Overview," plus the questions below.)

1. If you were a member of one of the first-century churches that first received a copy of this letter, and you decided to write a letter back to Peter after receiving this one, what would you include in the letter—what questions, comments, words of appreciation, etc.?

2. If this chapter were the only portion of Scripture you had access to, how could you use it to help answer this question: *What is the most powerful and effective way to improve my life?*

3. Look at each of these verses, and discuss which one you believe is the best candidate for "KEY VERSE" in the book of First Peter—the one which brings into sharpest focus what this book is most about: 1:6-7, 1:10-11, 4:12, or 4:13-14.

4. In James 1:23-24 we're told that "anyone who listens to the word but does not do what it says is like a man who looks at his face in a mirror and, after looking at himself, goes away and immediately forgets what he looks like." In what important ways has the book of First Peter been a "mirror" for you—showing you what you can and should do?

5. If you've decided on a starting point for applying something in this book more effectively to your life, what commitment would you be willing to make to others in your group regarding this?

6. How would you complete the following sentence as a word of advice to growing Christians? *Explore the book of First Peter if you want to learn more about...*

2 Peter

OVERVIEW

(Discuss these OVERVIEW questions both at the beginning of your study of Second Peter, and again after you've studied together all three chapters. Your answers may change significantly once you've looked more closely at the entire book.)

Startup: What does the word *apostasy* mean to you?

SEEING WHAT'S THERE

1. Look at 3:1-2, where Peter writes about his purpose for this letter. With those words in mind, what do you expect the subject matter of this book to look like?

2. What is the first *command* that Peter gives in this letter?

3. What is the first *encouragement* Peter gives in this letter?

4. Look also at the list of "Questions to Ask as You Begin Your Study of Each Book" on page 393.

CAPTURE THE ESSENCE

5. What previous impressions, if any, have you had about the book of Second Peter in regard to (a) its content, (b) its level of difficulty, and (c) its importance?

6. The book of Second Peter has been called "The Book of Christian Diligence," "Growing in the Lord's Grace and Power," and "Predictions of Apostasy." With that reputation for this book, what answers, guidelines, and solutions would you like to discover as you begin to examine it more closely?

7. While Paul has been called "the Apostle of Faith," and John "the Apostle of Love," Peter has been known as "the Apostle of Hope." Where in this letter do you see the theme of *hope* coming through?

FOR LIFE TODAY

8. When you get to heaven, if you have a long talk with the apostle Peter and he says to you, "By the way, what was most helpful to you in my second letter?" how would you like to be able to answer him?

9. How can you ensure that your study of Second Peter is not merely theoretical and intellectual, but is instead truly practical and relevant? Talk together about this. What can you do to help keep the process alive and interesting?

FOR GOING DEEPER

Look at Peter's words in 1:17, and compare this passage with the event recorded in Luke 9:28-36. What seem to be the most important things Peter learned from being a witness to this transfiguration of Jesus?

2 PETER 1

Startup: When you think of the term *God's promises*—which of His promises come first to mind?

SEEING WHAT'S THERE

1. How would you explain verses 3-4 to a young child?

2. In your own words, how would you explain the *process* which Peter teaches in verses 5-8?

3. SMALL, BUT IMPORTANT: In verse 8, notice Peter's use of the little word *if,* a word that signals a condition or supposition. What important condition does it highlight here?

4. Let the words of verse 11 form a picture in your mind, and then describe that picture.

5. In the last half of this chapter, what is it that Peter wants most for his readers to understand about him? And what is it that he most wants his readers to understand about Jesus?

6. Suppose that at the end of this chapter, Peter added this line: "If you remember only one thing from this chapter, let it be this:..." How do you think he would complete that sentence?

7. Look again at 3:1-2, where Peter gives his purpose for writing this letter. How does he begin accomplishing that purpose in chapter 1?

8. Look also at the list of "Questions to Ask as You Study Each Chapter" on page 392, which you may want to do for each chapter in Second Peter.

9. EYE FOR DETAIL— *If everyone in the group has read the entire chapter, try answering the following question without looking at your Bible:* The virtues listed in verses 5 to 7 begin with faith and end with love. There are six others in between. How many of them can you name?

CAPTURE THE ESSENCE

10. Many times we rob ourselves of the discovery of deeper truths in Scripture because we see a passage and say to ourselves, "I already know that." For which teachings in this chapter might it be easiest for Christians to fall into that trap?

11. In John 21, the resurrected Jesus said to Peter, "Feed my sheep." How would you describe the food that the sheep are getting from Peter in this chapter?

12. Look together at 2 Timothy 3:16, and compare what you see there with verses 20-21. Taking both passages together, what conclusions can you draw about the inspiration of Scriptures?

13. Notice the emphasis with which Peter begins his statement in verses 20-21. Why is this truth so important for us to understand?

14. From what you see in this chapter, what can we truly rely on God to do as we obey Him?

15. If you thought of this chapter as a roadmap for a Christian's life, what would be the safest "roads" to take, as taught in this chapter? And what would be the unsafe, dangerous roads to avoid?

FOR LIFE TODAY

16. Consider again verses 5-8. Get in mind a picture of yourself five years in the future, as a man or woman whose life truly reflects the process described in this passage. As this kind of person, what kinds of things do you see yourself doing?

17. What would you say is an especially good *starting point* for applying verse 10 more effectively to your life?

18. Suppose a new Christian asked you, "How can I become a stronger Christian like you?" How could you

use the verses in this chapter to help you give a meaningful answer?

19. If it's true that "you *become* what you *think*," then what are the most important thoughts from this chapter to plant firmly in your mind?

20. In light of how you're doing spiritually in your life today, which verse in this chapter do you think is the most important at this time—and why?

In verses 13-15, Peter speaks of his imminent death. His "departure," he says, was made clear to him by the Lord Jesus. What details do Jesus' words in John 13:36 and 21:18-19 reveal about Peter's manner of death?

2 PETER 2

Startup: When you think of the Bible characters Noah and Lot, what are your impressions of what their character was like?

1. As you read this chapter, what are the strongest impressions or images which it leaves in your mind?

2. What in this chapter do you think might be most surprising to a new Christian reading it for the first time?

3. In verses 1-3, notice what Peter tells his readers to be expecting. If you were one of the original recipients of this letter, what thoughts or questions or concerns would Peter's words raise in your mind?

4. Summarize what verses 4-9 say about God's *character* and His *ability.*

5. From what you see in this chapter, what is it that Peter most wants us to understand about false teachers?

6. Suppose the telegraph had been invented back in New Testament times, and Peter decided to send his readers a brief telegram of this chapter, in advance of the delivery of the full letter. In order to save money, he decided to send only the three most important verses from the chapter. Which three verses do you think Peter would have chosen?

7. Look once more at 3:1-2, where Peter writes about his purpose for this letter. How does he help accomplish that purpose in chapter 2?

8. EYE FOR DETAIL— *From what you recall seeing in this chapter, try answering the following question without looking at your Bible:* Three animals are mentioned in this chapter; what are they? (See verses 16 and 22.)

9. Would you say this is a chapter that especially requires *patience* as you

read and study it, in order to understand it? If so, why?

10. Try to "read between the lines" as you think about Peter's words in this chapter. What foundational principles would you say are the source of his teaching here? What is he most *concerned* about?

11. Recall again the words of the resurrected Jesus to Peter in John 21— "Feed my sheep." How would you describe the food that the sheep are getting from Peter in this chapter?

FOR LIFE TODAY

12. In what ways would you say Peter's description of false teachers in this chapter would fit anyone whom you're aware of today?

13. Which verse in this chapter do you think God wants you to understand best?

FOR GOING DEEPER

Peter's portrait of the false teachers (verses 1-18) who had invaded the church parallels a similar warning in Jude 8-16. Examine those two passages and cite the areas that most troubled these two church leaders.

2 PETER 3

Startup: How do you envision what *time* will be like in heaven?

SEEING WHAT'S THERE

1. Look again at verses 1-2. How would you say this chapter helps Peter fulfill his stated purpose for writing this letter?

2. In verses 3-4, notice again what Peter tells his readers to be expecting. Once more, if you were one of the original recipients of this letter, what thoughts or questions or concerns would Peter's words raise in your mind?

3. From what you see in verses 10-13, what should we be *expecting*, and what should we be *looking forward to?*

4. In your own words, summarize what Peter says about Paul in verse 15-16.

5. Which important details in this chapter do you think might be the easiest to overlook?

6. Suppose a band of armed terrorists stormed into the room where you're now meeting, then took you as hostages in a captivity that was likely to last for days or weeks. Just before they confiscated your Bibles, they allowed you to take one last look at the chapter open before you. Which verse in 2 Peter 3 would you most try to fix in mind before your Bible was snatched away, and why?

7. EYE FOR DETAIL— *From what you recall seeing in this chapter, try answering the following question without looking at your Bible:* How does Peter describe Paul in this chapter? (See verse 15.)

CAPTURE THE ESSENCE

8. From what you see in this chapter, what is the most important response we can have as we think about the "last days" and "the day of the Lord"?

9. From what you see in this chapter, what *expectations* can we rightly have of God?

10. *How,* exactly, does a person go about obeying the command given in verse 14?

11. If Satan wrote down some guidelines and commands to get people to do just the opposite of what this chapter teaches, how do you think his message might be worded?

12. Recall again the words of the resurrected Jesus to Peter in John 21—"Feed my sheep." How would you describe the food that the sheep are getting from Peter in this chapter?

FOR LIFE TODAY

13. In Psalm 119:47, these words are spoken to God: "I will *delight* myself in thy commandments, which I have *loved.*" At this point in your life, which commands in this chapter would be the quickest to bring you fulfillment and pleasure?

14. What kind of mental habits do you think could most easily block the truth of this chapter from staying alive in the minds and hearts of Christians today?

15. From what you see in this chapter, discuss together how you would complete this sentence: *What God really wants from me is…*

16. Imagine that you saw earlier today a message written in fire in the sky. It was addressed to you by name, then continued with these words: *Thus saith the LORD: "Read 2 Peter 3, for I have something for you there."* Which verses in this chapter do you think He most likely would be referring to?

17. In Philippians 4:8 we're given the following command: "Whatever is true, whatever is noble, whatever is right, whatever is pure, whatever is lovely, whatever is admirable—if anything is excellent or praiseworthy—*think about such things."* What food for thought can you find in this chapter that especially strikes you as being *true,* or *noble,* or *right,* or *pure,* or *lovely,* or *admirable,* or *excellent,* or *praiseworthy?*

18. What would you say is an especially good *starting point* for applying verse 18 more effectively to your life?

FOR GOING DEEPER

When Peter compared the Lord's second coming to the entrance of a thief (verse 10), he was using an image employed several other times in Scripture. How do the following Scriptures increase your understanding of this important word picture? (Matthew 24:43-44; 1 Thessalonians 5:2, 4; Revelation 3:3; 16:15.)

2 PETER:

THE BIG PICTURE

(Discuss again the questions in the "Overview," plus the questions below.)

1. If you were a member of one of the first-century churches that first received a copy of this letter, and you decided to write a letter back to Peter after receiving this one, what would you include in the letter—what questions, comments, words of appreciation, etc.?

2. If this letter were the only portion of Scripture you had access to, how could you use it to help answer this question: *What is the most powerful and effective way to improve my life?*

3. Look at each of these verses, and discuss which one you believe is the best candidate for "KEY VERSE" in the book of Second Peter—the one which brings into sharpest focus what this book is most about: 1:3, 1:20-21, 3:2, or 3:9-11.

4. In James 1:23-24 we're told that "anyone who listens to the word but does not do what it says is like a man who looks at his face in a mirror and, after looking at himself, goes away and immediately forgets what he looks like." In what important ways has the book of Second Peter been a "mirror" for you—showing you what you can and should do?

5. If you've decided on a starting point for applying something in this book more effectively to your life, what commitment would you be willing to make to others in your group regarding this?

6. How would you complete the following sentence as a word of advice to growing Christians? *Explore the book of Second Peter if you want to learn more about…*

1 John

OVERVIEW

(Discuss these OVERVIEW questions both at the beginning of your study of First John, and again after you've studied together all five chapters. Your answers may change significantly once you've looked more closely at the entire book.)

Startup: Discuss how much you agree or disagree with this statement: God wants all His children to know without a doubt that they will go to heaven after they die.

SEEING WHAT'S THERE

1. Start scanning this letter until you come to a verse that brings a question to your mind. What's the question?

2. Begin scanning the letter again until you come to a verse that gives you a smile or a sense of gratitude or joy. What is pleasing to you about this verse?

3. How many times in this letter do you see John using the words *command* or *commandment?* (Look for both the singular and the plural forms.)

4. How many times in this letter does John address his readers as "children"?

5. Suppose you were attending a citizens' meeting called by local school officials who were considering the removal of the Bible from the shelves of all school libraries in your community. You spoke up in favor of keeping the Bible available to students. Then another citizen rose to his feet and said, "I see no reason to keep it around. It's a forgotten book anyway. Even most Christians have no idea what's in it. For example," he said, then turned directly to you and asked, "Tell me what the book of First John is all about." In that situation, how would you respond?

6. Why did John write this letter? Discuss together the evidence you see in each of the following verses — 1:4, 2:1, 2:12-14, 2:21, and 5:13. Of the reasons you see in these verses, which one do you think was probably most important in John's mind?

7. What are the most important things you know about the apostle John, who wrote this letter, and about the circumstances that surrounded his writing of it?

8. What do you know about what the world was like at the time this letter was written? What would you guess to be the typical hopes and dreams and concerns of the people to whom John was writing?

9. Look also at the list of "Questions to Ask as You Begin Your Study of Each Book" on page 393.

CAPTURE THE ESSENCE

10. What previous impressions, if any, have you had about the book of First John in regard to (a) its content, (b) its level of difficulty, and (c) its importance?

11. The book of First John has been called "The Epistle of Knowledge and Assurance," "The Fellowship of the Father and His Children," and

"Living as Children of God." With that reputation for this book, what answers, guidelines, and solutions would you like to gain as you examine it more closely?

12. While Paul has been called "the Apostle of Faith," and Peter "the Apostle of Hope," John has been known as "the Apostle of Love." In which chapters of this letter do you see John teaching about *love?*

FOR LIFE TODAY

13. From what you see in this book and elsewhere in Scripture, what do you feel is the most important thing which you believe about Jesus Christ?

14. From what you see in this book and elsewhere in Scripture, what do you feel is the most important guideline for your relationship with other people?

15. How can you ensure that your study of First John is not merely theoretical and intellectual, but is instead truly practical and relevant? Talk together about this. What can you do to help keep the process alive and interesting?

16. When you get to heaven, if you have a long talk with the apostle John and he asks you, "What was most helpful to you in my first letter?" how would you like to be able to answer him?

FOR GOING DEEPER

John is known as the Apostle of Love, but what kind of person was he in his younger days? Look together at the following passages to see what you can discover — Matthew 4:21-22, Mark 3:17 and 10:35-45, Luke 9:51-56, and John 19:26-27 and 21:20-23.

1 JOHN 1

Startup: What's the darkest place you've ever been in? And what's the brightest place?

SEEING WHAT'S THERE

1. Notice how the tone of this chapter is one of *proclamation* or *declaration* or *announcement.* In your own words, summarize what it is that John is proclaiming or declaring or announcing.

2. SMALL, BUT IMPORTANT: In this chapter, how many times do you see the little word *if,* a word that signals a condition or supposition? And what important condition or supposition does it highlight each time?

3. How many times do you see the word *fellowship* in this chapter? And what does this word mean, in the way that John uses it here?

4. Look at verse 5. What does the word *light* mean, in the way that John uses it here? Does it also mean the same thing in verse 7?

5. From what you see in verse 7, when we "walk in the light," what impact does it have on our relationships?

6. In practical terms, what do you think the word *confess* means in verse 9?

7. If a young child heard you read verse 9, and then asked, "How does that work?"— how would you answer?

8. From what John says in this chapter, what does he most want us to understand about ourselves, and what does he most want us to understand about God?

9. Look ahead to 5:13, where John writes about his purpose for this letter. How does he begin accomplishing that purpose in chapter 1?

10. After looking over this chapter, which words or phrases or sentences here do you feel are the most difficult to understand?

11. Look also at the list of "Questions to Ask as You Study Each Chapter" on page 392, which you may want to do for each chapter in First John.

12. EYE FOR DETAIL— *If everyone in the group has read the entire chapter, try answering the following question without looking at your Bible:* John said he is writing this letter to make something full, or complete. What is it? (See verse 4.)

CAPTURE THE ESSENCE

13. Look again at verse 5. *Why* does God want us to know this truth?

14. In your own words, what does it mean to "walk in the light," as John says in verse 7?

15. From what John says in verses 5-10 (and look also at the first verse in chapter 2), how seriously does God view sin?

16. Picture this book of First John as a fast-moving train. Chapter 1 is the locomotive in front, and the other chapters represent railway cars that follow behind. From what you see here in chapter 1, what is the *energy* in the locomotive — the point or principle or theme that's the driving force for the locomotive and the entire train?

FOR LIFE TODAY

17. Think again about the words in verse 5 — "God is light." At this time in your life, how willing are you to let your habits and thoughts and attitudes and actions be examined under the pure light of God? To help you decide, use a scale of one to ten (one = "much less willing than ever," ten = "much more willing than ever").

18. What are some easy ways today that Christians can be tempted to "walk in darkness," as John speaks of in verse 6?

19. Consider again John's words in verse 7 about walking in the light. Practically speaking, what do you think is the strongest motivation for Christians today to walk in the light?

20. Notice again verse 8. Have you ever claimed to be without sin?

21. How would you use verse 9 to help a new Christian who felt guilt-ridden and unacceptable to God?

22. In Philippians 4:8 we're given the following command: "Whatever is true, whatever is noble, whatever is right, whatever is pure, whatever is lovely, whatever is admirable — if anything is excellent or praiseworthy — *think about such things.*" What food for thought can you find in this chapter that especially strikes you as being *true,* or *noble,* or *right,* or *pure,* or *lovely,* or *admirable,* or *excellent,* or *praiseworthy?*

23. Which verse in this chapter do you think God wants you to understand best?

24. What would you say is an especially good *starting point* for applying this chapter more effectively to your life?

FOR GOING DEEPER

What themes do you see in the first seven verses of this letter that you can recall also seeing in John's gospel? (You may want to scan together the first fourteen chapters of John to find them.)

1 JOHN 2

Startup: What would you say are the most important qualities for a father to have?

1. In verse 1, notice the description of the ministry of Jesus. Let these words form a picture in your mind, and then describe that picture.

2. Look also at the descriptions of His ministry in verse 2. How do verses 1 and 2 go together?

3. How many times do you see the word *know* in chapter 2?

4. How many times do you see the word *love* in chapter 2?

5. How many times do you see the words *true* or *truth* in chapter 2?

6. What are the "commands" or "commandments" which John mentions in verses 3-4?

7. SMALL, BUT IMPORTANT: The word *but* signals a contrast, or a change in direction. Look at the occurrences of this word in verses 5, 11, and 20, and identify the contrast or the change in direction that this word highlights.

8. For helpful background on the command John speaks of in verses 7-8, look at John 13:34-35 and 15:12, as well as Matthew 22:34-40 and Leviticus 19:18. What is *new* about this command, and what is *old* about it?

9. Look at verse 9, and discuss how much you agree or disagree with this statement: Any relationship between two believers is either *love* or *hate;* there is no such thing as a neutral relationship in the body of Christ.

10. If John's words in verses 12-14 represent different stages of spiritual maturity, how would you describe each level?

11. Notice the love John speaks of in verse 15. How is it like other kinds of love, and how is it different?

12. From what you see in verses 15-16, how much of worldliness is *internal,* and how much is *external?*

13. What does John mean by the term "last hour" or "last time" in verse 18?

14. How fully can you explain what John means by the term "anointing" in verses 20 and 27? (In some versions, the word is translated as "unction.") For helpful background, look together at John 14:16-17 and Acts 10:38.

15. Compare verses 20 and 27 again. Who is our teacher? And what does He teach us?

16. From what you see elsewhere in this letter, what is the "truth" John speaks of in verse 21?

17. Look again at 5:13, where John gives his purpose for writing this letter. How does he help accomplish that purpose in chapter 2?

18. After reading through this chapter, which words or phrases or sentences here do you feel are the most difficult to understand?

19. EYE FOR DETAIL— *From what you recall seeing in this chapter, try answering the following question without looking at your Bible:* In this chapter, who does John speak these words to: "You are strong"? (See verse 14.)

20. Compare verses 1-2 with verse 22. *What* is important to believe about Jesus, and *why* is it important?

21. When John tells of the ministry of Jesus in verses 1-2, notice how Jesus is described as being "righteous." In this context, what is the significance of that term?

22. Again with verses 1-2 in mind, discuss which one of the following

statements best describes the ministry of Jesus in the presence of God: (a) Jesus represents *love,* and God represents *justice;* as the advocate for our defense, Jesus pleads for God to have mercy upon us; (b) Jesus represents *justice,* for by His own death He has paid the penalty for our sin; God represents *love,* the love that desires to save mankind, and which sent His Son to earth to accomplish it.

23. Is John saying in verses 3-6 that a Christian never sins?

24. What exactly is the "beginning" which John speaks of in verse 7?

25. Notice again John's mention of *love* in verse 10. How do we define this love? Think about the following list of four words, each of which could be used in such a definition. Then rank them in the order of their importance in defining true love — *action, attitude, choice,* and *emotion.*

26. Look again at the command in verse 15. If you have a *love* for something or someone, how do you go about stopping that love?

27. Compare the three forms of worldliness mentioned in verse 16 with the three approaches Satan used in tempting Jesus (Luke 4:5-12). How closely do they match?

28. Compare verses 20 and 27 again, especially John's reference in verse 27 to not having a need for anyone to teach us. What is the best way to understand these words, in light of so many other Scriptures that provide for teachers and teaching in the church?

29. From what John says in this chapter, what does he most want us to understand about ourselves?

30. From what you see in this chapter, what *expectations* can we rightly have of God?

31. Think about the following question as you reflect on what you've seen so far in First John: Which is more important in the Christian life — what you *do,* or what you *don't* do? (Explain your answer.)

32. From what you've seen so far in this letter, answer this question as fully as you can: What are the most important "birthmarks" of someone who has been born again as a Christian? What is it that truly identifies him or her as a child of God?

FOR LIFE TODAY

33. If John's words in verses 12-14 represent different stages of spiritual maturity, into which level would you place yourself? And from what John says here, what is therefore true about you? (Express it in your own words.)

34. Look again at John's references to "fathers" in verses 13 and 14. Who are the "fathers of the faith" — the mature, proven Christians — who have had the most impact upon your life?

35. Keeping in mind John's words in verses 13-14 about fathers of the faith, what do you feel are the most effective ways to show respect and consideration for older, mature Christians?

36. Once more, compare verses 20 and 27. When it comes to letting the Holy Spirit be our teacher, what are the major *hindrances* to overcome, and what are the best *helps?*

37. Verse 29 is one of many in this letter in which John speaks about our "knowing" something. How well would you say you "know" what John speaks of in this verse?

38. From what you've seen so far in this letter, *why* should we not want to sin?

39. If a non-Christian friend said to you, "If a person believes truly in God,

and doesn't really see the need to also believe in Jesus, it doesn't make sense that God would condemn that person — since God is love, and since that person is truly sincere." How could you use what you've seen so far in this letter to help you give an answer?

40. How could you use this chapter in response to a new Christian who said to you, "There are some people I simply cannot and will not love."

41. Think about your most pressing struggle in life today — a fear, frustration, anger, or whatever. Which truth in this chapter would you say relates most directly to it?

42. Suppose you were discussing the gospel with a non-Christian friend, and he said to you, "What does Jesus really have to do with it? Aren't there other ways to God? What about all the other religions?" In your response, how could you use what John teaches in this chapter?

43. In Colossians 3:1 we read this command: "Since you have been raised with Christ, set your hearts on things above, where Christ is seated at the right hand of God." What have you personally observed about Jesus Christ in this chapter that would be worthy of setting your heart on?

44. Suppose you heard a voice from heaven saying to you, "Don't get over-ambitious and try to apply too much from this chapter to your life right now. Just pick one thing to focus on, and do it well." What one thing would you choose?

FOR GOING DEEPER

John uses one of his favorite words in verses 6, 10, 14, 27, and 28, a word that is translated as *abide* or *remain*. It appears many times in John's gospel and letters. From the following sample references, discuss the importance of this word to the Christian life — John 5:38, 12:46, 14:16, and 15:4-7; 1 John 3:6 and 3:24; and 2 John 9.

1 JOHN 3

Startup: What images come to your mind when you think of the term *child-likeness?*

SEEING WHAT'S THERE

1. How many times do you see the word *know* in chapter 3? Together, list aloud all the things in this chapter that John says we know.

2. From what you see in verse 24, what part does the Holy Spirit play in our "knowing"?

3. How many times do you see the word *love* in chapter 3?

4. From what you see in verse 2, what is the most important thing to know about what we'll be like in heaven?

5. Notice John's words in verse 3 about a purification process. How would you explain this verse to a young child?

6. Consider carefully John's message in verses 4-10. How would you compare that message with the popular phrase that goes, "Christians aren't perfect, just forgiven"?

7. In verse 8, John speaks of "the works of the devil," or "the devil's work." What is that work?

8. What is the "seed" which John speaks of in verse 9, and why is it important in his discussion of sin in this chapter?

9. Notice John's last statement in this chapter. How do you think the truth he gives here relates to the "seed" mentioned in verse 9?

10. Look together at the story of Cain and Abel in Genesis 4:1-15. How does it bear out John's interpretation here in verse 12?

11. Notice the two "hates" in verse 13 and 15. From what you see here and elsewhere in Scripture, what is the source of each one?

12. For helpful background on verse 15, look back at the words of Jesus in Matthew 5:21-22. To what degree would you say these two passages are saying the same thing?

13. How would you explain verse 16 to a young child?

14. Once more, look at John's words in 5:13 about his purpose for writing this letter. How does he help accomplish that purpose in chapter 3?

15. After reading through this chapter, which words or phrases or sentences here do you feel are the most difficult to understand?

16. EYE FOR DETAIL— *From what you recall seeing in this chapter, try answering the following question without looking at your Bible:* When John says our love should *not* be with word or tongue, how does he say our love should be? (See verse 18.)

CAPTURE THE ESSENCE

17. From what you see in verses 1-3, how would you state in your own words the most important facts about your identity?

18. Look again at the truth John states in the last part of verse 1. What light does this shed on our relationship with non-Christians?

19. What are the most important perspectives for a Christian to have about *sin,* according to what you see in verses 4-10?

20. How would you bring together what John says in verse 9 with what he wrote in the first verse of chapter 2?

21. From what you see in verses 12-16, discuss how much you agree or disagree with this statement: *Hate* is actually a love for one's self that causes you to ignore others; while *love* is actually hating (or ignoring) one's self in order to focus on others.

22. Keep verse 14 in mind as you discuss how much you agree or disagree with this statement: You cannot feel spiritually alive unless you are truly *focused* on loving other people.

23. From what you see in this chapter and elsewhere in Scripture, restate the principle in verse 17 in your own words, expanding it as broadly as the limits of Scripture allow.

24. From what you see in this chapter, what *expectations* can we rightly have of God?

FOR LIFE TODAY

25. It's been said that "the human heart resists nothing more than change." What truths in this chapter — truths that could require some changes in your life — cause some degree of hesitation and resistance inside you?

26. Look again at verse 1. In practical terms, what can help us to better understand and appreciate God's love?

27. In verse 2, look again at how John uses the word "know." How well do *you* know what it is that John is speaking of here? To help you decide, use a scale of one to ten (one = "I definitely do not believe it," ten = "I know it with total, personal certainty").

28. Now look in verse 5 at what John says we know. Do another personal rating, with the same scale of one to ten.

29. Now do the same rating with what John says in verse 14.

30. Look again at John's mention of *hope* in verse 3. Since this hope is so powerful in the way it brings purity to our lives, what would you say are the most important ways to keep that hope alive and strong in your mind and heart?

31. How susceptible do you think Christians in general are today to the de-ception which John warns against in verses 7-10?

32. Consider once more John's teaching about sin in verses 10-14. What would you say are the most important *choices* for a Christian to make in order to live in obedience to this passage?

33. Look again at verse 13. How often do you notice any hatred from the world, and how *surprised* are you to notice it?

34. Although the words *peace, freedom,* and *joy* are not found in verses 21-24, how could a Christian experience them more fully by obeying the guidelines and commands in these verses?

35. As you think about loving the people who are closest around you, in obedience to the command of Christ, what impact do you think your love should have upon their feeling of self-worth?

36. If it's true that "you *become* what you *think*," then what are the most important thoughts from this chapter to plant firmly in your mind?

37. Think again about the following question as you reflect on what you've seen so far in First John: Which is more important in the Christian life — what you *do,* or what you *don't* do? (Explain your answer.)

38. If God had written this chapter only for *you,* which words or phrases do you think He would have underlined?

FOR GOING DEEPER

How do James's strong-worded exhortations in James 1:22-26 and 2:14-17 give you a fuller picture of John's gentle prod in verse 18?

1 JOHN 4

Startup: What thoughts or images come to your mind when you think of the term *perfect love?*

SEEING WHAT'S THERE

1. How many times do you see the word *know* in chapter 4?

2. How many times do you see the word *love* in chapter 4?

3. From all that you see in this chapter, what are the most important truths for us to know about *love?*

4. What are the *spirits* that John speaks of in verses 1-3? And why do you think John uses that term?

5. From what you see in this chapter, what qualifies a Christian to be able to do the *testing* which we're commanded to do in verse 1?

6. Looking again at verses 1-3, what is the most important result to look for in testing the spirits?

7. In verse 18, John tells what perfect love does to fear. How would you explain the process by which this happens?

8. Which important details in this chapter do you think might be the easiest to overlook?

9. Again, look at John's words in 5:13 about his purpose for writing this letter. How does he help accomplish that purpose in chapter 4?

10. EYE FOR DETAIL— *From what you recall seeing in this chapter, try answering the following question without looking at your Bible:* How does John complete this sentence: "There is no fear…" (See verse 18.)

CAPTURE THE ESSENCE

11. Many times we rob ourselves of the discovery of deeper truths in Scripture because we see a passage and say to ourselves, "I already know that." For which teachings in this chapter might it be easiest for Christians to fall into that trap?

12. From what you see in this chapter, what is the *proof* of God's love, what is the *power* of God's love, and what is the *promise* of God's love?

13. Answer the following question as fully as you can from the evidence in verses 12-21: If God is really love, and He loves the world, how is the world supposed to know it?

14. From what you've seen so far in First John, discuss how much you agree or disagree with this statement: The only way a person can tell what he actually *believes* is to examine how he actually *behaves.*

15. Regarding the subjects that you've seen addressed so far in this book, what questions do you have that remain unanswered?

FOR LIFE TODAY

16. In verse 1, notice again what John tells us *not* to do. In what ways would you say Christians are most in danger of doing this?

17. In practical terms, what *confidence* do you gain from the truth John teaches in verses 4-6?

18. Suppose a friend heard you quote the phrase "God is love" from verse 8, and then asked you, "If God is love, why does He permit so much sin and suffering in the world?" how could you use other passages in this chapter to help you give a good response?

19. In verse 18, look again at what John tells us about perfect love and fear. What common fears can be done away with through love?

20. Think again about the following question as you reflect on what you've seen so far in First John: What is more important in the Christian

life — what you *do,* or what you *don't* do? (Explain your answer.)

21. If everyone in your church thoroughly understood this chapter, and had a passion for living out its truth in their lives, what kind of practical changes do you think would result?

22. Imagine that you saw earlier today a message written in fire in the sky. It was addressed to you by name, then continued with these words: *Thus saith the LORD: "Read 1 John 2, for I have something for you there."* Which verses in this chapter do you think He most likely would be referring to?

FOR GOING DEEPER

In verses 1-3, John warns about the "spirit of the antichrist" which is active in the world. Read 2 Thessalonians 2:3-12 and Revelation 13 as background for John's caution in verses 1-3. What does he mean by the "spirit of the antichrist" in this passage?

1 JOHN 5

Startup: In the way we read and study the Bible, what kind of mental habits can most easily block this book of First John from coming alive in our minds and hearts?

SEEING WHAT'S THERE

1. Scan this chapter together to determine how many times you see each of these key words — *know, love, life,* and *believe.*

2. From what you see in the first three verses alone, how would you explain the *motive* for love, and the *method* of love?

3. What *commands* is John speaking of in verses 2-3?

4. How would you explain verse 3 to a young child?

5. In verse 6, what does John mean when he mentions water and blood in connection with the coming of Jesus? Look together at the following passages to see how they help in understanding this verse — Matthew 3:13-17, Leviticus 17:11, Hebrews 2:14, and John 19:31-35.

6. In verses 7-8, John mentions how the Holy Spirit witnesses or testifies of Jesus. How does the Holy Spirit do this, and why is it important for us to know?

7. Look again at verse 13. How would you say this chapter helps John fulfill his stated purpose for writing this letter?

8. Compare verse 14 with what John said about prayer in 3:21-22. What is the most important thing that John wants us to understand about prayer?

9. In verses 16-17, what does John mean when he mentions sins that lead to death and sins that do not? Look together at the following passages to see how they help in under-

standing this verse — Mark 3:28-30, Acts 5:1-11, 1 Corinthians 11:27-30, and Hebrews 6:4-6.

10. According to verses 18-20, what is it that we *know?* From what you've seen elsewhere in this letter, why is each one important?

11. How does verse 20 put verse 21 into proper perspective?

12. EYE FOR DETAIL— *From what you recall seeing in this chapter, try answering the following question without looking at your Bible:* John asks only one question in this chapter. What is it? (See verse 5.)

CAPTURE THE ESSENCE

13. From what you see in verses 1-5, explain your answer to this question: Does love come from faith, or does faith come from love?

14. Look again at verses 1-5, and come up with a summary statement that includes these four words — *love, faith, obedience,* and *victory* — and explains how they all work together.

15. John speaks in verse 4 about "overcoming the world." What does this really mean, and why, exactly, do we need to do it?

16. In John's gospel, look at the words of Jesus in John 7:17. How would you say those words relate to what you see here in 1 John 5:10-12?

17. In verse 14, look at the condition attached to the promise about prayer. How can we know whether we are praying according to God's will?

FOR LIFE TODAY

18. Consider again verses 1-5, and recall the words of Jesus in John 15:5 — "Apart from me you can do nothing." Picture in your mind something good that could happen in your life in response to the teaching in these first five verses of 1 John 5, something that could clearly be accomplished only by the Lord's supernatural power. What would this be?

19. From what you see in this chapter and elsewhere in Scripture, what can you reasonably expect in life if you do *not* obey the command in verse 21?

20. From what you see in this chapter, discuss together how you would complete this sentence: *What God really wants from me is...*

21. If this chapter were the only portion of Scripture you had access to, how could you use it to help answer this question: *What is the most powerful and effective way to improve my life?*

22. Suppose a non-Christian friend asked you, "Can't a person become a Christian without believing that Jesus was God?" How could you use this chapter to help you give an answer?

23. If you were asked to write a discussion question to help your Bible study group apply something in this chapter to their lives, how would you word the question?

24. Of all that you see in this chapter, what one truth are you most *thankful* for, because of its personal significance to you?

FOR GOING DEEPER

Compare John's purpose for writing this letter (verse 13) with his stated purpose for writing the gospel of John (John 20:30-31). What was the driving force that caused John to put pen to paper?

1 JOHN:

THE BIG PICTURE

(Discuss again the questions in the "Overview," plus the questions below.)

1. Suppose that at the very end of this book, John added this line: "If you remember only one thing from this letter, let it be this:..." How do you think John would complete that sentence?

2. If you were one of the original recipients of this letter, and decided to write a letter back to John after receiving this one, what would you include in the letter — what questions, comments, words of appreciation, etc.?

3. Look at each of these verses, and discuss which one you believe is the best candidate for "KEY VERSE" in the book of First John — the one which brings into sharpest focus what this book is most about: 1:3-4, 2:15, 3:16, 4:19-21, or 5:11-13.

4. In James 1:23-24 we're told that "anyone who listens to the word but does not do what it says is like a man who looks at his face in a mirror and, after looking at himself, goes away and immediately forgets what he looks like." In what important ways has the book of First John been a "mirror" for you — showing you what you can and should do?

5. If you've decided on a starting point for applying something in this book more effectively to your life, what commitment would you be willing to make to others in your group regarding this?

6. How would you complete the following sentence as a word of advice to growing Christians? *Explore the book of First John if you want to learn more about...*

2 John

Startup: When you think of the word *antichrist,* what images come to your mind?

SEEING WHAT'S THERE

1. If this small book was the only portion of Scripture you had access to, what conclusions could you make from it about how to live the Christian life?

2. How many times do you see the word *truth* in this book? What do you think is uppermost in John's mind as he uses this word here?

3. Look also at the list of "Questions to Ask as You Begin Your Study of Each Book" on page 393, and at the list of "Questions to Ask as You Study Each Chapter" on page 392.

4. EYE FOR DETAIL— *If everyone in the group has read Second John, try answering the following question without looking at your Bible:* Which one of these doctrinal words is *not* included in this letter — *faith, grace, love, mercy, peace,* or *truth?* (See verses 1-3.)

CAPTURE THE ESSENCE

5. The book of Second John has been called "The Letter of Love and Truth" and "Caution: False Teachers." How well do you think those titles fit?

6. Imagine that you were the person carrying this letter from John to the "lady and her children" mentioned in verse 1. Along the way, you were attacked by a band of robbers who stripped you of all your valuables, including this letter. The leader of the robber band could not read, and when you asked him to return the letter, he replied, "Why? What's in it that's so important?" How would you answer him?

FOR LIFE TODAY

7. If the words in verse 8 were in a letter sent directly from God to you, how would you interpret its meaning?

8. Again with verse 8 in mind, what *rewards* are you looking forward to from God?

9. How would you translate verse 10 into a practical guideline for your life?

10. How would you complete the following sentence as a word of advice to growing Christians? *Explore the book of Second John if you want to learn more about...*

FOR GOING DEEPER

In verses 7-8 John warns believers to beware of "deceivers." What more can you learn about these deceptive teachers from 1 Timothy 4:1-2 and 2 Peter 2:1-3?

3 John

Startup: When you think of the word *hospitality,* what images come to your mind?

SEEING WHAT'S THERE

1. Make a summary list together of all the evidence you see in this brief letter concerning the character of these four men: Gaius, Diotrephes, Demetrius, and John.

2. How many times do you see the word *truth* in this book? What do you think is uppermost in John's mind as he uses this word here?

3. Look also at the list of "Questions to Ask as You Begin Your Study of Each Book" on page 393, and at the list of "Questions to Ask as You Study Each Chapter" on page 392.

4. EYE FOR DETAIL— *If everyone in the group has read Third John, try answering the following question without looking at your Bible:* Which one of these doctrinal words is *not* included in this letter — *grace, love, joy, peace,* or *truth?* (See verses 1-3 and 14.)

CAPTURE THE ESSENCE

5. The book of Third John has been called "The Epistle of Christian Hospitality," and "Helping Those Who Teach the Truth." How well do you think those titles fit?

6. Imagine that you were the person carrying this letter from John to his friend Gaius. Along the way, you were attacked by a band of robbers who stripped you of all your valuables, including this letter. The leader of the robber band could not read,

and when you asked him to return the letter, he replied, "Why? What's in it that's so important?" How would you answer him?

FOR LIFE TODAY

7. If God had written this letter only for *you,* which words or phrases do you think He would have underlined?

8. How would you complete the following sentence as a word of advice to growing Christians? *Explore the book of Third John if you want to learn more about...*

FOR GOING DEEPER

What might Diotrephes (verses 9-11) have learned if he had taken the time to study Philippians 2:1-8?

Jude

Startup: If someone was described as being "spiritually fit," what in your opinion would make that description accurate?

SEEING WHAT'S THERE

1. What do verses 3-4 indicate about the urgency of this letter?

2. From the evidence you see in this letter, what would you say is the most important thing Jude wants us to understand about God's judgment upon sin?

3. What are the most important things Jude wants us to understand about God's love and mercy?

4. Notice how we're told to pray at the end of verse 20. How exactly is this done?

5. Which verses in this letter leave the strongest images in your mind?

6. Look also at the list of "Questions to Ask as You Begin Your Study of Each Book" on page 393, and at the list of "Questions to Ask as You Study Each Chapter" on page 392.

7. EYE FOR DETAIL— *If everyone in the group has read all of Jude, try answering the following question without looking at your Bible:* Which one of these persons are *not* mentioned in this letter — Adam, Balaam, Cain, Enoch, Jacob, Korah, Michael, or Moses? (See verses 9, 11, and 14.)

CAPTURE THE ESSENCE

8. The book of Jude has been called "The Remedy for Apostasy," "Fighting for the Faith," and "Staying True to the Faith." With that reputation for this book, what answers, guidelines, and solutions would you like to gain as you examine it more closely?

9. Would you say this is a book that especially requires *patience* as you read and study it, in order to understand it? If so, why?

10. Look at the different responses indicated in verses 22-23. From what you see elsewhere in this book and elsewhere in Scripture, how does a Christian decide which of these actions is right toward what people and at what times?

11. If this small book was the only portion of Scripture you had access to, what conclusions could you make from it about how to live the Christian life?

12. If Jude had been able to write about the subject that he originally wanted to write about (as indicated in verse 3), what do you think he might have said, judging from what you see in the rest of this letter?

FOR LIFE TODAY

13. If it's true that "you *become* what you *think,*" then what are the most important thoughts from this letter to plant firmly in your mind?

14. Imagine that you saw earlier today a message written in fire in the sky. It was addressed to you by name, then continued with these words: *Thus saith the LORD: "Read the book of Jude, for I have something for you there."* Which verses in this book do

you think He most likely would be referring to?

15. Think carefully again about each of the commands in verses 20-21. Then imagine God evaluating you in these three categories: (a) *spiritual fitness,* (b) *spiritual prayer,* and (c) *intimacy with God.* On a scale of one to ten, in which ten equals the highest possible score, what score do you think He would probably assign to you in each of the three areas?

16. How would you complete the following sentence as a word of advice to growing Christians? *Explore the book of Jude if you want to learn more about...*

FOR GOING DEEPER

What common theme does Jude focus on in his opening words (verses 1-2) as well as his closing words (24-25)? Why, in this stern, bluntly-worded letter of warning, would he choose to begin and end with such a refrain?

Revelation

OVERVIEW

*(Discuss these OVERVIEW questions both at the be-
ginning of your study of Revelation, and again after
you've studied together all 22 chapters. Your answers
may change significantly once you've looked more
closely at the entire book.)*

Startup: What part, if any, has this book
had in your past Bible reading and
study?

SEEING WHAT'S THERE

1. Do a scan of Revelation together to
   see how often you find the word
   power. (You may want to divide into
   two groups—one group to start
   scanning at the beginning of the
   book, and the other to start at the
   end and work backwards.)

2. If this book of Revelation were not
   included in the Bible, how would
   you describe what would be missing
   in the total picture of the Bible's message?

3. Suppose you were attending a citizens' meeting called by local school
   officials who were considering the removal of the Bible from the shelves
   of all school libraries in your community. You spoke up in favor of
   keeping the Bible available to students. Then another citizen rose to
   his feet and said, "I see no reason to
   keep it around. It's a forgotten book
   anyway. Even most Christians have
   no idea what's in it. For example," he
   said, then turned directly to you and
   asked, "Tell me what the book of
   Revelation is all about." In that situation, how would you respond?

4. Look also at the list of "Questions to
   Ask as You Begin Your Study of Each
   Book" on page 393.

5. What do you know about the various approaches which Bible scholars
   have used to interpret the book of
   Revelation?

CAPTURE THE ESSENCE

6. What previous impressions have you
   had about the book of Revelation in
   regard to (a) its content, (b) its level
   of difficulty, and (c) its importance?

7. The book of Revelation has been
   called "The Book of Final Consum-
   mation," "The Coming of the Kingdom," "The Bible's Grand Finale,"
   and "How to Share Now in the Ultimate Victory." With that reputation
   for this book, what answers and
   guidelines and solutions would you
   like to gain as you examine it more
   closely?

8. What does Revelation have in common with the book of Genesis?
   What does it have in common with
   Daniel? What does it have in common with the gospel of John? And
   what does it have in common with
   the book of Acts?

9. If you could have *only one* of the following, which would you choose,
   and why? (a) A thoroughly detailed,
   step-by-step account of world events
   leading up to the return of Christ,
   including dates and times. (b) The
   Holy Spirit's intimate message to
   your heart about the power and glory
   of Christ, plus a personal guarantee
   that His power and glory will be

openly displayed for the entire world at an undisclosed future date.

FOR LIFE TODAY

10. When you get to heaven, if you have a long talk with the apostle John and he asks you, "What was most helpful to you in the book of Revelation?" how would you like to be able to answer him?

11. How can you ensure that your study of Revelation is not merely theoretical and intellectual, but is instead truly practical and relevant? Talk together about this. What can you do to help keep the process alive and interesting?

FOR GOING DEEPER

A PROMISED BLESSING—Note well the promise made in verse 3 of the first chapter. Then explore any of the following verses to help you put together a definition for the word *blessed*, as it's used in verse 3 in this chapter: Psalms 94:12-13, 112:1-3, 128:1-4, and 144:12-15; Jeremiah 17:7-8; James 1:12; and Revelation 19:9, 20:6, and 22:14.

1. because you discipline, teach + grant relief

2. because you fear Lord, delight in his commands; Children will be mighty, Generations upright; Wealth in his house + righteousness

REVELATION 1

Startup: How many different meanings can you give for the word *vision?*

SEEING WHAT'S THERE

1. Look closely at verse 1. Who is this book written to?

2. How many times do you see the word *seven* in this chapter?

3. What are the strongest visual images which you see in this chapter? Which ones do you recall seeing elsewhere in Scripture?

4. EYE FOR DETAIL— *From what you recall seeing in chapter 1, try answering the following question without looking at your Bible:* What *keys* does Jesus say He has? (See verse 18.)

5. Look also at the list of "Questions to Ask as You Study Each Chapter" on page 392, which you may want to do for each chapter in Revelation.

6. Suppose you were helping produce a feature film of the book of Revelation. To film what happens in this opening chapter, summarize all the scenes to be included, and the kinds of special effects, special scenery, background music, lighting effects, etc., you would use to meaningfully portray the central message and most important action.

CAPTURE THE ESSENCE

7. Recall again the full title of this book, as given in the opening phrase of verse 1—"The Revelation of Jesus Christ." What does chapter 1 reveal about *Jesus Christ?*

FOR LIFE TODAY

8. Look again at verse 1, at the mention made there of who this book is for. Are you assured that you are one of God's servants? If so, on what basis do you have that assurance? If you do *not* have that assurance, what is your reason for reading this book?

9. Notice again the promised blessing in verse 3. What can you do to "keep" or "take heed to" or "take to heart" the full message of this chapter?

10. In practical terms, how would you say the truth of our calling in verse 6 is best reflected in your life at this time?

FOR GOING DEEPER

John's vision of the glorified Christ in verses 12-17 parallels a much earlier experience in Matthew 17:1-7. How would you summarize the similarities and differences in these two stunning experiences in John's life?

ALSO: The book of Revelation has by far more imagery from the Old Testament than any other New Testament book. Suppose that in your Revelation film you decided to include some "flashbacks" showing scenes from earlier portions in Scripture, to help complement or "set off" this chapter's scenes in Revelation. What passages from the rest of the Bible would you consider including?

REVELATION 2

Startup: How would you describe your "first love" for the Lord when you were a new Christian?

SEEING WHAT'S THERE

1. How many times do you see the word *overcome* in this chapter? How would you describe the fullest meaning of this word, in the way it's used here?

2. What evidence can you find in this chapter that these words to specific churches are meant for all believers?

3. What are the *warnings* and *reprimands* in this chapter, and what is the right way for you and your church to respond to them?

4. What are the *promises* Jesus makes in this chapter, and what is the right way for you and your church to respond to them?

5. What are the strongest visual images which you see in this chapter? Which ones do you recall seeing elsewhere in Scripture?

6. EYE FOR DETAIL— *From what you recall seeing in chapter 2, try answering the following question without looking at your Bible:* Where is the tree of life? (See verse 7.)

CAPTURE THE ESSENCE

7. Look back again at the full title of this book, as given in the opening phrase of 1:1—"The Revelation of Jesus Christ." What does chapter 2 reveal about *Jesus Christ?*

8. In giving John a vision that concerns the end of this age and the final triumph over evil, why do you think Jesus gives such a prominent place to this intense examination of the church?

9. From what you see in this chapter, what does it mean to *follow Jesus Christ?*

10. From what you see in this chapter, what *expectations* does the Lord have of us, and what *desires* does He have for us?

FOR LIFE TODAY

11. Imagine that you saw earlier today a message written in fire in the sky. It was addressed to you by name, then continued with these words: *Thus saith the* LORD: *"Read Revelation 2, for I have something for you there."* Which verses in this chapter do you think He most likely would be referring to?

12. Look again at the promised blessing in 1:3. What can you do to "keep" or "take heed to" or "take to heart" the message of this chapter?

13. Which words in this chapter would be most accurate if they were in a letter written to *your* church?

14. If everyone in your group thoroughly understood this chapter, and you all had a passion for living out its truth in your lives, what kind of practical changes do you think would result?

FOR GOING DEEPER

The Lord's promise of "hidden manna" in verse 17 calls to mind the first appearance of manna in Exodus 16:13-18, as well as Jesus' reference to manna in John 6:48-51. How do those latter two references help you understand what Jesus may have been speaking about in this passage?

REVELATION 3

Startup: How do you respond to a job performance review or a similar kind of evaluation? Do you welcome the opportunity, or tend to dread it?

SEEING WHAT'S THERE

1. How many times do you see the word *overcome* in this chapter?

2. What are the *warnings* and *reprimands* in this chapter, and what is the right way for you and your church to respond to them?

3. What are the *promises* Jesus makes in this chapter, and what is the right way for you and your church to respond to them?

4. What are the strongest visual images which you see in this chapter? Which ones do you recall seeing elsewhere in Scripture?

5. Imagine again that you were helping to produce a film based on Revelation. To film what happens in this chapters 2 and 3, summarize all the scenes to be included, and the kinds of special effects, special scenery, background music, lighting effects, and so on, you would use to meaningfully portray the central message of these chapters.

6. EYE FOR DETAIL— *From what you recall seeing in chapter 3, try answering the following question without looking at your Bible:* Upon those whom He made pillars in the temple of His God, Jesus promised to write three names. What are these three names? (See verse 12.)

CAPTURE THE ESSENCE

7. Recall again the full title of this book given in the opening phrase of 1:1. What does chapter 3 reveal about *Jesus Christ?*

8. From what you see in this chapter, what does it mean to *follow Jesus Christ?*

9. From what you see in this chapter, what *expectations* does the Lord have of us, and what *desires* does He have for us?

10. From what you've seen so far in this book, discuss how much you agree or disagree with this first-person statement: "If this study of Revelation increases my mental knowledge about the coming end times, but does not give me a deeper faith, a braver hope, and a more selfless love, then I will have utterly missed the true meaning of this book."

11. What kind of mental habits do you think could most easily block the words in this chapter from staying alive in the minds and hearts of Christians today?

12. If God had written this chapter only for *you,* which words or phrases do you think He would have underlined?

13. Remember again the promised blessing in 1:3. What can you do to "keep" or "take heed to" or "take to heart" the message of this chapter?

14. Which words in this chapter would be most accurate if they were in a letter written to *your* church?

FOR GOING DEEPER

Verse 14 alone contains three names for the Son of God. Leaf through the pages of Revelation and note His many other titles in this book—1:8, 1:13, 1:18, 2:18, 4:11, 5:5-6, 7:17, 12:10, 19:11-13, 19:16, and 22:16.

ALSO: Suppose that in your Revelation film you decided to include some "flashbacks" showing scenes from earlier portions in Scripture, to help complement or "set off" this chapter's scenes in Revelation. What passages from the rest of the Bible would you consider including?

REVELATION 4

Startup: What are some of the different ways in which you picture heaven?

SEEING WHAT'S THERE

1. To help you capture the *movement* in this book, summarize what events have taken place in chapters 1— 4.

2. What are the strongest visual images which you see in this chapter? Which ones do you recall seeing elsewhere in Scripture?

3. EYE FOR DETAIL— *From what you recall seeing in chapter 4, try answering the following question without looking at your Bible:* There is a rainbow like an emerald in this chapter; what does it encircle? (See verse 3.)

4. Imagine again that you were helping produce a film based on Revelation. To meaningfully portray the central message and most important action in this chapter, summarize the kind of scenes you would include, plus special effects, special scenery, background music, lighting effects, and so on.

CAPTURE THE ESSENCE

5. What words or phrases in this chapter tell us the most about God's *character?*

6. What words or phrases in this chapter tell us the most about God's *purpose* and *plan* for His people?

7. What insights do you find in this chapter regarding the right way to approach God in worship?

FOR LIFE TODAY

8. In James 1:23-24 we're told that "anyone who listens to the word but does not do what it says is like a man who looks at his face in a mirror and, after looking at himself, goes away and immediately forgets what he looks like." In what important ways can you already see the book of Rev-

elation as a "mirror" for you—showing you what you can and should do?

9. Recall again the promised blessing in 1:3. What can you do to "keep" or "take heed to" or "take to heart" the message of this chapter?

10. Which verse in this chapter do you think God wants you to understand best?

FOR GOING DEEPER

John is given one of the most privileged and awesome sights in all the universe —a glimpse into the very throne room of heaven (verses 2-11). What are some common elements between this vision and that of the prophet Ezekiel (Ezekiel 1:4-28), who also beheld God's throne?

ALSO: Suppose that in your Revelation film you decided to include some "flashbacks" showing scenes from earlier portions in Scripture, to help complement or "set off" this chapter's scenes in Revelation. What passages from the rest of the Bible would you consider including?

REVELATION 5

Startup: Which image of Christ—Lion or Lamb—communicates best to you the nature of Christ?

SEEING WHAT'S THERE

1. To help you capture the *movement* in this book, make a summary of the events that have taken place in this chapter.

2. EYE FOR DETAIL— *From what you recall seeing in chapter 5, try answering the following question without looking at your Bible:* What question did the strong angel proclaim? (See verse 2.)

3. Imagine again that you were helping produce a film based on Revelation. To meaningfully portray the central message and most important action in this chapter, summarize the kind of scenes you would include, plus special effects, special scenery, background music, lighting effects, and so on.

CAPTURE THE ESSENCE

4. Recall again the full title of this book given in the opening phrase of 1:1. What does chapter 5 reveal about *Jesus Christ?*

5. What words or phrases in this chapter tell us the most about God's *purpose* and *plan* for His people?

FOR LIFE TODAY

6. What kind of mental habits do you think could most easily block the words in this chapter from staying alive in the minds and hearts of Christians today?

7. Keep in mind the promised blessing in 1:3. What can you do to "keep" or "take heed to" or "take to heart" the message of this chapter?

FOR GOING DEEPER

Read verse 8, and chapter 8 verses 3 and 4 in the context of Exodus 30:1-8 and

Psalm 141:2. How do reading these passages together help you understand the concept of believing prayer being like fragrant incense?

ALSO: Suppose that in your Revelation film you decided to include some "flashbacks" showing scenes from earlier portions in Scripture, to help complement or "set off" this chapter's scenes in Revelation. What passages from the rest of the Bible would you consider including?

REVELATION 6

Startup (for the "seven-seal" portion, chapters 6— 7): What is the most afraid you have ever been?

SEEING WHAT'S THERE

1. To help you capture the *movement* in this book, summarize what events have taken place in this chapter.

2. Look closely at the fear in verses 15-17. *Why* is there this fear? And why do you think God has given us this preview of it?

3. What are the strongest visual images which you see in this chapter? Which ones do you recall seeing elsewhere in Scripture?

4. Imagine again that you were helping produce a film based on Revelation. To meaningfully portray the central message and most important action in this chapter, summarize the kind of scenes you would include, plus special effects, special scenery, background music, lighting effects, and so on.

CAPTURE THE ESSENCE

5. What are the major questions *you* have in interpreting this chapter?

6. What words or phrases in this chapter tell us the most about God's *character?*

7. What words or phrases in this chapter tell us the most about God's *purpose* and *plan* for His people?

FOR LIFE TODAY

8. Consider carefully verses 9-11. What is the right balance between our desire for justice, and our patience until God accomplishes it? To maintain that balance, which do you need more of—a greater thirst for justice, or a more patient willingness to wait for God's timing?

God's inescapable day of wrath is described in verses 15-17, as well as in other passages such as Zephaniah 1:14-18 and 1 Thessalonians 5:1-3. From those three portions of Scripture, distill five words that best describe this dreadful epoch in human history.

ALSO: Suppose that in your Revelation film you decided to include some "flashbacks" showing scenes from earlier portions in Scripture, to help complement or "set off" this chapter's scenes in Revelation. What passages from the rest of the Bible would you consider including?

REVELATION 7

SEEING WHAT'S THERE

1. To help you capture the *movement* in this book, make a summary of the events that have taken place in the first seven chapters of Revelation.

2. EYE FOR DETAIL— *From what you've seen in the "seven-seal" portion of this book (chapters 6 and 7), try answering the following question without looking at your Bible:* When the earthquake came, what happened to the sun and the moon and the stars? (See 6:12-13.)

3. To review, retrace your way through the last few chapters. What has happened since the first seal was opened in 6:1?

4. Imagine again that you're producing a Revelation film. To meaningfully portray the central message and most important action in this chapter, summarize the kind of scenes you would include, plus special effects, special scenery, background music, lighting effects, and so on.

CAPTURE THE ESSENCE

5. If *hope* is defined as our "eager and confident expectation of what God has promised," then what in this chapter do you eagerly and confidently expect from God?

6. Keep in mind the full title of this book given in the opening phrase of 1:1. What does chapter 7 reveal about *Jesus Christ?*

7. In interpreting this chapter, what appear to be the easiest things to understand, and what are the most difficult things?

8. What words or phrases in this chapter tell us the most about God's *character?*

9. What words or phrases in this chapter tell us the most about God's *purpose* and *plan* for His people?

10. From this chapter of John's vision, what can we learn about the right way to worship God?

11. In Philippians 4:8 we're given the following command: "Whatever is true, whatever is noble, whatever is right, whatever is pure, whatever is lovely, whatever is admirable—if anything is excellent or praiseworthy—*think about such things.*" What food for thought can you find in this chapter that especially strikes you as being *true,* or *noble,* or *right,* or *pure,* or *lovely,* or *admirable,* or *excellent,* or *praiseworthy?*

12. If God had written this chapter only for *you,* which words or phrases do you think He would have underlined?

13. Remember again the promised blessing in 1:3. What can you do to "keep" or "take heed to" or "take to heart" the message of this chapter?

FOR GOING DEEPER

Does it seem strange to think that blood (verses 13-14) could wash a garment white and clean? For a wider picture of the blood-that-makes-clean, consider Romans 3:21-26 and 5:9-10, 1 Corinthians 6:11, Ephesians 1:7, Colossians 1:19-20, and Hebrews 9:11-13.

ALSO: Suppose that in your Revelation film you decided to include some "flashbacks" showing scenes from earlier portions in Scripture, to help complement or "set off" this chapter's scenes in Revelation. What passages from the rest of the Bible would you consider including?

REVELATION 8

Startup (for the "seven-trumpet" portion, chapters 8—11): When you think of the word *judgment,* what images come to your mind?

SEEING WHAT'S THERE

1. To help you capture the *movement* in the book of Revelation, make a summary of the events that have taken place in this chapter.

2. Imagine again that you're producing a Revelation film. To meaningfully portray the central message and most important action in this chapter, summarize the kind of scenes you would include, plus special effects, special scenery, background music, lighting effects, and so on.

CAPTURE THE ESSENCE

3. From what you see in this chapter, what *purposes* are served by the trumpet blasts?

4. What do verses 3-4 tell us about God's regard for our prayers?

FOR LIFE TODAY

5. Look again at verses 3-4. How many of these prayers will be *your* prayers?

FOR GOING DEEPER

The seven mighty trumpet blasts described in this chapter (and in chapters 9 and 11) join two other more hopeful end-time trumpet calls. Describe what the sound of God's trumpet in 1 Corinthians 15:50-52 and 1 Thessalonians 4:16-17 will mean to believers.

ALSO: Suppose that in your Revelation film you decided to include some "flashbacks" showing scenes from earlier portions in Scripture, to help complement or "set off" this chapter's scenes in Revelation. What passages from the rest of the Bible would you consider including?

REVELATION 9

SEEING WHAT'S THERE

1. To help you capture the *movement* in the book of Revelation, make a summary of the events that have taken place in this chapter.

2. Imagine again that you're producing a Revelation film. To meaningfully portray the central message and most important action in this chapter, summarize the kind of scenes you would include, plus special effects, special scenery, background music, lighting effects, and so on.

CAPTURE THE ESSENCE

3. What are the major questions *you* have in interpreting this chapter?

4. Look closely at verses 20-21. What do they reveal about human nature?

5. *Why* do you think God has given us a preview of what these judgments will be like for the wicked?

FOR LIFE TODAY

6. How possible could it have been for *you* to be a part of the crowd mentioned in verses 20-21?

FOR GOING DEEPER

While the "woes" described in this chapter prior to the second coming of Christ are the worst ever faced by mankind, the Lord Jesus gave warnings of "woe" to those who had rejected His credentials as Messiah in his first coming. In the book of Matthew alone, He pronounced these "woes" twelve times. For a representative sample, see Matthew 11:21, 23:13-16, and 23:23-29.

ALSO: Suppose that in your Revelation film you decided to include some "flashbacks" showing scenes from earlier portions in Scripture, to help complement or "set off" this chapter's scenes in Revelation. What passages from the rest of the Bible would you consider including?

REVELATION 10

SEEING WHAT'S THERE

1. To help you capture the *movement* in the book of Revelation, summarize what events have taken place in this chapter.

2. What do you learn about John in this chapter?

3. Imagine again that you're producing a Revelation film. To meaningfully portray the central message and most important action in this chapter, summarize the kind of scenes you would include, plus special effects, special scenery, background music, lighting effects, and so on.

4. What would be your guess about the things which John was prohibited from writing down in verse 4? What do you think the seven thunders might have spoken?

CAPTURE THE ESSENCE

5. What words or phrases in this chapter tell us the most about God's *character?*

6. What words or phrases in this chapter tell us the most about God's *purpose* and *plan* for His people?

FOR LIFE TODAY

7. Look again at verses 8-9. In what ways could you say that God has asked *you* to "eat" His Word?

FOR GOING DEEPER

The prophet Ezekiel had a "dining experience" similar to that of John's in verses 8-10. In Ezekiel 3:1-3 the prophet also ingested a sweet-as-honey heavenly scroll (without the resulting sour stomach). Both scrolls however, seemed to be served for the same purpose. Compare the job descriptions that followed the eating of each scroll in Revelation 10:11 and Ezekiel 3:4-9.

ALSO: Suppose that in your Revelation film you decided to include some "flashbacks" showing scenes from earlier portions in Scripture, to help complement or "set off" this chapter's scenes in Revelation. What passages from the rest of the Bible would you consider including?

REVELATION 11

SEEING WHAT'S THERE

1. To help you capture the *movement* in the book of Revelation, make a summary of the events that have taken place in this chapter.

2. EYE FOR DETAIL— *From what you've seen in the "seven-trumpet" portion of this book (chapters 8— 11), try answering the following question without looking at your Bible:* A Hebrew and a Greek name are given for a demon leader who is also called the "angel of the abyss" or the "angel of the bottomless pit." What were his Hebrew and Greek names? (See 9:11.)

3. To review, retrace your way through the last few chapters. What has happened since the first trumpet was sounded in 8:7?

4. Imagine again that you're producing a Revelation film. To meaningfully portray the central message and most important action in this chapter, summarize the kind of scenes you would include, plus special effects, special scenery, background music, lighting effects, and so on.

CAPTURE THE ESSENCE

5. Remember again the full title of this book (as given in 1:1). What does chapter 11 reveal about *Jesus Christ?*

6. In interpreting this chapter, what appear to be the easiest things to understand, and what are the most difficult things?

7. What words or phrases in this chapter tell us the most about God's *character?*

8. What words or phrases in this chapter tell us the most about God's *purpose* and *plan* for His people?

9. Which verse in this chapter do you think God wants you to understand best?

10. Recall again the promised blessing in 1:3. What can you do to "keep" or "take heed to" or "take to heart" the message of this chapter?

FOR GOING DEEPER

Verses 15-18 speak of the event toward which all history has been moving: the ultimate rule and reign of God over His rebellious creation. In Psalm 2, David also peered into the future to catch a glimpse of the final dominion of God and His Messiah over all the kings of the earth. What similarities can you see in the two passages?

ALSO: Suppose that in your Revelation film you decided to include some "flash-backs" showing scenes from earlier portions in Scripture, to help complement or "set off" this chapter's scenes in Revelation. What passages from the rest of the Bible would you consider including?

REVELATION 12

Startup (for the center portion of Revelation, chapters 12— 14): Look at the description of the dragon in verse 3 of this chapter. What further details would your imagination supply regarding this dragon's appearance?

SEEING WHAT'S THERE

1. To help you capture the *movement* in the book of Revelation, summarize what events have taken place in this chapter.

2. Imagine again that you're producing a Revelation film. To meaningfully portray the central message and most important action in this chapter, summarize the kind of scenes you would include, plus special effects, special scenery, background music, lighting effects, and so on.

CAPTURE THE ESSENCE

3. In interpreting this chapter, what appear to be the easiest things to understand, and what are the most difficult things?

4. What words or phrases in this chapter tell us the most about God's *character?*

5. What words or phrases in this chapter tell us the most about God's *purpose* and *plan* for His people?

FOR LIFE TODAY

6. If it's true that "you *become* what you *think,*" then what are the most important thoughts from this chapter to plant firmly in your mind?

7. Keep in mind the promised blessing in 1:3. What can you do to "keep" or "take heed to" or "take to heart" the message of this chapter?

FOR GOING DEEPER

Michael, a powerful angel, leads a cosmic battle against Satan and his demons in verses 7-9. What additional insights do you discover about Michael in the following passages—Daniel 10:4-14 and 12:1, and Jude 9?

ALSO: Suppose that in your Revelation film you decided to include some "flash-backs" showing scenes from earlier portions in Scripture, to help complement or "set off" this chapter's scenes in Revelation. What passages from the rest of the Bible would you consider including?

REVELATION 13

SEEING WHAT'S THERE

1. To help you capture the *movement* in the book of Revelation, make a summary of the events that have taken place in this chapter.

2. Look at the statement at the end of verse 10. In your own words, how would you explain this "patience" or "perseverance," as well as the "faith" or "faithfulness"? Why is each one needed?

CAPTURE THE ESSENCE

3. What are the major questions *you* have in interpreting this chapter?

4. Imagine again that you're producing a Revelation film. To meaningfully portray the central message and most important action in this chapter, summarize the kind of scenes you would include, plus special effects, special scenery, background music, lighting effects, and so on.

FOR LIFE TODAY

5. Look closely at the words of verse 9. How sensitive is your spiritual hearing? What are the most important things you are hearing from the Lord in this book of Revelation?

FOR GOING DEEPER

In verse 10, John employs one of the richest words in the New Testament language to describe the kind of attitude believers must exude when faced with trials of any kind— even the mind-boggling trials of the Great Tribulation. The word translated as "patience" or "endurance" is used in a wide variety of settings in the New Testament. Take time to sample a few such offerings from the following list—Luke 8:15 and 21:19; Romans 5:3-4, 8:25, and 15:4-5; 2 Corinthians 6:4 and 12:12; Colossians 1:11; 1 Thessalonians 1:3; 2 Thessalonians 1:4; 1 Timothy 6:11; 2 Timothy 3:10; Titus 2:2; Hebrews 10:36 and

12:1; James 1:3-4 and 5:11; 2 Peter 1:6; and Revelation 1:9, 2:2, 2:3, 2:19, 3:10, and 14:12.

ALSO: Suppose that in your Revelation film you decided to include some "flashbacks" showing scenes from earlier portions in Scripture, to help complement or "set off" this chapter's scenes in Revelation. What passages from the rest of the Bible would you consider including?

REVELATION 14

SEEING WHAT'S THERE

1. To help you capture the *movement* in the book of Revelation, make a summary of the events that have taken place in this chapter.

2. In your own words, how would you explain the "perseverance" or "patience" of verse 12, and *why* is it needed?

3. EYE FOR DETAIL— *From what you've seen in the center portion of this book (chapters 12— 14), try answering the following question without looking at your Bible:* Here in his vision, John sees the 144,000 standing with the Lamb on Mount Zion. What is written on their foreheads? (See 14:1.)

4. To review, retrace your way through the last few chapters. What has happened since the great wonder appeared in heaven in 12:1?

5. Imagine again that you're producing a Revelation film. To meaningfully portray the central message and most important action in this chapter, summarize the kind of scenes you would include, plus special effects, special scenery, background music, lighting effects, and so on.

CAPTURE THE ESSENCE

6. Recall again the full title of this book given in the opening phrase of 1:1. What does chapter 14 reveal about *Jesus Christ?*

7. In interpreting this chapter, what appear to be the easiest things to understand, and what are the most difficult things?

8. What words or phrases in this chapter tell us the most about God's *character?*

FOR LIFE TODAY

9. Remember again the promised blessing in 1:3. What can you do to

"keep" or "take heed to" or "take to heart" the message of this chapter?

FOR GOING DEEPER

The graphic depiction of God's wine press of wrath in verses 18-20 has parallels in Old Testament passages such as Isaiah 63:3-6, Lamentations 1:15, and Joel 3:11-13. What sorts of images are common to the four descriptions?

ALSO: Suppose that in your Revelation film you decided to include some "flashbacks" showing scenes from earlier portions in Scripture, to help complement or "set off" this chapter's scenes in Revelation. What passages from the rest of the Bible would you consider including?

REVELATION 15

Startup (for the "seven-bowl" portion, chapters 15— 16): What is the worst pain you've ever known?

SEEING WHAT'S THERE

1. How fully can you explain the significance of the message in verse 1?

2. To help you capture the *movement* in the book of Revelation, make a summary of the events that have taken place in the first fifteen chapters.

3. Imagine again that you're producing a Revelation film. To meaningfully portray the central message and most important action in this chapter, summarize the kind of scenes you would include, plus special effects, special scenery, background music, lighting effects, and so on.

CAPTURE THE ESSENCE

4. What words or phrases in this chapter tell us the most about God's *character?*

5. What words or phrases in this chapter tell us the most about God's *purpose* and *plan* for His people?

FOR LIFE TODAY

6. Recall again the promised blessing in 1:3. What can you do to "keep" or "take heed to" or "take to heart" the message of this chapter?

FOR GOING DEEPER

Verses 3-4 speak of a heavenly choir singing both the "song of Moses" and the "song of the Lamb." What event did the song of Moses in Exodus 15:1-19 celebrate? What does the song in this chapter celebrate?

ALSO: Suppose that in your Revelation film you decided to include some "flashbacks" showing scenes from earlier portions in Scripture, to help complement or "set off" this chapter's scenes in Revelation. What passages from the rest of the Bible would you consider including?

REVELATION 16

SEEING WHAT'S THERE

1. To help you capture the *movement* in the book of Revelation, summarize what events have taken place in this chapter.

2. Compare the bowl judgments in this chapter with the seven trumpet judgments in 8:2— 11:19. How are they alike, and how are they different?

3. What are the major questions *you* have in interpreting this chapter?

4. EYE FOR DETAIL— *From what you've seen in the "seven-bowl" portion of this book (chapters 15-16), try answering the following question without looking at your Bible:* When the seven angels came out of the temple carrying the seven plagues, what were the angels wearing? (See 15:6.)

5. To review, retrace your way through the last two chapters. What has happened since the seven angels with seven plagues appeared in 15:1?

6. Imagine again that you're producing a Revelation film. To meaningfully portray the central message and most important action in this chapter, summarize the kind of scenes you would include, plus special effects, special scenery, background music, lighting effects, and so on.

CAPTURE THE ESSENCE

7. What words or phrases in this chapter tell us the most about God's *character?*

8. What words or phrases in this chapter tell us the most about God's *purpose* and *plan* for His people?

9. *Why* do you think God has chosen to give us a glimpse of this coming destruction?

FOR LIFE TODAY

10. Keep in mind the promised blessing in 1:3. What can you do to "keep" or "take heed to" or "take to heart" the message of this chapter?

FOR GOING DEEPER

In verse 7, the altar itself raises a voice in praise to God. Compare this startling passage with the words of Jesus at His entrance to Jerusalem in Luke 19:37-40. Why might these two events call forth worship even from inanimate objects like an altar or a stone?

ALSO: Suppose that in your Revelation film you decided to include some "flashbacks" showing scenes from earlier portions in Scripture, to help complement or "set off" this chapter's scenes in Revelation. What passages from the rest of the Bible would you consider including?

REVELATION 17

Startup (for the "Babylon" portion, chapters 17— 18): What images come to your mind when you think of the word *Babylon?*

SEEING WHAT'S THERE

1. To help you capture the *movement* in the book of Revelation, summarize what events have taken place in this chapter.

2. In your own words, how would you explain the "mind of wisdom" in verse 9, and *why* is it needed?

3. Imagine again that you're producing a Revelation film. To meaningfully portray the central message and most important action in this chapter, summarize the kind of scenes you would include, plus special effects, special scenery, background music, lighting effects, and so on.

CAPTURE THE ESSENCE

4. In interpreting this chapter, what appear to be the easiest things to understand, and what are the most difficult things?

5. What words or phrases in this chapter tell us the most about God's *character?*

6. What words or phrases in this chapter tell us the most about God's *purpose* and *plan* for His people?

FOR LIFE TODAY

7. Look again at verse 14, and compare it with John 12:26. Where is Jesus now? And where are you?

FOR GOING DEEPER

In verse 8, John speaks of "the book of life." What does this passage teach about that book? What additional insights can you gain from the following verses in Revelation—3:5, 13:8, and 20:11-15?

ALSO: Suppose that in your Revelation film you decided to include some "flashbacks" showing scenes from earlier portions in Scripture, to help complement or "set off" this chapter's scenes in Revelation. What passages from the rest of the Bible would you consider including?

REVELATION 18

1. To help you capture the *movement* in the book of Revelation, summarize what events have taken place in this chapter.

2. What are the major questions *you* have in interpreting this chapter?

3. What are the strongest visual images which you see in this chapter? Which ones do you recall seeing elsewhere in Scripture?

4. EYE FOR DETAIL— *From what you've seen in the "Babylon" portion of this book (chapters 17— 18), try answering the following question without looking at your Bible:* What was the title written on the forehead of the woman who was drunk with the blood of the saints? (See 17:5-6.)

5. Imagine again that you're producing a Revelation film. To meaningfully portray the central message and most important action in this chapter, summarize the kind of scenes you would include, plus special effects, special scenery, background music, lighting effects, and so on.

CAPTURE THE ESSENCE

6. From the characteristics you see in this chapter, how is this Babylon like our world today?

7. What words or phrases in this chapter tell us the most about God's *character?*

FOR LIFE TODAY

8. Which verse in this chapter do you think God wants you to understand best?

FOR GOING DEEPER

The divine call in verses 4-5 is echoed in other portions of Scripture. Examine Genesis 19:12-13, Isaiah 52:11, and 2 Corinthians 6:17. What is the circumstance behind each of these "come out" directives?

ALSO: Suppose that in your Revelation film you decided to include some "flashbacks" showing scenes from earlier portions in Scripture, to help complement or "set off" this chapter's scenes in Revelation. What passages from the rest of the Bible would you consider including?

REVELATION 19

Startup: What are the most important lessons you've learned in your Christian life about *praise?*

SEEING WHAT'S THERE

1. To help you capture the *movement* in the book of Revelation, summarize what events have taken place in this chapter.

2. EYE FOR DETAIL— *From what you recall seeing in chapter 2, try answering the following question without looking at your Bible:* What names does Jesus have in this chapter? (See verses 11, 13, and 16.)

3. Imagine again that you're producing a Revelation film. To meaningfully portray the central message and most important action in this chapter, summarize the kind of scenes you would include, plus special effects, special scenery, background music, lighting effects, and so on.

CAPTURE THE ESSENCE

4. Recall again the full title of this book given in the opening phrase of 1:1. What does chapter 19 reveal about *Jesus Christ?*

5. What words or phrases in this chapter tell us the most about God's *character?*

6. What words or phrases in this chapter tell us the most about God's *purpose* and *plan* for His people?

FOR LIFE TODAY

7. Look at the command in verse 5. What can you learn from this chapter about *how* to praise God?

8. If *hope* is defined as our "eager and confident expectation of what God has promised," then where is *your* hope? What in this chapter can you eagerly and confidently expect from God?

9. Remember again the promised blessing in 1:3. What can you do to "keep" or "take heed to" or "take to heart" the message of this chapter?

10. If it's true that "you *become* what you *think,*" then what are the most important thoughts from this chapter to plant firmly in your mind?

11. What is *your* part in the victory revealed in this book? Describe it in your own words.

FOR GOING DEEPER

Discuss any similarities between the wedding feast mentioned in verses 6-9 with the parable Jesus told in Matthew 22:1-14.

ALSO: Suppose that in your Revelation film you decided to include some "flashbacks" showing scenes from earlier portions in Scripture, to help complement or "set off" this chapter's scenes in Revelation. What passages from the rest of the Bible would you consider including?

REVELATION 20

Startup: If you've thought previously about the last great battle between God's army and the forces of Satan, how did you picture it?

SEEING WHAT'S THERE

1. To help you capture the *movement* in the book of Revelation, summarize what events have taken place in this chapter.

2. EYE FOR DETAIL— *From what you recall seeing in chapter 20, try answering the following question without looking at your Bible:* As the chapter opens, and an angel descends from heaven, what does he hold in his hand? (See verse 1.)

3. Imagine again that you're producing a Revelation film. To meaningfully portray the central message and most important action in this chapter, summarize the kind of scenes you would include, plus special effects, special scenery, background music, lighting effects, and so on.

CAPTURE THE ESSENCE

4. What are the most important *certainties* revealed in this chapter?

5. What words or phrases in this chapter tell us the most about God's *character?*

6. What words or phrases in this chapter tell us the most about God's *purpose* and *plan* for His people?

FOR LIFE TODAY

7. Which verse in this chapter do you think God wants you to understand best?

8. If *hope* is defined as our "eager and confident expectation of what God has promised," then where is *your* hope? What in this chapter can you eagerly and confidently expect from God?

FOR GOING DEEPER

While verse 10 describes the unspeakable fate of Satan, two Old Testament passages may very well describe his stunning origin— as well as his first great fall. Ponder both Isaiah 14:12-15, and Ezekiel 28:11-19 for the beginning of the story to which this verse is the fitting finale.

ALSO: Suppose that in your Revelation film you decided to include some "flashbacks" showing scenes from earlier portions in Scripture, to help complement or "set off" this chapter's scenes in Revelation. What passages from the rest of the Bible would you consider including?

REVELATION 21

Startup: When do you remember first hearing about heaven?

SEEING WHAT'S THERE

1. What are the strongest visual images which you see in this chapter? Which ones do you recall seeing elsewhere in Scripture?

2. To help you capture the *movement* in the book of Revelation, summarize what events have taken place in this chapter.

3. EYE FOR DETAIL— *From what you recall seeing in chapter 21, try answering the following question without looking at your Bible:* What is written on the twelve gates of the new Jerusalem, and what is written on her twelve foundations? (See verses 12-14.)

4. Imagine again that you're producing a Revelation film. To meaningfully portray the central message and most important action in this chapter, summarize the kind of scenes you would include, plus special effects, special scenery, background music, lighting effects, and so on.

CAPTURE THE ESSENCE

5. Keep in mind the full title of this book given in the opening phrase of 1:1. What does chapter 21 reveal about *Jesus Christ?*

6. If a new Christian asked you, "What will eternity be like?" how could you use this chapter to help you give a meaningful answer?

FOR LIFE TODAY

7. Recall again the promised blessing in 1:3. What can you do to "keep" or "take heed to" or "take to heart" the message of this chapter?

8. If *hope* is defined as our "eager and confident expectation of what God has promised," then where is *your* hope? What in this chapter can you eagerly and confidently expect from God?

9. In verse 7, look at God's words about *overcoming.* At this time in your life, what must be overcome?

10. What kind of mental habits do you think could most easily block the words in this chapter from staying alive in the minds and hearts of Christians today?

FOR GOING DEEPER

Compare the opening verse of this chapter with the word picture in Hebrews 1:10-12. Discuss what images come to your mind as you contemplate the passing of the old heaven and earth and the coming of the new.

REVELATION 22

Startup: Practically speaking, what is the most important thing you want to do in the time you have remaining on earth?

SEEING WHAT'S THERE

1. Which important details in this chapter do you think might be the easiest to overlook?

2. What are the strongest visual images which you see in this chapter? Which ones do you recall seeing elsewhere in Scripture?

3. To help you capture the *movement* in the book of Revelation, summarize what events have taken place in this chapter.

4. What are the most important *changes* that you see described in the book of Revelation?

5. EYE FOR DETAIL— *From what you recall seeing in chapter 22, try answering the following question without looking at your Bible:* What word is spoken by "the Spirit and the bride"? (See verse 17.)

6. Imagine again that you're producing a Revelation film. To meaningfully portray the central message and most important action in this chapter, summarize the kind of scenes you would include, plus special effects, special scenery, background music, lighting effects, and so on.

CAPTURE THE ESSENCE

7. Remember once more the true title of this book, as given in the opening phrase of 1:1—"The Revelation of Jesus Christ." What does the Bible's final chapter reveal about *Jesus Christ?*

8. In what specific ways do these final chapters in Revelation bring to completion all the different aspects of the Bible's central message?

9. If there was a chapter 23 in Revelation, what do you think it would contain?

FOR LIFE TODAY

10. Think again of Philippians 4:8, where we're given this command: "Whatever is true, whatever is noble, whatever is right, whatever is pure, whatever is lovely, whatever is admirable—if anything is excellent or praiseworthy— *think about such things."* What food for thought can you find in the book of Revelation that especially strikes you as being *true,* or *noble,* or *right,* or *pure,* or *lovely,* or *admirable,* or *excellent,* or *praiseworthy?*

11. Remember once more the promised blessing in 1:3. What can you do to "keep" or "take heed to" or "take to heart" the message of this chapter?

12. If *hope* is defined as our "eager and confident expectation of what God has promised," then where is *your* hope? What in this chapter can you eagerly and confidently expect from God?

13. Of all that you see in this chapter, what one truth are you most *thankful* for, because of its personal significance to you?

FOR GOING DEEPER

Contrast the angel's command to John in verses 10-11 with the angel's command to the prophet Daniel in Daniel 12:4 and 12:8-10. Why might the instructions to each of these servants of the Lord have been so different?

ALSO: Suppose that in your Revelation film you decided to include some "flashbacks" showing scenes from earlier portions in Scripture, to help complement or "set off" this chapter's scenes in Revelation. What passages from the rest of the Bible would you consider including?

REVELATION:

THE BIG PICTURE

(Discuss again the questions in the "Overview," plus the questions below.)

1. Look together at each of these verses, and discuss which one you believe is the best candidate for "KEY VERSE" in the book of Revelation —the one which brings into sharpest focus what this book is most about: 1:3, 1:19, or 19:11-16.

2. If everyone in your church thoroughly understood this book, and had a passion for living out its truth in their lives, what kind of practical changes do you think would result?

3. If you've decided on a starting point for applying something in this book more effectively to your life, what commitment would you be willing to make to others in your group regarding this?

4. How would you complete the following word of advice to growing Christians? *Explore the book of Revelation if you want to learn more about...*

GUIDELINES FOR GREATER EFFECTIVENESS IN YOUR BIBLE STUDY DISCUSSION GROUP

➤ *Remember to pray,* both as you read and prepare, and later as you meet together and talk. Admit the truth: You really do depend on God's Holy Spirit to make the Word come alive in your mind and heart, so request His help. He *is* your teacher, and He will guide you into truth. (Pray for each other as well. The spiritual war rages, and each Christian's life is a battlefield.)

➤ *Don't dominate the discussion.* If necessary, keep asking yourself this question, and answering it honestly: *What do I enjoy more—presenting my own thoughts, or getting others more involved in discovering and discussing what the Bible says?*

➤ *Keep your focus on the Scriptures.* If you keep digging in with an honest desire for discovery, you'll *never* exhaust the Bible's treasures. It's natural for a group's discussion to occasionally wander down rabbit trails. Stay aware of that, and when it happens, speak up to restore the group's focus on the passage at hand. Then you'll often be surprised at the power Scripture has to quickly put tangents into true perspective.

➤ Don't get so wrapped up in *interpreting* what a passage might mean that you overlook two more important aspects of Bible study: *(1) simply seeing what the passage has to say,* and *(2) applying its message directly to your life.* Nothing kills effective Bible study more than the neglect of these two simple goals.

➤ *Truly encourage one another.* Show your genuine excitement when others relate their discoveries in God's Word. Respond in the same way Jesus would if He were bodily present in your group — for these are the voices of His children as they encounter the Scriptures that testify of Him.

Suggested Study Schedule

➤ Matthew: *30 weeks* — one for the overview, one for each chapter, and one for the "Big Picture" summary.

➤ Mark: *18 weeks* — one for the overview, one for each chapter, and one for the "Big Picture" summary.

➤ Luke: *26 weeks* — one for the overview, one for each chapter, and one for the "Big Picture" summary.

➤ John: *23 weeks* — one for the overview, one for each chapter, and one for the "Big Picture" summary.

➤ Acts: *24 weeks* — one for the overview, then group the chapters this way: •1 •2 •3 •4 •5 •6-7 •8 •9 •10-11 •12 •13 •14 •15 •16 •17 •18 •19 •20 •21-22 •23-24 •25-26 •27-28; plus a final week for the "Big Picture" summary.

➤ Romans: *17 weeks* — one for the overview, one each for chapters 1-16, and one for chapter 16 and the "Big Picture" summary.

➤ 1 Corinthians: *17 weeks* — one for the overview, one each for chapters 1-16, and one for chapter 16 and the "Big Picture" summary.

➤ 2 Corinthians: *14 weeks* — one for the overview, one each for chapters 1-12, and one for chapter 13 and the "Big Picture" summary.

➤ Galatians: *8 weeks* — one for the overview, one for each chapter, and one for the "Big Picture" summary.

➤ Ephesians: *8 weeks* — one for the overview, one for each chapter, and one for the "Big Picture" summary.

➤ Philippians: *6 weeks* — one for the overview, one for each chapter, and one for the "Big Picture" summary.

➤ Colossians: *6 weeks* — one for the overview, one for each chapter, and one for the "Big Picture" summary.

➤ 1 Thessalonians: *7 weeks* — one for the overview, one for each chapter, and one for the "Big Picture" summary.

➤ 2 Thessalonians: *5 weeks* — one for the overview, one for each chapter, and one for the "Big Picture" summary.

➤ 1 Timothy: *8 weeks* — one for the overview, one for each chapter, and one for the "Big Picture" summary.

➤ 2 Timothy: *6 weeks* — one for the overview, one for each chapter, and one for the "Big Picture" summary.

➤ Titus: *5 weeks* — one for the overview, one for each chapter, and one for the "Big Picture" summary.

➤ Philemon: *1 week.*

➤ Hebrews: *15 weeks* — one for the overview, one for each chapter, and one for the "Big Picture" summary.

➤ James: *7 weeks* — one for the overview, one for each chapter, and one for the "Big Picture" summary.

➤ 1 Peter: *7 weeks* — one for the overview, one for each chapter, and one for the "Big Picture" summary.

➤ 2 Peter: *5 weeks* — one for the overview, one for each chapter, and one for the "Big Picture" summary.

➤ 1 John: *7 weeks* — one for the overview, one for each chapter, and one for the "Big Picture" summary.

➤ 2 John: *1 week.*

➤ 3 John: *1 week.*

➤ Jude: *1 week.*

➤ Revelation: *16 weeks* — one for the overview, then group the chapters this way: •1 •2 •3 •4 •5 •6-7 ("Seven Seals") •8-11 ("Seven Trumpets") •12-14 (center chapters) •15-16 ("Seven Bowls") •17-18 ("Babylon") •19 •20 •21 •22; plus a final week for the "Big Picture" summary.

➤ ENTIRE NEW TESTAMENT: *289 weeks.*

Prayers & Promises from the Scriptures for Your Group and Personal Bible Study

➤ For the word that God speaks is alive and active: it cuts more keenly than any two-edged sword: it strikes through to the place where soul and spirit meet, to the innermost intimacies of a man's being: it exposes the very thoughts and motives of a man's heart. *(Hebrews 4:12, Phillips)*

➤ The words that I speak unto you, they are spirit, and they are life. *(John 6:63, KJV)*

➤ Let the Word of Christ, in all its richness, find a home with you. Teach each other, and advise each other, in all wisdom. *(Colossians 3:16, New Jerusalem Bible)*

➤ In a humble (gentle, modest) spirit, receive and welcome the Word, which implanted and rooted in your hearts contains the power to save your souls. *(James 1:21, Amplified Bible)*

➤ Do your best to present yourself to God as one approved, a workman who does not need to be ashamed and who correctly handles the word of truth. *(2 Timothy 2:15, NIV)*

➤ Everyone then who hears these words of mine and does them will be like a wise man who built his house upon the rock; and the rain fell, and the floods came, and the winds blew and beat upon that house, but it did not fall, because it had been founded on the rock. *(Matthew 7:24-25, RSV)*

➤ You are already clean because of the word which I have spoken to you. *(John 15:3, NKJV)*

➤ The seed is the word of God....And the seed in the good soil, these are the ones who have heard the word in an honest and good heart, and hold it fast, and bear fruit with perseverance. *(Luke 8:15, NASB)*

➤ Even more blessed are all who hear the Word of God and put it into practice. *(Luke 11:28, Living Bible)*